£29.50

Language and Globalization

Series Editors: **Sue Wright**, University of Portsmouth, UK, and **Helen Kelly-Holmes**, University of Limerick, Ireland.

In the context of current political and social developments, where the national group is not so clearly defined and delineated, the state language not so clearly dominant in every domain, and cross-border flows and transfers affect more than a small elite, new patterns of language use will develop. The series aims to provide a framework for reporting on and analysing the linguistic outcomes of globalization and localization.

Titles include:

David Block
MULTILINGUAL IDENTITIES IN A GLOBAL CITY
London Stories

Julian Edge (*editor*)
(RE)LOCATING TESOL IN AN AGE OF EMPIRE

Roxy Harris
NEW ETHNICITIES AND LANGUAGE USE

Clare Mar-Molinero and Patrick Stevenson (*editors*)
LANGUAGE IDEOLOGIES, POLICIES AND PRACTICES
Language and the Future of Europe

Clare Mar-Molinero and Miranda Stewart (*editors*)
GLOBALIZATION AND LANGUAGE IN THE SPANISH-SPEAKING WORLD
Macro and Micro Perspectives

Ulrike Hanna Meinhof and Dariusz Galasinski
THE LANGUAGE OF BELONGING

Leigh Oakes and Jane Warren
LANGUAGE, CITIZENSHIP AND IDENTITY IN QUEBEC

Forthcoming titles:

John Edwards
LANGUAGE AND SOCIAL LIFE

Diarmait Mac Giolla Chrióst
LANGUAGE AND THE CITY

Colin Williams
LINGUISTIC MINORITIES IN DEMOCRATIC CONTEXT

Language and Globalization
Series Standing Order ISBN 1–4039–9731–4
(*outside North America only*)

You can receive future titles in this series as they are published by placing a standing order. Please contact your bookseller or, in case of difficulty, write to us at the address below with your name and address, the title of the series and the ISBN quoted above.

Customer Services Department, Macmillan Distribution Ltd, Houndmills, Basingstoke, Hampshire RG21 6XS, England

Language, Citizenship and Identity in Quebec

Leigh Oakes
Queen Mary, University of London

and

Jane Warren
The University of Melbourne

© Leigh Oakes and Jane Warren 2007
Foreword © Gérard Bouchard 2007

All rights reserved. No reproduction, copy or transmission of this publication may be made without written permission.

No paragraph of this publication may be reproduced, copied or transmitted save with written permission or in accordance with the provisions of the Copyright, Designs and Patents Act 1988, or under the terms of any licence permitting limited copying issued by the Copyright Licensing Agency, 90 Tottenham Court Road, London W1T 4LP.

Any person who does any unauthorized act in relation to this publication may be liable to criminal prosecution and civil claims for damages.

The authors have asserted their rights to be identified as the authors of this work in accordance with the Copyright, Designs and Patents Act 1988.

First published in 2007 by
PALGRAVE MACMILLAN
Houndmills, Basingstoke, Hampshire RG21 6XS and
175 Fifth Avenue, New York, N.Y. 10010
Companies and representatives throughout the world.

PALGRAVE MACMILLAN is the global academic imprint of the Palgrave Macmillan division of St. Martin's Press, LLC and of Palgrave Macmillan Ltd. Macmillan® is a registered trademark in the United States, United Kingdom and other countries. Palgrave is a registered trademark in the European Union and other countries.

ISBN-13: 978–1–4039–4975–2 hardback
ISBN-10: 1–4039–4975–1 hardback

This book is printed on paper suitable for recycling and made from fully managed and sustained forest sources.

A catalogue record for this book is available from the British Library.

Library of Congress Cataloging-in-Publication Data

Oakes, Leigh.
    Language, citizenship, and identity in Quebec / by Leigh Oakes and Jane Warren.
       p. cm.—(Language and globalization)
    Includes bibliographical references and index.
    ISBN 1–4039–4975–1
      1. Citizenship – Québec (Province) 2. French language – Political aspects – Québec (Province) 3. Ethnicity – Québec (Province) 4. Group identity – Québec (Province) 5. Linguistic minorities – Québec (Province) 6. Nationalism – Québec (Province) I. Warren, Jane II. Title.

JL257.A2O25 2007
323.609714—dc22
                                                                                               2006047279

10 9 8 7 6 5 4 3 2 1
16 15 14 13 12 11 10 09 08 07

Printed and bound in Great Britain by
Antony Rowe Ltd, Chippenham and Eastbourne

*À nos amis québécois de toutes origines
qui nous ont fait découvrir le Québec*

Contents

List of Tables and Figures   ix

Foreword   x

Acknowledgements   xiii

1 Introduction   1
   1.1 Aims, methodology and structure of the book   2
   1.2 Social identity   6
   1.3 Ethnic identity, ethnicity and the ethnic group   10
   1.4 National identity, nationalism and the nation   13
   1.5 Globalisation   15
   1.6 Citizenship   18

Part I   New Challenges

2 From French Canadian to Quebecer   25
   2.1 From an ethnic past to a civic future   26
   2.2 Citizenship in Quebec or Quebec citizenship?   32
   2.3 Conceptions of citizenship and liberalism in Canada and Quebec   36
   2.4 A unique model of citizenship: intercultural citizenship   42

3 Redefining the Quebec Nation   44
   3.1 Dumont's ethnic model   45
   3.2 The civic models: Derriennic, Leydet, Caldwell, Bariteau   47
   3.3 Reconciling the ethnic and the civic: Bouchard, Seymour, Taylor   54
   3.4 Overcoming the taboo of ethnicity   60

4 Quebec in a Globalising World   62
   4.1 Quebec's international relations   63
   4.2 Quebec and the Americas   67
   4.3 Quebec, *la Francophonie* and cultural diversity   75
   4.4 Quebec as a global player   79

Part II A Common Language

5 French: A Language for All Quebecers — 83
  5.1 French in Quebec: from *langue commune* to *langue publique commune* — 84
  5.2 Status planning to motivate new Quebecers — 91
  5.3 'De-ethnicising' language? — 97
  5.4 Status planning for Quebecers of all ethnic origins — 104

6 Whose French? Language Attitudes, Linguistic Insecurity and Standardisation — 106
  6.1 *Est-ce qu'on parle bien, nous autres?* — 107
  6.2 The myth of 'international French' and the monocentric ideology of the standard — 112
  6.3 Identifying and describing a standard for Quebec French — 119
  6.4 Corpus planning for Quebecers of all ethnic origins — 126

Part III Diverse Experiences

7 Language, Immigration and Belonging — 131
  7.1 Quebec's role as host — 132
  7.2 Adult migrant experiences of language and belonging — 139
  7.3 *Les enfants de la loi 101* — 144
  7.4 'Pure new wool' Quebecers? — 148

8 Transformations of Anglophone Quebec — 150
  8.1 Who is an Anglophone Quebecer? — 152
  8.2 Are Anglophone Quebecers *des citoyens à part entière* ('fully-fledged citizens')? — 158
  8.3 Bilingualism: no problem(?) — 165
  8.4 A continuing rapprochement — 170

9 Linguistic Rights for Aboriginal Nations — 172
  9.1 Aboriginal nations and linguistic rights in Quebec — 174
  9.2 Aboriginal citizenship, new agreements and language — 180
  9.3 Language survival in practice — 186
  9.4 Shared interests, shared concerns — 192

10 Conclusion — 194

Appendix — 199

Notes — 200

Bibliography — 214

Index — 247

List of Tables and Figures

Tables

1.1	Attributes of ethnic groups and nations	13
5.1	Percentage of the population according to mother tongue, the language spoken at home and the language of public use (index) in the whole of Quebec, 1997	90
5.2	Percentage of workers according to the language used most often at work by mother tongue in the whole of Quebec	95
8.1	Size of the English-speaking community, according to various criteria, 1991 and 2001 Census data	156
8.2	Results of 2005 CROP-La Presse opinion poll: Quebecers and the choice of a premier	159
8.3	Ability to speak both official languages in Quebec, by mother tongue and Census year	167
9.1	Aboriginal nations in Quebec: demolinguistic background	177

Figures

1.1	The process of constructing social identity	7
4.1	Quebec in the Americas	68
6.1	A pluricentric conception of the French language	116
9.1	Aboriginal nations in Quebec	176

The authors have attempted to clear permission for use of all copyright items. In the event that any copyright holder has been inadvertently overlooked the publisher will make amends at the earliest opportunity.

Foreword

The numerous changes that took place in Quebec society during the second half of the twentieth century represent the most remarkable journey. A former colony of France and then England, long obsessed with the sense of its own fragility within an Anglophone and protestant North America, this cultural minority suddenly demonstrated a surprising confidence in its own destiny. With the Quiet Revolution of the 1960s–70s, the Francophone population set about establishing itself as a majority within the territory of Quebec and conceived an audacious project of political sovereignty. At the same time, not only did the nation radically redefine its identity by freeing itself from religion, it also redefined its relationship with France, the mother country, by asserting itself as a North American francophonie, out from under the cultural authority of France.

More remarkable still, the period 1960–90 saw the rise of a nationalist movement of unprecedented vigour, as well as the restructuring of national identity to take account of ethnic pluralism. Evolving out of its French Canadian identity, the nation became 'Quebecer', that is, open to all ethnic groups settled on its territory. It is worth underlining that this opening up of national identity was enshrined in law in 1975 by the adoption of a charter of rights and freedoms which established the legal equality of citizens. In other words, contemporary Quebec offers the rare example of an authentically liberal democracy. At the height of its force, instead of asserting itself at the expense of the Other, the new Quebec nationalism, on the contrary, committed itself to guaranteeing the Other an equal place.

It is difficult to overstate the scale, complexity and vigour of the debates that have accompanied all these changes right up to the present day. The work of Leigh Oakes and Jane Warren retrieves them with a precision, a clarity and an accuracy of vision which command admiration. Indeed, as well as talking with a number of key players, the authors give the impression that they have read all there is to read. They have in any case perfectly understood what is at stake and the surrounding controversies, they show a great deal of subtlety in their exposition and discussion, and throughout they display great erudition. It is well known that these qualities are not always in evidence when a society is viewed through a foreign lens. Here, on the contrary, the analysis is always careful, enlightened and perfectly pitched. As a Quebecer, I found in their analysis not only the very substance of our own debates but also the spirit and sensitivity which have animated them. This does the authors great credit.

The Anglophone public will no doubt also appreciate the originality of the approaches to civic identity that have been developed in Quebec, notably to accommodate ethnic diversity. I am thinking here, in particular, of the policy of interculturalism which pursues two objectives that are not easily reconciled, that is, the respect of diversity and the orchestration of interactions between ethnic groups. It is in this way that Quebecers seek to achieve the ideal of integration within pluralism. In the same spirit, one could give the example of the compromise which has been reached in the linguistic domain. Traditionally, the French language, along with Catholicism, constituted the essential element of French Canadian identity, so much so that the two seemed virtually indissociable from each another. In today's circumstances, this strictly unitary relation between language and identity has been considerably loosened, allowing all ethnic groups to adopt French (as their main, their second or their third language) to express their own culture through it, renegotiating their identity all the while as they see fit. On these subjects, as on many others, the work of Oakes and Warren offers concise and well informed analyses. A third example is to be found in the way in which Quebecers have rejected an overly radical and abstract version of the dichotomy of the civic nation and the ethnic nation, to arrive instead at a more flexible and realistic approach aimed at combining legal principles and identity.

Amongst the book's other achievements, the following are worth mentioning. Readers will appreciate, for example, the vantage point that the authors' status as outside observers confers on them. They introduce a comparative perspective on various subjects that is particularly welcome, given that this kind of approach is not widespread in local commentary. They also often shine new light on familiar subjects, subjects on which we, as Quebec intellectuals, had the (clearly mistaken) impression that we had said it all. In addition, readers will benefit from the array of points of view presented, which are often enriched by historical detail; the scope and the richness of the questions addressed; the useful discussions and theoretical clarifications (on identity, citizenship, nation ...); the considered attention given to Anglophones and Aboriginal peoples; all of which are based on a thorough bibliography and expressed in a very accessible, jargon-free language.

Finally, I would say that Oakes and Warren have clearly understood the current situation of Quebecers, as members of a minority culture which rejects insularity as much as ethnicism. In particular, they have made perceptive comments on the triple challenge that confronts this small, stateless nation, namely the necessity of negotiating viable and decent compromises in the face of (1) internal ethnic diversity, (2) Anglophone North America and (3) the dynamics of globalisation. Having said this, with the exception of citizens who belong to superpowers or to the well established nations of the old world, who would not recognise themselves in this particular set of circumstances?

It is to be hoped that this excellent synthesis of present-day Quebec soon finds its way into a French translation so as to ensure its widest readership in Quebec and elsewhere.

Professor Gérard Bouchard
Université du Québec à Chicoutimi
April 2006

Acknowledgements

The writing of this book was divided amongst the two authors. Oakes was responsible for writing Chapters 1, 2, 3, 5 and 6, Warren for Chapters 4, 7, 8, 9 and 10. By commenting on each other's work, both authors were nonetheless able to contribute to the book as a whole and take joint responsibility for its contents.

That said, the research on which this book is based owes much to many people. In particular, the authors wish to thank Claude Verreault (Université Laval), who not only proved to be a fount of knowledge personally, but also helped by providing research materials and introductions to other colleagues working in related fields. His generous support and hospitality during successive visits to Quebec are greatly appreciated.

The authors would equally like to express their gratitude to Gérard Bouchard (Université du Québec à Chicoutimi, UQÀC) who, in addition to having commented on a previous version of Chapter 5, kindly agreed to read the final version of the whole manuscript and write a foreword. Needless to say, it is an honour to have such a prominent local intellectual help us to introduce Quebec to the English-speaking world.

The research on which this book is based would certainly not have been possible without the involvement of many others as well, namely those who kindly gave up time to talk to the authors about the issues at hand, commented on chapters or related conference papers, provided reading materials, assisted with references and/or otherwise contributed to or supported the project in various ways. These include: Jocelyne Bisaillon, Denise Deshaies, Louis-Jacques Dorais, Jocelyn Létourneau, Simon Langlois, Conrad Ouellon, Wim Remysen and Diane Vincent (Université Laval); Michel Pagé and Michel Seymour (Université de Montréal); Anne-Marie Baraby, Richard Y. Bourhis, Daniel Chartier, Denis Dumas and Alain-G. Gagnon (Université du Québec à Montréal, UQÀM); Chantal Bouchard and Alan Patten (McGill University); Hélène Cajolet-Laganière and Louis Mercier (Université de Sherbrooke); Jean-Claude Corbeil (former secretary to the Commission des États généraux sur la situation et l'avenir de la langue française au Québec); Guy Dumas and Jacques Gosselin (Secrétariat à la politique linguistique); Pierre Georgeault and Michel Plourde (Conseil supérieur de la langue française); Gérald Paquette (Office québécoise de la langue française); Jean-Denis Gendron (former president of the Commission d'enquête sur la situation de la langue française et sur les droits linguistiques au Québec); Yvette Mollen and staff (Institut culturel et éducatif montagnais); Jack Jedwab (Association for Canadian Studies); Robert Laliberté (Association internationale des études québécoises); José Mailhot; Jeff Heinrich (*The Gazette*); André Pratte (*La Presse*); Deborah Hook (Quebec Community Groups Network); Madeleine Gaultier and Marie-Odile Magnan (Institut national de la recherche scientifique); Linda Cardinal (University of Ottawa); Noel Corbett and Raymond Mougeon (York University); Monica Heller and Martin Papillon (University of Toronto); Christine Fréchette (Forum sur l'intégration nord-américaine); Marc Levine (University of Wisconsin); Céline Gagnon and Denis Turcotte (Délégation générale du Québec à Londres); Bill Marshall (University of Glasgow); Martha-Marie Kleinhans (University of Reading); and Richard Cornes and David Marrani (University of Essex). In addition, the authors would like to thank Jill Lake and her team at Palgrave for their invaluable expertise with matters related to the overall production of this book; Jill Lake also took the photograph which appears on the cover. Oakes is grateful to Éric Darier in Montreal as well as Larry Sheehan, Martyn James and Ian Hogarth in Melbourne for their kind hospitality offered throughout the duration of this project; and Warren would like to thank Amanda Macdonald for her encouragement and good counsel during the writing process.

Finally, the research benefited greatly from the generous support provided to Oakes by the Arts and Humanities Research Council (AHRC) as part of their Research Grant (reference number 14547) and Research Leave (reference number 111715) schemes. The AHRC funds postgraduate training and research in the arts and humanities, from archaeology and English literature to design and dance. The quality and range of research supported not only provides social and cultural benefits but also contributes to the economic success of the UK. For further information on the AHRC, please see www.ahrc.ac.uk. Warren would like to thank the University of Melbourne for supporting study leave in Montreal and at Queen Mary, University of London, in the second half of 2004; the University of Melbourne's Research Unit for Multilingual and Cross-Cultural Communication (RUMACCC) for generously providing writing-up space and facilities; and the University's School of Languages for financing a research trip to Quebec in September 2005. In addition, publication of this work was assisted by a publication grant from the University of Melbourne, for which the two authors are very grateful.

L. O. and J. W.
London and Melbourne

1
Introduction

On 29 June 2000, the Parti Québécois government of Quebec created the Commission des États généraux sur la situation et l'avenir de la langue française au Québec (Commission of the Estates general on the situation and future of the French language in Quebec). Fearing that the future of French in Quebec might be threatened by such new realities as increased ethnic diversity and globalisation, the government armed the Commission with the following mandate (Gouvernement du Québec 2001a: i):

- to identify and analyse the main factors which influence the situation and future of the French language in Quebec;
- to determine the relevant avenues and priorities for action;
- to examine the sections of the Charter of the French language concerned;
- to make recommendations that aim to ensure the use, scope and quality of the French language in Quebec.

To carry out their task, President Gérald Larose and his team of nine commissioners and one secretary held a series of regional and national public hearings, themed conference sessions and an international conference in the last two months of 2000 and the first few months of 2001, which resulted in a long list of submissions and presentations which informed the Commission's deliberations.[1] In its final report, the Larose Commission, as it was commonly known, had become convinced that:

> more than ever, the language question must not be dealt with in a one-dimensional manner. Quebec is a plural society, and French, the official, common language, is a key factor in its social cohesiveness. Quebecers are ready to move on to another phase. There is a common will to work towards an inclusive social project, to construct a common life space and to lower the barriers that divide Quebec society according to ethnic origin. (Gouvernement du Québec 2001a: 4)[2]

While many of its 149 recommendations have not been acted upon, the report of the Larose Commission nonetheless constitutes a milestone. More than any other previous document, it squarely places Quebec language policy and planning within the framework of the new civic approach to national identity which seeks to unite Quebecers of all ethnic origins. As such, the report lays the foundation for a new approach to language policy and planning which is better suited to the realities of Quebec in the twenty-first century. That the Larose Commission has already served as an inspiration in this respect is evidenced by the new directions proposed in the recent publication *Le français au Québec. Les nouveaux défis* (French in Quebec: The New Challenges) (Stefanescu and Georgeault 2005).

1.1 Aims, methodology and structure of the book

Using the report of the Larose Commission as a point of departure, the present book wishes to contribute to the wider debate about the new civic approach to national identity within a global perspective. Much of the discussion has been dominated by the disciplines of political science, political philosophy and sociology. The authors seek to complement these perspectives by making a contribution informed by sociolinguistic preoccupations. Unlike some other studies not inspired by sociolinguistics, the present book thus never underestimates the role of language, which is regarded here as an important and inevitable component of national identity. Moreover, language is considered in all its dimensions: not only does the book focus on the macro issues of the sociolinguistic situation in Quebec (e.g., language planning, language attitudes), it also examines the micro level (e.g., linguistic variation, the standardisation of Quebec French), which is usually neglected in non-sociolinguistic treatments of language issues.

While other disciplines can benefit from a sociolinguistic contribution, sociolinguistics itself can also learn from other fields. In recent years, there has been a wave of sociolinguistic publications on national identity, nationalism and the nation. However, many of these make no mention of the useful theoretical paradigms that have been developed in other fields. One of the aims of the present study is therefore to do precisely this. In short, it is hoped that the pluridisciplinary approach adopted here will lead to a more comprehensive understanding of the complex relationship between language and national identity, not only in Quebec, but also in a broader sense.

Indeed, Quebec constitutes a unique laboratory for studying the relationship between language and nation in general, hence the reason why it is often cited in literature on the topic in other contexts around the globe. The amount of reflection on questions of language and/or national identity in Quebec is undeniably impressive. In the words of one commentator, '[f]rom a comparative point of view, there are not many places in the world where there have been so many innovative reflections about the politics of identity'

(Karmis 2004. 81). Some cynics may claim that this is a sign of Quebec's obsession with itself. Considering the highly critical nature of the debate at times, however, it is more likely that it is a sign of the search by Quebec society as a whole for some kind of social harmony.

Without a doubt, Quebec has a lot to teach the world; but it can learn a lot from the world too, and at times one cannot help but notice that a comparative dimension is lacking in the domestic debate. Another aim of the present study is therefore to introduce some elements of comparison with other contexts (albeit limited by space constraints), especially those about which the authors have first-hand knowledge. Moreover, while the perspective of insiders is crucial to obtain an in-depth understanding of the intricacies and subtleties of the situation, the role of outsiders is equally valid, ensuring, as it does, a more objective perspective. In this sense, the authors of the present study can benefit from being neither Quebecers nor English-speaking North Americans, at the same time as they are proficient enough in both French and English to be able to engage in the debate from both sides. Together with writing in English, this puts them in good stead to address a challenge identified by the Larose Commission:

> In Canada and abroad, Quebec language policy is too often perceived negatively. The business world and the media in particular know little about it. For their part, the Americans remain opposed to legislation which to them appears to reduce individual liberties and limit the use of English. For them, language and culture are two separate elements; they have difficulty seeing how the protection of Quebec culture also includes the protection of the French language, even though 25 American states have adopted declarations proclaiming English to be the official language. We therefore need to encourage the perception that Quebec culture is part of the North American heritage and needs to be protected. It is equally important to correct the erroneous perceptions regarding Quebec language legislation and its application. (Gouvernement du Québec 2001a: 184)

The research on which the present book is based made use of two methodologies. The main methodology involved the synthesis and analysis of primary and secondary materials. Primary sources included official publications and empirical studies; secondary sources included academic articles and monographs as well as debates in newspapers such as *Le Devoir*, *La Presse* and *The Gazette*. As a complement to the main methodology, the research also made use of semi-structured interviews with officials from various Quebec government bodies as well as academics specialising in fields of interest to the project (see Acknowledgements). These interviews were not the object of analysis *per se*, but rather served predominantly to obtain a more impressionistic idea of where Quebec is at and the direction in which it is heading with regard to questions of both language and national identity.

To be sure, it is possible to identify common ground in these areas, despite a variety of political opinions amongst the Quebec population at large. For example, with regard to language policy and planning, Gervais (2001) notes the fundamental similarities between the three main political parties in Quebec: the Parti Québécois (PQ), the Parti Libéral du Québec (PLQ) and the Action démocratique du Québec (ADQ). For the purposes of this book, it is thus of no major significance that a PLQ government was elected barely two years after the publication of the Larose Commission's report (see Appendix for the dates of office of recent Quebec premiers, as well as of federal prime ministers). Even if they disagree on detail, all three parties in fact favour state intervention in matters of language, efforts to improve the quality of French spoken in Quebec, the learning of other languages and increased powers for Quebec concerning immigration (the latter, as will be seen, concerning questions of language policy and planning as well as national identity). As for attitudes towards national identity in more general terms, despite the obviously varying degrees of affiliation to Quebec and Canada respectively, it has often been noted that '[even] Quebec federalists are Quebec nationalists, first and foremost' (Lucien Bouchard, former premier of Quebec, cited in Beiner 2003: 178). While the views of individual parties and/or governments are stressed in those cases where there are clear differences of opinion (e.g., regarding the notion of a Quebec citizenship), the relative overall consistency both in matters of language and national identity explains why mention is often made in this book simply to 'Quebec' or 'the Quebec authorities'.

Irrespective of political persuasion, Quebec as a whole is caught between two movements: an affirmation of difference, in its fight to promote an identity distinct from that of Anglophone Canada and the United States, and an opening up to the 'other', as immigration brings with it increasing ethnic and linguistic diversity, and as Quebec increasingly seeks some form of reconciliation with Aboriginal peoples and a rapprochement with Anglophones in the province. The challenge of finding the right balance between these movements is more important now than ever and is reflected in the main research questions of this study:

- In its effort to maintain a distinct national identity, how is Quebec dealing with the new realities of ethnic diversity and globalisation?
- What is Quebec doing to forge a sense of common identity through language?
- To what extent is official policy concerning these issues compatible with the diverse experiences of minorities in Quebec?

These three research questions form the basis of the three parts of the book. As the first of the three chapters included in Part I on the new challenges of ethnic diversity and globalisation, Chapter 2 traces the development of the civic, territorial conception of Quebec identity that began in the wake of the Quiet Revolution, when Quebec society underwent a major transformation as a result of modernisation and secularisation. In the post-1995 referendum period, this new civic identity has come to define itself predominantly in terms of citizenship, in particular the idea of a Quebec citizenship to exist alongside Canadian citizenship, and designed to foster an integrative attachment to Quebec and unite Quebecers of all ethnic origins.

Chapter 3 addresses the question of national identity in a more theoretical way, by examining some of the better-known and more developed models of nation that have been proposed for Quebec. The ethnic conception of nation especially prominent in the past has provoked attempts to redefine the nation in strictly civic terms. These latter, highly abstract conceptions of the nation have in turn triggered models which seek to reintroduce ethnic elements into an overall civic framework.

In addition to the challenge of accommodating ethnic diversity, contemporary Quebec also faces the realities of a globalising world where English is the global *lingua franca*. Chapter 4 evaluates to what extent Quebec is able to take advantage of the opportunities that globalisation throws up to 'act locally' through global cooperation, in order to further its own linguistic and cultural ends. The chapter focuses on significant linguistic and cultural issues raised in the two major global arenas of importance for Quebec, that of the Americas, as a site of linguistic and cultural plurality, and that of *la Francophonie*, viewed as an alternative global linguistic network to the English-speaking world.

As the first of two chapters included in Part II on the use of a common language to forge a sense of common identity, Chapter 5 examines the effect that the new civic approach to national identity in Quebec has had on efforts to maintain and promote the status of French there. Following a brief outline of the main milestones of status planning in Quebec, the chapter examines how the authorities hope to encourage the adoption of French as the language of public communications amongst a growing number of immigrants, the group of Quebecers upon whom the future of French is now understood to depend.

Chapter 6 focuses on the debate over the variety of French to be promoted in Quebec: French as commonly used in Quebec (also called *français d'ici*) or French as used in France (often confused with the notions of *français standard* and *français international*)? From the original myth of a French Canadian patois that arose in the nineteenth century, French-speaking Quebecers have suffered from a sense of linguistic insecurity because of the perceived lack of quality associated with their variety. With the more recent civic approach to Quebec identity, questions are now being asked about the kind of French that Quebec should offer its new immigrants and whether French-speaking Quebecers need to give up their particular variety and adopt a so-called 'international French' in order to be truly civic.

Part III contains three chapters which focus on the diverse experiences of minorities in Quebec. Chapter 7 examines specifically how immigrants themselves understand their relationship to Quebec society and explores the range of meanings that belonging can have for Quebecers of immigrant background, not least a sense of attachment to Montreal, rather than Quebec, and to multilingualism, rather than French alone.

Chapter 8 focuses on the extent to which Anglophone Quebecers can truly feel a sense of belonging to Quebec, and inversely whether the Francophone majority can fully accept Anglophones as 'true' Quebecers. The chapter also discusses the blurring of boundaries between the two groups, through growing bilingualism and mixing, particularly among the younger generation of Anglophones.

Chapter 9 examines how well official rhetoric on the linguistic rights of Aboriginal peoples in Quebec, as set out in policy documents and new agreements between the provincial and federal governments and various Aboriginal nations, squares with the vitality of Aboriginal languages within Aboriginal communities themselves.

A final chapter summarises the findings in terms of the three main research questions posed above. In addition, it considers how these questions may play out in the future, and suggests how the Quebec experience in these matters can inform other contexts around the globe. Before this book proceeds any further, however, it is necessary to define the main concepts that underpin the discussions in the various chapters: social identity, ethnic identity, ethnicity, ethnic group, national identity, nationalism, nation, globalisation and citizenship. These basic concepts are extremely complex and are the object of intense investigation themselves. Given space constraints, the treatments provided here focus on those aspects which are of most relevance to the topic at hand.

1.2 Social identity

If the word 'identity' derives from the Latin *idem* meaning 'same', the construction of identity is first and foremost about difference. Indeed, all identity is defined in contradistinction to other identities of the same type, a dynamic which is clearly demonstrated with regard to identities of a group or social nature (Eriksen 1993: 10, 62): Canadian identity is largely defined in contradistinction to American identity, gay identity in contradistinction to heterosexual identity, etc. This differentiation of oneself from the 'other' lies at the heart of theoretical considerations of social identity. Developed in the field of the social psychology of intergroup relations, social identity theory (Tajfel 1974, 1978; Tajfel and Turner 1986), for example, relies on a series of concepts which are linked together in a causal sequence. As part of the overall socialisation process, individuals learn from an early age to categorise themselves and others into social groups. From the individual's perspective, people either belong to the same group (ingroup) or another group (outgroup). The awareness that individuals have of their own social group and

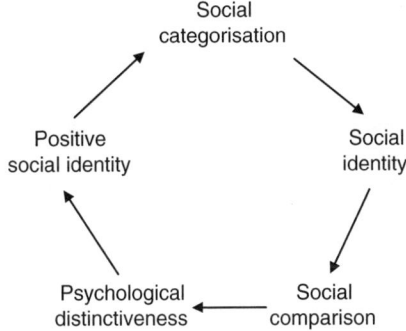

Figure 1.1 The process of constructing social identity (according to social identity theory)

the positive or negative values associated with membership in that group is known as their social identity (Giles, Bourhis and Taylor 1977: 319). According to the theory, when comparing social groups, individuals will favour the ingroup and discriminate against outgroups. This ingroup-centric behaviour, which makes use of popular myths and stereotypes, seeks to generate or maintain a state of psychological distinctiveness, which in turn leads to a positive social identity. A basic assumption of the theory is that social groups in Western societies strive to create and maintain positive identities. Moreover, identity is not something static; the phenomenon in question is better understood as an identification process (Hall 1990: 222; 1996: 4). As it is forever ongoing, the process of constructing social identity described above is thus naturally cyclical (see Figure 1.1).

Social identity theory also makes use of a distinction between 'secure' and 'insecure' identities (Tajfel 1978). Social comparisons and identities are said to be secure when 'status relations are perceived as immutable, a part of the fixed order of things' (Tajfel and Turner 1986: 22): the dominant group remains dominant and the minorities remain subordinate. More frequently, however, social comparisons and identities can be considered as insecure. The existence of 'cognitive alternatives' (Tajfel and Turner 1986: 22), which render other states of affairs conceivable, is what made it possible, for example, for French speakers in Quebec to become *maîtres chez eux* ('masters in their own home') by means of a struggle in the early 1960s known as the Quiet Revolution (see Section 2.1). But insecure identities do not only apply to subordinate groups, they can also affect majority groups: 'Any threat to the distinctly superior position of a group implies potential loss of positive comparisons and possible negative comparisons, which must be guarded against' (Tajfel and Turner 1986: 22). In insecure situations, dominant groups regarding their superiority as legitimate tend to intensify the existing differences to maintain their psychological distinctiveness and resulting positive social identity. This intensification of differences is usually manifested by a heightened sense of identity amongst the dominant group, and increased discrimination against minority outgroups. As for these latter groups, an insecure identity implies that the group no longer accepts its subordinate status. Attempts are made to improve this status and generate a more positive identity by employing one or more of the following identity strategies (Tajfel and Turner 1986: 19–20): individual mobility, social creativity and social competition.

Individual mobility refers to an individual's decision to dissociate him or herself from the ingroup and assimilate to the dominant outgroup. This is a strategy frequently observed amongst immigrants. For example, immigrants in Quebec tended in the past to assimilate to the English-speaking elite. Following language legislation introduced in the 1970s (see Chapter 5), more and more immigrants began to assimilate to the French-speaking (and now dominant) majority. Even though emphasis is today placed on integration as opposed to assimilation, individual mobility continues to be a strategy used by many immigrants, especially those of second and later generations (see Chapter 7).

As for social creativity, this is a strategy at the group level which can take three main forms. First, previously negatively-viewed symbols can be redefined in a more positive light. For instance, while indigenous populations, such as the eleven Aboriginal nations that exist within Quebec's territories (see Chapter 9), used to be dismissed because of their 'primitive' lifestyles, these same lifestyles can now be considered more ecological than those of consumer-orientated Western societies. Second, new positively-viewed symbols may be created: marginalised groups find new ways to distinguish themselves by creating new counter cultures. Such a strategy was observed by Roosens (1989) in his work on the Hurons in Quebec, in particular concerning the reinterpretation of history by Huron leaders in order to revive their dying culture:

> [T]hese Indians [sic.] had set out deliberately to develop a Huron *counterculture*. When I compared the characteristics of this neo-Huron culture with the culture depicted in the historical records, most of the modern traits, virtually everything, were 'counterfeit'; the folklore articles, the hair style, the mocassins, the 'Indian' parade costumes, the canoes, the pottery, the language, the music. (Roosens 1989: 46–7)

The last form of social creativity involves the selection of alternative, less favourable outgroups for comparison. For example, a minority may consider itself as the most dominant within a hierarchy of minorities in a given society. Indeed, Rosenberg and Simmons (1972) found that Blacks who made comparisons with other Blacks, rather than Whites, demonstrated a more positive social identity. Alternatively, social comparisons can be made on other dimensions, such as class rather than ethnicity.

The third strategy used by groups to generate a positive identity is known as social competition. Unlike social creativity, which has as a goal the improvement of the group's *subjective* social status, this strategy involves the competition for *objective* resources (Tajfel and Turner 1986: 20). A good example of this strategy was the desire of French speakers in Quebec to reverse the socio-economic inequality of the past: while in 1961, French Canadians were at the bottom of the salary scale of 14 ethnic groups, just above Italians and Aboriginal peoples, by 1980 a bilingual Francophone was earning on average more than a bilingual or monolingual Anglophone (Dion 1991: 297). As such resources are scarce, social competition can lead to conflict and antagonism between the groups in question. It is pursued nonetheless because of its ability to generate more favourable social comparisons, which in turn result in a positive social identity.

While social identity theory was designed to explain those instances when individuals choose to act as a group, it is nonetheless recognised that individuals sometimes desire to stress their personal identity, or even an identity at a higher level. Self-categorisation theory (Turner 1985; Turner et al. 1987: 42–67; Turner and Oakes 1989), which can be used in conjunction with social identity theory, was developed precisely to determine the level of identity – personal/individual, social/group or human – that a person emphasises at any given moment. Contrary to what one might initially think, social identity theory can also accommodate what is often called 'multiple identities'. This term is sometimes used to denote an individual's ability to simultaneously enjoy different social identities: he or she may belong to a certain ethnic group, but at the same time feel part of a larger religious community, a member of a certain socio-economic class, of a particular gender category, etc. (see A. D. Smith 1991: 4–8). Such phenomena pose no challenge to social identity theory, however, as the identification processes occur concurrently at these various levels of identity. The 'multiple identities' of interest here are those which exist *at the same level of identification*, when individuals belong to multiple groups *of the same nature*, for example when they are perceived to have two or more ethnic identities. On the surface, these are problematic for the theory, which implies that there is one positively-viewed ingroup, while all outgroups are considered unfavourably. What of those Quebecers, for example, who do not have difficulty in reconciling their Quebec and Canadian identities? Social identity theory would seem at first to assume that one of these identities must be viewed negatively. This would be the case if indeed we were talking about two separate identities, but in fact the term 'multiple identities' is somewhat of a misnomer: while one can indeed speak of multiple affinities or loyalties, individuals only ever have one identity. As Maalouf (1998: 34) stresses: 'identity is made up of multiple allegiances; but it is essential to equally stress the fact that it is one, that we experience it as a whole.' Even if they are hybrid in nature, so-called 'multiple identities' are nonetheless separate entities distinct from other identities. In practice, this means that the identity of a Quebecer who feels both Quebecer and Canadian is constructed in contradistinction to the identities of both those who feel only Canadian and those who feel only Quebecer.

1.3 Ethnic identity, ethnicity and the ethnic group

As a form of social identity, ethnic identity is constructed in opposition to other ethnic identities. Indeed, '[t]o speak of an ethnic group in total isolation is as absurd as to speak of the sound from one hand clapping' (Eriksen 1993: 9).

> A community which enters into no contact whatever with other races, languages, and cultures thinks of itself as representing the human species rather than any of its branches. This fact is reflected in the ethnic names which primitive [sic.] peoples like to give themselves when asked who they are: 'men.' On first contact with people of another breed, the initial reaction is to treat them as ancestors. (Pipes 1975: 454)

Such an observation raises questions about the very nature of ethnicity. Primordialist approaches insist that ethnicity is a 'given' of human existence, the product of blood ties, meaning that ethnic identity is an immutable property of the group (Shils 1957; Geertz 1973). As such, primordialism has today 'acquired pejorative connotations of fixity, essentialism and naturalism' (A. D. Smith 2001: 53). By contrast, situational or constructivist accounts view ethnic identity as malleable, varying with the particular situation and dependent on how individuals wish to portray themselves at particular times (A. Cohen 1974a). The latter approach opens the way for an instrumental or political use of ethnicity, for example by elites who wish to mobilise large groupings to support their pursuit of power (Brass 1991; see also A. D. Smith 1991: 20; Bulmer 2001: 71). However, as many commentators point out, if ethnic identities were created wholly through political processes, then it would be possible to convince individuals that they were of another ethnicity: 'Since such a feat is evidently not possible, ethnicity must have a non-instrumental, non-political element' (Eriksen 1993: 55). Clearly, a combination of both primordialism and situationalism must be included in any definition of an ethnic group, such as that given by A. D. Smith (1991: 20):

> An ethnic group is a type of cultural collectivity, one that emphasizes the role of myths of descent and historical memories, and that is recognized by one of more cultural differences like religion, customs, language or institutions. Such collectivities are doubly 'historical' in the sense that not only are historical memories essential to their continuance but each such ethnic group is the product of specific historical forces and is therefore subject to historical change and dissolution.

Somewhat related to the primordialism/situationalism debate, another difficulty involved in the definition of ethnicity concerns its relationship with culture. At one extreme are those narrow definitions of ethnicity which clearly distinguish it from culture on account of its putative link to biological descent (e.g., Poole 1999: 39). Not only is this view supported by certain scholars, it also tends to dominate in certain languages. For example, '[t]he connotations of *ethnie* ("ethnic group") in French are sometimes uncomfortably close to obsolete notions of race or reifying notions of "cultures" ' (Eriksen 1993: 161). The reality is that most ethnic groups cannot speak so much of biological descent as a *mytho*-biological descent, a 'fictive' or 'metaphoric kinship' (Eriksen 1993: 34, 68; see also A. D. Smith 2001: 52). At the other extreme are those commentators who collapse ethnicity and culture completely. For example, A. Cohen (1974b) argues that London stockbrokers can be considered as an ethnic group since they are relatively endogamous (they tend to marry within the same socio-economic class) and share a sense of culture. To be sure, it is often difficult to draw the line between the two concepts. As G. Bouchard (1999: 26) points out:

> it seems that there does not exist a precise definition of ethnicity which clearly brings out its specificity in relation to culture in a global sense. Consequently, these two notions overlap and it is never clear to what extent realities which pertain to one are also included in the other. (see also G. Bouchard 1997: 128)

In light of this difficulty, the present study adopts a position halfway between the two extremes described above by understanding ethnic identity in a broad sense, which implies a significant amount of overlap with cultural identity. It nonetheless clearly distinguishes the two concepts because of the myth of common descent, the '*sine qua non* of ethnicity' (A. D. Smith 1986: 24).

That common descent should be understood in mythical terms highlights the fact that ethnic identity relies to a great extent on subjective attributes. Indeed, other characteristics of ethnic groups, such as shared historical memories and the attachment to a certain territory that is sometimes present, also have a largely mythical and subjective quality (A. D. Smith 1991: 22–3). Owing to the importance of this subjective dimension, a useful way of looking at ethnic identity is in terms of boundaries (Barth 1969). This approach has the effect of shifting the emphasis from objective cultural content, which is in fact quite fluid over time, in order to focus on the subjective attitudes and representations of individual group members. As such, 'Barth further argues that cultural variation may indeed be an *effect* and not a *cause* of boundaries' (Eriksen 1993: 39). In a sense, Barth's approach can thus be considered situational in nature; it explains how cultural content can be manipulated or politicised in order to maximise psychological distinctiveness *vis-à-vis* other ethnic groups. As the sociologist explains himself, 'some cultural factors are used by the actors as signals and emblems of differences, others are ignored, and in some relationships radical differences are played down and denied' (Barth 1981: 203).[3]

With the help of social identity theory, Barth's observation can explain, for example, why it is language which has become the primary attribute of Quebec culture. Since the Quiet Revolution, when Quebec underwent a rapid process of liberalisation and modernisation (see Section 2.1), many French-speaking Quebecers feel that the only thing that separates them from Anglophone Canadians both inside or outside Quebec is their language (Dion 1991: 304): 'language provides the best fit for self-categorization in terms of maximising the contrast in differences between and similarities within groups in contemporary Québec' (Sachdev and Bourhis 1990: 218–19).

A final consideration about ethnic identity is that it is not merely for minorities. Even if they prefer to speak of national identity or patriotism (see Section 1.4), 'majorities and dominant peoples are no less "ethnic" than minorities' (Eriksen 1993: 4). As such, we can speak of both an English and a French Canadian ethnic group (Breton 1988). With the decline of the concept of French Canada (see Section 2.1), some commentators have rejected the latter, considering the term 'French Canadian' as outdated and laden with negative connotations. There has been much debate about what to call the ethnic majority in Quebec instead; alternatives include *Québécois* (as opposed to 'Quebecer') (Adelman 1995; Feldstein 2003: xvii–xviii), 'Francophone Quebecers' (Bouchard, Rocher and Rocher 1991), 'Franco-Quebecers' (G. Bouchard 2001a: 31) and 'Quebecers of French-Canadian background' (Létourneau 2001: 61). The first of these terms merely perpetuates a uniquely ethnic definition of Quebec identity as a whole. Since it cuts across the efforts of successive Quebec governments over the last few decades to create an open, inclusive society, it is not used in the present study, which refers only to 'Quebecers'. The second alternative does not refer to ethnicity so much as language. As Juteau (2001: 211) points out, '[i]t is important to distinguish between French Canadians and francophones, as there are Quebec francophones who are not French-Canadian' (see Sections 3.4 and 5.3 for further discussions on the importance of recognising the ethnic identity of the majority group in Quebec). The third suggested term is ambiguous: does 'Franco' refer to the French language or a 'French' ethnic group? As for the fourth option, while this is technically correct, it is somewhat awkward on account of its length. In the present study, reference is simply made to 'French Canadians' for two main reasons. First, as the study is limited to Quebec, there can be no confusion with French speakers in other parts of Canada. Second, and more importantly, it is recognised that the French Canadian ethnicity of former times is not the same as French Canadian identity today. This is the argument used by Juteau (2001: 125), who also favours the reintroduction of the term 'French Canadian' to designate the ethnic majority component of the Quebec nation.

1.4 National identity, nationalism and the nation

As another type of collective cultural identity, national identity is somewhat akin to ethnic identity, in the same way that nations overlap conceptually with ethnic groups. Like ethnic identity and ethnic groups, national identity and nations do not rely solely on objective characteristics (e.g., language, religion, customs, territory, institutions); they also depend on subjective features (e.g., attitudes, sentiments, perceptions), making the nation a kind of 'imagined community' (Anderson 1983). Nations are equally subjected to the same primordialism versus instrumentalism debate, linked to which is the question of whether they are either perennial or a product of the modern era, however defined (Anderson 1983; Gellner 1983; Hobsbawm 1992), or in fact both of these, namely modern phenomena that are nonetheless based on pre-modern ethnic cores (A. D. Smith 1986, 1991: 37–42). But while the nation and the ethnic group share many attributes (see upper part of Table 1.1), they can also be distinguished from each another by their important differences (see lower part of Table 1.1).

Nations can thus be distinguished from ethnic groups in so far as they typically have a public culture common to all members and usually occupy their territorial homelands (which may or may not form a state); they also have common legal codes with common rights and duties for all, and exhibit a common division of labour or economic unity (see also A. D. Smith 1991: 40). As it meets these criteria, Quebec clearly constitutes a nation and only a minority of people attempt to claim otherwise (e.g., Nemni 1998).

In studies of the nation and nationalism (understood here broadly as any expression or manifestation of national identity[4]), it is customary to distinguish two ideal types: the so-called ethnic variety and the so-called civic variety. Ethnic nationalism considers the nation very much as an extension of the ethnic group. As is the case for the latter (see Section 1.3), however, the common origins shared by members of the nation are usually understood in a metaphoric sense. This is the reason why this type of nation is sometimes called the cultural nation. At the other extreme of the often-cited

Table 1.1 Attributes of ethnic groups and nations

Ethnic group	Nation
Proper name	Proper name
Common myths of ancestry, etc.	Common myths
Shared memories	Shared history
Cultural differentia(e)	Common public culture
Link with homeland	Occupation of homeland
Some (elite) solidarity	Common rights and duties
	Single economy

Source: A. D. Smith (2001: 13).

dichotomy is civic nationalism, which unites people from various ethnic groups around common values and institutions, thus giving rise to a nation which is more territorial or political in nature (see Renan 1990).[5] Some commentators argue that this is not nationalism at all, but rather patriotism, 'an emotional attachment to one's state or country and its political institutions' (Connor 1993: 374).

Despite its continued popularity, the ethnic/civic dichotomy has been the object of much criticism in recent years, not least in Quebec in the context of the debate about which model of nation to adopt. For example, Venne (2001b: 8) speaks of a 'false dichotomy [that] has been largely superseded', while Bourque (2001: 98) claims that 'the outdated opposition between the civic and the ethnic is no longer an adequate starting point for understanding Quebec nationalism'. Perhaps the most vociferous critic is Seymour, who, together with his colleagues, argues that the dichotomy has given rise to accounts that 'trace a truncated picture, and yield in important ways a distorted understanding, of the complex phenomenon that nationalism has become' (Seymour *et al.* 1996: 2). The main objection of these and other commentators, such as Taylor, is that the dichotomy leads to essentialist interpretations which obscure the fact that most nations function in reality on both ethnic and civic dimensions:

> [T]he famous distinction between 'ethnic' and 'civic' regimes [...] does not apply to our situation, as most democratic societies these days are in fact hybrid creations. While strongly rooted in a 'republican' liberalism, they also define themselves according to their core ethnic group or groups. (Taylor 2001: 20)

Schnapper (1996: 233) makes the same observation as Taylor, noting that 'different nations are all both "ethnic" and "civic", but are differently "ethnic" and "civic".' But while Schnapper is of the opinion that one needs to move beyond the ethnic/civic opposition, by using these terms herself she paradoxically affirms the view of her opponents in the debate who claim that the dichotomy remains nonetheless a 'very useful analytic and heuristic tool' (A. D. Smith 1996/1997: 9). The fact that all nations exhibit varying degrees of ethnic and civic elements is not a reason to reject these notions; it is not the dichotomy *per se* which is outdated, rather the belief that nations can be exclusively ethnic or civic. In other words, the dichotomy remains of value, as Schnapper demonstrates, not to categorise nations as either ethnic or civic in an absolute sense, but rather to describe the different dimensions of a single nation, the multitude of objective and subjective components used to construct it throughout different periods in time.

It is also useful at this point to separate the concepts of nation and nationalism. While there is no such thing as a purely ethnic or purely civic *nation*, the terms 'ethnic' and 'civic' can still be used to describe the different *nationalisms* of conceptions of a single nation that exist either at various points throughout history (e.g., compare the different conceptions of the nation promoted by successive governments) or at any one point in time (e.g., compare the different representations of the nation at the grassroots and official levels). As will be seen in Section 2.1, there are diachronic differences between the variants of nationalism promoted throughout Quebec's history. The existence also of synchronic differences is clearly observed in the following document drafted by the Bloc Québécois, the political party at the federal level devoted to the promotion of sovereignty for Quebec:

> A Quebecer is someone who lives in Quebec. This definition is inclusive. It links Quebec identity to the act of belonging to the same political community. It bases this identity on citizenship. However, this conception has not been completely internalised by the population. There still remains a too widely held view according to which being a Quebecer means: 'old-stock French-speaking Quebecer' or Quebecer of French Canadian origin. (Bloc Québécois 1999, cited in Canet 2003: 136)

Instead of *transcending* the ethnic/civic dichotomy outright, one should therefore be attempting to *reconcile* its two poles: the ethnic and the civic should not be considered as mutually exclusive, but rather as acting in tandem, notwithstanding an irreducible degree of tension between them. Seymour *et al.* (1996: 6) argue that such attempts at reconciliation remain nonetheless 'under the spell' of the dichotomy and merely serve to enhance its importance (see also Karmis 2004: 81, 92). Yet even these fervent critics of the dichotomy cannot resist making reference to it themselves, either explicitly or implicitly, throughout their writing, such is its usefulness and general acceptance by many.

1.5 Globalisation

As evidenced by the abundance of literature on the topic, there is a great desire amongst scholars in a wide range of disciplines to understand globalisation, the phenomenon that has all but become the 'cliché of our times' (Held *et al.* 1999: 1). Yet the more this concept has become an object of study, the more its meaning has become vague and difficult to define (Meyer and Geschiere 1999: 1; Nederveen Pieterse 2004: 8). Much of the confusion results from the different realities that scholars are in effect describing; in many cases, '[i]t is not clear whether the different parties invoking globalization mean the same thing or even if they are addressing the same issue' (Ferguson 1992: 69). Moreover, globalisation is often confused with, or at least not clearly distinguished from, internationalisation (see Jucquois 1995: 80). However, as Giddens (1998: 137) explains: 'Globalization, it should be stressed, is not the same as internationalization. It is not just about closer ties between nations, but concerns processes, such as the emergence of a global civil society, that cut across the borders of nations.'

Considering the confusion with internationalisation, it is understandable that opinions differ greatly about when globalisation first began.[6] Following Giddens, the present study considers it as a more advanced stage of internationalisation (see also Jucquois 1995: 317, 322), and therefore as a relatively recent phenomenon. The emerging global – as opposed to international – order which the advent of neo-liberalism helped create was boosted by the 'opening-up' of Eastern Europe that followed the end of the Cold War in the late 1980s, a time when the word 'globalisation' first began to appear in academic and media circles (Giddens 1998: 28).

With regard to culture, which is of interest here, reactions to globalisation can be grouped according to three categories (Held *et al.* 1999: 3–10). 'Hyperglobalizers' (e.g., Hamelink 1983; Reich 1992; Ohmae 1995) consider that the impact of Western media and consumerism will lead to cultural homogenisation. Whether this homogenisation is welcomed as a means of creating a 'global village' (McLuhan 1962), or rejected as a form of Western cultural imperialism, both positions agree that the world is moving rapidly towards uniformity. Indeed, it would be impossible to deny that the global flow of mass cultural consumption has already resulted in some degree of homogenisation, which many consider synonymous with global Americanisation (Schiller 1985; Hall 1991: 28; Ritzer 1997). However, this extreme view of globalisation 'fails to take into account the ways in which cultural products are locally consumed, locally read and transformed in the process' (Held *et al.* 1999: 373). Unlike hyperglobalisers, 'transformationists' (e.g., Giddens 1990) thus predict the 'indigenisation' (Appadurai 1990: 295) of global culture, or the emergence of new 'creolised' (Hannerz 1990, 1991) or 'hybridised' (Nederveen Pieterse 1995, 2004) cultures. Finally, there are the 'sceptics' (e.g., Hirst and Thompson 1996), who question whether the impact of global culture has been, and will continue to be, as profound and enduring as is often assumed.

The present study situates itself somewhere between the last two positions, those of the transformationists and the sceptics. In other words, it considers that the theories of globalisation advanced by hyperglobalisers have tended to neglect the importance of culture, and in particular the power of cultural identity (Castells 1997). As more attention has progressively been paid to the sociocultural dimension of globalisation (e.g., Featherstone 1990; Hannerz 1991; Robertson 1992; Appadurai 1996; Tomlinson 1999; Nederveen Pieterse 2004), it has become increasingly clear that the homogenising tendencies that appear inherent to globalisation paradoxically encourage 'continued or even reinforced cultural heterogeneity' (Meyer and Geschiere 1999: 2). As one scholar explains, 'ethnic and cultural fragmentation and modernist homogenization are not two arguments, two opposing views of what is happening in the world today, but two constitutive trends of global reality'

(Friedman 1990: 311). In other words, '[g]lobal and local are the two faces of the same movement' (Hall 1991: 27; see also Beiner 2003: 23), so much so that Robertson (1995: 26) even suggests the replacement of the term 'globalisation' with 'glocalisation'.

By 'local' is often meant 'regional' nationalist movements, such as those in Quebec, Catalonia and Scotland (Giddens 1998: 31–2). According to some commentators (e.g., Nguyen 1998: 103), these movements are weakening the nation-state from below. Such a threat was implied by the then Canadian Minister of Foreign Affairs, Pierre Pettigrew, when he described the intervention of what he termed 'non-states' as one of the main characteristics of globalisation, as opposed to internationalisation (*Le Devoir*, 2 September 2005). Indeed, Canadian federalists lament what they perceive as the decline of the Canadian nation, at the same time as they paradoxically try to convince Quebecers of the irrelevance of the Quebec nation in an era of globalisation. The fact is that globalisation has not been shown to have undermined national sentiment in any context around the world. On the contrary, in a study of national identity conducted in 1998 amongst 2,500 young people in Quebec as well as France, Belgium, Burundi, Poland, Russia and Zaire, it was found that the nation was still the 'place of belonging' and 'primary reference point', a 'springboard from which to cast oneself elsewhere' (Létourneau 1998: 412–13).

The continued or even increased relevance of national identity at the present time can be regarded as a perfectly natural and predictable consequence of globalisation. Giddens (1985: 218) considers a stronger nationalist sentiment as a reaction to the 'ontological insecurity' of modern times whereby individuals resort to 'regressive forms of object-identification', such as the classic symbols of national identity (e.g., national languages, religions, currencies, flags, anthems, etc.). Not all would agree, however, with Giddens' choice of the term 'regressive' to describe such instances of nationalist sentiment: 'Nationalist movements [...] are not anachronistic manifestations but rather extremely modern signs. They are not the relic of a disappearing past or a banal primitive remnant, but foreshadow the future of our societies' (Dieckhoff 2000: 31).

In other words, the greater the homogenising pressure that globalisation exerts on national cultures in the future, the more nations are likely to accentuate the differences which remain. This tendency can already be observed in Quebec where, according to what has been termed 'Tocqueville's paradox' (Dion 1991), the convergence of attitudes and life-styles amongst Quebecers and other Canadians witnessed in recent decades has been accompanied by a greater awareness of a distinct Quebec national identity (Taylor 1992: 181–214; Kymlicka 1995: 88; Norman 1995: 141–2). Such a reaction is completely consistent with social identity theory (see Section 1.1): a heightened sense of national identity can thus be explained in terms of a desire to express national distinctiveness, a condition which is especially important considering the shift from an era characterised by internationalisation to one marked by globalisation (Oakes 2001: 147). Not only does globalisation encourage a heightened sense of national identity; the increased awareness of ethnic diversity which has accompanied it also raises questions about who belongs to a given society, that is, questions about citizenship.

1.6 Citizenship

Ever since the French Revolution and the birth of the modern nation centred on the state, citizenship has tended to be regarded as synonymous with nationality (in its legal or political sense).[7] No longer did sovereignty lie with the monarch; the democratisation of politics now placed sovereignty with the people, who had become 'nationally defined citizens' (Heater 1999: 96–7). Historically and conceptually, however, there is an important distinction to be made between the two terms. Nationality in its legal or political sense has to do with the state to which one belongs. It has traditionally been acquired according to the principles of *jus sanguinis* ('blood right') or *jus soli* ('soil right'), a distinction similar to that between ethnic and civic nationalism (see Section 1.4). By contrast, citizenship in its classical sense refers to certain duties and rights associated with one's membership of the polity. It has traditionally not been granted automatically to all nationals: initially, only those 'possessing sufficient reason and property' were considered eligible for citizenship; even today, 'the mentally disabled and minors are not citizens, although they are nationals' (Fieschi and Varouxakis 2001: 22).

Far from being an anachronism, the distinction between citizenship and nationality is becoming relevant again as multiple and transnational citizenships become increasingly visible for a variety of reasons, many of which are associated with globalisation (see Section 1.5): the rise of neo-liberalism and the effect it has on the equity of citizens, accelerated human migrations, greater nationalist awareness amongst some minorities, and regionalism such as European integration that is perceived by some as a threat to the legitimacy of the nation-state (Heater 1999: 2–3). The new circumstances have naturally led to questions being raised about the criteria for belonging to a given society. Such concerns are not limited to ethnic and national minorities, but also to those groups that differ in terms of religious beliefs, gender and sexual orientation. As J. A. Cohen (2001: 109) notes:

> Citizenship here refers to the political logic at work in the management of diversity – that is, to the modes of recognition or nonrecognition of distinct identities within the broader fabric of a national mode of cohesion, when indeed such cohesion holds true.

With its emphasis on inclusion, citizenship thus pertains to the social and political relationship that an individual has with a given society. Weinstock

(2000: 16–17) explains that there are at least three dimensions to this relationship. First, citizenship is a judicial status:

> A citizen, unlike a mere resident, is the bearer of certain rights. In principle, only a citizen has the right to vote or stand for public office. And, again ideally, only the citizen of a political entity can profit from economic and social benefits provided by the political entity in question: a citizen also has certain responsibilities which do not apply to the mere resident. For example, only the citizen can be called upon to sacrifice himself or herself in times of war. In this way, even if the mere resident and the citizen are linked to a political entity by certain common judicial ties (they both pay taxes and are subject to the same criminal code), the citizen benefits from certain rights and carries certain additional responsibilities. (Weinstock 2000: 16)

Second, citizenship also refers to a series of practices: 'A citizen is someone who, beyond his or her mere judicial status, actively participates in the life of political institutions and in the shaping of the common good' (Weinstock 2000: 16). Depending on their level of engagement, individuals can thus be content with a 'passive' or 'minimal citizenship' or opt for a 'supererogatory citizenship' that entails a much more active participation than required by law. Third, citizenship comprises an identity dimension:

> This dimension of citizenship is fully realised when the attachment to a collectivity designated by citizenship status is of subjective importance to the individual, when he or she is prepared to act on various situations, or to react to them, at least in certain cases as a citizen of such and such a collectivity rather than, for example, as a member of such and such a gender or class, etc. In other words, a fully-fledged citizen according to this affective dimension is someone who, in the event of a conflict, will at least on a good number of occasions give priority to the citizenship dimension of his or her identity, as opposed to other politically relevant dimensions of it. (Weinstock 2000: 17)

Not only do these three elements of citizenship interact causally, they can also be arranged in a variety of ways so as to give rise to different conceptions or models of citizenship. In Western political philosophy, two conceptions of citizenship have traditionally dominated: the liberal and the civic republican (Heater 1999: 4; Weinstock 2000: 18).

The liberal conception of citizenship places emphasis primarily on the judicial dimension of citizenship:

> Citizens are above all bearers of certain rights, which allow them to commit themselves actively to the public sphere if they so desire, but which

nonetheless have the main function of protecting their autonomous private sphere from the encroachment of fellow citizens and, especially, from the state itself. This conception thus minimises the importance of truly civic activity and recognises that the activity of the citizen will be focused on the economic as well as the private spheres. (Weinstock 2000: 18)

As for the identity dimension, this is, at least in principle, also kept to a minimum in the liberal model of citizenship: 'there is no sense that the state has any organic existence, bonding the citizens to it and to each other' (Heater 1999: 6); 'it is considered as perfectly normal that citizens identify first and foremost with their family or profession' (Weinstock 2000: 19). Such a minimal or procedural definition of citizenship was facilitated by the rise of capitalism in the late eighteenth century, in particular the right of individuals to acquire property (Heater 1999: 7–9). Since then, it has progressively been developed as a concept to include other types of rights. In his famous essay *Citizenship and Social Class* first published in 1950, T. H. Marshall defines citizenship as being composed of three types of rights: civil (e.g., freedom of movement and expression, and the right to property), political (e.g., the right to vote and hold public office) and social (e.g., the right to welfare and to partake in the heritage of society) (Marshall and Bottomore 1992: 8). More recently, the liberal conception of citizenship is represented in the work of theorists such as Rawls (e.g., 1999).

The other main conception of citizenship in Western political philosophy is the civic republican:

By 'republic' is meant a constitutional system with some form of sharing out of power to prevent concentrated arbitrary and autocratic government; and 'civic' means the involvement of the citizenry in public affairs to the mutual benefit of the individual and the community. (Heater 1999: 44)

Unlike liberal citizenship, this model of citizenship thus places great emphasis on 'the citizen's direct participation in the collective debate on questions of public interest and on his or her active participation in the pursuit of the common good' (Weinstock 2000: 19). While the liberal interpretation of citizenship 'emphasises rights', civic republicanism thus 'places its stress on duties' (Heater 1999: 4). Not surprisingly, a relatively high degree of identification with the state is also expected from citizens in the latter model: together, the state and its citizens form 'a community, an organic society, not merely a collection of individuals' (Heater 1999: 55). The civic republican conception of citizenship is much older than the liberal one, with its origins in the work of Aristotle and Cicero, and later in that of Machiavelli during the Renaissance. Thanks to Rousseau, it became particularly popular in the eighteenth century, before being eclipsed by the liberal conception. It was kept alive in the nineteenth century by such figures as Hegel and Tocqueville, and is currently experiencing a revival 'as a counterbalance to the perceived defects of liberal citizenship' (Heater 1999: 51–2). With its concern for collective rights, Quebec is also experiencing a renewed interest in this model of citizenship, as will be seen in Chapter 2.

Part I
New Challenges

Part I examines how Quebec is dealing with the new challenges of ethnic diversity and globalisation. Chapter 2 traces the development of the civic, territorial conception of Quebec identity that began in the wake of the Quiet Revolution, when Quebec society underwent a major transformation as a result of modernisation and secularisation. In the post-1995 referendum period, this new civic identity has come to define itself predominantly in terms of citizenship, in particular the idea of a Quebec citizenship to exist alongside Canadian citizenship, and designed to foster an integrative attachment to Quebec and unite Quebecers of all ethnic origins.

Chapter 3 addresses the question of national identity in a more theoretical way, by examining some of the better-known and more developed models of nation that have been proposed for Quebec. The ethnic conception of nation especially prominent in the past has provoked attempts to redefine the nation in civic terms. These latter, highly abstract conceptions of the nation have in turn triggered models which seek to reintroduce ethnic elements into an overall civic framework.

Chapter 4 evaluates to what extent Quebec is able to take advantage of the opportunities that globalisation throws up to 'act locally' through global cooperation, in order to further its own linguistic and cultural ends. The chapter focuses on significant linguistic and cultural issues raised in the two major global arenas of importance for Quebec, that of the Americas, as a site of linguistic and cultural plurality, and that of *la Francophonie*, viewed as an alternative global linguistic network to the English-speaking world.

Part 1
New Challenges

2
From French Canadian to Quebecer

> *Après avoir emprunté, ces dernières décennies, la voie de la modernisation de l'appareil étatique et celle de la maîtrise du développement économique, social et culturel, le Québec approfondit actuellement la voie identitaire pour s'affirmer face au reste du Canada, de l'Amérique et du monde. D'où le projet de citoyenneté québécoise qui prend forme actuellement, inclusive et accueillante. Issue des valeurs démocratiques centenaires, puisant au respect des autres, pétrie de culture québécoise et de langue française, cette citoyenneté encore à définir cristallise le besoin des Québécoises et des Québécois de se solidariser et de sortir de l'anonymat auquel la mondialisation condamne les petits États. [...] La citoyenneté québécoise, née d'un besoin de cohésion sociale, s'impose parce que nous vivons une période de grands bouleversements et une époque de confusion sur les plans de la langue et de l'appartenance.*

After having in recent decades modernised the machinery of government and mastered its economic, social and cultural development, Quebec is now thoroughly examining its identity in order to assert itself *vis-à-vis* the rest of Canada, North America and the world. Hence the proposal for an inclusive and welcoming Quebec citizenship which is currently taking shape. Stemming from centuries-old democratic values, drawing on respect for others and steeped in Quebec culture and the French language, this citizenship, yet to be defined, crystallises the need of Quebecers to act in solidarity and overcome the anonymity to which globalisation condemns small states. [...] Quebec citizenship, born out a need for social cohesion, is necessary because we are experiencing a period of great upheavals and of confusion with regard to language and belonging. (Gouvernement du Québec 2001a: 11–12)

Contemporary debates about citizenship, like that raised by the Larose Commission cited above, are no longer about rights, as they were in the immediate post-war period, so much as the role citizenship can play in cementing social cohesion (Helly 2000: 119; Labelle and Salée 2001: 289; Beiner 2003; see also Section 1.6). Citizenship is now seen as the means of reinforcing a sense of community or solidarity that many feel has suffered since the late 1980s–early 1990s, not least as a result of the perceived excesses of globalisation: 'A bit like if, by a swing of the pendulum, one suddenly realised that neo-liberalism had gone too far' (Lacroix 2000: 54). While this phenomenon is witnessed around the globe, it is especially apparent in the context of Quebec, where the efforts of successive Quebec governments to create a strengthened sense of solidarity by means of a common public culture coincide with a desire to ensure the survival of a language spoken by a mere two per cent of the North American continent. The consolidation of a common public culture must be reconciled, however, with the ethnocultural diversity that characterises modern-day Quebec. The desire of the authorities to be as inclusive as possible has led to the progressive 'de-ethnicisation' of Quebec identity, a process which has also served to reinforce the legitimacy of the nationalist movement in this era of (neo-)liberalism (Keating 2001b: 72).

This chapter examines the shift from an ethnic to a more civic and inclusive conception of national identity in Quebec. After tracing the initial stages of this progression, it investigates how the civic project has expressed itself more recently through the notion of citizenship, and in particular the idea of a formalised Quebec citizenship to exist alongside Canadian citizenship and within Canadian nationality. Opposition to this idea can be explained to a large extent by the confusion between citizenship and nationality, as well as by the different conceptions of citizenship that exist in Quebec and Canada and which reflect different versions of liberalism. Irrespective of whether it is formalised or not, the model of citizenship under construction in Quebec offers a useful compromise between the extreme conceptions defended by classical liberalism with its (albeit often merely token) commitment to multiculturalism on the one hand, and by French-style civic republicanism and politics of non-differentiation on the other.

2.1 From an ethnic past to a civic future

The development of a nationalism based on the ethnic identity of French Canadians was largely a product of the failure of the Patriot revolt of 1837–38 (Dufour 2001: 161). Predominantly of French descent, but also including others of English and Irish extraction, the Patriots favoured the establishment of an independent, bilingual and secular Canadian nation, constructed around political principles and inspired by the French and American republics. In the autumn of 1837, the revolt degenerated into armed conflict, which was quickly quashed by the intervening British army. Lord Durham was subsequently sent from London to investigate. In his report from 1839, he suggested a series of measures (e.g., the immediate need to populate Lower Canada with subjects loyal to Her Majesty, the Act of Union of 1840 which united Upper and Lower Canada), all designed to put French Canadians in a position of subordination in the hope that they would be assimilated. It was in order to survive as a people that French Canadians sought refuge in an ethnic nationalism founded on traditional Catholic and rural values (Mathieu 2001: 24–6).

Not until the 1950s did this ideology of *survivance* ('survival') of French Canadian culture begin to be challenged from within. Writers such as Guy Frégault, Maurice Séguin and Michel Brunet who made up the so-called Montreal School sought to establish a nationalism better suited to an urban, industrial and modern society (Maclure 2003: 23–5). Adopted later by contributors to the journal *Parti pris* (1963–68), this neo-nationalism provided a major impetus for the Quiet Revolution of the early 1960s, a period which resulted in the emergence of a new, secular, modernised and territorially-defined Quebec nation. No longer did the French speakers of Quebec wish to be considered as a minority in Canada, but rather as a majority in their own context. In line with identity strategies available to minorities according to social identity theory (see Section 1.2), the term *Québécois* was re-evaluated as a positive symbol of identity, as noted by the sociologist Marcel Rioux in 1975: 'Although the term always existed, it is only roughly in the last decade that *Québécois* has been re-evaluated to the point of becoming a sort of symbol of self-affirmation, self-determination and national liberation' (M. Rioux 1990: 9).

As became clear at the États généraux du Canada français (Estates general of French Canada) of 1967, this identity transformation dealt a major blow to the concept of French Canada: French Canadians were now divided into Quebecers on the one hand, and *francophones hors Québec* (Francophones outside Quebec) (e.g., *Franco-Ontariens, Franco-Manitobains, Fransaskois*, etc.) on the other (Frenette 2000: 326; Thériault 2000: 255; C. Bouchard 2002: 238).[1] In Quebec, the 'territorialisation' of identity was to set in motion the gradual 'de-ethnicisiation' of the Quebec nation. In 1975, the Quebec Charter of Human Rights and Freedoms introduced an important civic dimension to the representation of the Quebec nation, by recognising the right of ethnic minorities to preserve and develop their culture and by outlawing discrimination on the grounds of language or ethnic background (*Charter of Human Rights and Freedoms*, R.S.Q. c. C-12, s. 10). Following its rise to power in 1976 under the lead of René Lévesque, the overtly sovereigntist Parti Québécois also began to distance itself from an ethnic interpretation of Quebec culture, as evidenced in its White Paper of 1978 entitled *La politique québécoise du développement culturel* (Quebec Policy on Cultural Development):

> A French society first and foremost, Quebec must also find a source of vitality in its minorities. Fortunately these days, the model of the 'melting

pot', as illustrated by American society, is increasingly being called into question. The total assimilation of all new immigrants is not a desirable objective. [...] [T]he common good and even that of minority groups requires the integration of these diverse groups into an essentially French-speaking Quebec totality. But once this fundamental requirement has been established and respected, the existence of dynamic and active minority groups can only be an asset to Quebec as a whole. (Gouvernement du Québec 1978: 63)

This document was also used to promote the Parti Québécois' policy of *culture de convergence* (culture of convergence) (G. Bouchard 1999: 12), defined as the culture which constitutes 'the rallying point of all others' (Dumont 1997: 70). While the document did not explicitly accord a central place to French Canadian ethnicity as had been the case in the past (Levine 1997: 364), there was nonetheless a considerable overlap between the *culture de convergence* and that of the French Canadian majority (see Section 3.1). As such, it is perhaps no surprise that the term *Québécois* continued to be largely limited to those Quebecers of French Canadian descent until at least the 1980s (G. Bouchard 2001b: 169–71).

From this time, Quebec identity entered a new phase in its history, as immigrants and ethnic minorities increasingly began to take on the role traditionally played by *les Anglais* as the significant 'other' for French Canadian identity (Breton 1988: 100). This new phase can be divided into two periods, the starting points of which are marked by the referenda on sovereignty in 1980 and 1995 (Juteau 2002). The first period witnessed the relaunching of the Ministère de l'Immigration (Ministry of Immigration) founded in 1968: from 1981, this became known as the Ministère des Communautés culturelles et de l'Immigration (Ministry of Cultural Communities and Immigration).[2] In its action plan published in the same year under the title *Autant de façons d'être Québécois* (Québécois. Each and Everyone) (Gouvernement du Québec 1981), the new Ministry introduced elements of its preferred model of integration which was later to become known as interculturalism.

Quebec's interculturalism seeks to foster dialogue and exchange between the various ethnic groups in general, and between the 'cultural communities', that is those groups of immigrant descent, and the dominant French Canadian ethnic group in particular. Because this takes place in French, some have argued that there is in fact little difference between Quebec's interculturalism and the US and Canadian models of integration:

Quebec's interculturalism appears similar to the models adopted by the United States and Canada, in that, while the latter two countries look more like anglo-conformity in practice, Quebec's interculturalism often translates into franco-conformity in everyday life. Dominant-conformity triumphs once again. (Fournier, Rosenberg and White 1997: 108)

However, most claim that interculturalism is distinct from both the US monocultural melting pot and the Canadian multicultural mosaic, the latter treating the various components that make up Canadian society as merely juxtaposed and largely isolated entities (Juteau 1999: 157–8; Bissoondath 2002). Unlike both these other models, interculturalism involves 'the meeting of cultures, their mutual interpenetration and the reciprocal recognition of their respective contributions, within a common civic culture and a French-speaking framework' (Anctil 1996: 143; see also Gagnon 2000; Gagnon and Iacovino 2002: 325–9, 2004: 373–8).

Despite its good intentions in this direction, *Autant de façons d'être Québécois* nonetheless clearly distinguished between members of the Quebec nation on the one hand, and those of the cultural communities on the other (Juteau 1999: 158–9, 2002: 444). Not until the next major immigration policy document published by the Liberals in 1990 – *Au Québec, pour bâtir ensemble. Énoncé de politique en matière d'immigration et d'intégration* (Let's Build Quebec Together: Vision: A Policy Statement on Immigration and Integration) (Gouvernement du Québec 1991) – was this changed so that Quebecers were now defined as all those who lived in Quebec, irrespective of ethnic origin. Central to the *Énoncé* was the idea of a 'moral contract' between immigrants and the host community. This contract is guided by three principles that reflect the 'social choices that characterise modern Quebec' (Gouvernement du Québec 1991: 16), namely that Quebec is:

- a society in which French is the common language of public life;
- a democratic society where everyone is expected and encouraged both to participate and contribute;
- a pluralist society that is open to multiple influences within the limits imposed by the respect of fundamental democratic values and the need for intergroup exchanges.

Of the three principles, the acceptance of French as the language of public life is the only one that is truly specific to Quebec's distinct society (Carens 1995a: 56, 2000: 131). Moreover, as the document explains, the onus in this matter is not just on the immigrants, but also on the host community:

The host community therefore expects immigrants and their descendants to be open to the French fact, to make the necessary effort to learn the official language of Quebec and to acquire over time a feeling of commitment with regard to its development.

In return, the Government recognises that although linguistic integration depends first and foremost on the provision of adequate services, it also relies on a concerted effort in promoting the use of French, in being open to others as the host society and in developing harmonious intergroup relations. Only under these conditions can the French language become the common heritage of all Quebecers. (Gouvernement du Québec 1991: 17)

As for the *Énoncé*'s second principle regarding democracy, Quebec's demands are no different to those of other liberal democracies, especially those that adopt more republican-like models of citizenship (see Sections 1.6 and 2.3). Finally, Quebec's commitment to pluralism stated in the third principle goes beyond that of multicultural societies, because of Quebec's preferred model of interculturalism: 'The Quebec position on intercultural relations aims [...] to avoid extreme situations where different groups would maintain their culture and traditions in an integral and rigid fashion and coexist in reciprocal ignorance and isolation' (Gouvernement du Québec 1991: 19).

Quebec's concern for the protection of minorities and immigrants was also asserted repeatedly in the report of the Commission on the Political and Constitutional Future of Quebec (see Ajzenstat 1995: 122). Established in 1990 following the failure of the attempt at Meech Lake in 1987 to reform the federal constitution and recognise Quebec as a 'distinct society' (see Edwards 1994: 26–41), the Bélanger-Campeau Commission, as it was more commonly known, recommended a bill authorising a referendum on Quebec sovereignty (Commission sur l'avenir politique et constitutionnel du Québec 1991). Disappointed by the failure of the Meech Lake Accord, even the Quebec Liberal Party called for the decentralisation of a list of substantial powers to the provinces in its Allaire Report (Comité constitutionnel du Parti Libéral du Québec 1991). In the wake of another unsuccessful attempt to break the constitutional impasse with the Charlottetown Accord in 1992, and after the subsequent return to power of the Parti Québécois in 1994, a referendum on sovereignty was finally held on 30 October 1995, but this had the unintentional result of highlighting an obstacle in Quebec's efforts to create a more civic conception of nation.

In his now infamous declaration, Premier Jacques Parizeau expressed his disappointment at the failure of the independence cause despite the very close results (50.58 per cent for the 'no' and 49.42 per cent for the 'yes' campaigns respectively): 'It's true that we were beaten, but in the end by what? By money and ethnic votes. [...] We want a country and we will have it' (cited in *La Presse*, 31 October 1995). With his clearly ethnic definition of 'we', Parizeau drew attention to the fact that the civic project was not as advanced as one might have been led to believe in some quarters. First, as witnessed by the existence of the expressions *Québécois de souche* ('old stock

Quebecers') and *Québécois pure laine* ('true Quebecers'), not all Quebecers of French Canadian extraction had embraced the civic project with as much vigour as the Ministry of the Cultural Communities and Immigration (Carens 1995a: 68). Even if extreme views are limited to 'a few loose canons' (Nielsen 1999: 127; see also 1998: 155), it was surely unfortunate that such a public figure as the premier was seen to be making comments in this direction (Beiner 2003: 155). Second, the fact that around 95 per cent of non-French Canadian Quebecers had voted 'no' revealed that the majority of these did not identify with Quebec enough to vote for independence.

Indeed, as will be seen in Section 7.2, research conducted amongst immigrants confirms a gulf between grassroots attitudes and official civic rhetoric. Despite the Parti Québécois' adoption in 1996 of a definition of the *peuple québécois* ('Quebec people') as all those living in Quebec (see Bariteau 2001: 139), official rhetoric was not mirrored in actual attitudes at the grassroots level (Mathieu 2001: 13). This was to become only too apparent again in 2000 with the passing of Bill 99 (*Act respecting the exercise of the fundamental rights and prerogatives of the Quebec people and the Quebec State*, R.S.Q. c. E-20.2), a counter-measure to the federal government's *Clarity Act* (2000, c. 26) attempting to limit the possibility of a victory for the independence campaigners in any subsequent referendum (Lajoie 2004). The reference made in the Quebec act to a *peuple québécois* comprising all residents of Quebec was rejected by many non-French Canadians living in Quebec, not least the Aboriginal peoples (see Chapter 9).

Quebec's difficulty in shaking off its ethnic past has traditionally been hindered by the political discourse of the federal government, which 'legitimises and feeds ethnic differentiation and the obsession with ethnicity' (Bouthillier 1997: 14–15). Seymour (1999c) describes this strategy of the federal government as one which 'aims to ethnicise Quebec':

> Quebec must be ethnicised in order to delegitimise the independence project and to counteract it in this way. [...] While Quebec is said to be a closed, ethnic and inward-looking society, Canada is claimed to be civic, inclusive, pluriethnic and multicultural. (Seymour 1999c)

Similarly, the English Canadian press frequently aims to discredit Quebec nationalism by comparing it to tribalism, ethnic cleansing, racism, apartheid, xenophobia and the like (see Bouthillier 1997: 161; Venne 2000b). This phenomenon is not unique to Quebec, but rather reflects the pejorative way in which minority nationalisms have traditionally been conceptualised by the majorities in the states where they occur (Keating 2001a: 25–6). In the particular context of Quebec, the accusations have played on the 'guilty conscience' of nationalists, with Quebec governments and certain intellectuals now actively distancing themselves from the notion of ethnicity because of its negative connotations (J. Beauchemin 2001: 156, 2002; see also Brière 2002). This desire to emphasise only the civic virtues of the nationalist project led to the emergence of a new defining characteristic of Quebec identity in the post-1995 period: citizenship.

2.2 Citizenship in Quebec or Quebec citizenship?

In 1996, the Ministère des Communautés culturelles et de l'Immigration was renamed the Ministère des Relations avec les citoyens et de l'Immigration (Ministry of Relations with Citizens and Immigration). The government now wished to emphasise inclusion in a *culture publique commune* (common public culture) and avoid reference to cultural communities, which it considered divisive (Juteau 2002: 448; Molinaro 2005: 100–1). In 1997, the *Semaine interculturelle* (Intercultural week) was also renamed accordingly; rather than adopt the suggestion made by the Conseil de relations interculturelles (Council of Intercultural Relations) of a *Semaine de la citoyenneté et des relations interculturelles* (Citizenship and intercultural relations week), the new Ministry opted simply for a *Semaine québécoise de la citoyenneté* (Quebec citizenship week) (Juteau 2002: 448).[3] The latter became an annual event consisting of activities such as a welcoming ceremony for the newly-arrived and the awarding of the *prix québécois de la citoyenneté* (Quebec citizenship awards) to 'honour individuals, organizations, and public and private corporations for their exceptional contribution to strengthening democratic life and the exercise of citizenship in Quebec' (Gouvernement du Québec 2004c). In more recent years, emphasis has increasingly been placed not only on citizenship in a general sense, but on the idea of a Quebec citizenship in particular.

Opinions differ greatly over whether one can talk about a Quebec citizenship at all in the absence of an independent Quebec state. In this way, even the sovereigntist Claude Bariteau (2000: 136; see also Section 3.2) affirms that 'Quebec citizenship does not exist. [...] One is a citizen of a sovereign state normally recognised on the international stage. Not of a province.' Similarly, Duchastel (2000: 37) claims that while one cannot associate the adjective 'Quebec' with the concept of citizenship, 'one can certainly ponder over citizenship in a broad sense, such as it is experienced in Quebec.' Such beliefs are even more common in English Canada, where 'citizenship' and 'nationality' are almost exclusively considered synonymous, as tends to be the case in other parts of the English-speaking world as well (e.g., Australia, the UK). However, such considerations do not take into account the historical and conceptual distinction between citizenship and nationality mentioned in Section 1.6 and maintained in Quebec government documents, such as that prepared for the Forum national sur la citoyenneté et l'intégration (National Forum on Citizenship and Integration) held in 2000:

> Citizenship designates above all a person's legal capacity to participate in the exercise of power by way of the right to vote and of eligibility for public office. [...] As for nationality, this relates to the international domain.

it sanctions, with regard to another state, the link between an individual and the state that provides diplomatic protection. (Gouvernement du Québec 2000: 13–14)

In other words, citizenship exists independently of nationality. Indeed in federations such as the US and Switzerland, there exist several layers of citizenship within a single nationality (Heater 1999: 123–6). Inherent in American nationality, for example, is citizenship of the individual states as well as citizenship of the Union or State (to use the capitalisation convention followed by some). In Switzerland, citizenship exists simultaneously at the federal, cantonal and even municipal levels. Although it is a federation, Canada does not have an equivalent tradition of referring to citizenship at the provincial level; with regard to the right to vote and eligibility for public office in Quebec, for example, reference is merely made to *Canadian* citizenship and the need to have been domiciled in Quebec for at least 12 months (*Election Act*, R.S.Q. c. E-3.2, s. 54). But in at least two respects, one could in effect speak of a Quebec citizenship which exists alongside Canadian citizenship and within Canadian nationality. As one specialist on citizenship argues:

> One may argue that the enfranchised inhabitants of, say, Brittany or Catalonia or Scotland are not truly citizens of those regions in the same way as the enfranchised inhabitants of, say, Texas, Bavaria or New South Wales are citizens of their states. In a devolved structure Bretons, Catalans and Scots, for example, are not legally citizens of those provinces. Even so, on at least two key criteria they may be accorded that title: they may well have a deep sense of allegiance to their region, and they certainly have the civic right to vote for and serve in their assemblies. (Heater 1999: 132)

The problem with the Forum document is that it stresses Quebec's political right to self-determination, that Quebec's National Assembly is 'the ultimate site of the democratic expression of the Quebec people' (Gouvernement du Québec 2000: 13–14). For this reason, some have argued that the Quebec citizenship project is not purely limited to citizenship in the strict sense, but also connotes nationality (Juteau 2002: 450; see also Thériault 2002b: 31). As the editor of *Le Devoir*, Michel Venne, wrote about the then Minister of Relations with the Citizens and of Immigration, Robert Perreault, '[i]f he wants a discussion about [sovereignty], let him do so openly, not under the cover of an alleged debate about citizenship' (Venne 2000a). Because of this link with the sovereignty project, it was no surprise that the work of the Forum quickly became politicised (Gagnon 2001).

The next push for a Quebec citizenship came a year later from the Larose Commission, which recommended '[t]hat a Quebec citizenship be officially and formally instituted to reflect the attachment of Quebecers to the entire array of patrimonial and democratic institutions and values that they have in common' (Gouvernement du Québec 2001a: 21).

Quebec citizenship as described here serves two purposes: first, it reinforces the civic as opposed to ethnic nature of Quebec identity; second, it emphasises that Quebec is somehow different from the rest of Canada, meaning that the Quebec citizenship project can be considered as the perpetuation of previous attempts to have Quebec recognised as a 'distinct society'. In line with its mandate, the main difference that the Larose Commission wanted to highlight was the linguistic one. Indeed, as will be seen in Section 5.2, the idea behind this recommendation was to create an integrative motivation amongst new Quebecers that would lead them to adopt French as their language of public communications.

Recognising nonetheless that the proposal to formalise a Quebec citizenship was beyond the scope of her portfolio, the Minister responsible for the Charter of the French language at the time, Diane Lemieux, handed the issue over to her new counterpart in the Ministère de Relations avec les citoyens et de l'Immigration, Joseph Facal. While the latter had previously rejected the idea of setting up a national commission on citizenship (Facal 2001; see also Gagnon 2001; Maclure 2001), he nevertheless appointed a group of experts to examine the feasibility of the Quebec citizenship proposal (*La Presse*, 21 August 2001). A lively debate followed in the media: 'Quebec is not Switzerland', claimed Jean-Marc Léger (2001), stressing that the idea was unrealistic in the current political and judicial climate. While being sympathetic to the proposal, Jean-François Lisée also recognised the potential difficulties:

> If the Landry government envisages going down this road, it should know that this is a major undertaking which, however salutary, will cause considerable upheaval, going as it does to the heart of Quebec problem – past, present and future. We would no longer be caught up in flights of fancy [in French, *angélisme*], but in the realms of realpolitik and, in many respects, of suffering. (Lisée 2001)

Other objections made included: that English Canada would never buy the idea in the same way that it never accepted the notion of a 'distinct society'; that Quebec citizenship in a federal context would not attract non-Francophones because its function would be to promote a sense of belonging to Quebec to the detriment of other forms of identity; and that the idea would still be too linked to sovereignty since it would need to be promoted by a sovereigntist government (Venne 2001a).

In light of its politically sensitive nature, it is no surprise that the proposal to formalise a Quebec citizenship was not taken up by the Parti Québécois government. Since the arrival in power of Jean Charest and his Liberal Party in 2003, reference to citizenship in official discourse is rare and there has been a shift in focus back to cultural communities. Indeed, this is the case in the new immigration and integration action plan for 2004–07 entitled *Des valeurs partagées, des intérêts communs. Pour assurer la pleine participation des Québécois des communautés culturelles au développement du Québec* (Shared Values, Common Interests: To Ensure the Full Participation of Quebecers from Cultural Communities in the Development of Quebec), a document which also alludes to the replacement of the *Semaine québécoise de la citoyenneté* with a *Semaine québécoise des rencontres culturelles* (Quebec week for intercultural contacts) (Gouvernement du Québec 2004a: 83). Somewhat confusingly, in June 2005, the Ministère des Relations avec les citoyens et de l'Immigration also resorted to its original name, albeit with the two elements inverted, to become the Ministère de l'Immigration et des Communautés culturelles (Ministry of Immigration and Cultural Communities). As for the specific notion of a Quebec citizenship, this was supplanted for a brief period by 'democratic citizenship', a term which is more clearly distinct from nationality and which is already accepted on the international scene in the context of civic education (see e.g., Council of Europe 2004). More recently, however, even this latter term seems to have disappeared from the political landscape.[4]

Despite the potential difficulties with formalising a Quebec citizenship, such a creative use of citizenship is not as uncommon as it might seem. European citizenship exists alongside the nationalities and citizenships of individual member states of the European Union. In the same way that we can conceive of a citizenship at the supranational level, we can also consider it at the subnational – or rather substate or 'non-sovereign' (Balthazar 1988) – level. Even in the 'one and indivisible' France (see Section 2.3 below), a Caledonian citizenship for New Caledonia was introduced with the 1995 amendment of the Constitution (new art. 77) and then organised by the *Loi organique n° 99–209 du 19 mars 1999 relative à la Nouvelle-Calédonie* (art. 4 and 188) following the *Accord de Nouméa* (Leclerc 2005d). A similar design should follow for a Polynesian citizenship for French Polynesia since an amendment of the Constitution was proposed in 1999 (future art. 78) together with a *loi organique* (art. 4), which has, however, still not been adopted (Leclerc 2005e). As the then President of the government of French Polynesia declared, Polynesian citizenship 'is a citizenship within French nationality' (Flosse 2001: 21). One important difference between Quebec on the one hand and New Caledonia and French Polynesia on the other is the quasi-colonial relationship the latter continue to have with France. For this reason, a better comparison may be between Quebec and Corsica, which is more integrally part of France than the overseas territories of the South Pacific. Indeed, recognition of a 'Corsican people, component of the French people' was famously rejected in 1992 by the Conseil constitutionnel, who argued that 'the expression "the people", when applying to the French people, must be considered as a unitary category that cannot be subdivided by virtue of the law' and that 'consequently any mention made by the legislator to the "Corsican people, component of the French people" is contrary to the Constitution, which recognises only the French people composed of all French citizens irrespective of origin, race or religion' (Décision n° 91-290 DC of 9 May 1991, *Loi portant statut de la collectivité territoriale de Corse*, Rec. 50, cons. n° 11 and 13; see also Nguyen 1998: 98–9; Koubi 2004: 197). That said, substantial powers were granted to the provincial assembly of the island with the *Loi n° 2002-92 du 22 janvier 2002 relative à la Corse*, particularly with regard to education, culture, language and communication (Leclerc 2005a).[5]

The point being made here is that citizenship in the legal sense is not an immutable concept, but can be used creatively to respond to a wide range of demands for recognition. Not only is the content of the rights instituted by New Caledonian and Polynesian citizenship different in each case (predominantly political rights in the former, and social and economic rights in the latter), the desired outcome of these measures also varies: while the provision of a referendum to be held between 2014 and 2019 may lead to independence for New Caledonia (in which case Caledonian citizenship would be integrated into a new Caledonian nationality), Polynesians clearly wish to remain French (Flosse 2001). In a similarly creative way, a formalised Quebec citizenship could be limited to rights which seek solely to preserve the French language and which need not be seen as a separatist plot. Unfortunately, the possibility of such a citizenship has not yet been explored. The discussion which followed the Larose Commission's proposal has tended to concentrate on the form (i.e., citizenship or nationality?), to the detriment of a real reflection about the content of what could constitute a formalised Quebec citizenship. The difficulty stems not only from the confusion between citizenship and nationality which pervades in the minds of many, but also from the different conceptions of citizenship that exist in Canada and Quebec and which reflect different versions of liberalism.

2.3 Conceptions of citizenship and liberalism in Canada and Quebec

As noted in Section 1.6, two models of citizenship dominate modern Western political philosophy: the so-called liberal and civic republican conceptions. As a whole, Canada subscribes to the former, giving priority as it does to individual rights (Juteau 2002: 445). By far the main representative in Canada of this type of classic, individualist liberalism was Pierre Elliott Trudeau. Before he even became prime minister, Trudeau, the intellectual, embarked on a crusade against nationalism, not least in articles published in the journal *Cité libre*, which he co-founded in 1950 as a forum of opposition to the authoritarianism and conservatism of the Duplessis government in Quebec (1936–39 and 1944–59). 'Anglo-Canadian nationalism produced, inevitably, French Canadian nationalism', Trudeau (1977: 163) claimed, and the latter was now, in his view, holding French Canadians back from modernity, enlightenment and reason, qualities they could find in federalism (see Karmis 2004: 83). Yet while he was critical of the type of federalism that had existed until then and which merely perpetuated the dominance of English Canada, Trudeau was nevertheless against the granting of collective rights which, in his opinion, were by definition ethnocentric and therefore undemocratic: 'a truly democratic government cannot be "nationalist", because it must pursue the good of all its citizens, without prejudice to ethnic origin. The democratic government, then, stands for and encourages good citizenship, never nationalism' (Trudeau 1977: 169).

In his White Paper of 1969, this belief even led Trudeau to make the case for the complete assimilation of Aboriginal peoples, so that they would become Canadians like all other Canadians (Maclure 2004: 98). He was eventually forced to back down in the face of protests from indigenous groups. Nonetheless, Trudeau's individualist liberalism and anti-nationalism continued to underpin his policies during his time as prime minister (1968–79 and 1980–84). According to his vision, 'there is no Quebec people, no Quebec national community. There are only individuals, only citizens like you and me, who happen to live in the province of Quebec' (G. Laforest 1995: 46). The irony was that his repatriation of the Constitution and subsequent establishment of a Canadian Charter of Rights and Freedoms in 1982 represented the beginning of a new Canadian nationalism.

Trudeau's legacy is apparent in the work of contemporary scholars, as exemplified by Leydet (1995), who similarly argues that only a minimalist or procedural approach to citizenship is legitimate:

> It is in fact not up to the state nor to a theory of citizenship to claim to prescribe specific feelings of allegiance, solidarity or co-citizenship. These can only be born of actual practice, of the common ways that citizens experience their institutions. (Leydet 1995: 129)

These are somewhat puzzling words coming from a theorist, whose task is precisely to favour the normative over the practical dimension of such questions. Indeed as will be seen in the next chapter, the specific model of nation proposed for Quebec by Leydet is highly abstract and neglects the reality of practices at the grassroots level. For example, like many supporters of a liberal conception of citizenship, Leydet (1995: 120) questions the relevance of national identity in a post-national world where the nation is just one of many identity reference points amongst gender, religion, sexuality, etc. However, as noted in Section 1.5 and as will be seen further in Chapter 4, globalisation has not entailed the decline of nation-states or national identities, not even amongst young people as Leydet claims in particular.

Moreover, classical liberalism is hypocritical in so far as it takes for granted the very nation that it claims to reject. In Canada, despite the much-vaunted policy of multiculturalism first announced in 1971 and enshrined in the *Canadian Multiculturalism Act* (R.S., 1985, c. 24 (4th Supp.); see Edwards 1994: 53–62), it is often forgotten that 'there is no mosaic without cement, [and] in this case, it is English Canada which is the cement' (Bouthillier 1997: 188). While it is true that multiculturalism is an important factor in distinguishing the image of Canada from that of the metaphoric melting pot of its southern neighbour, the differences between the US and Canadian models of integration are certainly overestimated, with both encouraging a certain degree of Anglo-conformity (Kymlicka 1995: 14; Norman 1995: 154; Gagnon and Iacovino 2002: 330–1, 2004: 385). As the social psychologist John Edwards observes about his native country: 'the multicultural *symbol* is what appeals, not a reality which might actually alter things' (Edwards 1994: 59; see also Breton 1986).[6] Moreover, unlike Quebec's interculturalism, Canadian multiculturalism places all groups apart from the dominant one on the same footing, without distinguishing between historically rooted Aboriginal peoples and French speakers on the one hand, and ethnocultural groups of immigrant origin on the other (Gagnon 2000: 15). From Quebec's perspective, Canadian multiculturalism is thus quite simply 'a denial of the distinct status of Quebec and its ability to govern itself as a host society' (Gagnon 2000: 24; see also Bourque and Duchastel 2000: 159); it 'has been and continues to be a product of nation-building efforts rather than a genuine commitment to the main tenets of ideological multiculturalism' (Gagnon and Iacovino 2004: 385). According to what is termed the 'liberal paradox', classic liberalism thus often denies the communitarian base on which it is built (Seymour 2000: 2). Not only does this have the effect of discrediting the concept of ethnicity, by further reinforcing the fallacy that only minorities have ethnic identities (see Sections 1.3 and 2.1), it also places liberalism in the hypocritical position of favouring the culture of the majority by default. As liberal defenders of nationalism rightly point out, a purely civic nation is a myth and liberal-democratic states are not as ethnoculturally neutral as they claim (Kymlicka 1995: 110–55, 1998: 25, 1999, 2001: 24; Tully 1995: 5–7; Nielsen 1999: 125; Yack 1999; Karmis 2004: 74–5; see also Section 5.3 for state claims to neutrality with regard to language). 'Like in a game of shifting mirrors, the civic nation to some becomes the ethnic nation in the eyes of the other. This is so because ethnicity cannot be driven out of politics by ideal political arrangements' (Arel 2001: 76). As such, the best one can hope for is for the state to be evenhanded with regard to ethnocultural identity (Carens 2000).

Unlike Canada as a whole, Quebec has clearly opted for a model of citizenship which more closely resembles the civic republican conception, emphasising the practical and identity dimensions of citizenship and 'stressing integration to a common culture' (Juteau 2002: 445). Indeed, the document prepared for the National Forum on Citizenship and Integration states that '[c]itizenship is never a pure abstraction. It is embedded in a context, history and culture which give it its meaning and primary impetus' (Gouvernement du Québec 2000: 10). As for the Larose Commission, it defines citizenship as:

> Full participation of individuals in the social, economic, cultural and political life of a collectivity, i.e. the recognition and actual exercise of various rights and freedoms for their benefit. Normally associated with this are civil rights (e.g. freedom of expression, the right to property), political rights (e.g. universal suffrage), social rights (e.g. social protection, healthcare services), and cultural rights (e.g. the protection of heritage, linguistic rights) as well as the obligations these entail. (Gouvernement du Québec 2001a: 224)

This definition is clearly inspired by that of T. H. Marshall (see Section 1.6). But whereas the latter identifies three types of rights which together constitute citizenship (civil, political and social), the Commission divides the last of these into two, presumably in order to stress cultural, and in particular linguistic, rights. Despite having borrowed Marshall's liberal framework for its formal definition, the Commission nonetheless clearly intends a civic republican conception of citizenship, as evidenced by its discussion of the notion elsewhere:

> It is not a question of a citizenship in the sole sense of the legal capacity to participate in the exercise of power, but in the broader sense of belonging to a living heritage, founded on the sharing of common political and cultural references and on a shared identity. (Gouvernement du Québec 2001a: 12)

It is true that the Commission favours a substantive as opposed to a procedural conception of citizenship; however, this is quite different from an ethnically-defined notion of citizenship, and there is no reason why it need be at odds, as some commentators claim (e.g., Thériault 2002b: 30), with the establishment of an inclusive citizenship. Indeed, as seen in the above citation, the Larose Commission, like the Forum document, stresses the dynamic nature of culture and that citizenship is a '*living* heritage' to which all Quebecers contribute irrespective of their ethnic background.

More valid criticisms of the civic republican model of citizenship are provided by post-nationalists (e.g., Juteau 2002), who claim that the promotion of a common identity, however inclusive, still occurs at the expense of individual ethnic identities:

> In the case of Quebec, the attempt to foster and institutionalise a strong, shared national identity has subordinated particularistic identities, which are now seen as divisive. The rise of the citizen has de-ethnicised the community, in spite of recommendations made by the CRI [Conseil des relations

interculturelles] to take ethnicity into account (CRI, 1997). While pluralism is not abandoned, what now stands out is a commitment to a diversity without boundaries and the decline of institutional pluralism. (Juteau 2002: 449)

Juteau's claim in the last sentence above evokes the civic republicanism defended by scholars in France. For example, Koubi (2004) argues that the French model of non-differentiation of ethnic, religious and other identities in the public sphere represents an original means of managing cultural diversity. While the primary emphasis is placed on territory, the 'one and indivisible' republic, 'the approach is subtle and allows culture to *emerge from behind* territory' (Koubi 2004: 213). Many would argue, however, that such a *laissez-faire* approach is not sufficient to defend minority cultures from the dominant one. When French intellectuals vehemently defend the republican model of integration against what they call the ' "ethnisation" of public life' (Schnapper 1994: 98), for example when it comes to considering the rights of ethnic minorities, they are according preferential status to the ethnicity of the majority. In the words of Seymour (2000: 5), 'Jacobin Republicans who relentlessly denounce minority claims are most often unconscious nationalists.' As such, the republican model is linked to nationalism, if not of the overtly ethnic variety, at least of the civic kind with all its hypocrisies. Indeed, behind the civic façade, the reality is that French national identity is often conceived in ethnic terms not only at the grassroots level, but even to a large degree in official and academic circles too (Oakes 2001: 99–100). One of many examples is the irrefutably ethnic interpretation of French history taught to school children and embodied in the well-known dictum '*nos ancêtres, les Gaulois*' ('our ancestors, the Gauls') (Citron 1991: 30–1). In the light of such examples, it is no surprise that the very nature of French civic republicanism is considered to have paradoxically produced 'a tightly-knitted ethnicity' (G. Bouchard 1999: 40).

It is true that the complexities of the republican model are often misunderstood (J. A. Cohen 2001; Birnbaum 2004). Many commentators stress the need to appreciate its necessarily utopian nature, that it is merely a theoretical ideal, 'that in practice we have no choice but to settle for scaled-down and less ambitious forms of civic life' (Beiner 2003: 7). Koubi (2004: 198) goes as far as to claim that, considering its unique historical development, French republicanism in particular cannot be analysed using imported 'Anglo-Saxon' concepts. Nonetheless, beyond the normative rhetoric, the reality is that France today suffers from the same problems of ethnic discrimination that are observed in so-called Anglo-Saxon countries. Ardagh (1999: 225) cites the example of the

> *de facto* discrimination practised by white residents of HLMs,[7] who will try to move out of a block if it becomes too full of immigrants. This has

tended sometimes to create Maghrebi or black ghettos, which the official French policy of integration expressly seeks to avoid. [...] The State promotes an integration which the public then obstructs; the public stresses cultural differences which the State refuses to recognize. [...] On the one hand the State regards all citizens as equal, with the same full rights, and turns a blind eye to any distinctions between them of race or culture. But the French public, in its mass, does *not* regard immigrants as fully or equally French, and will constantly remind them of their otherness.

French-style civic republicanism renders the state largely powerless to tackle such ethnic discrimination head on. Rather than recognising ethnic identities, and thereby putting the state in a position to acknowledge the marginalisation felt by immigrants and their descendents, the French model rejects what it indiscriminately labels as 'communitarianism'. It was this mindset that lay behind the state's uncompromising reaffirmation of the cherished republican principle of *laïcité* (secularism) in the return of the debate over the wearing of the *hijab* (Islamic head-scarf) in public schools in 2003–04 (Maclure 2004).

The civic republican model of citizenship promoted in Quebec is clearly distinguishable from that which exists in France (May 2001: 231). Unlike the latter, Quebec has opted for a 'measure to address discrimination and a tool for integrating particular needs' known as *accommodement raisonnable* (reasonable accommodation) (Gagnon and Jézéquel 2004):

> The notion of reasonable accommodation contributes to making the law receptive to the particular needs of minorities and is driven by a desire for equity which breaks with a homogenising conception of equality. It is also justified by Quebec's policy of integration based on a 'moral contract to integrate' which makes the host society and immigrants jointly responsible for resolving conflicts of norms in a way which brings together the right to equality and the right to a cohesive host society. (Gagnon and Jézéquel 2004)

Such policies that accommodate and respect pluralism at the same time as promoting a common identity or culture are completely in line with liberal principles. Indeed, liberal practices such as those of Quebec have challenged classical liberal theory to the point that the latter has been forced to find ways to accommodate a desire for a sense of community. Dagger's (1997) notion of 'republican liberalism', for example, seeks to 'strengthen the appeal of duty, community, and the common good while preserving the appeal of rights' (Dagger 1997: 5). In the particular case of Quebec, the type of community desired by many Quebecers, and especially those of French Canadian descent, is of course national, and it is no surprise that there is now also a growing body of literature that demonstrates that liberal nationalism is not an oxymoron (Tamir 1993; Miller 1993, 1995; Carens 1995b, 2000; Kymlicka 1995, 1998, 1999, 2001; Levinson 1995; Nielsen 1998, 1999). Many commentators claim that, from a theoretical perspective, this is not a kind of nationalism at all so much as 'a form of liberalism that is not indifferent to concerns about national identity' (Beiner 2003: 111). Be this as it may, it does not detract from the fact that certain versions of liberalism and many forms of nationalism are mutually compatible in practice. Such is the case in Quebec, where the two ideologies have even developed in tandem:

> Before the Quiet Revolution, the Québécois generally shared a rural, Catholic, conservative, and patriarchal conception of the good. Today, after a rapid period of liberalization, most people have abandoned this traditional way of life, and Québécois society now exhibits all the diversity that any modern society contains – e.g. atheists and Catholics, gays and heterosexuals, urban yuppies and rural farmers, socialists and conservatives, etc. [...] Far from displacing national identity, [this] liberalization has gone hand in hand with an increased sense of nationhood. Many of the liberal reformers in Quebec have been staunch nationalists, and the nationalist movement grew in strength throughout the Quiet Revolution and afterwards. (Kymlicka 1995: 87–8)

All the signs indicate that this compatibility between liberalism and nationalism will continue, irrespective of whether Quebec remains in the federation or ultimately becomes independent.

2.4 A unique model of citizenship: intercultural citizenship

In his submission to the Larose Commission on 13 December 2000, the Parti Québécois candidate for the seat of Mercier, Yves Michaud, made some remarks which were quickly seized upon by opponents of Quebec nationalism. He argued that not a single voter of Côte-Saint-Luc, a predominantly English-speaking and Jewish district on the Island of Montreal, had voted for sovereignty in the 1995 referendum. He reiterated his views that the Jews were not the only people to have suffered; so too had Palestinians, Armenians and Rwandans. Finally, he also described the Jewish organisation B'Nai Brith as extremist, anti-Quebec and anti-sovereigntist, comments he made in the full knowledge that the mayor of Côte-Saint-Luc and member of B'Nai Brith was also present in the audience. Michaud was condemned by a unanimous *Assemblée nationale* the following day; Premier Lucien Bouchard also made it known that he no longer wanted Michaud to stand for the seat of Mercier. When Bouchard eventually resigned on 11 January 2001 – although purportedly for different reasons – 72 per cent of Quebecers claimed in a poll that they had agreed with the position taken by the former premier throughout the so-called Michaud affair (*La Presse*, 16 January 2001). The views of Premier Bouchard and a majority of Quebecers demonstrate that, despite the outbursts of a minority of old-guard sovereigntists, Quebec is slowly but surely making its way down the civic road, a journey which is rarely ever fast or without difficulty. As one commentator noted nearly two decades ago about this very progression: 'If the history of the evolution of English Canada can be any guide as to what we can expect in Quebec in this connection, a long and stressful process is to be anticipated' (Breton 1988: 100).

With its primary aim of inclusion, the civic project naturally leads to questions of citizenship. Irrespective of whether it is formalised or not, the model of citizenship under construction in Quebec is unique. Underpinned by a liberal nationalism born out of the ideologies of successive Parti Québécois and Liberal governments since the Quiet Revolution, it not only rejects the purely ethnic definition of the past, but also promotes a model of cultural pluralism that represents 'a third way between the (French) republican and (Canadian) multicultural forms of belonging' (Gagnon and Jézéquel 2004; see also Mc Andrew 2001). Modifying Kymlicka's (1995) notion of 'multicultural citizenship' to take into consideration Quebec's preferred model of integration and its unique form of civic-republicanism, one can speak of 'intercultural citizenship' (Tully 1995; Allegritti 2003). Unlike postnational theories of citizenship, Quebec's intercultural citizenship clearly belongs to the realms of realpolitik in that it is anchored in the nation – the notion of community which is still relevant to most people in Quebec, or indeed in Canada and elsewhere (Labelle and Rocher 2001: 74). This is not the same as to say that the idea of a Quebec citizenship is necessarily linked to the question of sovereignty, and a distinction can still be maintained between citizenship on the one hand and nationality on the other. What the Quebec conception of citizenship does require, however, is the establishment of a new model of nation for Quebec which considers 'the individual as the point of departure for reflection on citizenship, as Western tradition now desires, without necessarily overlooking the fact that the individual is inevitably anchored in a community' (Lacroix 2000: 57). The next chapter examines the development of such models, as well as alternatives that have been proposed over the last few decades.

3
Redefining the Quebec Nation

> *Délaissant l'attitude défensive des minoritaires, rejetant le caractère diviseur et ethnique du multiculturalisme, la nation québécoise mise de plus en plus sur le potentiel rassembleur d'une culture commune, fruit de la créativité de chacun de ses membres, pour accroître chez tous la conscience de partager une même citoyenneté.*
>
> Abandoning the defensive attitude characteristic of minorities, rejecting the divisive and ethnic nature of multiculturalism, the Quebec nation is counting more and more on the unifying potential of a common culture, born of the creativity of each of its members, to raise everyone's awareness that they share the same citizenship. (Gouvernement du Québec 2001a: 14)

As seen in the previous chapter, since the Quiet Revolution of the early 1960s, there has been a progressive shift in Quebec from a predominantly ethnic to a more civic conception of the nation. In the opinion of one commentator, '[t]he shift from a French Canadian to a Quebec representation of the nation is of such significance that, rather than of a transformation or reworking, one should speak of a rupture' (Dufour 2001: 164). Considering the extent of the change, it is no surprise that there has been much debate about which model of nation is most suitable. While most agree with the Larose Commission that Quebec is right to abandon 'the defensive attitude characteristic of minorities' and stress a 'unifying common culture', opinions vary about the balance that should be struck between the two main issues in question: the recognition of the ethnic pluralism of present-day Quebec on the one hand, and the continuity of the French language and culture in North America on the other. A good example of the collective debate was the initiative taken by the newspaper *Le Devoir* in 1999, which led to a series of articles, a conference and ultimately to the publication of *Penser la nation québécoise* (Vive Quebec! New Thinking and New Approaches to the Quebec Nation) (Venne 2000c, 2001c), a volume outlining the definitions of nation of seventeen Quebec intellectuals.

The present chapter focuses on some of the better-known and more developed models of nation that have been proposed for Quebec. The ethnic conception of nation defended by Dumont in particular has provoked attempts to redefine the nation in strictly civic terms (e.g., Derriennic, Leydet, Caldwell, Bariteau). These latter, highly abstract conceptions of the nation have, in turn, triggered models which seek to reintroduce more ethnic-orientated elements into an overall civic framework (e.g., G. Bouchard, Seymour, Taylor). In so far as all of these representations of the nation already coexist amongst Quebecers, this chapter can be said to be descriptive in nature. However, as one of the above-mentioned commentators points out, self-representations also have a normative character: 'Conceptualising the nation can help us to begin thinking about what we want to be, not merely to provide an image of what we are already' (Seymour 1999a: 98). The chapter therefore ends with the present authors' own views about which models are best suited to the reality of Quebec in the new century, namely those which seek to overcome the taboo of ethnicity and reconcile the latter with civic values.

3.1 Dumont's ethnic model

In seminal works such as *Genèse de la société québécoise* (1996) and *Raisons communes* (1997), Fernand Dumont outlines his model of the French nation in America. This nation is not limited to French speakers in Quebec, but rather to all French speakers in America (Dumont 1997: 57), even if he considers that 'Quebec is the "main home" and "centre of gravity" of this nation' (Dumont 1997: 67).

Dumont's French nation has its origins in the early days of colonisation in New France, in particular the rupture with the mother country (see also Section 4.3):

> As the settlement in the new country continued, as generations succeeded one another on the same soil, as the permanent residents differentiated themselves from those passing through, *Canadiens* became different from French people from across the Atlantic. This national sentiment was reinforced by the effects of the Conquest: the presence of a foreign power, the perils confronting the institutions, the coexistence of two societies. The time had now come when this sentiment would express itself, when the community would take shape and dedicate itself to representations. (Dumont 1996: 155)

As seen in Section 2.1, these representations were to converge around the ideology of *survivance* ('survival') of French Canadian culture. While he recognises that it would be pointless to attempt to draw up an exhaustive list of the elements which define any nation, Dumont does mention some of the defining characteristics of this French culture in America: the French language,

Catholicism and civil law. These are to be understood as cultural institutions or traditions, hence the importance Dumont also attributes to memory or historical consciousness (Dumont 1997: 55).

Dumont reacts strongly against attempts to define the nation in civic terms. This is manifested in his criticism of the attempts of the Patriot movement of the 1830s to construct a new, independent, bilingual and secular Canadian nation, founded on political principles and inspired by the French and American republics (see Section 2.1). Unlike in the past where genealogy alone defined a French Canadian, it was envisaged that political allegiance to the new republic would be equally valid. Dumont attributes the failure of the Patriot project to its lack of cultural grounding, its incompatibility with the defence and promotion of French culture in America:

> [T]he idea of nation cannot be reduced so easily, all the more because it is older than political consciousness. How can the old discourse of *survivance* be reconciled with the republic? This can only be done with difficulty. Founded on the sovereignty of the people, the republic presupposes implementing integral democratisation and introducing liberalism at all levels and in all institutions; but the national institutions that one seeks to maintain are historical legacies, customs, traditions. How can one justify the perpetuation of the [French] language itself, which is an exception on the continent, other than as a legacy of the past? It is no more democratic in its essence than other languages. (Dumont 1996: 175)

Dumont recognises that change is needed for the French language and culture to survive in North America, but he feels that French Canadians will disappear as a distinct cultural entity if they give up their cultural characteristics in the name of great political principles. He therefore urges his compatriots not to rely too heavily on the conception of the nation founded on the Quebec state that has progressively spread since the Quiet Revolution (Dumont 1997: 67–8). In his view, 'Quebec is not a nation' (Dumont 1997: 57), but rather a political community which comprises Francophones, Anglophones, Aboriginal peoples as well as the 'cultural communities':

> It is common to speak of a *Quebec nation*, which is a mistake, if not a myth. If our English fellow citizens of Quebec do not feel that they belong to our nation, if many Allophones are repelled by it, if the Aboriginal peoples reject it, can I include them in it by the magic of vocabulary? History has created a French nation in America; by what sudden decision can be transformed into a Quebec nation? To define the nation by territorial boundaries is to claim that the state is identified with it. This is a completely rhetorical and entirely artificial construction invented by political tacticians. (Dumont 1997: 66)

As part of his criticism of the concept of a Quebec nation, Dumont rejects the idea of a *culture publique commune* (common public culture) intended to unite Quebec's different ethnic or national groups:

> This is insufficient to create a community; the latter assumes cultural references with which individuals identify. [...] [I]t is no use juggling with different recipes, in which ingredients taken from here and there are meticulously measured in order to artificially manufacture a hybrid culture. (Dumont 1997: 69–70)

Instead, Dumont prefers his own notion of *culture de convergence* (see Section 2.1). In the political community that is Quebec, Dumont claims that this must be French Canadian culture: 'If a culture of convergence is to exist one day, it will not be a compound made in a laboratory or following a fixed set of rules; it will be French culture' (Dumont 1997: 70). With regard to language, this means that French is not considered as 'a mere mechanism of communication', but rather as 'a language in its fullest sense, that is, a culture' (Dumont 1997: 70).

In his critique of this model, Seymour (1999a: 61) claims that the so-called cultural nation of Dumont should not be confused with an ethnic nation. By this, Seymour means that Dumont's model is not ethnic because it includes those Quebecers of English, Scottish, Irish, Italian and other descents. Indeed, to emphasise that his nation is not defined by race, Dumont (1997: 53–4) cites the famous 1882 lecture by Ernest Renan, who is often considered to be the father of the civic nation (see Section 1.4). But is it not rather the case that the descendants to which Dumont is referring have merely assimilated to the French Canadian ethnic majority? Indeed, as Seymour somewhat paradoxically claims himself later, one has to assimilate to be a part of Dumont's nation (Seymour 1999a: 67). Moreover, in so far as there is substantial overlap between the concepts of culture and ethnicity as defined in a broad sense (see Section 1.3), Dumont's model can clearly be considered as ethnic in nature. Indeed G. Bouchard (1999: 42–61) refers to it not as the model of the cultural nation, but as the 'theory of ethnic nations' (see Section 3.3), while Mathieu (2001: 130) observes that 'because it is linked to the culture of the majority group, this conception comprises a relatively significant degree of ethnicity.'[1] It is in reaction to ethnic conceptions of the nation such as Dumont's that a wave of civic models of nation have been proposed for Quebec.

3.2 The civic models: Derriennic, Leydet, Caldwell, Bariteau

In his *Nationalisme et démocratie* (1995), Jean-Pierre Derriennic makes a plea for an 'individualistic conception of the nation and a non-national one of the state' (Derriennic 1995: 138). He believes that 'in politically civilised societies, the ultimate value must not be the nation, but citizenship' (Derriennic 1995: 107). Like religious beliefs, national identities should thus be confined to the private sphere. Whereas nationalism based on ethnicity or identity 'presents the greatest potential for division among fellow citizens' according to Derriennic (1995: 19), in its civic variant, he claims that it is 'a source of social cohesion, justice and civil peace' which has many virtues, especially in societies with heterogeneous populations:

> Civic nationalism has allowed for the amelioration of numerous identity-based conflicts, especially religious conflicts, those which were for a long time the most dangerous. It has facilitated the integration of immigrants, in the United States of course, but also in France: all those survivors of poverty or persecution from Eastern and Southern Europe, who became citizens of the Republic over the last century. [...] Civic nationalism has been a source of solidarity and justice. It encouraged the acceptance of equality regarding the right to vote, income tax and compulsory schooling paid for by taxpayers, including those who do not have children. It even helped in the struggle against tuberculosis. (Derriennic 1995: 19)

Derriennic's use of France as an example is partially explained by the fact that he is French himself; like many French intellectuals, he idealises the distinctly French model of integration. Together with his cosmopolitan background, his veneration of this highly abstract civic model of nation leads him to make claims that are uncharacteristic of most French people, such as when he states that 'the victory of a Belgian or Irish person in the Tour de France gives me more satisfaction than that of a French person' (Derriennic 1995: 27). In light of such statements, one cannot help but endorse Cantin's (2001b: 54) criticism of certain intellectuals in their ivory towers disconnected from the grassroots level by their theoretical approaches and like-minded colleagues.

In his country of adoption, Derriennic's ideology has translated into support for Quebec's remaining within a civic and federal Canada. Indeed most of his essay constitutes an attack on what he brands as the ethnic nationalism of Quebec sovereigntists. While Derriennic is willing to accept that the current model of nation in Quebec is predominantly civic, and that if Quebec had become independent sometime in the past it would most likely also be civic now,[2] he believes that the process of becoming independent today would necessarily involve ethnonationalist arguments in order to distinguish the independence option from the *status quo*:

> I think that in an independent Quebec, as in the federated Quebec that we know, nationalism could be civic, but that, in order to separate Quebec from Canada, arguments based on identity nationalism will be unavoidable.

[...] The arguments based on identity nationalism will return because, in the end, these are the only ones which highlight a difference between the two civic nationalisms, Quebec and Canadian. (Derriennic 1995: 39–40)

As pointed out by Seymour (1999a: 20), Derriennic's main thesis is that 'identity-based nationalism and democracy make strange bedfellows.' While Derriennic claims that these doctrines are at first glance compatible, 'if we analyse the consequences that they have had in those places where they were put into practice, it is clear that nationalism and democracy are profoundly antinomic: nationalisms produce confrontational situations which are resistant to democratic decision-making procedures' (Derriennic 1995: 16). Moreover, about countries like Denmark, 'where culture and law are individualistic' (Derriennic 1995: 137), Derriennic implies that national identity is unimportant there, even though studies show that this is a serious misinterpretation (e.g., Zølner 2000).[3] Considering that civic approaches are usually claimed to be driven by purely rational concerns, it is surprising that Derriennic makes such an emotional and often ungrounded plea for his model of nation. His essay is highly speculative and makes little reference to any other authors, and especially not to the extensive body of new literature that demonstrates the mutual compatibility of certain versions of liberalism and many forms of nationalism, such as that in Quebec (see Section 2.3).

This problem does not dog the model advanced by Dominique Leydet (1995), who is much more theoretically rigorous. Leydet favours a civic nation which reflects a minimalist or procedural definition of a *culture publique commune* and which rests on principles that satisfy three conditions:

> First, these principles must be able to be applied generally, that is, they must be able to be legitimately accepted by all members of the society in question irrespective of their community of origin. Second, these principles must be able to be justified according to juridico-political principles that form the basis of liberal democracy. Third, adherence must be voluntary, in other words, through rational choice. (Leydet 1995: 127)

With regard to membership of a certain society, these three conditions make up the 'conditions of entry', which should be clearly distinguished, in Leydet's view, from the 'conditions of allegiance', that is, 'the reasons why such and such an individual acknowledges an obligation of loyalty to the society of which he or she is a member' (Leydet 1995: 126). In other words, while the former relate to citizenship in a purely procedural sense (see Section 1.6), the latter have to do with questions of 'identification with a collective destiny, with a culture' (Leydet 1995: 127).

Leydet criticises the position of the Quebec authorities, in particular their attitude which she describes as: 'you must act like this, because this is how we, the majority community, choose to act' (Leydet 1995: 123). As an example, she cites the *Enoncé de politique en matière d'immigration et d'intégration*. As seen in Section 2.1, this document defines Quebec as: 'a society in which French is the common language of public life'; 'a democratic society where everyone is expected and encouraged both to participate and contribute'; and 'a pluralist society that is open to multiple influences within the limits imposed by the respect of fundamental democratic values and the need for intergroup exchanges' (Gouvernement du Québec 1991: 16). Leydet claims that while the principles of democracy and pluralism are non-negotiable, can be applied generally and are therefore morally legitimate, the requirement that French be the *langue publique commune* of Quebec is more problematic. If the use of a particular language can be defended in terms of a community's need for a common means of communication, it should not be justified in identity terms (Leydet 1995: 124–7):

> Thus, it is not the same thing to ask a Pakistani immigrant to learn French by virtue of an argument concerning the conditions of full participation in Quebec democratic life as to demand of this immigrant that he or she feel the same sense of attachment and commitment to this language as do a majority of French-speaking Quebecers. In the latter case, it is the identification of the immigrant to the destiny of a particular collectivity which is called into question. To be sure, such an identification may develop over time, as the immigrant develops a sense of belonging to the host society, but it cannot be a requirement. (Leydet 1995: 127)

Unlike Miller (1993, 1995; see Section 2.3) and others who defend a substantive definition of *culture publique commune*, Leydet is left with the dilemma of how to distinguish a certain nation from any other liberal democracy. As she herself admits: 'In fact, the principles evoked in the *Énoncé* are essentially those which form the basis of all liberal democracies, yet I do not feel a particular sense of allegiance to the German or English political societies' (Leydet 1995: 128).

But Leydet stops short of attributing the differences among liberal democracies to those of national identity; rather, in her view, variation can be explained by the fact that the principles are shaped by certain necessarily specific histories, institutions and practices (Leydet 1995: 128). The histories, institutions and practices to which Leydet refers are not so much those of the dominant ethnic group of a particular society, but rather those that all citizens, irrespective of ethnic background, are in the process of creating. This is clearly demonstrated by her claim that the only legitimate justification for using French as the *langue publique commune* of Quebec is that it reflects the decision of the majority of citizens *at a particular point in time*:

> Let's suppose that the massive arrival of immigrants significantly modifies the sociological composition of Quebec society and that after a democratic debate, a majority of Quebecers come out in favour of modifying the

Charter of the French language and decide to opt for the choice of two official languages. Such a change would be perfectly legitimate. (Leydet 1995: 130; see also Carens 2000: 132)

Unlike Ledyet, Gary Caldwell (1988, 2001; Caldwell and Harvey 1994) accords a much greater sense of permanency to French as the *langue publique commune*: 'In Quebec, this language can only be French, because every public culture is also the product of a specific historical experience' (Caldwell 1988: 709). For this reason, one could claim that his model maintains a minimal degree of ethnicity (Mathieu 2001: 129), but this assertion needs to be qualified in two respects. First, the 'greater cultural tradition' that Caldwell says feeds this 'specific historical experience' is not limited to French Canadian ethnicity, but is also made up of elements from other ethnicities (e.g., Quebec's British-inspired political institutions). Second, Caldwell is not valuing ethnicity *per se*; the importance he attributes to the 'greater cultural tradition' is more for the sake of history than ethnicity.

Unlike the notion of *convergence culturelle*, in which the majority culture takes up practically all the space (Caldwell and Harvey 1994: 789), the definition of *culture publique commune* advocated here is therefore still very much a procedural one. While it is clearly a product of history, it is nonetheless predominantly defined in terms of traditional civic means. Basing themselves on Caldwell's (1988) earlier work, Caldwell and Harvey (1994: 790-3) define the content of Quebec's *culture publique commune* in terms of three levels (see also Caldwell 2001). First, the 'rules of the communitarian game in Quebec' involve freedoms (e.g., of speech, of religion, of movement, etc.), political rights (e.g., right to vote, right to stand in elections), judicial rights (e.g., equality before the law, presumption of innocence), social rights (e.g., right to education, right to receive medical treatment, right to language of public use), and economic rights (e.g., right to the fruits of one's labour, right to property). Second, these 'rules of the game' are underpinned by certain principles (e.g., individuals are responsible for their own acts; society is responsible for the well being of all its members, especially the less fortunate; the state and the Church are separated; there should be no discrimination on the grounds of race, colour, sex, religion, language, ethnic origin or socio-economic situation). Finally, a further exploration of these principles reveals more fundamental 'articles of faith which support our culture' (e.g., everyone has an intrinsic value; freedom of choice exists; we are part of a continuity of generations, even if there is still freedom of development; all humans are part of the same humanity and can develop a sense of solidarity). Caldwell (1988: 708) explains that the intensity with which these rules and principles have been internalised clearly varies according to ethnocultural belonging. Nonetheless, they represent what Quebecers all have in common, that is, the *culture publique commune*:

> It is the element of culture that all citizens, wherever they are, be they French, from one of the eleven Amerindian peoples, or Anglo-Quebecers

of old or new descent. At the same time, this will allow for the shift from a series of ethnic nationalisms to a territorial nationalism common to all. (Caldwell and Harvey 1994: 789)

Like Caldwell, Claude Bariteau (1996, 1998, 2001) too asserts that French should be the *langue publique commune* in Quebec. However, he insists that '[i]n a political project in a multicultural environment, it is important not to link language and cultural belonging' (Bariteau 1998: 163; see also 1996: 159); rather, the French language should be dissociated from the French Canadian cultural memory (see also Lamoureux 1995a: 68; Section 5.2). Bariteau epitomises the political framework most frequently associated with a procedural definition of *culture publique commune*, namely Habermas's Jacobin-inspired theory of constitutional patriotism (Habermas 1994, 1996). Developed originally as a new model of nation for post-war Germany, but now applied to other contexts such as the European Union and Quebec, constitutional patriotism is

> a mechanism in line with the principles of a liberal and democratic society allowing for the de-ethnicisation of citizenship by replacing cultural affiliations, which are by definition specific, with an allegiance to institutions and political symbols that are potentially universal in nature. (Lamoureux 1995b: 132)

In order to apply a model based on constitutional patriotism to multiethnic or multicultural societies, and for it to succeed in creating a 'founding myth' for all citizens, Bariteau (1996: 148; 1998: 146) explains that five rules need to be respected. First, the law needs to be distinguished from substantively defined ethical practices; in other words, it should be neutral. Second, there should be a clear distinction between the *culture publique commune* to which all citizens integrate and the specific cultures to which groups or sub-groups can integrate for identity reasons. Third, the Constitution should reject all fundamentalist practices. Fourth, immigrants should integrate to the *culture publique commune*, and not to the culture of the dominant group or groups. Finally, the *culture publique commune* should be 'respectful of the differences that characterise the communities which make up the nation.'

While recognising that specific ethnocultures exist and should be respected, constitutional patriotism nonetheless requires that individual rights should have primacy:

> Individual rights and the right to difference cannot be put on an equal footing, in the same way that individual rights cannot be equated with the affirmation of a particular culture. These are two realities which it is important to distinguish. (Bariteau 1996: 152)

Following Habermas (1994), Bariteau thus rejects the ethnocultural nation of Dumont and in particular the 'politics of recognition' of Taylor (1994; see also Section 3.3). Such approaches lead to the 'escalation of demands for group rights' (Bariteau 1998: 138) and all the problems that these entail. In the case of Quebec's English speakers, Bariteau (1996: 155) highlights the potential for secessionist claims if Quebec became independent. Moreover, in his view, this group does not even constitute a nation: 'Quebec's English minority is strictly of a linguistic nature and comprises several culturally distinct groups with few affinities among them. It is thus a misuse of the term to speak of a "nation" ' (Bariteau 1996: 155). As for Aboriginal peoples, he points out the difficulty in granting rights to groups that are not limited to the territory of Quebec, but which also live in neighbouring provinces (Bariteau 1996: 156). Bariteau's opinion on the cultural communities is somewhat contradictory. All the while rejecting group rights, he believes that sovereigntists have traditionally only been concerned with integrating immigrants and have not paid them enough attention (Bariteau 1996: 153–4). Nonetheless, the recognition of specific cultures should be clearly limited to the private sphere; Bariteau thus stops short of favouring a policy of multiculturalism, such as that which exists in Canada:

> Applied to Quebec, [multiculturalism] would be, as it is already, more a source of division than of efforts to find common goals. That said, there is no reason why cultural communities and ethnic minorities cannot be recognised, why their contribution to the flourishing of Quebec cannot be acknowledged and why ways cannot be found for their members to feel part of all facets of Quebec civil society. Such recognition in no way implies the defining of group rights. (Bariteau 1996: 154–5)

Bariteau's strictly civic conception of nation has led him to claim that the Quebec nation does not yet exist and will only come into being once Quebec becomes independent. He once claimed that Quebec is at best a virtual 'nation', and Quebecers of French origin constitute a 'national' minority within the Canadian nation (Bariteau 1996: 136). More recently, however, Bariteau seems willing to accept the idea that a Quebec nation in the civic sense does already exist: 'There is indeed a political nation in Quebec which is distinct from the Canadian political nation' (Bariteau 2001: 137). Nonetheless, elements of his previous claim that it is 'virtual' are still present when he states that '[t]he Quebec political nation has manifested itself in Quebec's territory for some time. The problem is not that it needs to be invented, but that it hesitates to recognize itself and act on its own behalf' (Bariteau 2001: 137).

The fact that Bariteau is a sovereigntist distinguishes his model from that of others such as Derriennic. Unlike the latter, who considers that an independent Quebec would necessarily have recourse to ethnic nationalism,

Bariteau (2001: 138) maintains that the independence movement has been instrumental in encouraging new civic conceptions of the Quebec nation. This does not imply that he rejects the ethnic/civic dichotomy; rather, he considers it all the more important for this reason:

> This is a fundamental distinction. Far from being a false dichotomy, as some people have tried to persuade Quebecers, this distinction needs to be made to clarify the direction and destiny of the sovereignty proposal. More to the point, this is the only way of preventing sovereignists from mixing together 'cultural identity' and 'political subject' into an explosive brew, as many of them tend to do. (Bariteau 2001: 138)

3.3 Reconciling the ethnic and the civic: Bouchard, Seymour, Taylor

Like Bariteau, the historian Gérard Bouchard (1997, 1999, 2001a) also considers the ethnic/civic dichotomy important because it 'very clearly indicates the direction to follow in the overall endeavour that consists of reworking the nation in order to situate it within diversity' (G. Bouchard 1999: 42). Bouchard is often considered as defending a civic model of nation, since he criticises the 'theory of ethnic nations' of Dumont and others who divide Quebec up into three ethnic nations or parts thereof: French Canadians, English Canadians and Aboriginal peoples (G. Bouchard 1999: 44).[4] In particular, he believes that a return to a French Canadian conception of the nation would entail several risks (G. Bouchard 2001a: 35–6): the risk of putting an end to thinking about Quebec in its entirety as a Francophone society; the risk of marginalising all non-French Canadians by relegating them to minority status; the risk of creating a climate that favours divisions, stereotypes, and ethnic and racial tensions; the risk of playing into the hands of Trudeau's idea of multiculturalism; the risk of enclosing the sovereignty project in an ethnocentric box; the risk of regressing to the inward-looking vision associated with the old *survivance*-inspired nationalism; the risk of strengthening the idea of 'old stock' origins and making the nation a barricade rather than a meeting place; the risk of needlessly formalising the majority status of the French Canadian ethnic group in the public sphere; and the risk of perpetuating the privileges that this group has granted itself in this sphere (e.g., its quasi-monopoly over employment in the civil service).

Bouchard thus proposes to 'open the circle of the nation' (1997), to create a 'national coalition' founded on five principles (G. Bouchard 2001a: 32): respect for already existing ethnic groups and identities; the need to promote interaction between these groups; concerted interaction (through public debates of various kinds); multiple identities (something that all Quebecers have long had experience of); and adherence by affiliation (transfers, individual choices) as well as by filiation (attachment to one's ethnic group of origin). With regard to this last principle, Bouchard (2001a: 32) notes that '[s]o far, in reference to the coalition project, we have concentrated on adherence by filiation, but adherence by affiliation is no less important.'

Bouchard's model rests on two pillars. The first is that French should be the common denominator of the Quebec nation. As the language that roughly 93 per cent of the population claim to be capable of speaking – 'exactly the same as the proportion of Americans who currently say they can speak English' (G. Bouchard 2001a: 30) – French allows all Quebecers to participate fully as citizens in the life of the nation, thereby contributing to a sense of common identity:

> Some people will raise the reasonable objection that a common language in itself is not an adequate basis for an identity, let alone a national culture. But these things need to be seen in a dynamic, long-term perspective. Language, as a common denominator, needs to be looked at here as a point of departure. It is a *sine qua non* of the new identity – the new culture to be promoted by investing in all the diversity of traditions and cultures that already exist in our society. Language is the vector that opens the way to interactions, initiatives and common experiences whose destiny over the long haul will be to foster a true Quebec identity. [...] In short, just as law does not create society but establishes the boundaries for it, so language does not take the place of culture but prepares the ground for it. (G. Bouchard 2001a: 30)

Bouchard explains that the Francophone *enfants de la loi 101* (children of Bill 101) represent a perfect example of this culture or identity in formation (G. Bouchard 2001a: 30; see Chapter 5 on the relationship between affinity with Quebec and the adoption of French as a language of public communication).

The second pillar of Bouchard's model rests on *américanité*, the idea that an element of the Quebec nation is North American in nature (see Section 4.3). Some commentators reject this idea in so far as it breaks with 'the idea of a Quebec culture whose destiny is inevitably tortuous because it is so radically alone in America' and that it consists of 'uprooting French-Canadian culture from the soil that nourished it and replanting it in the diversity that is now such a prominent feature' (J. Beauchemin 2001: 159). But the criticism from Beauchemin and others (e.g., Cantin 2001a) is somewhat harsh considering that Bouchard in fact rejects strictly civic models of nation, such as that proposed by Bariteau:

> I do not think that the model of civic nation as proposed is sociologically viable. To be sure, it indicates an ideal to follow, but it is more a question of utopia (in the noble sense of the term: an affirmation of civilised values,

a necessary direction) than of true social engineering. The problem results from the fact that it proposes a simplistic vision of society, too narrowly centred on the rationality of law and the privileges of the individual. However, the individual remains no less part of a collectivity with which he or she develops attachments that cannot be relegated to a secondary or optional level, as can everything which falls within the private sphere. In particular, because of the divisions and structural constraints that it creates, the collective dimension is an important, necessary and universal component of an individual's life and it is obvious that neither the state nor the law can be indifferent to it. (G. Bouchard 1999: 22)

Unlike others (e.g., J. Beauchemin 2001, 2002), Bouchard may reject a substantive definition of *culture publique commune*, considering the latter to be a 'culture in motion' (G. Bouchard 1999: 66); he nonetheless recognises that 'the prospect of a zero ethnicity is quite simply not realistic' (G. Bouchard 1999: 31):

It is unrealistic to think that the *common* culture [...] can be constructed completely from scratch. The Quebec cultural space is not blank, it is highly structured by virtue of a nearly four-century-old collective dynamic, within which the French component has always mattered the most because of its number, age and vigour. It is sociologically impossible for this massive component to retreat suddenly from the symbolic areas that it has developed throughout history (language, customs, symbols, and the rest) and in a way relinquish what it is. Consequently, it is inevitable that the *common* culture is heavily impregnated by the old French Canadian culture – and the latter has nothing to apologise about. (G. Bouchard 1997: 130)

In other words, Bouchard believes that even a new civic nation in Quebec cannot and should not escape some degree of ethnicity, which is not to say that it is ethnicist or ethnocentric in nature.[5] In subsequent refinements of his model of the Quebec nation as a North American *francophonie*, he claims to have reduced the 'ethnicity coefficient' to language alone (G. Bouchard 1999: 64, 71). His acknowledgement that language cannot be 'de-ethnicised' (see Section 5.3) means that his conception of the nation

is more akin to the reality of the Quebec experience as it accepts from the start that French as the *langue publique commune* is, for the Francophone majority of French Canadian descent, their *langue identitaire* ['identity language'] and that through which they express their cultural identity, which means that it is an essential expression, the most essential even, of their ethnicity. (Pagé 2006: 37)

Bouchard's model is therefore not a purely civic one, as some claim, but rather one which endeavours to reconcile the ethnic and civic aspects of national identity, by bringing together in a single model elements of French Canadian culture (be it merely the French language or more) and liberal democratic principles such as equality, inclusiveness and respect for diversity.

As seen in Section 1.4, others believe that such attempts at reconciliation remain nonetheless 'under the spell' of the ethnic/civic dichotomy and merely serve to enhance its importance (Seymour *et al.* 1996: 6). Instead, they prefer to seek to 'transcend' or 'surpass' the opposition completely. Such is the aim of the 'sociopolitical nation' proposed by Michel Seymour (1998, 1999a, b, 2001):

> The sociopolitical nation is a political community which has specific sociological traits. It is first and foremost composed of a national majority but also, in many cases, of national minorities and individuals with different national origins. Finally, the population of this political community must also conceive of itself as being constituted in this way. This conception is sociopolitical because it brings into play considerations that relate both to the existence of a political community and to the sociological composition of the group. The two key concepts are the national majority and the political community. As the first is sociological and the second political, I call this conception sociopolitical. (Seymour 1999b: 158)

Seymour criticises the abstract nature of what he calls Dumont's 'cultural' definition of the nation, which does not take into consideration the political dimension of national identity, as manifested, for example, by the effects of the Quiet Revolution on the identity of Francophones in Canada (see Section 2.1). He explains that, on the one hand, the majority of Francophone Quebecers now consider that their identity is distinct from that of French speakers outside Quebec; on the other hand, the latter nowadays feel little affinity with Quebec, but rather identify with the Canadian nation, or the Acadian nation in the case of French speakers in New Brunswick. While one can still find people who do identify with a French Canadian nation, he argues that these are mainly older people and that they constitute a minority. For this reason, Seymour (2001: 151) claims vehemently that '[t]he French-Canadian nation no longer exists!' Moreover, the Quebec nation, as Seymour sees it, includes for the most part all groups that belong to the Quebec political community who, in turn, have a moral obligation to accept that they belong to this nation (Seymour 1999a: 73–4).[6] While there exist certain institutions specific to the various groups that make up this nation (e.g., *Le Devoir*, the Université du Québec, the Université de Montréal, etc. for French speakers; *The Gazette*, McGill University, etc. for English speakers), there are nonetheless a number of institutions which all Quebecers share and which contribute to a common Quebec identity (e.g., Quebec's parliamentary system, the *Assemblée nationale*, the *Bibliothèque nationale*, the *fête nationale*, etc.) (Seymour 1999a: 63–5). This sense of shared identity amongst all Quebecers is confirmed by popular opinion: Seymour explains that not only do French speakers consider Quebec's English speakers and new Quebecers as belonging to the Quebec nation, the majority of English speakers also claim to be Quebecers (Seymour 1999a: 65, 69), even if some of them feel a certain reticence (see Section 8.2).

Despite his difference of opinion with Dumont over the importance of the political dimension of national identity, Seymour does agree that the definition of a nation should also include a sociological element. For this reason, he criticises strictly civic conceptions of the nation such as those discussed in Section 3.2:

> We should clearly reject an exclusively civic model that would make the national majority of francophone Quebecers disappear into a sterilized political community. Whether in the form of Jacobin republicanism imported from France or constitutional patriotism imported from Germany, an exclusively civic – even postnational – identity is not well suited to the particular situation of Quebec. The Quebec identity should not be dissolved in a civic identity that ignores the presence of a national majority of francophones. The grounding of the common civic identity of all Quebecers in the language, culture (as a meeting place of specific influences) and history of the francophone national majority needs to be recognized. (Seymour 2001: 152)

Not only does Seymour stress the importance of the Francophone majority, his model also accords rights to the other groups that make up the Quebec nation, in particular the Anglo-Quebecers, through a policy of multiculturalism.[7] The question is: what sort of groups is he talking about? No doubt because of the negative connotations of ethnicity in Quebec and Canada, Seymour is at pains to 'de-ethnicise' his conception of the nation, preferring instead to define the constituent groups in terms of language, history, culture and a desire to live together (Seymour 1999a: 100). However, as seen in Section 1.3, these are all considered important elements of ethnicity when defined in a broad sense. Even if Seymour's narrow definition is adopted instead – the ethnic nation 'assumes either the existence of a common ancestral origin or the belief in such a common origin' (Seymour 1999b: 156) – it is difficult to see how ethnicity can be avoided, considering that Seymour claims to defend a model of nation 'that does not deny its origins' (2001) and defines the constituent groups in those terms:

> [The Quebec nation] includes the francophone national majority (francophones of French Canadian origin or through assimilation), the anglophone

national minority (anglophones of Anglo-Saxon origin or through assimilation) and people who are of other national origins (allophones, new Quebecers, members of cultural communities, and people who belong simultaneously to more than one of these categories). (Seymour 2001: 152)

Whether one takes a narrow or broad definition of ethnicity, it is therefore not surprising that Seymour has been described as defending 'a conception of the nation in which ethnicity plays a key role' (Mathieu 2001: 131). Seymour may be guilty of terminological gymnastics, by expressing in terms of sociology what others would describe in terms of ethnicity. However, it is somewhat harsh to claim, as does Mathieu (2001: 82–3), that his model does not offer a real alternative to Dumont's: Seymour clearly does differ from Dumont in the value he attributes to the political dimension of national identity. For this reason, it would seem more accurate to describe Seymour's model as one which seeks not to transcend the ethnic/civic dichotomy so much to reconcile its two poles.

Another model of nation for Quebec which also has the effect of reconciling the dichotomy is that progressively being developed by Charles Taylor. In the past, Taylor has described French speakers in terms of a cultural nation, sharing Dumont's belief that the French-speaking nation in question was not limited to Quebec. For example in 1970, he claimed that '[t]he great majority of French Canadians fundamentally identify with what is rightly called *the French Canadian nation*' (Taylor 1992: 36). He reiterated this position in 1990:

> Quebec is a distinct society, the political expression of a nation, the great majority of which live within its borders. [...] Quebec is the main home of this nation, whose branches have established themselves elsewhere in North America, principally in Canada. (Taylor 1992: 162)

In more recent writings, Taylor still refers to the 'French Canadian nation' (Taylor 2001: 19), but he seems completely open to the idea of a Quebec nation defined in political terms, even if his preference is for this to be within the Canadian nation, and even if he admits that '[a]n inclusive Quebec political nation has not yet fully come into being' (Taylor 2001: 26). What is interesting to note is that Taylor's notion of a Quebec political nation extends well beyond the bounds of what is normally associated with civic nations. His belief in the 'politics of recognition' (Taylor 1994) leads him to see even the political nation as the meeting place for sociocultural differences. In the context of Quebec, any political nation would need to be composed of three essential elements: a political ethic, essentially defined by human rights, equality and democracy; French as the common public language; and a certain relationship with history (Taylor 2001: 22). Even if he stresses that this must not be considered as fixed, the emphasis Taylor places in particular on this last element, history, clearly demonstrates his desire not to banish the ethnic dimension from any definition of the Quebec nation:

> This is part of the 'ethnic' dimension of our hybrid democracy (which is also highly civic in nature): that we must ask new immigrants to assume our history as their own, as it is the formative matrix of the society that they are to take part in. And this is an ethnic history, largely the history of the majority French-Canadian ethnic group, but also that of Aboriginal nations, and more recently, of the 'English.' (Taylor 2001: 24; see also 1996: 359)

It is because of this recognition that Taylor accords ethnicity within an otherwise civic framework that we can describe his model for a Quebec nation, like those of Bouchard and Seymour, as one which seeks to 'reconcile the two forms of cohesion' (Taylor 1996: 360).

3.4 Overcoming the taboo of ethnicity

So-called liberal culturalists are quick to point out that one should not confuse ethnicity with culture: Quebec is a cultural nation, they argue, not an ethnic one (e.g., Nielsen 1998, 1999; Kymlicka 1999: 132–3). However, closer inspection reveals that it is indeed the culture of ethnic groups they are referring to: 'this idea that liberal-democratic states (or "civic nations") are *ethno*culturally neutral is manifestly false' (Kymlicka 2001: 24, emphasis added). While Kymlicka and others are right to claim that Quebec nationalism is no longer purely ethnic, the implication that cultural nationalisms are void of ethnic elements is clearly problematic.[8] In light of the difficulties in maintaining a rigid distinction between culture and ethnicity (see Section 1.3), it would seem wiser – and certainly less disingenuous – to recognise that all nations have ethnic elements, even if they choose to express these within an overall civic framework. Rather than reject ethnicity as illegitimate, as do the purely civic and Jacobin-inspired models of nation outlined in Section 3.2, one should instead seek to overcome the taboo which this concept has come to represent in Quebec and elsewhere. The 'reclaiming' of ethnicity in this way would not only benefit minority groups, who clearly desire to express their ethnic identities (see Chapter 7), but also the French Canadian majority. In the words of Juteau (2004: 97):

> The dominant *ethnie* could instead choose to recognize ethnicities, subordinate and dominant. It would then be in a better posture [*sic.*] to establish a more egalitarian society. In addition, *Québécois* of French-Canadian ethnicity would no longer dilute their own specificity under the cover term Francophone *Québécois* and no longer deprive themselves

of a name designating their own distinct and mobile identity within the *Québécois* community of citizens.

What Juteau forgets to mention when she talks of French Canadians depriving themselves of a name is that the promotion of a civic identity which refuses to recognise French Canadian ethnicity also risks alienating the dominant group, potentially causing it to withdraw into itself and become defensive. Such an outcome would completely cut across the original goal of redefining the nation in more inclusive terms. The challenge facing Quebec is therefore not just to create an inclusive, civic society that values and encourages the ethnic identities of indigenous and immigrant minorities, but also one which combines this with respect for the ethnicity of the majority French Canadian population. In the view of the authors of this book, the models proposed by Seymour and Bouchard, as well as the conception of the Quebec nation being developed by Taylor, are the best suited to this purpose.

Of course, the challenge that Quebec faces is not limited to its borders. The balance that needs to be struck between being open to other cultures on the one hand, and feeling able to express the more ethnic-orientated elements of its identity on the other, also applies to Quebec's relations with other nations in North America and on the international scene in general, as will now be seen in Chapter 4.

4
Quebec in a Globalising World

> *Il fallait la poussée déferlante de la mondialisation pour faire prendre conscience aux États de la menace que représente pour les cultures et les langues du monde l'hégémonie anglo-américaine. Tout à coup, la résistance qu'avaient toujours opposée les Québécoises et les Québécois à l'uniformisation culturelle et langagière du continent, loin d'être une exception, s'avère d'une extraordinaire modernité et les projette à l'avant-garde d'un courant planétaire en faveur de la diversité des cultures. Ce sursaut de conscience mondiale est salutaire. Il ne peut que favoriser la cause québécoise et celle de tous les peuples, en particulier les petits, dont la culture et la langue sont plus fragiles.*
>
> It took the sweeping rise of globalisation to make states aware of the threat that Anglo-American hegemony represents for the cultures and languages of the world. The resistance that Quebecers have always put up to the cultural and linguistic standardisation of the continent, far from being an exception, suddenly proves to be extraordinarily modern and propels them to the forefront of a planetary movement in favour of the diversity of cultures. This surge of world conscience is salutary. It can but further the Quebec cause and that of all nations, in particular small nations, whose culture and language are more fragile. (Gouvernement du Québec 2001a: 8)

The Larose Commission's framing of Quebec's struggle for survival as a longstanding resistance to the threat of Anglo-American hegemony corresponds to an understanding of globalisation which pits local forms of resistance against the global homogenising force of Western, and particularly US, culture and its linguistic expression, English: far from being a backwater exception to current world trends, Quebec's fight for cultural and linguistic survival places it at the forefront of a global movement to protect and promote cultural diversity. Globalisation, in this reading, has produced the conditions prompting other governments and states to follow in Quebec's footsteps, as they increasingly recognise the overwhelming capacity of the US 'to project its culture and values globally' (Sonntag 2003: 19), and the dangers of English as 'the main bearer of American economic and technological hegemony' (Holborow 1999: 4). Globalisation, then, legitimises Quebec's longstanding bilateral struggle by making it a universal one – all the world against a common foe.

But globalisation can be construed in terms other than those of Anglo-American hegemony (see Section 1.5). In a compelling analysis, the sociologist Roland Robertson, one of the first scholars of the modern phenomenon of globalisation, considers it as 'the compression of the world as a whole', which has as its basis 'the linking of localities' (Robertson 1995: 34). He argues that the local is an aspect of globalisation, not its opposite. This construction of globalisation is about contact, not threat or invasion, about 'space', not language. Scholars sympathetic to Robertson's insight have demonstrated that the interpenetration of the global and the local gives rise to a growing necessity for transnational collaborations and activities to promote local concerns, in a world where the interests and spheres of influence of nation-states – and other political entities – within their territory are becoming more restricted (Lash and Urry 1994: 280). This proliferation of alliances and collaborations has been described as structural hybridisation, 'a pluralization of forms of co-operation and competition as well as [...] novel mixed forms of co-operation' (Nederveen Pieterse 1995: 52).

By working from the premise that the global entails the local, rather than simply viewing the local and the global in opposition, as the Commission does, this chapter shows that, far from either being caught in or choosing heroically to wage a constant fight against the global, Quebec is able to take advantage of the opportunities that globalisation throws up to 'act locally' through global cooperation, in order to further its own linguistic and cultural ends. The chapter focuses on significant linguistic and cultural issues raised in the two major global arenas of importance for Quebec, that of the Americas, as a site of linguistic and cultural plurality, and that of *la Francophonie*, viewed as an alternative global linguistic network to the English-speaking world. Within each of these arenas, Quebec's relationship to the dominant players – the US in the Americas, and France in *la Francophonie* – has major consequences for Quebec in terms of language and of identity formation. Underlying these relationships is, of course, perhaps Quebec's most fundamental one, that with Canada.

4.1 Quebec's international relations

In order to situate the various strands of Quebec's active exploitation of the local within the global, it is useful to consider Quebec's presence and status internationally and its relationship with Canada. Since the Quiet Revolution, successive Quebec governments have been aware that international relations are crucial (Gouvernement du Québec 2001b: 21), and Quebec, as a non-sovereign actor (see Balthazar 1988), has since been engaged in what have been termed 'systematic trans-sovereign activities' (Duchacek 1988: 14). As is the case of other non-sovereign governments, Quebec's international action has taken place in various areas – economy, environment, tourism, education, cultural exchanges, among others – but, distinct perhaps from other non-sovereign entities, its contacts with other national groups and states 'have always contained some political ingredients even when the party in power has not been committed to separatism' (Duchacek 1988: 14). During the 1960s, Quebec's international presence was limited, but, as political scientist Daniel Latouche argues, this presence was essential in giving Quebec 'a degree of autonomy which only outside actors could provide. In the end, the Quebec state must have existed because it was being taken into account by other states, most notably that of France' (Latouche 1988: 36). Canada's objection to Quebec's international presence simply confirmed Quebec's distinctiveness, and as time went by, Quebec's international positioning also became 'an essential component of the Quebec strategy to legitimize its claim to a different constitutional treatment' within the Canadian polity (Latouche 1988: 37).

The intensification of globalisation, in particular over the last ten or fifteen years, has not only provided Quebec with increased opportunities to act transnationally, but has also modified the set of 'others' and 'outside' elements against which Quebec defines and constructs itself (Latouche 1995). Canada, which Latouche terms Quebec's 'privileged other', 'remains a central element of the Quebec imaginary landscape' (1995: 127), but, as well as Ottawa and the federal government, now includes English Canada as a whole; *la Francophonie* has joined France as a central element of 'Quebec's French international connection' and has become 'an important feature of Quebec's vision of what is happening in the rest of the world'; the US, predominantly through the free trade agreements, first with Canada, then with Canada and Mexico as partners, has become an increasingly visible part of Quebec's 'out-there'; Quebec's immigrants constitute an internal 'other' (Latouche 1995: 127–8); and the Americas are becoming a significant element in the make-up of Quebec's external environment.

In line with previous Quebec governments, regardless of their political persuasion, Liberal Jean Charest, who was elected premier in 2003, reiterated the general importance of the international arena: 'Societies like Quebec, which do not have the advantage of numbers, have a duty to be daring. Our economy and our culture depend on our ability to make ourselves known on every continent' (cited in Michaud 2003: 948): in contradistinction to the quotation with which this chapter opened, Quebec is here extremely committed to the potential of globalisation for its own ends. Quebec's imperative 'to make itself known on every continent' is reflected in its push for representation in world organisations. Within what could be called traditional international organisations made up of nation-states, Quebec, as a province of Canada like any other, is represented officially by the Canadian government. The one international organisation in which Quebec participates independently, and one of the few in which it can define its own concerns as distinct from those of Anglophone Canada, is the Organisation internationale de la Francophonie (OIF) (Neathery-Castro and Rousseau 2001/2002: 18). Since 1971, Quebec has had the status of 'participating government' within *la Francophonie*, thus raising the province's international profile and prestige (see Section 4.3). The importance of this recognition for a non-sovereign state such as Quebec cannot be overestimated, and demonstrates the continuing power and reach of such organisations. As Croucher (2004: 17) points out, 'much of what constitutes global interaction and exchange is mediated through or in some way shaped by states and the state system', this in spite of the claim made by many that globalisation tends to diminish the importance of the nation-state (see Section 1.5).

Whether or not the ultimate protection of Quebec's language and cultural distinctiveness is through its accession to statehood, it is worth noting that Quebec already benefits from considerable powers which are normally considered the purview of fully-fledged states, including language laws, and control over immigration – at least in part. Add to this a network of delegations and offices in the US, the Asia-Pacific region, Latin America and the West Indies, Europe, and Africa and the Middle East;[1] international agreements; ministerial missions; and various international programmes and forms of cooperation (Gouvernement du Québec 2001b; Fry 2003a: 952), some of which have been in place since the 1960s (see Fry 2003b for a detailed historical account of Quebec's international relations). Quebec has indeed set an example for the new global order, not so much for nation-states, but rather for those non-sovereign entities like itself – other Canadian provinces, US states, among others, which have sought to emulate Quebec's achievements in the international arena (see e.g., Feldman and Feldman 1988; Latouche 1995: 130).

Quebec has been pushing for some time for a more independent role from Canada in the area of international representation, and this has caused tensions between the Quebec and Canadian governments. The Strategic Plan for 2001–04 of Quebec's Ministère des Relations internationales makes clear the degree of difficulty that Quebec's relationship with Canada creates in Quebec's continuing development of international ties and agreements, as well as its representation in international bodies (Gouvernement du Québec 2001b). Outside *la Francophonie*, Quebec must negotiate with the federal government in order to have a voice in governmental international organisations in which Canada is the accredited state (Gouvernement du Québec 2001b: 21), this in spite of the fact that as early as 1965 Quebec passed the Gérin-Lajoie doctrine, which asserted the province's right 'to assume at the international level the extension of its domestic responsibilities' (Gouvernement du Québec 2001b: 21).

The principle of the Gérin-Lajoie doctrine, which has subsequently been reaffirmed by the passage in Quebec's National Assembly of Bill 99 in 2000 (*Act respecting the exercise of the fundamental rights and prerogatives of the Québec people and the Québec State*, R.S.Q. c. E-20.2; see Section 2.1) and Bill 52 in 2002 (*Act to amend the Act respecting the Ministère des Relations internationales and other legislative provisions*, S.Q. 2002, c. 8), has not sat well with Canada for obvious reasons. It undermines the authority of the Canadian state, and has the potential to cause ambiguities in Canada's relations with other states, as well as create resentment in Canada's other provinces. From time to time, the federal government does allow some latitude to Quebec, as illustrated by Ottawa's approval of the November 2004 trade mission to Mexico by Quebec and France, led by the French Prime Minister Jean-Pierre Raffarin and Quebec's Premier Jean Charest. However, approval for the trip from Ottawa did not guarantee its acceptance in the rest of Canada, where there was some criticism of the federal government's approval as it was seen to be conferring special privileges on Quebec (Séguin 2004). Quebec's view of itself as a quasi-state, then, regularly pushes the boundaries of its relationship both with Canada and with the other provinces.

One of the few areas in which Quebec and Canada have acted in concertation, with the same goals, has been the cultural diversity agenda. Even here, tensions have re-emerged, as was evident at the time of the debates on UNESCO's Draft Convention on the Protection of the Diversity of Cultural Contents and Artistic Expressions, in Paris in September 2004. Both Canada and Quebec were represented – by the Canadian Heritage Minister, Liza Frulla, and by the Quebec Minister of Culture, Line Beauchamp, respectively. Liza Frulla let it be known that Quebec could occasionally speak in the name of Canada at international meetings on cultural diversity, given that the voices of Quebec and Canada were virtually interchangeable on the issue of cultural diversity (*Le Devoir*, 23 September 2004). She was swiftly corrected by the Canadian Minister of Intergovernmental Affairs, Lucienne Robillard, who made it very clear that no province would replace Canada's voice abroad (*Le Devoir*, 1 October 2004). However, there does seem to be some possibility of progress in the extension of asymmetric federalism beyond Canada's boundaries, and the very fact that Quebec was able to participate in the UNESCO cultural diversity talks in its own right has a symbolic value (*Le Devoir*, 2–3 October 2004).

Among non-sovereign states, then, Quebec can be viewed as one of the most engaged in the international arena (e.g., Dutrisac 2002: 669). In addition to its activities within what can be termed 'traditional' international instances, Quebec is home to more informal, and in some cases novel, transnational forums, which are precisely the kind that globalisation is now prompting; at the same time, these forums represent one of the few collaborative partnerships in which a non-sovereign nation such as Quebec can take part, given its exclusion from most traditional nation-state groupings. In this sense, globalisation is a positive and legitimising force for Quebec's interests, expanding the range of arenas in which issues of mutual concern in the region can be addressed. As an illustration, a non-governmental organisation founded by Christine Fréchette in 2002 and based in Montreal, the North American Forum on Integration, has as its mandate 'to encourage debate among the partners of NAFTA [North American Free Trade Agreement] on the political, economic and social stakes of integration and to focus the attention of decision-makers on the importance of the challenges at hand' (Pastor and Fréchette 2003: 982). The issue of the political, cultural and social fallout of trade agreements with the US as principal partner is a central one with regard to Quebec's positioning in the Americas.

4.2 Quebec and the Americas

It is generally agreed that economics is an essential motor of globalisation (e.g., Croucher 2004: 14). Quebec's increasing economic interconnectedness in the Americas is realised formally through its participation, as a province of Canada like any other, in trade agreements in which the US is the major player. The first of these agreements was the Canada–United States Free Trade Agreement in 1988, followed by NAFTA between the US, Canada and Mexico in 1992. The most recent agreement proposed, the Free Trade Area of the Americas (FTAA), which seeks to unite all the countries of North, Central and South America with the exception of Cuba, was set for 2005. However, reservations by a minority of countries – Brazil, Argentina, Paraguay, Uruguay and Venezuela – resulted in the talks stalling towards the end of 2005 (*Le Devoir*, November 2005). In spite of this setback, it is clear that in an era of US economic dominance, the US constitutes a prime economic partner for many countries around the globe, and Quebec is no exception, especially given its North American location (see Figure 4.1).

Both the Quebec government and Quebecers have on the whole been favourable to trade agreements with the US, far more so than their Anglophone counterparts in the rest of Canada, although there are recent signs of a more nuanced attitude towards such agreements, in part due to their possible negative consequences in the areas of culture and the environment (Fréchette 2005: 36). It remains the case, however, that the French language can be viewed as a linguistic shield, which allows Quebec a degree of proximity to US cultural values and practices not tolerated by Anglophone Canada and which creates the right conditions for a generally favourable position on North American integration (see Salée 1997). In other words, in Giles' (1979) terms, the French language in Quebec is a hard linguistic boundary, which allows the softening of other, non-linguistic boundaries. There may be a certain degree of linguistic mistrust expressed in Quebec towards English as the common foe, as seen in the opening quotation to this chapter, and it has to be remembered that Quebec has continued to live with

Figure 4.1 Quebec in the Americas

the dominance of the 'English fact' since the 1759 Conquest. However, their fundamental linguistic difference gives Francophone Quebecers a degree of confidence in their cultural identity that Anglophone Canadians lack.

It is clear that Quebec's survival as a distinct culture and society is dependent in no small part on the strength of its economy, and thus increasing trade with the US is welcomed. However, although economic integration has generally had a positive effect on Quebec's economy in key areas such as information technology, engineering and telecommunications (Balthazar and Hero 1999), and with 84 per cent of Quebec's total exports going to the US in 2002 (Fry 2003a: 953), some commentators argue that the social and cultural consequences of integration have not received enough attention: 'Quebec [...] increasingly has to bear the social and cultural consequences of growing regional integration, without there having been any debate on the topic' (Legaré 2003: 14).

There are positive signs of activity on the cultural and social fronts at the pan-American level, both in traditional nation-state organisations, and in new forms of cooperation, which are often initiated by Quebec, either officially or by various actors within the province. As an example of the former, the Organization of American States (OAS) is becoming more aware of the need to discuss the cultural impact of economic integration, and the Ministers of Culture of participating OAS states held their first meeting in 2002 to discuss cultural and linguistic issues arising from it. As an example of the latter, the North American Forum on Integration has highlighted one of the challenges of NAFTA that those in charge have not faced: how to integrate a developing country like Mexico into a trade agreement with two of the most developed countries in the world, the US and Canada (Pastor and Fréchette 2003). Over a decade on from the signing of NAFTA, it is clear that Mexico has hardly benefited economically or socially from its NAFTA participation. The Quebec historian Gérard Bouchard articulates the similar challenge that faces the countries of the Americas – how to create a community of interests and a common global vision, given the very considerable social and economic heterogeneity apparent in the Americas, as well as the dominance of the US:

> In [the Americas] there is [...] a centre-periphery relationship that is the reflection if not the cause of the imbalances of globalisation. How can such a space – one of the most unequal on the planet – be developed in such a way that all actors are able to reach their full potential within it? After all, US imperialism currently constitutes the main relationship that unites this continent; yet it is precisely this relationship that people would wish to modify. That being the case, how will it be possible to establish a community of interests with a common vision of the world? (G. Bouchard 2002: 18)

In 'one of the most unequal spaces on the planet', the Americas, there are other concerns that are pressing for a non-sovereign nation that is already fighting to make its voice heard above English on the North American continent. How will it be possible for Quebec to maintain French, faced not only with the juggernaut of the Anglophone US but also with seventeen Spanish-speaking states, at a moment in history when the Spanish language is globally on the rise?

Bouchard's solution to the conundrum he poses above is 'a rapprochement among the small nations with the aim of constituting not a new economic space but rather an alliance focused on cooperation and political intervention' (G. Bouchard 2002: 19). This kind of cooperation between minority cultures is, of course, exactly the kind of structural hybridisation described by Nederveen Pieterse (1995), and is also the course of action suggested in the opinion of Quebec's then Conseil de la langue française entitled *Language Issues in the Integration of the Americas* (Fréchette 2001). Fréchette argues that continental developments like the proposed FTAA, far from making states more vulnerable to the homogenising influence of English through increased contact and connection with the US, actually represent an opportunity to create 'new collaborations and [...] new forms of solidarity' (Fréchette 2001: 6).[2]

On the issue of language, such 'new forms of solidarity' must deal with the question of linguistic diversity in the Americas. In discussions and documents on linguistic integration coming out of Quebec, four languages have been targeted as the major languages of the Americas: English, Spanish, Portuguese and French (see e.g., Beaudoin 2001; Fréchette 2001; Georgeault 2003; G. Dumas 2004), languages which represent the legacy of the region's colonial history. In spite of the fact that there are an estimated 1,000 languages spoken in the Americas, by a total population of about 780 million people (Fréchette 2001: 7), only a few of these languages have official status throughout a sovereign state – Spanish, English, French, (Haitian) Creole, Dutch, Guaraní and Portuguese – and only four have official status in intergovernmental organisations within the region: English, Spanish, Portuguese and French (Fréchette 2001: 8). In terms of numbers of speakers, it is clear that English and Spanish are in a league of their own: nearly 40 per cent of the region's population speak Spanish and 38 per cent speak English, with 20 per cent speaking Portuguese and barely 2 per cent speaking French. However, Quebec can call on the trump cards of the international prestige of French, its existing status as an official language of many international organisations, and even the *Francophonie* network, to support its assertion of French as one of the *major* languages of the Americas (Fréchette 2001) and it negotiates effectively along these lines.

Quebec realises the fundamental importance of creating alliances between itself and the Spanish- and Portuguese-speaking states, in an attempt to create both formal and informal supranational structures that will support the protection and the promotion of linguistic and cultural diversity at the national and local levels. Indeed, it is clear that it is no longer possible to elaborate a national language policy without considering the supranational level (Georgeault 2003: 4) in a world that is increasingly organised around the transnational and the global. This point is echoed in the recommendations of Fréchette's 2001 report mentioned above, which focus on three areas: (1) supranational cooperation through the development of inter-American institutional multilingualism and the setting up of official forums and networks for the promotion of languages in the Americas; (2) the protection of consumers through commercial multilingualism; and (3) the development of individual multilingualism, often termed plurilingualism (for the full list of recommendations, see Fréchette 2001: 49–52). There has already been uptake of Fréchette's recommendations in the area of supranational cooperation, with the first Inter-American Languages Management Seminar organised by the Conseil supérieur de la langue française in Quebec City in August 2002. This was considered a great success, with more than 120 participants of various ranks from more than 12 countries in the Americas (Georgeault 2003: 2).[3] The second seminar was held in Paraguay in 2003, with the third in Brazil in May 2006, demonstrating that other countries in the region are taking an active interest in the issues surrounding linguistic diversity.

However, the route towards ensuring that French, given its demographic status, has equal place with the other three languages is beset with obstacles, and demonstrates the tenacity that will be needed to ensure that the Americas will be a quadrilingual space. The stakes are high, as the economic integration of the Americas will necessarily impose 'new linguistic demands which will weaken the balance between the languages of the four main linguistic groups which do not all have the same weight' (G. Dumas 2004). As an illustration, Quebec had to fight hard to ensure that the documents for negotiations on the FTAA at the 2001 Summit of the Americas, held in Quebec City, were provided in French. This struggle mirrors that between Quebec and Canada with regard to Quebec's insistence on a certain degree of autonomy.

The two languages that lag behind are Portuguese and French. In her address to the 2001 Summit, the then Minister of International Relations, Louise Beaudoin, emphasised the necessity that Portuguese and French have equality with English and Spanish institutionally and commercially within the Americas (Beaudoin 2001). The current status of the four languages of the Americas within inter-American organisations exemplifies their inequality. A 2001 survey by the then Conseil de la langue française on multilingualism in four inter-American organisations showed that overall

> [a]lthough most of these organisations would like to give the impression that they operate in four languages, it seems clear that [they] do not devote all the necessary efforts to enhancing multilingualism and to ensuring the equality of the official languages. (Fréchette 2001: 30)

On the corresponding internet sites, quadrilingualism is not very present beyond the home pages, with the bulk of documents and reports available only in English and Spanish. Maurais (2003: 26) claims that 'only the adoption of the systematic translation of official texts in the main official languages of the region is possible', and he warns both French and

Portuguese speakers of the need to be 'vigilant in order to assure the presence of their languages in future institutions'.

The rising importance of Spanish in the region, and globally, may well have an impact on Quebec's hopes for French in the linguistic integration of the Americas. Indeed, it is not clear to what extent the Spanish-speaking countries share Quebec's concerns, perhaps understandably, given the strength of Spanish both demographically and geographically. Some have gone as far as to claim that the Americas will be transformed into 'an English–Spanish bilingual zone' (Maurais 2003: 23, drawing on Graddol 1997: 58). Spanish is also gaining ground in the educational sector, not least in Quebec, where Spanish is now taught at secondary level (Maurais 2003: 25). There is not, conversely, a corresponding rise in the teaching of French in Latin America (Maurais 2003: 26), which has been going into decline across the Americas. Globalisation is also changing Quebec's relationship to English. From a situation in which English was seen as the language of the oppressors, there is now a growing awareness of its linguistic capital (see Bourdieu 1982), in spite of lingering Francophone concerns. This is illustrated in the decision of the Jean Charest's Liberal government to introduce the teaching of English from Grade 1 at primary level (age 6) from 2006 (Boileau 2005). Quebec, too, is showing greater interest in taking advantage of the multilingualism within its own borders, as growing numbers of immigrants bring with them a wealth of languages (e.g., Fréchette 2005: 72–7; see also Sections 5.2 and 7.1).

Overall, at this stage, it is extremely difficult to pinpoint accurately the effects of economic integration on the major languages spoken in the Americas, as these effects 'tend to be indirect and diffuse' (Morris 2003: 144). Part of the complexity of North American integration is the blend of informal and formal integration, which creates a rather unstable and potentially polemical situation, and makes '[m]anagement of cultural and language issues to mutual advantage [...] especially difficult' (Morris 2003: 146). The spread of English has been uneven, in spite of Anglophone US being the dominant economic partner. English 'has not displaced the established national language in any North American country or territory outside the USA' (Morris 2003: 154), and in fact language policies in various localities have so far limited its influence. Although it appears that '[t]here is no consensus among the three NAFTA partners about how to deal with cultural and linguistic issues' (Morris 2003: 155), there are encouraging signs, as already mentioned, from the Organization of American States and the meeting of the Ministers of Culture in 2002, that pan-American concern is being expressed in some official quarters about questions of linguistic and cultural diversity in the region. At the meeting, the Ministers of Culture underlined the importance of promoting linguistic and cultural diversity and of the cultural contribution of various linguistic groups to the Americas (Lortie 2002: 5).

Any discussion of Quebec's integration in the Americas needs to address, however briefly, the concept of *américanité*. This term has been used in various ways to tease out the complexities of Quebec's attachment to the US and to the Americas in general. This attachment is a tangled affair, full of twists and paradoxes, not least that at the same time as voicing loud and clear its claim to a distinctive culture, Quebec simultaneously participates in some, if not many, of the cultural practices of a country that it also considers the source of cultural homogenisation. To a certain extent, it is no surprise that Quebec – and Canada – shares certain cultural traits with the US, from playing and watching ice hockey and eating donuts to US TV and film production values and forms. Indeed, it would be impossible not to be influenced, given US physical proximity and the worldwide distribution of US popular culture. However, Quebec can rightfully point to numerous instances of unique cultural practices, not least a healthy local TV industry, which, in spite of US influence, produces a host of hugely popular, specifically Quebec sitcoms, dramas and *téléromans* (Nguyên-Duy 1999), a flourishing theatre, exemplified in the work of Robert Lepage, and overall a distinctive cultural production that is the envy of Anglophone Canada. And, of course, there is the French language, which, as described earlier, affords Quebec a proximity to US cultural values and practices that Anglophone Canada cannot allow itself.

In terms of the view of globalisation as the interpenetration of the global and the local, the rise of discourses of *américanité* in various realms of Quebec public life points to the growing importance of the US in particular, and of the Americas in general, both in Quebec's construction of itself and, more importantly for the present discussion, in the way it strategically places itself in the world for maximum local return. In order to understand how *américanité* is used, it is useful to take as a starting point the distinction between *américanité* and *américanisation* as conceived by the historian Yvan Lamonde in his understanding of the cultural impact of the US on Quebec.[4] He views *américanité* as an openness to continental belonging to the Americas, whereas *américanisation* is a process of acculturation to US culture, the former necessarily viewed as positive, the latter as negative:

> the *américanisation* of Quebec [...] is a process of acculturation whereby US culture influences and dominates both Canadian and Quebec culture – and world culture – whereas *américanité*, which includes both Latin and Anglo America, is a concept of openness and mobility which expresses Quebec's acceptance of its continental belonging. (Y. Lamonde 1996: 11)

Bouchard, who is one of the leading academic lights of *américanité* along with Lamonde, explores further the notion of continental belonging, and argues that Quebec has rooted itself in the Americas as 'a new collectivity'

(G. Bouchard 2001b). Bouchard characterises Quebec and other European settler societies such as the US, Canada, Australia, New Zealand, and the countries of South America as having a similar founding experience on a new continent based on a rupture with the mother country and new, politically emancipated beginnings.[5] The US is taken as the model 'new collectivity', distinguished among other things by a clear rupture from Britain. Quebec, on the other hand, has a distinct trajectory understood as a cycle of rupture and continuity (see G. Bouchard 2001b: 77–182 for a detailed description of this cycle). Of particular note in Bouchard's analysis, as well as in Lamonde's work, is the distinction made between the elites and the masses, the former with allegiances to France and a European way of life, and the latter living a US way of life through their cultural practices, particularly since the Second World War (J. Beauchemin 2002: 70).

The notion of *américanité* as conceived by Lamonde and Bouchard has not been without its critics (see e.g., Thériault 2002a; J. Beauchemin 2002), but their arguments are not central to the present discussion. What is important here is the way in which ideas of continental belonging have been exploited by various groups within Quebec for their own ends. Nationalist politicians have used *américanité* to express 'Quebec's economic openness to globalisation' and in particular an openness to free trade agreements with the US (Thériault 2002a: 12). The strength of the discourse of *américanité* at the governmental level is illustrated in the decision of Quebec's Ministère des Relations internationales to call the first decade of the twenty-first century 'The Decade of the Americas' (Gouvernement du Québec 2001b). Historians and social scientists have taken the term to describe variously the 'American' birth of Quebec society, the implantation of Quebec on the North American continent, as seen above, and participation of Quebecers in US mass culture;[6] and artists have used the term to express abroad the specificity of Quebec culture, particularly in France (Thériault 2002a: 12).

How does this brief discussion of *américanité* help in understanding Quebec's global positioning and ability to advance its cultural and linguistic agenda? To begin with, it is certainly the case that Quebec's economic integration with the US has given it the opportunity to participate in the global economy as well as in 'modern technological civilisation' (Thériault 2002a: 76) – *américanité* indistinguishable from *américanisation*. There is no doubt, either, that there is, or has been, a need to re-evaluate Quebec identity in terms of its continental belonging, and to legitimise an aspect of its identity formation that had tended to be omitted from national history and myth-making. In addition, the notion of belonging to the Americas – and not simply to North America – becomes a crucial element of an imagined shared past and future as Quebec endeavours to create new alliances and bonds with countries and regions in Central and South America. However, as already indicated, Quebec's positive re-evaluation of its historical and cultural ties to the Americas also carries within it a potential legitimisation of what could be viewed as Quebec's increasing cultural integration with the US. Quebec's path towards the Americas is a perilous one that involves among other things the difficult task of side-stepping that region's economic and cultural giant. Indeed, if a 'civilization of the Americas' is to make any sense, to paraphrase Daniel Latouche, Quebec and the other members of the Americas outside the US are essential 'to provide an outlook on the world that is not limited to the outlook of the United States' (Latouche 1995: 137).

The recent swing towards continental belonging in debates on Quebec identity is reflected in Bouchard's analysis of Quebec's trajectory as one of rupture and continuity, the 'pendulum swing' between Europe and the Americas, between France and the US, both in the evolution of Quebec's self-definition and in its attempts to find allies in its fight to assert itself. The 'reconfiguration of geography' (Scholte 2000: 16) that is globalisation may have swung the pendulum towards the Americas – and more specifically the US – and away from France and Europe, but France remains an important force, not only in Quebec's understanding and construction of itself, but also in its dealings with the world. It is the question of cultural diversity that has dominated much of Quebec's recent collaboration with France and its activities within *la Francophonie*.

4.3 Quebec, *la Francophonie* and cultural diversity

Quebec's preoccupation with linguistic diversity in the Americas is mirrored by its current focus on the international recognition of cultural diversity through the global arena that is *la Francophonie*. Quebec's investment in diversity in the two arenas is a clear example that 'global' in fact means, in practical-political terms, 'local': Quebec's concern with its 'local' language and culture is translated at the international level by arguing for a rich 'global' tapestry, precisely in order to guarantee the survival of its own small part of that tapestry. In the Americas, as seen already, linguistic diversity for Quebec at this stage translates primarily as the maintenance of French as one of the four major languages of the region. Within the alternative geopolitical configuration of *la Francophonie*, Quebec seeks to harness both its status as a major player and its close alliance with France in order to further the global protection of cultural diversity, with what it hopes will be subsequent local payoffs.

Quebec was very active from the start in the building of the community of French-speaking nations known as *la Francophonie*, as part of its bid to survive as a French-speaking society and 'to flourish at the international level' (Judge 1996: 26).[7] The first Francophone governmental organisation, l'Agence de coopération culturelle et technique, was set up in 1971, and Quebec was granted the status of participating government within this organisation, although not without a struggle. Currently, the main governing body of *la Francophonie* is the Organisation internationale de la Francophonie (OIF). The OIF comprises 53 member states and governments and 13 observer states. Its current mandate is to promote the French language as well as linguistic and cultural diversity; to promote peace, democracy and human rights; to support education and research; and to develop cooperation through sustainable development (http://www.francophonie/org/oif/missions/cfm).

Within *la Francophonie*, the relationship between France and Quebec has been a significant one, and collaboration and exchanges between the two countries contributed 'to the advancement of the Francophone project, and to its inspiration and evolution' (Léger 1987: 128). France, too, was instrumental in gaining Quebec the status of 'participating government' in 1971. At the time, there was conflict between Quebec and Canada over the exact status of Quebec within the organisation, with the Canadian government arguing that only sovereign states should be able to adhere. France was a firm supporter of Quebec's push for greater status, and proposed the category of participating government, a solution which was finally accepted by Canada (Chatton and Bapst 1991: 31). It has been argued that Quebec's engagement in the *Francophonie* movement has in some sense compelled Canada to become more involved itself, less perhaps at the level of ideas or projects than in terms of financial support (Léger 1987: 131).

Quebec's very survival as a Francophone nation is dependent on 'the success of the great Francophone project' (Léger 2000: 338). The interdependence between Quebec and *la Francophonie* has become even more apparent in the global movement for the recognition of the importance of cultural diversity. Indeed, the interests of Quebec, France, Canada, and the *Francophonie* movement in general seem to have coincided on this issue. Cultural diversity for Quebec is about 'the necessity for states and governments to support their national cultures' (Ministère des Relations internationales 2003a). The defence of cultural diversity ensures 'the right of governments to equip themselves with policies and measures aimed at promoting and preserving their cultures' (Ministère des Relations internationales, 2003a). This approach to cultural diversity echoes that of France, which continues to be a staunch defender of its national culture and which promoted the issue of *l'exception culturelle* in the 1980s as a way of fighting US cultural hegemony (see e.g., Neathery-Castro and Rousseau 2001/2002). However, it should be noted that the issue of cultural diversity is not simply a preoccupation of 'first-world' nations, and *la Francophonie* – which can also be characterised as one of the 'unequal spaces on the planet' – has shown the lead by underlining the importance of cultural industries to the development of African countries (Beaudoin 2004b).

In advancing its cultural diversity agenda, Quebec has both exploited state-based international frameworks and made use of more innovative and hybridised forms of collaboration. At the international level, Quebec has worked within the state-based body of the OIF, primarily in concertation with France and Canada, as well as through other international agencies (Ministère des Relations internationales 2003b). *La Francophonie* was the first international organisation to vote in favour of cultural diversity, at the Moncton Summit in 1999 (Beaudoin 2004a). This was followed by the Declaration of Cotonou at the third Francophonie Ministerial Conference on Culture in 2001, which reinforced *la Francophonie*'s commitment to safeguarding and promoting cultural diversity, and affirmed the principle that cultural goods and services are carriers of a nation's identity and cannot be reduced to their economic dimension (Gouvernement du Québec 2001a: 172–3). It was at the 2002 Summit in Beirut that the decision was made to ask UNESCO to take over the cultural diversity dossier (Beaudoin 2004a).

At the bilateral and multilateral levels, Quebec has proceeded in partnership with France through the Franco-Quebec Working Group on Cultural Diversity. One of the most important outcomes of this working group was a joint report by jurists Ivan Bernier and Hélène Ruiz Fabri on the legal feasibility of an international instrument on cultural diversity (Bernier and Ruiz Fabri 2002), which served as the basis for subsequent work within UNESCO. In addition, the cultural diversity debate has brought Quebec and Canada together (see Section 4.1), both at the governmental and grassroots levels (see e.g., Baillargeon 2001). An example of grassroots activity is the Coalition for Cultural Diversity, which was established from within the cultural milieu in Quebec and regroups around 30 Canadian cultural and communications associations, and which is funded in part by the Quebec and Canadian governments. Along with the equivalent group in France, an international liaison committee was created to support coalitions elsewhere, which now exist in a dozen countries (Ministère de la Culture et des Communications 2004). UNESCO formally took up the global fight in 2003, and out of various propositions, chose to draw up a Convention on the Protection and Promotion of the Diversity of Cultural Expressions, which was adopted by an overwhelming majority in October 2005 (UNESCO 2005b).[8]

Quebec, then, has been very successful in its advocacy for cultural diversity. Globalisation, here, is reinforcing old alliances and channels of action, primarily through *la Francophonie*, as well as creating the conditions for new collaborations at more informal levels. However, it can be argued that Quebec is to some extent a victim of its own success: while it has been focusing on the elaboration of an instrument for the recognition of *cultural* diversity, the issue of *linguistic* diversity escaped notice (Pierre Georgeault, personal communication, August 2004). But surely 'culture' necessarily includes language? Certainly UNESCO thinks so in its Universal Declaration on Cultural Diversity, which makes very clear the intimate link between culture and language – the Action Plan has among its objectives 'Safeguarding the linguistic heritage of humanity and giving support to expression, creation and dissemination in the greatest possible number of languages', 'Encouraging linguistic diversity – while respecting the mother tongue – at all levels of education, wherever possible', and 'Promoting linguistic diversity in cyberspace' (UNESCO 2002).

However, some were taken aback by the lack of reference to language and to linguistic issues in the draft Convention, which came out in 2004 (Fréchette 2005: 46–7; Prujiner 2005: 381). Language was only mentioned once, under Article 6, which discusses the measures member states can take to protect and promote diversity of cultural expression within their territory (UNESCO 2004: 5); linguistic diversity was also mentioned just once, in passing, in an annex on cultural policies.[9] Support for including linguistic diversity in the Convention arrived from an unexpected source in the shape of the US, whose delegation was surprised to find the concept of language missing from the document, given that language is a fundamental element of cultural diversity (Fréchette 2005: 47). The US suggestion, that language should be mentioned in the preamble, seems to have been taken on board – the final version of the preamble includes the following: '*Recalling* that linguistic diversity is a fundamental element of cultural diversity, and reaffirming the fundamental role that education plays in the protection and promotion of cultural expressions' (UNESCO 2005a: 2, italics in original). Nevertheless, there is still no additional reference to language or to linguistic diversity in the body of the final version, and the annex in which reference was made to linguistic diversity has been cut.[10]

One of the challenges that faces global linguistic diversity, according to Bernier (2001), is precisely that of ensuring that the close link between language and culture is transposed to the international fight for cultural diversity:

> If it is true, in fact, that the fight for linguistic diversity cannot be won by disregarding the international dimension of the problem, it is equally true that the efforts undertaken in favour of cultural diversity at the international level can but gain by taking into account the linguistic dimension of the question in a more dynamic way. (Bernier 2001)

Bernier argues that although the question of cultural diversity was linked very early on to the threats inherent in the globalisation of the economy, this has not been the case for linguistic diversity, and both would benefit from being considered together.

In addition, the question of global linguistic diversity has generally been taken up to direct world attention towards protecting those minority languages that are considered endangered. Although its culture may be considered 'endangered' in some sense, Quebec's language remains a first world language, not an endangered one. From Quebec's point of view, however, the focus on endangered languages has drawn attention away from the predicament of lesser-used national languages. As Georgeault (2003: 7) points out, 'in the context of globalisation that we are experiencing, national languages are the most poorly treated' (see also Bernier 2001). This is particularly the case for national languages such as French in Quebec, which does not benefit from a sovereign state framework.

Louise Beaudoin was involved in 2004 in spreading the word internationally about the draft Convention as Quebec's official representative to the OIF. She saw the challenge as a major one, given resistance by various countries to the cultural diversity agenda: 'While the countries of *la Francophonie* generally understand what is at stake in an international convention on cultural diversity and are mostly in agreement with the principle, things are less clear in Latin America, Asia or Anglo-Saxon countries, many of which are positively opposed to the project' (Beaudoin, cited in Boucher 2004). The global fragmentation that Beaudoin identifies goes to the heart of differences in Quebec's own arenas of activity: in *la Francophonie* it has a set of allies who are receptive to its concerns; in the Americas, it is far more difficult for Quebec to identify allies who share similar goals.

4.4 Quebec as a global player

In September 2005, Monique Gagnon-Tremblay, Quebec's Minister for International Relations, set out a list of demands presented to the federal government to enable Quebec to speak in its own right in international forums. These demands included the following: (1) 'access to all information on the negotiation of any international treaty concerning provincial competencies and participation in the elaboration of the Canadian position'; (2) a Quebec representative on Canadian delegations with the right to participate in discussions; (3) freedom for Quebec to speak in its own right in United Nations forums, for example, UNESCO; and (4) 'the right of Quebec to give its assent to a treaty before it is signed by Canada' (*Le Devoir*, 15 September 2005). These demands were accepted on 5 May 2006 to the extent that Ottawa and Quebec signed an agreement on a formal role for Quebec in UNESCO, and illustrate Quebec's view of itself as a global player.

Indeed, by constructing Quebec as a victim of Anglo-American hegemony, the Larose Commission disregards the very real achievements of Quebec in exploiting the global for local ends. Globalisation is working to Quebec's advantage on more than one level. In the Americas, it is bringing a new legitimacy to Quebec's efforts to protect and promote its language and its culture. In *la Francophonie*, it is reinforcing old alliances, as well as creating the conditions for new collaborations in which Quebec can advance its cause, both at official and more informal levels. In addition, Quebec faces certain challenges, particularly in terms of convincing current and potential partners around the world of the validity and urgency of focusing on issues of cultural and linguistic diversity. In the Americas, Quebec's bid to create a multilingual space within the region, in which French has equal status to Spanish, English and Portuguese, faces the challenge of the world dominance of English and the increasing global importance of Spanish, as well as the fact that Quebec's particular concern with linguistic diversity is not necessarily shared. Within the network of *la Francophonie*, Quebec has been able to advance its cause, particularly through concerted action with France and Canada on the protection and promotion of cultural diversity at the global level. However, it remains to be seen to what extent the UNESCO Convention on the Protection and Promotion of the Diversity of Cultural Expressions will afford Quebec the protection it seeks.

But perhaps Quebec's biggest achievement, as a non-sovereign state, has been its use of one order of globality – *la Francophonie* – to operate within another semi-global or hemispheric arena – the Americas; in other words, its strategic exploitation of 'hegemonic' or major Frenchness to push minoritarian Francophone causes in its home region. These two orders of globality will come together on Quebec soil in 2008, when the 12th Summit of *la Francophonie* will take place, to coincide with the 400-year anniversary of the founding of Quebec City. This symbolic moment will be a timely reminder to the Americas of the resilience of French in the region, and of its global reach.[11] The next chapter takes up the question of the resilience of French itself within Quebec through an examination of recent efforts to promote French as the common public language.

Part II
A Common Language

Part II focuses on Quebec's use of language planning as a means of finding a voice for itself which is distinct both from France and within North America. Chapter 5 examines Quebec government interventions from the 1960s to protect and promote the status of Quebec French, a type of language planning traditionally referred to as status planning (Kloss 1969). Following a brief outline of the main milestones of status planning in Quebec, the chapter examines how the authorities hope to encourage the adoption of French as the language of public communications amongst a growing number of immigrants, the group of Quebecers upon whom the future of French is now understood to depend.

Chapter 6 analyses language attitudes in Quebec and the debate about the quality and variety of French to be promoted within a civic society, questions that fall within the field of language planning known as corpus planning. From the original myth of a French Canadian patois that arose in the nineteenth century, French-speaking Quebecers have suffered from a sense of linguistic insecurity because of the perceived lack of quality associated with their variety. With the more recent civic approach to Quebec identity, questions are now being asked about the kind of French Quebec should offer its new immigrants and whether French-speaking Quebecers need to give up their particular variety and adopt a so-called 'international French' in order to be truly civic.

Both chapters include discussions of a third type of language planning termed acquisition planning (Cooper 1989), an activity which seeks to encourage knowledge of a particular language or variety, in this case (Quebec) French and English as a global *lingua franca*.

5
French: A Language for All Quebecers

> *Toute personne habitant le territoire du Québec, quelle que soit son origine, reçoit en partage la langue officielle et commune du Québec. Le français devient ainsi la voie d'accès privilégiée au patrimoine civique (valeurs, droits, obligations, institutions, etc.) commun à l'ensemble des Québécoises et des Québécois et sur lequel se fonde leur citoyenneté. La langue française devient le lieu de recherche et de développement des valeurs propres à l'ensemble de la société québécoise. Elle est aussi le lieu d'un vouloir-vivre collectif, l'espace public commun où chacun peut rencontrer l'autre.*

> The official and common language of Quebec is passed on to everyone living in the territory of Quebec, whatever his or her origin. In this way, French becomes the privileged means of access to the civic heritage (values, rights, obligations, institutions, etc.) common to all Quebecers and on which their citizenship is founded. The French language offers a site for the exploration and development of the particular values of the whole of Quebec society. It is also the site of a collective will to live together, the common public space where everyone can meet. (Gouvernement du Québec 2001a: 13)

It is well known that ethnic forms of nationalism have recourse to language as a symbol of national identity: in the view of the German Romantic Johann Gottfried Herder, for example, language is considered as an essential and immutable element of a people's *Volkgeist*, what unites those of the same ancestry or blood. But as the above citation from the Larose Commission shows, civic nationalisms also make use of language as a symbol of the nation by emphasising a different function: language provides the 'privileged means of access to the civic heritage common to all' and is where an otherwise ethnically diverse population expresses its 'collective will to live together'. Language is thus 'less exclusive than ethnicity' (Castells 1997: 52); indeed, it 'is not an instrument of exclusion: in principle, anyone can learn any language. On the contrary, it is fundamentally inclusive, limited only by the fatality of Babel: no one lives long enough to learn all languages' (Anderson 1983: 122). This is a view that has come to mark language planning in Quebec on account of the shift from an ethnic to a more civic conception of national identity there.

This chapter examines the effect that the new civic approach has had specifically on those efforts that aim to promote and maintain the status of French in Quebec. While the response of new Quebecers to this status planning will be examined in Chapter 7, the discussion here remains at the macro or ideological level, focusing on the overall intentions of successive Quebec governments since the 1990s in particular. With the realisation that the future of French now depends on a growing number of immigrants, the challenge that the authorities face is how to encourage the adoption of French as the language of public communications. The task is rendered all the more difficult because, while the idea of French as a *langue publique commune* for all Quebecers assumes that French can somehow be 'de-ethnicised' to become the property of all ethnic groups, a more thorough analysis of the situation in Quebec and elsewhere only confirms the inextricable link between language and ethnicity. These two challenges form the basis of this chapter: How can new Quebecers be motivated to adopt French as their language of public communications? And can language be completely 'de-ethnicised' as much of the official and academic discourse surrounding the concept of *langue publique commune* implies? Before examining these questions more closely, it is useful to consider first the history of status planning in Quebec. The discussion which follows is intended as a brief summary only, with a particular focus on the effects of the more civic discourse now emanating from official circles. For full details of the complexities of language legislation in Quebec past and present, readers are referred to the acts themselves and the many in-depth studies devoted to this topic (e.g., Bourhis 1984; Plourde 1993; Chevrier 1997, 2003; Levine 1997; Woehrling 2000, 2005).

5.1 French in Quebec: from *langue commune* to *langue publique commune*

Ever since the 1960s–70s, reference has been made in official circles to the idea of making French the *langue commune* (common language) of Quebecers. For example, in the *Livre blanc sur la politique culturelle* (White paper on cultural policy) (Gouvernement du Québec 1965), the Ministry of Cultural Affairs spoke of the need to declare French the 'priority language' of Quebec and empower the Office de la langue française (French Language Office), set up at the same time as the Ministry in 1961, 'to ensure the establishment of French as a common language in all sectors of human activity' (cited in Bouthillier and Meynaud 1972: 691). Similarly, in its 1972 report, the Commission d'enquête sur la situation de la langue française et sur les droits linguistiques au Québec (Commission of Inquiry on the Situation of the French Language and Linguistic Rights in Quebec), otherwise known as the Gendron Commission, recommended

> that the Government of Quebec set itself the general objective of making French the common language of Quebecers, that is, the language which, known by all, can serve as an instrument of communication in contact situations between French-speaking and non-French-speaking Quebecers. (Gouvernement du Québec 1972: 154)

The Gendron Commission had been set up in the midst of the Saint-Léonard crisis of 1967–68, which saw school commissioners of this Montreal neighbourhood adopting a resolution requiring immigrants to send their children to monolingual French-medium primary schools instead of the bilingual ones set up in 1963 (Levine 1997: 117–45; Larrivée 2003a: 170–1).[1] This decision was based on the observation that, instead of promoting integration into French-speaking circles, the bilingual classes merely encouraged the majority of the children of immigrants (more than 85 per cent) who finished their primary studies to go on to English-medium secondary schools in the area concerned (Levine 1997: 118; Robert 2000: 244). Faced with a wave of protests from Anglophones throughout the province, and after an initial failed attempt to overturn the decision of the school commissioners with Bill 85, the Union nationale government of Jean-Jacques Bertrand sponsored Bill 63, which was passed in 1969 (*Act to promote the French language in Quebec*, S.Q. 1969, c. 9). Despite its name, this Act upheld the free choice of parents with regard to language of instruction for their children; it did, however, require those children attending English-medium schools to have a 'working knowledge' of French, as well as give the authorities the responsibility of ensuring that immigrants learned French soon after, or even before, their arrival in Quebec, as well as send their children to French schools. However, these measures were not enough to alleviate the mounting linguistic tensions which, combined with other factors, contributed to the October Crisis of 1970.[2]

While Bertrand and his government chose not to wait for the recommendations of the Gendron Commission, the new Liberal government under Robert Bourassa took some of these into consideration when drafting its Bill 22, passed in 1974 (*Official Language Act*, S.Q. 1974, c. 6). The latter declared French the official language of Quebec, but only in the first of the three domains of use mentioned was this taken seriously: French was to be 'the ordinary language of communication in the public administration'. In the workplace, employees would be able to speak French amongst themselves and with their bosses at work, while French was also to be 'omnipresent' in company management, corporate names, public signage and contracts. But as Levine (1997: 165) notes, 'the promotion of French in the business world relied on optional rather than compulsory measures.' For example, while companies wishing to have dealings with the provincial government were required to obtain francisation certificates administered by what had now become the Régie de la langue française (French Language Board), these were awarded in many cases to completely Anglophone businesses. Finally, on the question of language of instruction, freedom of choice was again maintained, but those students wishing to attend English-medium schools would now have to pass tests to demonstrate a 'sufficient knowledge' of this language. In the end, the Official Language Act satisfied no one: while dealing a major blow to the Anglophone vision of an officially bilingual Montreal, the measures proposed fell nonetheless well short of making French the common language of Quebec.

On its arrival in power in 1976, the Parti Québécois quickly announced its intention to implement new, more ambitious language legislation. In a White Paper entitled *La politique québécoise de la langue française* (Quebec's policy on the French language), the Minister for Cultural Development, Camille Laurin, explained:

> The Quebec that we want to build will be essentially French. The fact that the majority of its population is French will finally be visible: in the workplace, in communications and in the landscape. [...] There will no longer be any question of a bilingual Quebec. (Gouvernement du Québec 1977: 36–7)

As an indication of how important the Parti Québécois considered the language question, Laurin's ideas were granted the honour of constituting the government's very first bill, Bill 1, which was given the name Charter of the French language. The latter made many references to the fact that French was the language of the Quebec people, thus implying that non-French speakers were not true Quebecers (Levine 1997: 194). Faced with potential Liberal opposition, Bill 1 was withdrawn and subsequently resubmitted in a more moderate form as Bill 101, written in a way so as to include non-Francophone Quebecers. Adopted on 26 August 1977, the Charter of the French language once again declared French the 'official language of Quebec' (*Charter of the French language*, R.S.Q. c. C-11 [hereinafter Charter], s. 1). After listing a series of fundamental linguistic rights, its authors also stipulated how French was to become the *langue commune* in six areas.

According to the Charter, which remains Quebec's main language law to date, French is the language of the legislature and the courts in Quebec. Since the Blaikie decision of the Supreme Court of Canada (*A.G. (Quebec) v Blaikie et al* [1979] 2 S.C.R. 1016), however, bills and laws are also translated into English; the latter can also be used in Quebec courts. French is equally the language of public administration, the only language that can be used by the government, its ministries and affiliated agencies. In the remaining four domains of use, which are not under the immediate control of the state, the

Charter stipulates that French should be the 'normal and everyday language' (*Charter*, preamble). Semi-public agencies, such as public utility enterprises (e.g., transport authorities, electricity, water, gas providers, when they are not already government agencies) and the professional orders (e.g., doctors, lawyers, accountants), 'must arrange to make their services available in the official language' (*Charter*, s. 30). In the workplace, written communications to staff and offers of employment must be in French. Employers are also prohibited from requiring knowledge of a language other than French, unless this is necessary for the particular employment.

In the field of commerce and business, French must be used in product labelling, including restaurant menus; where other languages are used as well, these must not be given greater prominence than French. All computer software and operating systems must be available in French, unless no French-language version exists. Similarly, toys and games that rely solely on languages other than French are prohibited, unless a French-language version is also available on the Quebec market. Originally, public signage and commercial advertising was to be in French only, with exceptions for the cultural activities of ethnic groups and non-profit organisations. With the Ford decision of 1988 (*Ford v A.G. (Quebec)* [1988] 2 S.C.R. 712), the Supreme Court of Canada ruled that the prohibition of any language other than French in public signage and commercial advertising was contrary to freedom of speech, as stipulated both in the Quebec Charter of Human Rights and Freedoms of 1975 (R.S.Q. c. C-12, s. 3) and the Canadian Charter of Rights and Freedoms (*Constitution Act, 1982*, s. 33). Quebec decided to use the notwithstanding clause contained in the Canadian Charter to pass Bill 178 (*Act to amend the Charter of the French language*, S.Q. 1988, c. 54), according to which other languages were now permitted in public signage and advertising inside commercial buildings, provided that French was predominant. Outside, however, French monolingualism would continue to reign. The notwithstanding clause being valid for a maximum of five years, the Quebec government was forced to find a more permanent solution. This came in 1993 in the form of Bill 86 (*Act to amend the Charter of the French language*, S.Q. 1993, c. 40), which amended the Charter of the French language so as to permit bilingual signage anywhere on the condition that French was 'markedly predominant'. A bone of contention for many years, the status of French as a common language in public signage is now 'firmly rooted in the minds of a majority of Quebecers' (Chevrier 2003: 146), irrespective of ethnic background.

Finally, with regard to education, the field which has sparked the most tensions, the Charter states that '[i]nstruction in the kindergarten classes and in the elementary and secondary schools shall be in French' (*Charter*, s. 72), a requirement which applies to both state schools and those private schools partially funded by the Quebec state. Abolishing the freedom of choice regarding language of instruction, the Charter as originally drafted allowed attendance of English-medium schools only for Anglophones with historical links to Quebec, namely those children whose mother or father received their primary education in Quebec in English. This had the effect of excluding three categories of people: immigrants, including those whose mother tongue was English; Francophones; and Canadians from other provinces (Woehrling 2000: 287). Despite their immediate disapproval, the federal authorities nonetheless had no means to combat what was known as the 'Quebec clause' since it was not incompatible with the Constitution Act, 1867, which continued to be in force at the time. Written in a way as to invalidate the Charter precisely on this point, the new Canadian Charter of Rights and Freedoms included in the Constitution Act, 1982 resulted in a Supreme Court of Canada decision in 1984 which replaced the 'Quebec clause' with the 'Canada clause' (*A.G. (Quebec) v Quebec Protestant School Boards* [1984] 2 S.C.R. 66). Nowadays, education in English is permitted even for the children of Canadian citizens who received their primary schooling in English elsewhere in Canada (*Charter*, s. 73).

Following recommendations made by the Larose Commission (Gouvernement du Québec 2001a: 71), the Quebec government passed Bill 104 (*Act to amend the Charter of the French language*, S.Q. 2002, c. 28) in 2002 to close a loophole whereby attendance of a private school not subsidised by the state, even for a short period, was enough to guarantee subsequent passage into the English-medium state-funded school system. The Act also reorganised the language agencies set up under the Charter, the main ones now being: the Office québécois de la langue française (Quebec Office of the French Language), charged with, amongst other things, the awarding of francisation certificates to companies with 50 employees or more, and the investigation of alleged infringements of the Charter; and the Conseil supérieur de la langue française (Higher Council of the French Language), the mandate of which is to conduct research on language in Quebec and advise the Minister responsible for the administration of the Charter on any matter relating to this topic.

As is clear from the six domains of use mentioned, the Charter is concerned with public communications only; at no time does it try to enforce the use of French in the private sphere. Indeed, the White Paper that preceded the Charter was careful to distinguish the new policy of making French the common language of Quebec from one of linguistic assimilation:

> The total assimilation of all new immigrants, to the extent that they have lost all ties to their country of origin within one or two generations, is not a desirable objective. A society that allows its minority groups to maintain their language and culture is a society that is richer and probably better balanced. (Gouvernement du Québec 1977: 26, cited in Béland 1999: 9–10)

Although not deliberately assimilationist, the new language policy could, however, be seen as forming part of the broader policy of promoting a *culture de convergence*, whereby immigrants in particular were encouraged to 'converge' towards the culture of the ethnic Francophone majority (see Section 2.1).[3] With the abandonment of this policy, and the new concern for ethnic diversity that arose in the 1990s in particular, it became necessary to state even more explicitly that 'common language' meant 'common *public* language', as is clearly manifested in official documents of the time:

> This valorisation of French as the common language and language of public life does not, however, mean that one should confuse the mastering of a common language with linguistic assimilation. Indeed, as a democratic society, Quebec respects the right of individuals to adopt the language of their choice in communications of a private nature. Moreover, it considers that the development of heritage languages constitutes an economic, social and cultural asset for the whole Quebec population. (Gouvernement du Québec 1991: 17)

In its 1996 report, the Comité interministériel sur la situation de la langue française (Interministerial committee on the situation of the French language) advocated an approach which put more emphasis on the language used in the public sphere, thus allowing for a better evaluation of the aims of the Charter of the French language. With this aim, a 'new definition of the linguistic integration process' (Levine 1997: 361) was advocated to replace the traditional categories used in censuses of the time, namely *langue maternelle* (mother tongue) and *langue d'usage* (the language spoken at home):

> In order to determine whether French has progressed as the 'normal and everyday language' of public activities in Quebec, it is clear that we cannot rely on data about the *langue maternelle*; what is not clear, however, is that we should limit ourselves to data about the *langue d'usage*, since the language spoken at home is not necessarily the language used at work or in public communications. Consequently, it is clear that we should use data relating to the common language (or civic language), but these data are not yet available. This can therefore lead to an underestimation of the number of 'French-speaking Quebecers', especially amongst Allophones (if they use French in their public communications more than at home). (Gouvernement du Québec 1996: 10)

To this end, the Committee introduced the notion of *langue d'usage public* (language of public use) and called for the creation of a real instrument of measurement for this new concept. In 1997, a study was therefore carried out by what was then the Conseil de la langue française, in collaboration with the Secrétariat à la politique linguistique (Secretariat for Language Policy), the Office de la langue française, the Ministère des Relations avec les citoyens et de l'Immigration and the Ministère de l'Éducation, 'to evaluate the public use of languages and to elaborate a global index of the linguistic behaviour of Quebecers' (Béland 1999: 4). An 'indicator of the languages of public use' was constructed based on statistical information relating to the use of languages in various public domains: formal communications, the workplace, shops, health establishments, etc. As the Comité interministériel sur la situation de la langue française had hoped, the new index has resulted in more positive statistics: whereas only 83 per cent of Quebec's population used French at home in 1997, 87 per cent could be said to use French as their main *langue d'usage public* (see Table 5.1).

It must be noted that the 'indicator of the languages of public use' has been criticised especially by statisticians and demographers. In addition to the criticisms of the methodological procedures used in the 1997 study (Roy 2001), it has been claimed that the *'faux-fuyant'* ('red herring') or 'chimerical' (Castonguay 2002b: 13) nature of the *langue d'usage public* concept conceals the actual precarious position of the French language, especially on the island of Montreal. Unlike *langue maternelle* and *langue d'usage*, the *langue d'usage public* indicator does not provide information about language maintenance and language shift tendencies (both amongst native speakers and new Quebecers), the only reliable data, in Castonguay's view, that can be used to evaluate the vitality of French in Quebec (Castonguay 2003).

Despite such criticism, the notion of *langue d'usage public* is popular in official circles *precisely because* it distances itself from the assimilationist connotations of the concept of language shift, thereby proving better attuned to the more civic approach to language and nation now promoted. Not surprisingly, then, it has come to form one of the major cornerstones of status planning in Quebec. For example, in its *Plan stratégique en matière de politique*

Table 5.1 Percentage of the population according to mother tongue, the language spoken at home and the language of public use (index) in the whole of Quebec, 1997*

Language	Language category			
	Mother tongue	Language spoken at home	Language of public use	Main Language of public use
French	82	83	82	87
French and English	N/A	1	8	N/A
English	8	10	8	11
Other	9	6	1	1

* The population was 18 years or older and native or immigrated before 1995, and was required to declare one mother tongue only. N = 13,295.
Source: Béland (1999: 46).

linguistique 2005–2008 (Strategic Plan regarding Language Policy 2005–2008), the government stated its desire to 'ensure the permanence of the French language in Quebec, *to reinforce its public use*, to enhance its mastery and to improve its quality' (Gouvernement du Québec 2005b: 6, emphasis added). In a recent publication on the new challenges that face French in Quebec, the Conseil supérieur de la langue française also stated that:

> The primary basis for analysis of [Quebec's] linguistic dynamics can only be the *langue d'usage public*. Since all Quebecers can use the language of their choice in the private sphere and because the adoption of French as the *langue d'usage* in the home is not a requirement in order to be recognised as adhering to the objectives of the Charter, the *langue d'usage public* becomes the key variable of analysis. The *langue d'usage public* must be seen as the language of integration. It allows for the measurement of the current attraction of French in collective life. (Stefanescu and Georgeault 2005: 594)

But how does this attraction work in reality? How can new Quebecers be motivated to adopt French as their language of public communications?

5.2 Status planning to motivate new Quebecers

It is often claimed that the only difference between the civic nation being proposed in Quebec, and that which supposedly already exists in the United States for example, is that the common public culture into which immigrants are expected to integrate is not English- but French-speaking (see Arel 2001: 75). Yet as far as second language acquisition is concerned, it is unwise to compare French and English in these two contexts when the languages do not enjoy the same power of attraction, when immigrants are not motivated to learn them for the same reasons.

Although opinions vary, most contemporary researchers agree with Gardner and Lambert (1972) that there are two main kinds of motivation involved in second language acquisition: instrumental and integrative.

> The first assumes that individuals are interested solely in acquiring sufficient communicative ability to satisfy their own specific goals, usually economic targets, while the second is based on the desire of individuals to associate themselves ever more closely with a target community to the point, eventually, of assimilating to it. (Ager 2001: 109)

A similar instrumental versus sentimental opposition has also been used to account for an individual's loyalty or attachment to the nation-state (Kelman 1972: 188).

Applying this dichotomy to the US context, Ager (2001: 114) explains that, despite variation between countries of origin and individual circumstances, instrumentalism is generally the primary motive behind the desire to emigrate to this country. Regarding language, this means that immigrants learn English in order to attain socio-economic mobility, so that they can more easily find employment. Moreover, the instrumental reasons at play in this case extend beyond the borders of the US. Learning English will improve one's employment prospects anywhere on the North American continent or indeed in the world, thanks to the language's current *de facto* status as a global *lingua franca*. By contrast, French in Quebec does not benefit from this degree of instrumental motivation: it is not the dominant language of the Canadian state, it is only spoken by two per cent of North America's population and has far fewer speakers than English world-wide. To make things worse, immigrants do not always make the psychological distinction between Canada and the US, not to mention between Canada and Quebec. Indeed, as Levine (1997: 98) notes about the situation during the pre-Charter period: 'For the newly arrived, North America rather than Quebec was their point of reference. Immigrants considered that knowledge of English was indispensable to get on in North America and consume mass culture circulated in English.'

Faced with this situation, the Quebec authorities set about improving the instrumental value of French by means of language legislation to make it the common language of public administration, education, the workplace, etc. (see Section 5.1). The instrumental motivations would result not only from the simple increase in status that French would enjoy in these fields, but also from the real 'added value' it would offer immigrants in the workplace once salary discrepancies between English and French speakers had been rectified.[4] More importantly perhaps, it was hoped that the instrumental motivations created would in time spill over into integrative ones, thus further reinforcing the commitment of immigrants to learning French.[5] In this way, many believe that the increased number of the so-called *enfants de la loi 101* (children of Bill 101) who were born and grew up there under the influence of the Charter of the French language can be expected to result in a greater affinity with Quebec and the French language (Baum 2001: 83). Others are less certain about the long-term effectiveness of compulsory schooling in French for immigrants and argue that 'maintaining the distinct society may well depend on their having a deeper, less instrumental commitment than that' (Carens 2000: 133). Such concerns are all the more real because the Charter only requires instruction in French at primary and secondary levels, not at the levels of CEGEP (*collège d'enseignement général et professionnel*, college of general and vocational education)[6] or university:

> It is doubtful that, in the long term, school alone can guarantee the *francisation* of immigrants. To be sure, there are more immigrants who learn

French at primary and secondary school, but this obligation does not apply to college level and it is noteworthy that when they have the choice, a majority of youngsters with immigrant backgrounds invariably opt for English schools at college and university levels. This has a much greater impact upon social and professional integration. (Monière 2003: 23)

While language legislation has enjoyed a fair degree of success in the past, it is now generally accepted that the survival of French in the twenty-first century, especially in Montreal, depends rather on fields that cannot be easily regulated by language legislation, such as immigration and integration policy (Levine 1997, 2000, 2002). Whereas in the beginning, the authorities preferred to concentrate on improving the instrumental value of French, possibly because minority languages are often dismissed as 'anti-instrumental, as merely "carriers" of "identity" ' (May 2003: 137), they soon realised the potential benefits of encouraging an affective attachment to the host society as an additional source of motivation. For example, the *Énoncé de politique en matière d'immigration et d'intégration* viewed French both in its instrumental function and in its capacity to engender a sense of belonging to Quebec:

> [L]anguage is not only an essential instrument which makes participation, communication and interaction with other Quebecers possible, it is also a symbol of identification. For immigrants, the learning of French supports the development of their sense of belonging to the Quebec community. (Gouvernement du Québec 1991: 17)

This sentiment was echoed in 1996 by the Comité interministériel sur la situation de la langue française, which explained that '[t]his expression *"langue commune"* evokes the dual idea of "communication" and "community" ' (Gouvernement du Québec 1996: 239). It was thus now hoped that, in addition to having a communicative function, French would also be an expression of identity for new Quebecers. For even if French is a second language instead of a mother tongue for the latter, at least for the first generation, it does not follow that the attachment to this language must be purely instrumental: 'second languages can play a significant role in one's linguistic identity' (Joseph 2004: 185).

The importance of integrative motivations has only been further stressed by the more recent debates about the redefinition of the Quebec nation. For example, the Larose Commission pointed out the need to explain to new arrivals that, 'in strictly linguistic terms, arriving in Quebec is not equivalent to arriving in Canada' (Gouvernement du Québec 2001a: 19):

> In Quebec, the *langue commune* is French. Elsewhere in Canada, English is the *langue commune*. The Commission deems it of the highest importance that the Quebec state takes the necessary measures so that, from the

moment of their welcoming, the message new arrivals receive about the characteristics of their host society, where French is the official and common language and the language of participation in civic life, is reiterated at the time of obtaining Canadian citizenship. (Gouvernement du Québec 2001a: 19)

How the Commission proposed to do this was with the aid of a common Quebec citizenship to exist alongside Canadian citizenship and with French as the key element (see Section 2.2). Considering that the intercultural model favoured in Quebec sees citizenship 'as the explicit recognition of belonging to a nation, a community of individuals who choose to live together and share a common culture' (Gouvernement du Québec 2001a: 14), this means that knowledge of French is itself considered by the Larose Commission as the main form of attachment to the Quebec nation. This marks a shift from the 1990 *Énoncé* in which French was described simply as 'supporting the development' of a sense of belonging to Quebec.

As seen in Section 2.2, the idea of formalising a Quebec citizenship was eventually rejected without any real reflection about the possible content it could have entailed. Recalling that Quebec is a mere province of Canada, Monière (2003: 23–4) claims that '[t]he motivation for adopting French is necessarily weak and transitory among immigrants in a country which is officially bilingual and where English is the language of economic and social success.' In a similar fashion, G. Bouchard (2001a: 38) claims that sovereignty is one of the necessary conditions or prerequisites for the full realisation of his model of the Quebec nation built around French as the common denominator (see Section 3.3). This may eventually prove so, but in the short term, an alternative to sovereignty could have been found in the formalisation of a Quebec citizenship. Focused solely or predominantly on language, and conceived in a way which was acceptable to Quebecers of all ethnic origins, the latter could have had the potential to create the integrative attachment to Quebec needed to ensure the status of French as the *langue publique commune*.

While the strategy of a Quebec citizenship may have been rejected, the ultimate goal of creating an integrative motivation to learn French by having recourse to civic values nonetheless remains. For example, the Liberal government's immigration and integration Action Plan for 2004–2007, *Des valeurs partagées, des intérêts communs* (see Section 2.2), stresses once again that the mastery of French by immigrants is in itself considered an expression of belonging to a society 'which has become their own' (Gouvernement du Québec 2004a: 65). As stated in the same document, one of the aims of the 'francisation services' offered to immigrants is also 'to develop a sense of belonging thanks to knowledge of the *langue publique commune*' (Gouvernement du Québec 2004a: 66).

Despite all these efforts and the optimism of governmental rhetoric, a recent report on the role of French in the workplace notes that in 2001 only

43 per cent of Allophones declared French as the language they used most often at work (see Table 5.2).

In other words, notwithstanding measures to increase the integrative motivations for learning and using French, the instrumental motivation to use English persists (Molinaro 2005: 102; see also Section 7.1). This is because, as Pagé explains:

> [i]n general, in their everyday life, people do not refer constantly to a collective identity. The identity dimension of integration is only one dimension of the fundamental motivation to be French-speaking and it is perhaps not the most salient.
>
> Other factors which give rise to this tendency in everyday life are much closer to daily personal preoccupations than the collective preoccupations evident at 'major gatherings'. Linguistic choices in a multilingual society are also, or especially, motivated by considerations that are very close to personal interests. (Pagé 2005: 216–17)

In the case of immigrants, these 'personal interests' are closely linked to the reasons for immigration to North America mentioned at the beginning of this section. It may also be that, following the framework of self-categorisation theory (see Section 1.2), economic migrants attribute more importance to the personal (individual) rather than the social (group) dimension of their identity for these same reasons. Moreover, it has been claimed that immigrants are more likely to adopt English for reasons of socio-economic mobility as a result of the exodus of educated and wealthy Francophones to the Montreal suburbs, which leaves immigrants on the island of Montreal with fewer middle-class Francophone role models (Leclerc 2005b). Indeed, urban planning is the other main area in addition to immigration policy that will undoubtedly

Table 5.2 Percentage of workers according to the language used most often at work by mother tongue in the whole of Quebec*

Mother tongue	French	French and English**	English	Other	N
French	92	4	4	0	3,219,540
English	22	9	69	0	300,195
French and English	49	33	17	0	22,330
Other*	43	14	36	7	396,450
Total	82	5	12	1	3,938,510

* Also includes those who declared a third mother tongue in addition to French and English.
** Also includes those who claimed to use a third language at work in addition to French and English.
Source: Statistics Canada, Canadian Census of 2001 (cited in Lapierre Vincent 2005: 17).

have an impact on the status of French in the Quebec of tomorrow (Levine 1997, 2000, 2002).

To be sure, 'we are a long way from the situation of the past when integration to the Francophone group meant acquiring a devalued identity' (Pagé 2005: 219). However, the attraction of English today no longer lies in the fact that it is the language of a socio-economically advantaged minority in Quebec, but rather in its status as the language of socio-economic success on the North American continent, not to mention as the current *lingua franca* of an increasingly interconnected world (Stefanescu and Georgeault 2005: 591). As Edwards (2003: 41) observes: 'globalization and its linguistic ramifications are welcomed by many who see in it upward mobility – physical, social, psychological.' This is a fact that language planning in Quebec needs to take into consideration if it is not to run counter to the aspirations of new Quebecers or, for that matter, of all Quebecers, irrespective of mother tongue. Even with state backing, language policies are rarely successful if they do not have support at the grassroots level, where actual language practices determine the 'real language policy' (Spolsky 2004: 222-3):

> [A]ll the evidence to date suggests that governments are unable to legislate top-down about acquisition of lingua francas. Although language learning on an ideological basis was achieved in nation building, this was because top-down and bottom-up movements coincided: the spread of the national language was central to nation building; acquisition of the language was useful for individual success and social mobility. Such dual pressure is not present for any policy that tries to limit English-language spread. (Wright 2004: 169–170)

Quebec is not alone in having to find a difficult balance between promoting the national language at the same time as encouraging knowledge of the global *lingua franca*. For example, in Sweden, where English has traditionally enjoyed a privileged status in many fields of language use, a nationalist revival has resulted in a new desire to promote the Swedish language, but not at the expense of English (Oakes 2005).

Unlike Sweden, Quebec does not have the luxury of an independent state to protect its language. Nonetheless, the challenge is the same: if they are to be successful, language planning measures that seek to promote national languages need to be consistent with polices that promote knowledge of a *lingua franca* that will allow members of the population in question to compete in the global market. Pagé (2005: 222) is right to say that 'francisation is compatible with knowledge of English'. Of course, how the learning of English is promoted is a matter for debate, as witnessed by the range of reactions to the Charest government's decision to introduce the teaching of English as a second language into the first cycle of primary school (Boileau 2005; see also Section 4.2). Moreover, there is no reason why francisation should not be considered compatible with the promotion of other languages as well, including those already spoken by immigrants. While it is true that the latter are attached to their multilingualism (see Sections 7.2 and 7.3), their resistance to monolingualism 'need not be read as an obstacle to the generalization of French as the common public language of Quebec' (Molinaro 2005: 110). As an increasingly active presence on the global scene (see Chapter 4), Quebec can only benefit from making full use of the linguistic potential of its ethnolinguistically diverse population, and this need not necessarily undermine the status of French in Quebec (Fréchette 2005). One of the major challenges for status planning in Quebec in the future is therefore to find a way of coexisting in harmony with acquisition planning that favours the learning of other languages, not least English. Only by finding a suitable balance between desires to learn and maintain other languages on the one hand, and to promote French on the other, can the latter become 'a language which is not imposed, but which imposes itself' (Stefanescu and Georgeault 2005: 593).

As seen throughout this chapter so far, the principal aim of status planning in Quebec over the last few decades has been to motivate new Quebecers to adopt French for sentimental or integrative reasons. In order to facilitate the desired outcome, the Quebec authorities have been engaged in efforts to dissociate French from French Canadian ethnicity (Molinaro 2005: 91). Such attempts to 'de-ethnicise' language are not unique to Quebec but can also be observed in other similar contexts around the world where large-scale immigration has to be reconciled with a desire to promote a minority language. In Catalonia, for instance, increased immigration both from other regions of Spain and the Maghrebi countries in particular, coupled with a falling birth rate amongst indigenous Catalans, has led the authorities there to attempt to dissociate Catalan language and ethnicity: 'Too much insistence on that bond is likely to alienate those whose first language is not Catalan, and it may encourage them to insist that their linguistic rights take precedence over Catalan self-ascription' (Hoffmann 2000: 435).

A good example of rhetoric that seeks to 'de-ethnicise' language in Quebec is provided by the title of the Larose Commission's report: *Le français, une langue pour tout le monde* (French: A Language for Everyone). No longer is French to be considered the property of the French Canadian majority, but rather as a language for all Quebecers irrespective of ethnic origin. But while one must accept a 'dynamic model' of language that takes into account the new ways of relating to French (Pagé 2006), one must also wonder how far the 'de-ethnicisation' process can go. Can language be completely 'de-ethnicised', as much of the official and academic discourse implies?

5.3 'De-ethnicising' language?

Perhaps the first person since the Quiet Revolution to attempt to dissociate the French language from French Canadian ethnicity was Pierre Trudeau, as demonstrated by his rejection of the idea of a bicultural Canada favoured by the Commission d'enquête sur le bilinguisme et le biculturalisme (Commission of Inquiry on Bilingualism and Biculturalism, 1963–71), also known as the Laurendeau-Dunton Commission:

> Trudeau opted instead to adopt a policy of official multiculturalism in a bilingual framework [established by the Official Languages Act introduced in 1969]. As such, it was believed that language could be dissociated from culture, and individuals would be free to decide whether or not to endeavour to preserve their ethnic identities. (Gagnon and Iacovino 2002: 323; see also Dumont 1997: 40)

Trudeau's preference was for language policy based on the principle of personality, according to which individuals are free to obtain services throughout an entire state in the language of their choice. Notwithstanding the fact that services in French are limited in a large part of the country, Trudeau's vision of a bilingual Canada 'from coast to coast' has failed in so far as it has only encouraged Quebec to develop language policy based on the principle of territoriality, according to which services are only (or mostly) offered in the language of the (ethnic) majority of the population in a given territory.[7] But while it assumes a strong link between language and ethnicity, even this latter type of policy as it existed in Quebec was predicted to lead to

> the progressive dissociation of language from ethnicity, as more and more people of different ethnic origins adopt the French language. The imposition of 'franco-conformity' will progressively yield the same results with regard to French as those brought about by the imposition of 'Anglo-conformity' with regard to English. In fact, to a considerable extent, a 'francophone' is already socially defined as someone who speaks French; not as someone who belongs to an ethno-cultural group. In other words, French will become less and less the distinctive cultural attribute of an ethnic community and more and more the means of communication of an economic and political collectivity. (Breton 1988: 97–8)

Over 15 years on, it is now possible to examine Breton's predictions more closely. It is true that, while the children of immigrants to Quebec may not easily be able to become ethnic French Canadians, they can become fully-fledged Quebecers by becoming Francophones (G. Bouchard 2001a: 33). However, the use of language as opposed to ethnicity as a parameter of social categorisation by no means weakens the link between these two concepts. Indeed, '[t]he majority of ethnic groups have the right to their own *phone*: italophone, hellenophone, hispanophone, not forgetting creolophone' (Bouthillier 1997: 84).

Moreover, the term 'Francophone' demands closer attention. A quick survey of dictionaries of Quebec French reveals that a broad perspective is usually adopted when defining this word. For example, the *Dictionnaire du français plus à l'usage des francophones d'Amérique* (1988: 706) describes a Francophone as someone 'for whom French is the mother or official language', the *Dictionnaire québécois d'aujourd'hui* (1992: 513–14) as someone '[w]ho speaks French, either as a mother, official or second language' and the most recent *Dictionnaire québécois-français* (Meney 1999: 864) simply as a '*personne de langue française*' ('a person who speaks French'). However, anyone spending time in Quebec will notice that the word is often used, at the grassroots level in particular, with a more narrow meaning to describe an ethnic, rather than purely linguistic reality (see also C. Bouchard 2002: 238). For example, the above definitions undeniably include immigrants from France, yet the latter are usually referred to as 'French' and not 'Francophones', a term by and large reserved for those of French Canadian descent.[8]

Even within official and academic circles, this traditional definition of Francophone persists. For example, the Larose Commission defines a Francophone as a '[p]erson whose mother tongue is French or who uses this language most often in his or her *private life* and public communications' (Gouvernement du Québec 2001a: 225, emphasis added). This definition is inconsistent with the more civic or integrationist approach adopted overall by the Commission Larose since, 'in order to be included in the category of Francophone, one needs to have undergone language shift to French in one's private life as well' (Pagé 2006: 42). Even those calling for a more inclusive definition of Quebec identity still have a need to refer to those who have French as a mother tongue, the *francophones de souche* ('old stock' Francophones) (e.g., G. Bouchard 1999: 69, 77) or *Franco-Québécois*, defined not as all those Quebecers who speak French, but as those Quebecers of French Canadian descent or whose ancestors assimilated to this group (G. Bouchard 2001a: 198). If the new approach is to emphasise that everyone using French in the public sphere is a Francophone, why are these distinctions still made?

The answer to this question is two-fold. First, however strong the civic aspirations of a society may be, ethnicity cannot simply be banished; the fact remains that there is still a French-speaking ethnic group in Quebec, designated throughout this book as French Canadian, and there is a need to refer to this group on occasion (see Section 1.3). Second, while they sometimes choose to give precedence to their personal over their social identity (see Sections 1.2 and 5.2), history has shown that people do want to distinguish themselves along ethnic lines, especially in those circumstances where their ethnicity is perceived as threatened. As such, ethnicity is indeed exclusive, in so far as social identities are invariably constructed in contradistinction to others. This is not to imply, however, that individuals cannot assimilate to the majority group if so desired (e.g., there are many cases of Irish and

Scottish people having assimilated to the French Canadian majority), no more than it hinders members of different ethnic groups from living as equals in the same society or nation, depending on how the latter is defined. Indeed, as Létourneau explains, the fact that immigrants in Quebec can usually be identified by the way they speak need not necessarily lead to discrimination:

> 'Betrayed' by their language (accent, phrases, lexis, etc.), Quebecers of French, Belgian or Romanian origin who have lived in Quebec for a long time and who hold Canadian nationality will thus be identified in practice as coming from 'elsewhere'. The same is true for Anglophones born in Quebec and who speak French with ease, albeit with a 'particular pronunciation'. Whether they like it or not, recently arrived immigrants to Montreal will be put into the same generic category on opening their mouth: they will belong to the world of 'audible minorities'. They will be assuredly and indisputably Quebecers (or in the process of becoming so if they have undertaken the legal process that leads to Canadian nationality). But they will be approached and welcomed as 'external members' of the group, which does not mean that they will experience marginalisation or social relegation, let alone ostracism. (Létourneau 2002: 90–1)

To recall the warning of G. Bouchard (1999: 30; see Section 3.3), ethnicity should not be confused with ethnocentrism or ethnicism. In other words, rather than deny the desire of group members to *differentiate* themselves on ethnic grounds, one should condemn ethnocentrism and ethnicism; it is these phenomena which drive individuals to *discriminate* against members of other ethnic groups, irrespective of how much the state promotes a common culture and language.

In France, for example, the strong civic model of non-differentiation (see Section 2.3) has not succeeded in eliminating – and one could argue may even have encouraged – ethnic discrimination through language. About the French spoken by foreigners, Kristeva (1988: 58) has observed that

> [e]ven when he is legally and administratively accepted, the foreigner is not for all that accepted into [French] families. His untoward usage of the French language discredits him, consciously or not, in the eyes of the natives who identify themselves more than in other countries with their polished and cherished speech.

Vassberg (1993) makes a similar observation, this time about a variety of French indigenous to France: '[A]n Alsatian accent when pronouncing French usually produces very negative judgments of the speaker: "an accent" is considered unrefined, ungraceful, crude, ridiculous, a mark of lower-class origins and a lack of education' (Vassberg 1993: 170). Empirical research has shown that such 'evaluations of language varieties do not reflect intrinsic linguistic or aesthetic qualities so much as the levels of status and prestige that they are *conventionally* associated with in particular speech communities' (Giles and Coupland 1991: 37-8). As the status of a language is closely associated with the status of the speakers of that language, it follows that negative opinions about different varieties of French reflect negative views about the ethnic groups that speak them.

In the United States, too, calls heard since the mid-1980s to make English the official language not just of individual states, but also at the federal level, have equally been shown to be motivated by ethnicism, or what is often termed in the US the new nativism (Nunberg 1997; May 2001: 204-24; Schmid 2001: 41-3). Similarly in Sweden, where nationalist rhetoric has been played down since the 1930s, language offers a convenient means of discrimination against immigrant others, when criteria such as race or ethnicity are not deemed politically correct (Oakes 2001: 114-15). That language is used for this purpose highlights the purely theoretical nature of Anderson's (1983: 122) claim mentioned in the introduction to this chapter, that language is not an instrument of exclusion.

Not only is ethnic identity invariably expressed through the fabric of language, there is an inextricable link between language and ethnicity on a macro level as well. This is demonstrated by the patently false claims that civic models of nation can be ethnoculturally neutral (see Section 2.3) which are also made with regard to language. As Kymlicka (2001: 24-5) reveals about the US:

> Consider the actual policies of the United States, which is the prototypically 'neutral' state. Historically, decisions about the boundaries of state governments, and the timing of their admission into the federation, were deliberately made to ensure that anglophones would be a majority within each of the fifty states of the American federation. This helped establish the dominance of English throughout the territory of the United States. And the continuing dominance of English is ensured by several ongoing policies. For example, it is a legal requirement for children to learn the English language in schools; it is a legal requirement for immigrants (under the age of 50) to learn English to acquire American citizenship; and it is a *de facto* requirement for employment in or for government that the applicant speak English. (Kymlicka 2001: 24-5)

In France, too, the choice of French as a common public language is far from being ethnoculturally neutral, as speakers of minority languages who have long fought for official recognition of their languages know all too well (see Oakes 2001: 88-97, 116-18).

More than choices about other symbols of national identity (e.g., flags, holidays, etc.), where there are a number of options, choices about language are inexorably linked to ethnicity. Considering that all modern states have language policies, be they *de jure* or *de facto* in nature, some ethnic (or national) groups are necessarily favoured over others (Walker 1999: 154; Carens 2000: 53–4; Patten 2003). This is all too apparent in the European Union, where difficult choices that favour some member states and not others will need to be made in the future if the EU is to limit the number of official and working languages it uses as a solution to the problem of mounting interpreting and translation costs (see Oakes 2001: 131–6). Supporters of English as a global language also base their arguments on the false belief that the language is neutral (see Fishman 1977: 118), especially since those who speak it as a second or foreign language significantly outweigh those who have it as a mother tongue.[9] Yet these arguments have not succeeded in convincing many around the world, for instance those with a particular knowledge of the Third World. While English may be used as a *politically* neutral language in some cases, for example in India and Nigeria, it is certainly not *ethnoculturally* neutral (Carens 2000: 78). Indeed, Gandhi (1965) was vehemently opposed to the use of English in India, likening this practice to a form of mental slavery, while the Nigerian writer Chinua Achebe (e.g., 1988) has opted for a strategy of subversion, rather than outright rejection of English, by using 'the language of the colonizer to convey the Igbo experience of that colonization' (Slattery 1998).[10]

Just as choices about official languages in other contexts cannot be ethnoculturally neutral, the decision to make French the official language of Quebec is no more civic than had another language been chosen. To recall the words of Dumont about the republican aspirations of the Patriot movement in 1837–38, French 'is no more democratic in its essence than other languages' (Dumont 1996: 175; see Section 3.1). Walker makes the same point about creating a Francophone *'visage linguistique'* ('linguistic face') in Montreal:

> Arguments about protecting culture cannot by themselves justify using majority rule to replace the institutions of this formerly bilingual, and still multicultural city, so as to give it a francophone *visage linguistique*. Such a change could only be justified by reference to the needs of a particular ethnic group. Only an argument that shows that the needs of the French-speaking Québécois ethnic group justify their usage of Montreal for their particularist cultural goals would support the promotion of a francophone *visage linguistique* on the island of Montreal. An argument for the protection of the specific cultural 'context of choice' what we find on the island of Montreal would lead to quite a different result: to the protection of the *multi*-cultural character of Montreal against the policies of the largely homogenous population on the territory around. [...] It is only if we give primacy to a model of ethnic hegemony that we can justify the process of cultural de-differentiation involved with giving Montreal a francophone *visage linguistique*. (Walker 1999: 152–3)

Irrespective of whether one agrees or not with Walker's advocacy of an active policy of multilingualism in the public sphere in Montreal, he does nonetheless make the valid point that it is difficult to justify choices about language without making reference to ethnic culture. This is possibly the reason why French is rarely referred to as the 'national language' in Quebec in the same way that Quebec City is considered as the *capitale nationale*, the new library as the *bibliothèque nationale* and 24 June as the *fête nationale* of all Quebecers. Considering that all national culture is usually based on that of the dominant ethnic core (see A. D. Smith 1986, 1991: 37–42; Section 1.4), any reference made to French as the *langue nationale* would be tantamount to recognising officially that the language of the ethnic majority is being favoured over those of the ethnic minorities.

If the complete 'de-ethnicisation' of language is problematic in general terms, this endeavour is all the more doubtful in the specific case of Quebec where, since the secularisation of society that followed the Quiet Revolution (see Section 2.1), it is language which has come to replace the Church as the main bearer of French Canadian memory (Cantin 2001b: 55):

> [I]n Quebec, as elsewhere in the world, language – French in this case – is not only a vehicle of communication. It is much more than this, namely the mode of expression *par excellence* of a culture that has its own memory and that, by means of this memory carried by language, seeks to express itself to the world in its specificity and its universality, in its heritage and its projects. Language is not in fact simply and solely a means of communication. For a group that finds and invests in it a significant part of its *être-au-monde* ['being in the world'], language is memory and self-image. Hence the problem that one can envisage and which often ensues: speaking a language does not *a fortiori* make the speaker, if he or she comes from an 'other' culture, a fiduciary of the memory and representations of a particular group, of its *être-au-monde* and its expectations for the future. (Létourneau 2002: 80–1)

Moreover, the relationship between language and ethnicity is mutually reinforcing: not only is the French language 'vested with all the French Canadian cultural heritage' (G. Bouchard 1997: 120), French Canadian ethnicity is one of the major driving forces behind the maintenance of the French language in North America. Yet this fact is clearly ignored by the strictly civic models of nation that have been proposed (see Section 3.2), such as Bariteau's application to Quebec of Habermas's theory of constitutional patriotism:

> Civic approaches like Bariteau's are void of underlying motivation if they cannot be understood as being motivated by the desire to ensure the survival of a common public culture of French expression. Now, despite the warnings of Dumont and Bouchard, new conceptions of the 'Quebec nation' seem to want to keep this motivation which drives them in the

dark. They believe that, simply by underlining in passing that French will be the language of citizenship of the new sovereign state, they can solve the problem of the survival of the French language in the few acres of snow lost in America, as well as the linguistic quarrels which arise on its territory. These positions are either naive or dishonest. (Dufour 2001: 198; see also Mathieu 2001: 128-9)

In other words, even if language could be completely 'de-ethnicised' as a matter of principle, one should not attempt to do so if French is to have a chance of survival in North America. Ethnicity provides a necessary motivation for the maintenance of French, which reference to civic principles alone cannot inspire. In this light, it is somewhat extraordinary that the Larose Commission, whose recommendations sought to ensure the continued use and expansion of French, makes no mention of the fact that French is an important – if not the most important – symbol of identity for the French Canadian majority in Quebec.

5.4 Status planning for Quebecers of all ethnic origins

Since the 1960s-70s, status planning in Quebec has undergone a radical transformation. While its ultimate goal of ensuring the survival of the French language remains the same, it no longer focuses exclusively on the needs of the French Canadian majority; rather, it is predominantly shaped today by the desire to accommodate a growing number of immigrants, the group of Quebecers upon whom the future of French now depends. With the aid of the concept of *langue (publique) commune*, attempts have been made by successive Quebec governments especially since the 1990s to motivate immigrants to learn French for integrative or affective reasons, as a linguistic expression of their allegiance to the host society. This requires a new dynamic model for status planning in Quebec, which takes into account the different ways that new Quebecers relate to French as well as the fact that the language is now used as a vehicle for widely different cultural values, some of which may not be congruent with those of the majority French Canadian group (Carens 2000: 129). Another challenge for status planning in Quebec is to reconcile the promotion of French with acquisition planning measures that favour the learning of other languages, including English. Not only will these measures meet the needs of new Quebecers, who are both concerned about maintaining their heritage languages and want to learn the language of socio-economic mobility in North America, they will also benefit native French- and English-speaking Quebecers, by providing them with the skills to work and live in an increasingly globalised world.

Any new model of status planning also needs to recognise, however, that one of the ways of relating to French in Quebec results from its role as a carrier of French Canadian identity. Various non-ethnic arguments are often used to justify the decision to make French the official language of Quebec, for example that it is the main *langue d'usage public* of 87 per cent of the population or that it is worth defending the language for the sake of maintaining linguistic diversity in the world. Nonetheless, the fact remains that French is also the mother tongue of the French Canadian ethnic majority, which is clearly a more obvious reason for its defence, not to mention a major force behind its maintenance. To ignore this reality is not only disingenuous, it also risks alienating French Canadians from the civic project. Unfortunately, the ethnic function of French in Quebec seems doomed to non-recognition as long as the concept of ethnicity remains taboo. This is why language policy has to be developed in association with the establishment of a new model of the Quebec nation which, within an overall civic framework, nonetheless recognises the different ethnic identities of all Quebecers, not least that of the French Canadian majority. These are important challenges not only for status planning, but also for corpus planning, which is the focus of the next chapter.

6
Whose French? Language Attitudes, Linguistic Insecurity and Standardisation

> *Comme le soulignait le grand architecte de la* Charte de la langue française, *Camille Laurin,* « le statut de la langue est lié à sa qualité et l'amélioration de sa qualité ne fera que renforcer le statut de la langue. » *Cela s'avère encore exact aujourd'hui. Plus que jamais, le statut de la langue dépend de notre volonté de promouvoir ici, au Québec, un français de qualité qui, tout en prenant en compte nos spécificités, correspond à la norme internationale. C'est à cette condition que les Québécoises et les Québécois seront fiers de leur langue, qu'ils donneront le goût aux autres locuteurs de la parler et qu'ils contribueront à verser dans le patrimoine mondial linguistique et culturel une langue de qualité, pétrie des réalités de son continent.*

As highlighted by the great architect of the Charter of the French language, Camille Laurin, 'the status of a language is linked to its quality and the improvement of its quality will only reinforce its status'. This is still true today. More than ever, the status of the [French] language depends on our desire to promote here in Quebec a French of quality which, while all the while taking into account our specificities, corresponds to the international norm. Only in this way will Quebecers be proud of their language, will they inspire others to speak it and will they add to the global linguistic and cultural heritage a language of quality, shaped by the realities of its continent. (Gouvernement du Québec 2001a: 78)

As Gérald Larose and his team of commissioners were well aware, questions of status planning are inextricably linked to those of corpus planning. In other words, the recommendations made by the Commission with the view to ensuring the continued use and scope of French in Quebec cannot escape questions about the nature of the French to use. Since the nineteenth century, Francophones in Quebec have been dogged by the thorny matter of whether to adopt French as commonly used in Quebec (also called *français d'ici*) or French as used in France (often confused with the notions of *français standard* and *français international*). While the latter has always enjoyed great social prestige in Quebec, this has traditionally not been the case for the former, hence concerns about the quality of language, such as those expressed in the citation above. But as C. Bouchard (2005: 387) notes, '[t]he notion of quality of language is relative, because quality can only be measured in relation to a norm'. While it was originally supposed that only French as used in France could assume the role of a prestigious social norm, the last few decades have witnessed a re-evaluation of Quebec French. More precisely, a third possibility has arisen, namely a socially acceptable, locally-defined variety which has come to be known as Standard Quebec French. As a compromise between the two previously proposed models, the latter attests to the desire of French-speaking Quebecers to remain part of *la francophonie*, yet at the same time express their unique identity within this arena. As such, it has the potential to relieve French-speaking Quebecers of their linguistic insecurity *vis-à-vis* the French of France. However, this is not the only stake to consider. In the efforts to define Standard Quebec French, care must be made not to scare off immigrants (Poirier 1998: 149). As seen in the last chapter, it is on this group of Quebecers that the future of French depends.

This chapter therefore examines the debate about the quality of language and the variety of French to be espoused, with particular regard to the new civic approach to Quebec identity. What kind of French should Quebec offer its new immigrants? Do French-speaking Quebecers need to give up their particular variety and adopt a so-called 'international French' in order to be truly civic? Or can a third, halfway solution be found in a new pluricentric conception of the French language? These questions are examined here both from a theoretical perspective and in the context of the concrete efforts of lexicographers over the last two decades to describe the emerging standard for Quebec French. Most recently, this challenge has been taken on by a team of researchers at the Université de Sherbrooke whose new 'national dictionary' is set to appear in 2007. In order to contextualise the reactions from all sides that this latest initiative has provoked, it is useful to outline first the history of language attitudes in Quebec. This historical background will allow for a better understanding of the question which many Quebecers continue to ask themselves: *Est-ce qu'on parle bien, nous autres*? Do we Quebecers speak well?

6.1 *Est-ce qu'on parle bien, nous autres?*

From the arrival of the first settlers in the early seventeenth century and throughout all of the eighteenth century, attitudes towards the variety of

French spoken in New France were positive. The accounts of travellers from Europe frequently made claims of the type:

> [N]owhere else is our language spoken more purely. No accent is to be heard here. (Father Pierre-François-Xavier de Charlevoix 1720, cited in Charlevoix 1744: 79)
>
> There is no *patois* in this country. All Canadians speak a French like ours. (d'Aleyrac 1755, cited in d'Aleyrac 1935: 31)
>
> I observed that Canadian peasants speak very good French. (Marquis de Montcalm 1756, cited in Montcalm 1895: 64)
>
> It is remarked of the Canadians that [...] they speak the French in the greatest purity, and without the least false accent. (Jefferys 1761: 9)
>
> The people here speak perfectly well without a bad accent. Although there is a mixture of almost all the provinces of France, one cannot distinguish the idiom of any of them in [the speech of] Canadian women. (Bacqueville de la Potherie 1700, cited in Bacqueville de la Potherie 1753: 279)[1]

The settlers had emigrated from certain parts of France; from Île-de-France, the northwest and the west in particular. Because of the various idioms that they spoke, some scholars claim that New France experienced a '*choc des patois*' ('*patois* choc') (Barbaud 1984) which ultimately led to the rapid adoption as a *lingua franca* of what was known then as *françoys*:

> In its early stages, the act of populating the colony under the French Regime was an undertaking which had the effect of abruptly and suddenly removing native speakers from the age-old order of linguistic practices. Uprooted from their country of birth, transplanted to a living space as virgin as it was confined, these speakers were confronted with difficulties of verbal communication in its most vernacular form. They were the actors of a linguistic disorder which must have lasted for some time. But the urgent need to return to a more stable order drove them to modify their linguistic behaviour, amongst other things. They learned to become bilingual. In the end, they opted for *françoys* monolingualism. (Barbaud 1984: 183)

However, a majority of scholars working on the history of French in Quebec now agree that the use of the so-called *patois* in New France was not as common as first believed (e.g., Asselin and McLaughlin 1994; Poirier 1994; see also Marcel 1973: 27). They claim that, when the emigrants were not already from towns in France where French was more widely spoken, the lengthy periods spent in ports such as La Rochelle and Nantes offer a more likely explanation for the early adoption of French in the new colony. Whatever the reason, by the end of the seventeenth century, and by the early eighteenth century at the latest, New France was perceived to have attained a degree of linguistic uniformity that was purportedly lacking in the mother country where, according to Abbé Grégoire, at least six million people, especially in the countryside, did not know the national language (Certeau, Julia and Revel 1975: 302). It is quite likely that it was this relative linguistic uniformity of New France that lay behind the positive evaluations of the language spoken there; for while the latter may have been French, it was on the whole not the French of the aristocracy and classical authors (Cajolet-Laganière and Martel 1995: 40–1). The language of administrators aside, the French spoken in New France in the middle of the eighteenth century would probably have resembled that used by the lower classes of the 'Frenchified' parts of France, especially in the northwest (C. Bouchard 2002: 47).

Following the Treaty of Paris of 1763, New France became a British possession cut off from the mother country. This rupture was to have a significant effect on life in the former colony in many respects (see also Section 4.3). Linguistically, the isolation from France meant that the variety of French spoken in Canada began to differ significantly over the next century. Not only was the latter removed from the effects that the Revolution had on language in France, the contact with English led to an influx of anglicisms in the form of direct borrowings, so-called *calques* or syntactic borrowings, English pronunciations, imitations of English punctuation, etc. Once again, it was the foreign travellers who made the first observations. In his *Travels through Canada and the United States of America in the Years 1806, 1807 and 1808*, John Lambert noted that

> [The] intercourse between the French and English has occasioned the former to ingraft many anglicisms in their language, which to a stranger arriving from England, and speaking only boarding-school French, is at first rather puzzling. The Canadians have had the character of speaking the purest French; but I question whether they deserve it at the present day. (Lambert 1814: 87–8)

The writings of Michel Bibaud (e.g., his columns on language from 1817 in *L'Aurore*) and Thomas Maguire's *Manuel des difficultés les plus communes de la langue française* (1841) represent early indications of an awareness amongst the French Canadians themselves that their French no longer resembled that spoken in France. However, it was not until the second half of the nineteenth century that it became of real concern that foreigners, and especially English speakers on the continent, considered Canadian French to be a *patois* far removed from the prestigious variety of French spoken in Paris. Having begun to re-establish links with France after a century of rupture, it was members of the elite who were first affected by what has become known as the 'myth of French Canadian Patois' (C. Bouchard 2000: 198, 2002).[2] Figures of the likes of Arthur Buies, Louis Fréchette, Joseph-Amable Manseau and Oscar Dunn began to write an impressive number of books, pamphlets and newspaper columns in which they denounced the use of anglicisms especially.[3] In his *L'anglicisme, voilà l'ennemi* (Anglicisms are the enemy), Jules-Paul Tardivel (1880), for example, warned of the particular danger of semantic anglicisms, that is, of giving English meanings to French words (e.g., *faire une application* instead of *poser sa candidature*, 'to make an application', e.g., for a job):

> If we do not watch out, it is possible that with time the language of the province of Quebec will become a real *patois* which will only be French in name, a jargon that we would be better to abandon faced with the impossibility of reforming it. [...] This habit that we have gradually contracted of speaking English with French words is all the more dangerous because we are generally unaware of it. [...] In my view, barbarisms, neologisms, tautologies and errors of syntax and orthography are mere peccadilloes compared with anglicisms which are, as it were, sins against nature. (Tardivel 1880: 5–7)

In the beginning, it was the urban bourgeoisie who were targeted because of their close contact with English, but the criticism soon spread to the lower classes as industrialisation forced the latter into the English-dominated cities in search of work (C. Bouchard 2000: 201). Even the dwindling number of true peasants or *habitants* did not remain immune for long on account of the archaisms that differentiated Canadian French in general from that spoken in France at the time. Buies, Fréchette and other purists pushed for the modernisation and realignment of Canadian French with French as spoken in France, rejecting the widely-held belief that the former was in fact purer because it was closer to the classical French of Louis XIV's seventeenth-century France (C. Bouchard 2002: 93–5). Other commentators saw in these archaisms 'old family jewels' to be conserved (E. Gagnon 1916 [1802], cited in C. Bouchard 2002: 91), a view shared by Dunn (1880) and Clapin (1894) who adopted more nuanced, descriptive approaches to Canadian French in their respective glossaries.

By the end of the nineteenth century, the 'myth of French Canadian Patois' had reached the public at large, who now began to feel a deep sense of linguistic insecurity in two respects: not only did they feel inferior by not speaking the dominant English language, they were now being told that they did not even speak French, but rather a mere *patois*. Fearing that French Canadians would opt for assimilation rather than a stigmatised identity, many commentators now sought in a more active fashion to counter the negative attitudes amongst French Canadians and foreigners alike by stressing the legitimacy of the local variety of French (C. Bouchard 2002: 101). It was in this context that the Société du parler français du Canada was founded in 1902 by Adjutor Rivard, Stanislas Lortie and others such as

Camille Roy and Jules-Paul Tardivel (Mercier 2002b). While still denouncing the use of true anglicisms, the Société aimed to raise the profile of certain particularities of Canadian French, using historical studies to reveal that many of these were not anglicisms, as some falsely believed, but rather remnants of old French and certain dialects spoken in France. This legitimisation exercise characterised the majority of the Société's numerous activities, which included: the *Bulletin du parler français au Canada*, the first linguistic journal in French Canada, which later became *Le Canada français*; the organisation of two Congrès de la langue française au Canada in 1912 and 1937, and its (albeit less significant) participation in two more in 1952 and 1957; as well as its *Glossaire du parler français au Canada* (Société du parler français au Canada 1930), described as 'one of the centrepieces of Quebec lexicography' (Mercier 2002b: 99). Nonetheless, the efforts of the Société and others to improve the standing of Canadian French was not enough to stem the linguistic insecurity felt by most French Canadians, a phenomenon which reached its peak during the period from 1940 until 1960 when attitudes towards French had never been as negative (Pöll 2001: 113–14; C. Bouchard 2002: 85).

Then came the Quiet Revolution of the early 1960s (see Section 2.1). The myth of French Canadian Patois was replaced by debates about *joual*, a distortion of the word *cheval* ('horse') taken from the expression *parler cheval* ('to speak badly'). In his now famous *Les insolences du Frère Untel*, Jean-Paul Desbiens denounced what he considered to be this 'decomposition', this 'absence of language that is *joual*' (Desbiens 1960: 24), which he claimed epitomised the collective alienation of French Canadians: 'Our pupils speak *joual*, write *joual* and don't want to speak or write in any other way. [...] The vice is therefore profound: it involves syntax. It also involves pronunciation' (Desbiens 1960: 24). In the absence of any scientific definition, there was much confusion in the early days about what *joual* actually referred to. Before it emerged that *joual* was little more than a register used especially by the lower, urban classes, the term was used with a variety of meanings, with many even equating it with Quebec French in its entirety (see Gagné 1979: 49; Saint-Jacques 1990: 232; Cajolet-Laganière and Martel 1995: 67–8). In the words of one commentator: 'What therefore is *joual*? In the final analysis, it is the vision or mental representation that certain groups of individuals have of the Francophone linguistic reality of Quebec' (N. Beauchemin 1976: 9). As such, it was no surprise that the debate around the concept provoked lively reactions from all directions (see Verreault 1999a; Brochu 2000). Writers grouped around the journal *Parti pris* (e.g., Gérald Godin, André Major, Paul Chamberland and Laurent Girouard; see also Section 2.1) used *joual* in their works, as did Jacques Renaud in his 1964 novel *Le cassé* and Michel Tremblay in his play *Les belles-soeurs*, first performed in 1968. The decision made by these authors to use *joual* as a means of artistic expression did not aim to legitimise *joual* so much as to highlight the socio-economic and political domination and alienation of French-speaking Quebecers that it represented (G.-R. Lefebvre 1984; C. Bouchard 2002: 240–1). Others such as Turi (1971) and Bélanger (1972), however, embraced *joual* for its own value as a symbol of Quebec identity, what distinguished Quebecers from English-speaking North Americans and the French alike. In her *La deffence & illustration de la langue québecquoyse*, the poet Michèle Lalonde (1973) argued that the popular variety of French spoken in Quebec needed to be defended and promoted in the same way that Joachim du Bellay (1549) sought to improve the ability of French to overcome the dominance of Latin in sixteenth-century France (Poirier 1998: 131; Verreault 1999a). Others still declared a Quebec language distinct from the French spoken in France (e.g., L. Bergeron 1981). Indicative of an identity strategy available to minorities to generate a positive identity (see Section 1.2), such acts sought to reinterpret in a more positive light the previously negatively-viewed symbol of Quebec identity that was *joual*. In other words, '[w]hat was scorned becomes a source of pride' (Corbeil 1979: 28).

This was not the view of the establishment, however. The Royal Commission of Inquiry on Education in the Province of Quebec, known more commonly as the Parent Commission (1961–66), attacked the poor quality of French in schools (Maurais 1985b: 48), while Pierre Trudeau, then federal Minister of Justice, famously declared in 1968 that French speakers in Quebec should not be granted further rights as long as they continued to speak 'lousy French' (C. Bouchard 2002: 265). As for the newly founded Office de la langue française, it sanctioned a mere 62 specifically Canadian words or *canadianismes de bon aloi*, favouring on the whole an alignment with what was called 'international French' (Office de la langue française 1965, 1969). Replacing former references to Parisian French, the new term caught on fast and was promoted by the anti-*joual* camp throughout the 1960s and 1970s. For example, in his denunciation of *joual* as a Trojan horse that would lead to linguistic assimilation, Jean Marcel (1973) argued that the best defence lay in a re-alignment with 'international French'. But why has the term 'international French' enjoyed such success? And what does it actually refer to?

6.2 The myth of 'international French' and the monocentric ideology of the standard

C. Bouchard (2002: 245) explains the introduction of the concept of 'international French' in the 1960s in terms of several phenomena. First, following the Second World War, there was a growing awareness in Quebec of other French-speaking countries, which allowed Quebecers to envisage an opening up of their culture to a vaster and more diversified world. Second, it was during the 1960s that the Quebec government made its first international contacts, opened its first delegations abroad and became active in the international Francophone movement. One could also include the fact that Quebec was the centre of international focus in 1967 because of its hosting of

World Expo (D. Dumas 2001: 241). Third, there was also a rejection amongst Quebec intellectuals, artists and writers of the cultural domination of Paris.

To Bouchard's list, we can add that the term 'international French' is in line with the civic approach to national identity that has its origins in the Quiet Revolution of the 1960s and which is the focus of the present study. Detached from the ethnic identity of the majority French Canadian group, the notion of 'international French' is clearly not only compatible with this type of civic approach to identity in Quebec, it also actively contributes to it. While *joual* was seen by many as enclosing Quebecers in their own linguistic world, the adoption of 'international French' is considered as a display of civic openness. As the Institut de diction française au Québec noted in the submission it presented in 1970 to the Gendron Commission (see Section 5.1):

> Given that, of all the so-called French-speaking peoples, the French Canadian people speak French the worst ... ; given that it is not in line with the dignity of free men to impose on immigrants, who have freely consented to enriching our country with their contributions, a language, *joual*, which is either rubbish or counterfeit, the Institute recommends that the authorities ensure that immigrants master authentic or international French. (cited in Saint-Jacques 1990: 230)

No wonder, then, that 'international French' also figures prominently throughout the Larose Commission's report. Indeed, only by considering the term as an ideological tool, as part of the new civic rhetoric, can one make any sense of the model of French advocated for Quebec by the Larose Commission; for as a linguistic concept, 'international French' is completely abstract in so far as it refers to the language of no defined group of speakers (C. Bouchard 2002: 244). This is not unique to French, but is a property of any so-called 'international language'. For example, if, when talking to an American or British person, an Australian refers to the *sidewalk* or the *pavement*, rather than the *footpath*, it is because he or she chooses to use the American or British words over the Australian one for the sake of comprehension. Clearly, this is not a case of a fictitious 'international English', but of a phenomenon that is governed by the dynamics of speech accommodation theory (Giles *et al.* 1987; Giles and Coupland 1991: 60–93). Moreover, as this example shows, it makes little sense to speak of a common international English, since in this case there is no common term at all. Rather, one should speak of different standards or 'world Englishes' (Kachru 1986, 1992) that nonetheless share a common linguistic core, with regard in particular to morphosyntax and *basic* vocabulary.

These same issues have been observed with regard to French:

> But who could therefore claim to speak international French? On the one hand, as soon as they open their mouths, all Francophones are identified,

if only by their accent, as coming from or belonging to a particular sociocultural community. On the other hand, supposing even that this international French could be defined as being exclusively composed of what is common to all Francophones, it is evident that this common part could not by itself constitute a linguistic system sufficient for expressing the different visions that each of the particular communities that make up *la francophonie* have of the world. Consequently, the mere notion of international French pertains more to myth than reality. (Verreault 1999b: 28; see also M. Laforest 2002: 81; Mercier 2002a: 58)

The only reality is that international French is used as a euphemism for the French of France:

'International French' is preferred to 'French from France' because it does not make reference to the linguistic hegemony of Paris; in reality, everyone knows that international French is nothing more than the French of Paris as described in common grammar books (e.g. Grevisse-Goosse) and French dictionaries (e.g. *Le Robert*). (Cajolet-Laganière and Martel 1995: 68)

Not only does the term 'international French' not refer to any linguistic variety in its own right, it has the adverse effect of hindering a real reflection around the notion of linguistic variation in French (Lockerbie 2005: 22). Unlike with English, German, Spanish and other languages, there is a long tradition of viewing French as a 'monocentric' as opposed to a 'pluricentric' language (Lüdi 1992). The origins of this perception lie in the social history of the language in France, in particular the role French has played in the construction of national identity in that country (Lodge 1993; Bourhis 1997: 307–14; Oakes 2001: 53–64, 88–104). As noted at the beginning of this chapter, status planning is inextricably linked to corpus planning. In other words, the promotion of French in France has usually entailed the promotion of one particular variety of French which has come to be symbolised by the notion of *bon usage* (Lüdi 1992: 152–5).[4] Defined by Vaugelas in the seventeenth century as the way of speaking of 'the most sensible part of the court', *le bon usage* is not so much a linguistic norm as a social norm (Martel and Cajolet-Laganière 1996: 73). Others speak of an internal, objective or statistical norm versus an external, subjective or fictive one (e.g., Houdebine 1982, 1993; Deshaies 1984). The same distinction is made by Garmadi (1981: 64–72; see also Lodge 1993: 154–6), who distinguishes between a simple norm and what he calls a *sur-norme*. Whereas the former is the result of an implicit linguistic consensus needed for communicative purposes and which allows for some degree of linguistic variation, the latter is much stricter, prescribing and proscribing as it does for socio-political rather than communicative reasons. More precisely:

It is a set of instructions defining what should be chosen if one wishes to conform to the aesthetic or sociocultural ideal of a social group enjoying prestige and authority, and the existence of this set of instructions implies the existence of forms that are banned. (Garmadi 1981: 65)

Like the notion of 'international French', *le bon usage* is thus somewhat of a myth. The standard for which it forms a basis is a mere ideology (Berrendonner 1982), a 'fantastical idealisation' (Houdebine 1995: 100), 'an idea in the mind rather than a reality – a set of abstract norms to which actual usage may conform to a greater or lesser extent' (Milroy and Milroy 1999: 19). As another scholar explains:

> In fact, it is extremely doubtful that this so-called 'usage of Paris' corresponds to an existing sociolect. Nor does the French taught in French schools always match the norms of the *bon usage*. Instead, there is plenty of evidence to show that we are facing an illusion here, an imaginary object of an utopian discourse. However, this phantasm belongs to the linguistic representations of most speakers of French, even those who do not know it. (Lüdi 1992: 155)

Indeed, as noted in Section 6.1, the ideology of standard French has historically been part of the linguistic representations of French and English Canadians alike.

Despite the strong monocentric ideology that continues to surround it, French is in reality a pluricentric language (Valdman 1983; Lüdi 1992). In the context of Quebec, this is not only demonstrated by the linguistic facts (see Section 6.3 below), but also by Quebec's different political reality and the desire of a majority of Quebecers to express their linguistic autonomy (as opposed to linguistic sovereignty or separatism) within the French-speaking world. What is therefore needed is a new pluricentric conception of the French language, such as that proposed by Verreault (1999b: 27; see Figure 6.1).

Verreault's model is an accurate representation of the current reality in several respects. It establishes a hierarchy which clearly shows the social position of the various geographical varieties of French in relation to each other and the relationships of power that exist between them, what has been referred to the 'architecture' of a language (Paquot 1990: 181). Depending on the reference point, the varieties further up the hierarchy act as supranorms, while those towards the bottom function as infranorms (Corbeil 1986: 57). Unlike other models (e.g., Martel and Cajolet-Laganière 1996: 68–9, 87), the one proposed by Verreault also considers that Quebec French belongs to the level of language, as opposed to discourse (Verreault 1999b: 24). In other words, Quebec French is itself an abstraction which has its own structured internal variation at lower levels of abstraction, not to mention the variation that arises at the surface level that is discourse. Moreover, the different levels or categories of variation are clearly distinguished in this model. For example, Verreault makes an important distinction between national varieties and

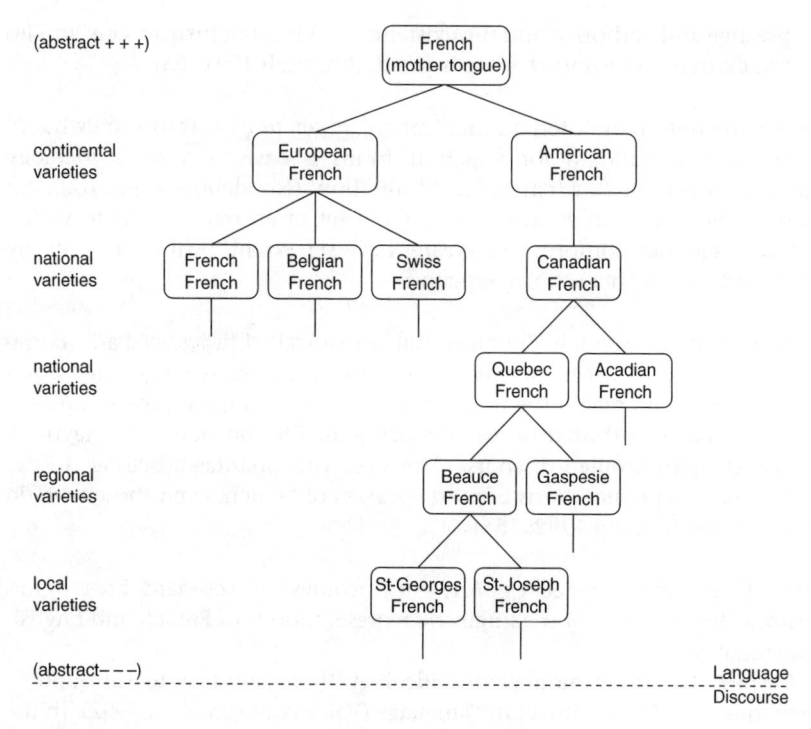

```
                              ┌──────────────┐
(abstract +++)                │   French     │
                              │(mother tongue)│
                              └──────┬───────┘
                         ┌───────────┴───────────┐
continental        ┌──────────┐            ┌──────────┐
varieties          │ European │            │ American │
                   │  French  │            │  French  │
                   └────┬─────┘            └─────┬────┘
              ┌─────────┼─────────┐              │
national   ┌──────┐ ┌───────┐ ┌───────┐     ┌─────────┐
varieties  │French│ │Belgian│ │ Swiss │     │ Canadian│
           │French│ │French │ │French │     │  French │
           └──┬───┘ └───┬───┘ └───┬───┘     └────┬────┘
              │         │         │         ┌────┴─────┐
national                                ┌───────┐ ┌────────┐
varieties                               │Quebec │ │Acadian │
                                        │French │ │ French │
                                        └───┬───┘ └────┬───┘
                                      ┌─────┴─────┐    │
regional                          ┌────────┐ ┌────────┐
varieties                         │ Beauce │ │Gaspesie│
                                  │ French │ │ French │
                                  └───┬────┘ └────┬───┘
                                ┌─────┴───┐       │
local                       ┌──────────┐┌──────────┐
varieties                   │St-Georges││St-Joseph │
                            │  French  ││  French  │
                            └─────┬────┘└─────┬────┘
                                                              Language
(abstract---) ------------------------------------------------ ────────
                                                              Discourse
```

Figure 6.1 A pluricentric conception of the French language
Source: Adapted from Verreault (1999b: 27).

regional varieties. Until the early 1980s, Quebec French was perceived as a regional variety of French (Martel and Cajolet-Laganière 1996: 69).[5] From then on, it became increasingly clear that, in so far as Quebec does not constitute a region of France, it was more appropriate to refer to Quebec French as a national variety of the language, which in fact has its own regional variation (Hausmann 1986; Poirier 1987; Verreault and Mercier 1998; Pöll 2001: 31). It may be that the concept of 'national variety' is better suited to certain Francophone contexts than others. Indeed, reservations have been expressed regarding its applicability to the French-speaking communities of Belgium (Francard 1998) and Switzerland (Thibault 1998). However, with regard to Quebec, the concept of 'national variety' reflects the desire of the majority of Quebecers to perceive themselves as a nation. As seen in Section 1.4 and Chapter 3, nations can be defined in a variety of ways. As such, both Canadian French and Quebec French can be described as national varieties of French depending of the definition of nation used (Verreault 1999b: 26).

One major obstacle to the acceptance of such a pluricentric conception of the French language is the reluctance of the French, who constitute the largest group of native French speakers, to relinquish sole ownership of the language and to accept the reality of linguistic variation (Pöll 2001: 32). Quebec may have been successful in persuading France to modify its proposed amendment to article 2 of its constitution in 1992: the original wording 'French is the language of the Republic' implied that France was the sole proprietor of the language and was eventually replaced by the more neutral 'the language of the Republic is French' (Conrick 2002a: 254). However, as Gadet (2001: 8) notes:

> Even if, by some nice paradox, they are proud of the international *francophonie*, [the French] confusingly tend to consider that the other Francophones of the world can know no better gift than access to their language as they, the French, speak it.

This attitude was clearly apparent in the opposition of the Académie française to the feminisation of profession titles introduced in Quebec from the 1970s and in Belgium in 1993–94 (Moreau 1999: 43–4; Conrick 2002b: 208, 213).[6] Behind such concerns is the fear of the fragmentation of the French language, that the recognition of linguistic variation will result in the same fate for French as that suffered by Latin and which, according to some unenlightened commentators (e.g., de Saint Robert 2000: 25), now threatens English. Far from being a weakness, the reality is that the acceptance of the geographical diversity of a language is a strength, since it allows the latter to serve both as a means of communication for a speech community as large as *la francophonie* and to satisfy the important identity needs of its speakers.

It may be that it will prove the responsibility of other Francophones to have a pluricentric model of French accepted. As the only significantly large group of native speakers outside Europe, French-speaking Quebecers are in a unique position to take on this challenge if they can overcome their own linguistic insecurity. As confirmed by language attitude studies, the linguistic insecurity of French Canadians that began in the mid-nineteenth century was still very present in the 1960s–early 1970s (see Gagné 1979: 49; 1983: 468; Bourhis and Lepic 1993: 361–4; Bourhis 1997: 318). From the mid-1970s, however, more positive attitudes towards Quebec French began to emerge (see Laporte 1984; Pöll 2001: 115). While the French of France still enjoyed important status on the whole, Quebec French was now rated more favourably on solidarity dimensions.[7] In other words, the 'overt prestige' of the French of France now had to compete with what Labov (1972) would call the 'covert prestige' of Quebec French being a symbol of Quebec national identity. As one commentator noted already in 1974:

> In Quebec, to speak the French of France is, according to the degree of politeness of the comment, 'to speak effeminately', 'to speak like a

Parisian', or 'to speak with a mouth like a hen's arse'; to speak Québécois is 'to speak with good sense', to speak with virility (Saint-Jacques 1990: 235; see also Moreau 1999: 50)

The origins of the more positive attitudes lie no doubt in the cultural revival that Quebec was undergoing, as well as in the greater overall self-confidence felt by Quebecers from this time, as witnessed by the rise of the Parti Québécois in 1976 and the introduction of the Charter of the French language in 1977 (see Section 5.1). Gendron (1990a) describes the change as one which led to the 'repatriation of sociolinguistic attitudes', a desire amongst Francophone Quebecers to exercise autonomy with regard to matters of language (see also Gendron 1990b, c). This is not to say that the quality of French spoken in Quebec has not continued to be denounced by some overly puristic members of the elite (see Section 6.3 below). As far as the general public is concerned, however, research carried out in 1989 and 1993 attests to much improved attitudes amongst Francophones *vis-à-vis* the perceived quality of their French (see Cajolet-Lagnière and Martel 1995: 31–2).

More recently, in a study conducted in 1998 amongst 1,591 French speakers, it was found that 'few Francophones wish to speak "like French people from France" (4%) or "like the majority of politicians in Quebec" (6%), the others being divided between the speech of Radio-Canada news readers (44%) and that of ordinary people (47%)' (Bouchard and Maurais 1999: 96). The same study showed that even Anglo-Quebecers, who have in the past preferred 'Parisian French', now tend to favour some form of a locally-defined standard for French: 36 per cent were in favour of a totally Quebec model, 33 per cent of an intermediary Quebec-French model, and 31 per cent of a French model (N = 292). Only the Allophones tended to prefer a totally French-defined model: 54 per cent, as opposed to 27 per cent in favour of the intermediary Quebec-French model and 19 per cent of a totally Quebec model (N = 324) (Bouchard and Maurais 1999: 114). The latter results highlight the particular challenge that immigrants pose to the acceptance of a new pluricentric conception for French: the conception of French amongst immigrants, especially those with previous contact with the language, is invariably more monocentric than that of their Quebec-born fellow citizens and can lead to less than positive attitudes towards Quebec French. Clearly, much work needs to be done to persuade new Quebecers of the value of a new pluricentric approach to the French language.

While providing some indication that French-speaking Quebecers are beginning to overcome their linguistic insecurity, the findings of Bouchard and Maurais nonetheless need to be interpreted with caution. As revealed in a previous study of language attitudes in Quebec (d'Anglejan and Tucker 1973), results obtained through direct elicitation (e.g., by means of a questionnaire such as that used by Bouchard and Maurais) are not always confirmed by those obtained through indirect methods (e.g., matched-guise technique) (see also Bourhis and Lepicq 1993: 363-4; Pöll 2001: 116). Quebecers may well be beginning to feel more linguistically secure, but they still suffer from a fair degree of linguistic insecurity, as evidenced by the difficulty they continue to have in achieving even 'semi-endonormativity' (Ammon 1989; see also Clyne 1992: 462), that is, the partial definition from within of their own socially acceptable national variety of French.

6.3 Identifying and describing a standard for Quebec French

In 1977, the Quebec Association of French Teachers proposed a compromise in the debate over *joual* by declaring that the French used in schools should be *'le français standard d'ici'*, Standard Quebec French. This was defined as 'the socially prestigious variety of French that the majority of Quebecers tend to use in formal communication situations' (Association québécoise des professeurs de français 1977: 11). Since then, a broad consensus has formed regarding the existence of this standard (e.g., C. Lefebvre 1984; Maurais 1985a, 1986; Gendron 1986, 1990a, b, c; Hausmann 1986; P. Auger 1988; Corbeil 1988; Martel 1990; Simard 1990; D. Smith 1990: 50).

Standard Quebec French represents a halfway model between the two models that were previously proposed, as clearly manifested in its linguistic characteristics. In its oral form, commonly referred to as Radio-Canada French after the French-language branch of the federal government-owned broadcaster, it avoids the most stigmatised features of French as spoken in Quebec (e.g., diphthongisation of long vowels). It nonetheless includes many phonetic and phonological traits of French spoken in Quebec that are now considered socially neutral (e.g., so-called 'assibilation' of /t/ and /d/ before high, front vowels and semi-vowels; the maintenance of the phonemes /ɑ/ and /ɛ̃/) (D. Dumas 1987, 2001; Gendron 1990c; Ostiguy and Tousignant 1993). In its written form, a standard for Quebec French has traditionally been more difficult to identify, with many Quebecers adopting a social norm that approximates that which exists in France (Papen 1998: 163). This has prompted some commentators (e.g., Nemni 1993, 1998; Paré 1993) to claim that Standard Quebec French is little more than a myth. Nonetheless, its existence is confirmed by characteristics that touch all aspects of language, albeit some more than others (Martel and Cajolet-Laganière 1996: 96–112; see also Martel, Vincent and Cajolet-Laganière 1998): orthography (e.g., *canoé* 'canoe' in Quebec as opposed to *canoë* in France); typography (e.g., accents, diereses and cedillas placed on upper case letters unlike in France, the capitalisation of names of institutions and the titles of films and books, as demonstrated in the French works cited in the bibliography of this study); morphology (e.g., feminisation of profession titles which are often different if not non-existent in France); syntax (e.g., *avoir voulu, j'aurais fini plus vite* 'had I wanted to, I could have finished faster' as opposed to *si j'avais voulu* in France – a socially acceptable syntactic peculiarity of Quebec French that even supporters of 'international French' (e.g., Marcel 1973: 71) are willing to admit); and semantics (e.g., *baccalauréat* referring to a university degree not a secondary school qualification as in France).

Perhaps the most obvious characteristic of both oral and written Standard Quebec French concerns lexis. Quebec has come a long way since the Office de la langue française recognised a meagre 62 *canadianismes de bon aloi* in 1969 and a significant number of words are now recognised as forming part of Quebec's own *bon usage*. What has traditionally been considered as distinguishing Quebec French from the French of France are: regionalisms (e.g., *champlure* 'tap') and archaisms (e.g., *achalandage* 'patronage') that have remained from the language of the first settlers; direct borrowings from English (e.g., *tire* from the American spelling of 'tyre'); a small number of borrowings from indigenous languages (e.g., *atoca* 'cranberry'); *faux amis* or semantic borrowings (e.g., *supporter* 'to support'); *calques* or syntactic borrowings (e.g., *fin de semaine* 'weekend'); and *québécismes* or innovations (e.g., *dépanneur* 'convenience store'). However, many of these characteristics are limited to more colloquial forms of Quebec French, the number of regionalisms, archaisms and direct borrowings from English in particular figuring much less frequently in Standard Quebec French. Indeed in a study of the formal register of French used by three Quebec newspapers (*Le Devoir*, *La Presse* and *Le Soleil*) and the French daily *Le Monde*, it was found that French regionalisms and archaisms represented less than 10 per cent of those lexical items specific to the Quebec press, while direct borrowings from English accounted for only 11 per cent of these same words (Villers 2005: 406). What distinguished the Quebec press the most from *Le Monde* was the number of lexical innovations or *québécismes*: 70 per cent of the lexical forms specific to the Quebec dailies examined (Villers 2005: 412). Words such as *traversier* and *commanditaire* are preferred in most contexts in Quebec, including the most formal, whereas *ferry-boat* and *sponsor* are used in the same contexts in France (Martel and Cajolet-Laganière 1996: 109–12). As Maurais (1986: 83) notes, '[t]he rejection of anglicisms – especially lexical anglicisms – is part of the [social] norm of Quebec French' (see also Maurais 1985a). This leaves us with non-lexical, indirect borrowings, the *faux amis* and *calques*, which are less obviously compatible with Standard Quebec French. While many of these are eschewed when recognised, a significant number of them are nonetheless used unconsciously even in formal registers. Indeed, 70 per cent of the *faux amis* and *calques* listed in the *Répertoire d'emprunts critiqués à l'anglais* (Repetoire of criticised borrowings from English)[8] were found in the pages of the Quebec dailies studied by Villers (2005: 407–10). Clearly, many of these indirect anglicisms have become part of Quebec's linguistic culture, so much so that they could even be considered as a type of *québécisme* or innovation (see also Cajolet-Laganière and Martel 1995: 49–58). However, there is much disagreement about whether they are considered 'correct', as demonstrated by the anecdote about a *motelier* ('motel owner') in Sainte-Anne-de-Beaupré in the mid-1980s (Bienvenue 1990).

The motel owner was brought before the court charged with using an anglicism, the word *office*, which he displayed outside the reception of his motel. Such use of English in public signage was proscribed by the Charter of the French language introduced in 1977. The first instance judge upheld the charge, basing his opinion on the evidence presented to him by a linguistic adviser from the Commission de protection de la langue française. After consulting several dictionaries, the adviser concluded that this word was indeed an anglicism when used with the meaning of one's place of work or, in this case, a reception of a motel. But while the Charter of the French language may have declared French the 'official and habitual language of Quebec', it made no mention of the variety of French to be used, thus leaving the way open for a multitude of interpretations of what constitutes French. The linguistic adviser had of course relied on dictionaries from France, in particular *Le Petit Robert*. When appealing the judgement, the motel owner called upon the expertise of Léandre Bergeron, author of the *Dictionnaire de la langue québécoise* (L. Bergeron 1980). For Bergeron, the Quebec language, as he called it (see Section 6.1), 'comprises the French language in its entirety, but also all the linguistic heritage of the Quebec people's 300 years of belonging to the North American continent' (cited in Bienvenue 1990: 356). Indeed, Bergeron was able to point to several glossaries and dictionaries which confirmed that, although most likely a borrowing from English in the beginning, the word *office* with the meaning of 'place of work' was widespread and had been used in Quebec for at least 100 years. Convinced by Léandre's argument, the Superior Court quashed the conviction on the grounds that the word was indeed part of Quebec usage. This does not mean, however, that it necessarily belongs to what many would consider to be 'correct' usage.

It was such questions of 'correctness' of usage or register which led to the wave of criticism following the first two real attempts to describe Quebec French in the context of a pluricentric conception of the French language: the *Dictionnaire du français plus* (1988) and the *Dictionnaire québécois d'aujourd'hui* (1992). Unlike the so-called differential approaches which had dominated up until then, the global or general methodologies used for these dictionaries considered Quebec French as an autonomous whole, limiting geographical markings to *francismes* as opposed to the *québécismes* used previously.[9] By this was not meant that the editors attempted to sever the linguistic link with France; in fact, their dictionaries were adaptations of dictionaries that already existed in France. The autonomy implied merely that the reality of Quebec be better reflected in the usages included. However, the inclusion of items from colloquial and popular language, such as anglicisms and swear words, resulted in much criticism of the two dictionaries, which were eventually denied the endorsement of the Ministry of Education.

Subsequent analyses of the critiques of these two works have shown that what is needed is a dictionary which provides a detailed picture of the social hierarchisation of the various usages of French as spoken in Quebec, that is, information about what words are appropriate for which situations. Indeed, it was the lack of such a description which allowed Georges Dor, in his many tirades throughout the mid- to late 1990s (e.g., 1996, 1997, 1998), to reduce all of Quebec French to an inferior register by means of simplistic, haphazard observations questioned by linguists in and outside Quebec:

> In a very simplistic way, the speech of the working class of one city, Montreal, is still depicted as the ONLY type epitomising Quebec French and is contrasted with the speech of the bourgeois class of one city, Paris, which is depicted as the ONLY type epitomising international French. (M. Laforest 1997:9)

In all his books, Dor uses fanciful spellings that ridicule and render almost incomprehensible the examples described; he portrays them as if they represent the only way of saying things, rejecting the idea that these forms have their place in informal conversations but that Quebecers replace them with more standard forms in more formal situations; and he treats with disdain the warnings of linguists who try to set these examples back into a historical and sociolinguistic context that does them justice (J. Auger 2005: 67).

In an endeavour to add emotional support to their arguments, Dor and other purists (e.g., D. Lamonde 1998, 2004; Nemni 1998) attempt to revive the spectre of *joual*, which they use as a 'shorthand term by which the Québec variety of French in general is demonized' (Lockerbie 2005: 21). But *joual* is now an anachronistic concept, belonging to a particular ideology of the 1960s–70s that no longer exists. Contemporary linguists prefer the more neutral *français populaire* to refer to this informal register of language. Moreover, questions about quality of language, such as those raised by Dor (e.g., about the language of younger generations and that used on television), are present in all societies, including France (Maurais 1985c). They should therefore not be confused with the very separate issue of defining an emerging Standard Quebec French. This is the view of the Quebec authorities who, while still endeavouring to improve the quality of French spoken in Quebec, are nonetheless now firmly behind the project of producing a new 'national dictionary'.

Following two conferences organised on the topic (Conseil de la langue française 1990a, b), the Conseil de la langue française submitted an opinion to the Minister responsible for the Charter for the French language in which it supported the compilation of such a dictionary with three main aims (Conseil de la langue française 1991):

- to describe the usages of Quebec French and their sociolinguistic hierarchisation;

- to maintain contact with the rest of *la francophonie*;
- to include geographical information about where words are used.

In the same document, the Conseil also noted the benefits that the proposed dictionary would bring to Quebecers of all origins, and even to foreigners outside Quebec:

> The existence of such a work would certainly have the consequence of increasing the linguistic security of Quebecers; it would provide foreigners with an awareness of how the French language has adapted to Quebec; it would allow immigrants in the process of becoming French speakers to benefit from a solid, formally documented reference which would demonstrate the existence and legitimacy of a Standard Quebec French; it would allow Allophones who, at least at the beginning of their stay, get by with a sort of 'interlanguage', made up of their mother tongue and the language of the host community, to acquire a tool that can only facilitate their integration to Quebec society. Indeed, the integration of immigrants into the French fact has become more and more talked about; reasserting the value of Quebec French, by showing that there exists a Standard Quebec French which is legitimate, can only facilitate this integration. (Conseil de la langue française 1991)

A decade later, with work on the dictionary still not having begun, the Larose Commission reiterated the importance of instruments of reference for Quebec French, such as a dictionary (Gouvernement du Québec 2001a: 89), and stressed once again the link between the promotion of a standard for Quebec French and efforts to increase the language's power of attraction amongst immigrants.[10]

Not surprisingly, the FRANQUS research team at the Université de Sherbrooke, who were ultimately granted the responsibility of producing the new dictionary, also conceive their dictionary in terms of the new civic approach to national identity currently being promoted.[11] In particular, the FRANQUS team stress that their dictionary, unlike the general dictionaries published previously, is based on a database composed totally of texts written by Quebec authors, thereby providing unique access to Quebec culture.[12] As the website of the project explains:

> The dictionary serves as a guide of *bon usage* or the legitimate usage accepted and recognised by the elites of French-speaking America. It will also be a powerful factor of integration for immigrants and Anglophones who acquire French as a second language. In this dictionary, the latter will be able to find descriptions and citations that truly correspond to what they read in our newspapers, magazines, technical and economic texts,

and books, at the same time as being in a position to make the link with the French used by other Francophones. (FRANQUS n.d.)

While it is true that the dictionary will provide Quebecers of non-Francophone backgrounds with cultural and linguistic references needed for their integration, the question is to what extent full integration can be achieved by reading newspapers, magazines, and technical and economic texts. Does the integration process not take place more informally, by talking to one's neighbours, the owner of the local *dépanneur*, etc.? This reality has not been addressed by the FRANQUS team, who have specifically stated that their dictionary will focus on Standard Quebec French only. Apart from the fact that a standard is also defined by indirect means (i.e., by describing words that are not considered standard), the exclusion of terms from informal registers of language will deprive non-Francophone Quebecers of these equally important tools of integration. The latter of course figure in the many glossaries aimed at laymen currently available on the market. However, these works often tend to ridicule the variety of French in Quebec and do not provide reliable information about register that allows Quebecers of non-Francophone backgrounds to use informal terms and expressions in appropriate contexts (Mercier and Verreault 2002: 103).

Unfortunately, a dictionary which seeks to define Standard Quebec French with the aid of both standard and non-standard terms does not seem to be viable at the present time on account of the current state of the linguistic insecurity in Quebec. Indeed, even before its publication, the national dictionary has already received criticism from a small, yet vocal minority of purists for merely attempting to define a locally-defined variety of French. Once again reducing Quebec French in its entirety to an inferior register, D. Lamonde (1998: 85), for example, claims that '[t]here has in fact never been a greater act of legitimising *joual* as that undertaken today by the supporters of the general dictionary of Quebec French.'

Another ardent supporter of 'international French' who has been fiercely critical of the FRANQUS project is the linguist Lionel Meney, who, it is worth adding, is of French origin. In numerous newspaper articles and an open letter sent to Premier Jean Charest, Meney warns of the 'linguistic ghettoisation' of Quebec and denounces the 'linguistic separatism' and 'francophobic nationalism' of what he scornfully labels the *aménagistes* ('language planners') (Meney 2003a, b, 2004a, b, c, d, 2005a, b, c). But as another Quebec linguist points out:

> The act of recording Quebec usages in a dictionary does not sanction a rupture with the French of France but allows those who are interested in our cultural production to have access to our cultural universe and, more broadly, to our vision of the world. This gesture seems to me to lead more

to an opening up to the world than to the ghettoisation of Quebec society. (Poisson 2002: 107)

In reality, it is Meney himself who could be accused of linguistic separatism in light of his *Dictionnaire du québécois-français* (Meney 1999). Despite claiming that 'Québécois is not a distinct language totally different from French', Meney admits nonetheless that his work was conceived 'on the model of a bilingual dictionary' (Meney 1999: v), an approach clearly visible in the title. Moreover, because he has turned his back on the more contemporary general or global methodology, he describes only the differences between Quebec French and the French of France. Whether intentionally or not, this leads him to provide misleading information about some entries, for example that the words *autobus* (bus) and *radio* (when referring to a radio receiver) are only ever heard in Quebec with the feminine and masculine genders respectively (Mercier and Verreault 2002: 88). While it is true that these usages can be heard in Quebec, they belong to colloquial or popular registers, and are certainly not part of Standard Quebec French. Not only does Meney's outdated differential methodology risk exacerbating the linguistic insecurity of Quebecers by focusing only on such deviations, it denies them the right to define their own norm from within. Meney claims that Quebec's small population size does not warrant an endo- or semi-endonormative model for Quebec French like it does for English as spoken in the US, Spanish in South America or Portuguese in Brazil. Not only would this argument be considered offensive to New Zealanders, Australians and English Canadians, who all have their own dictionaries despite their relatively small populations compared with the UK and the US, it does not convince the majority of Quebecers either, and this, irrespective of political persuasion. When awarding the second instalment of funds to the FRANQUS project, the Liberal Minister of Culture, Line Beauchamp, stated that

> it is worth recalling that the French language has had a similar evolution to that of, for example, Spanish, English and Portuguese in North and South America. These three languages which originated in Europe have developed differently on these continents and have given rise to distinct varieties of the source language. Some of the states concerned have deemed it necessary and completely legitimate to elaborate dictionaries which describe their specific usages. [...] I consider it fundamental that our usages [...] like those of other states of *la Francophonie*, be disseminated and potentially shared by all French-speaking communities. (Beauchamp 2004)

Far from evoking a mentality of cultural isolation, such an attitude of openness is completely in line with the type of civic model of nation that Quebec is in the process of defining. For as seen in Chapter 3, the models of nation which are best suited to Quebec's reality are not strictly civic, highly abstract ones, but those that nonetheless recognise the ethnicity of the dominant French Canadian group within an overall civic framework.

6.4 Corpus planning for Quebecers of all ethnic origins

On the occasion of the 25th anniversary of the Charter of the French language in 2002, the Quebec government released a TV advertisement to remind Quebecers, especially those of the younger generation, of the importance of the Charter and the gains it had brought them over the last two and a half decades. To the tune of Yves Duteil's *La langue de chez nous*, Quebecers of all ethnic origins could be seen coming together to celebrate the French language, demonstrating once again the more civic model of nation advocated in Quebec. But the choice of a song written by a Frenchman – even if he had Quebec in mind – was not without controversy, with some commentators (e.g., Monette 2002) arguing that the language being celebrated was not *la langue de chez nous* but rather *la langue de chez eux*, that is, not the French of Quebec but the French of France.

As this example shows, in the aftermath of the debate surrounding *joual* in the 1960s–70s, there is now a desire amongst many Quebecers to express linguistic autonomy in the French-speaking world, not linguistic separatism as some commentators claim. Slowly but surely, French-speaking Quebecers are overcoming the linguistic insecurity that has dogged them for over a century, and the new national dictionary currently under construction will help this process along further. Irrespective of whether the latter receives criticism on methodological grounds, which is surely to be expected if the case of previous dictionaries is anything to go by, its publication in 2007 can nonetheless only be welcomed. As the first real attempt to describe a socially prestigious, locally-defined variety of French, the dictionary will assist in promoting a new pluricentric conception of the French language, which recognises that the language spoken by the majority in Quebec is indeed French, even if the standard in use there is different from that used in France, and elsewhere.

Perhaps more importantly, however, the new dictionary also has the potential to improve the power of attraction of Quebec French amongst immigrants. Considering the declining birth rates amongst native French speakers, it is on this group of Quebecers that the future of French depends. Not only will the dictionary present new Quebecers with a socially acceptable, locally-defined standard for Quebec French, thereby demonstrating that the latter should not simply be reduced to *joual*, it will also facilitate their integration by giving them direct access to Quebec's unique linguistic and cultural heritage, albeit that of a more formal nature. As such, the dictionary can in no way be considered as promoting solely the interests of the dominant French Canadian ethnic group; on the contrary, it actively contributes to the more civic model of nation that Quebec has chosen for itself. Ultimately, however, the extent to which Quebecers of non-French Canadian backgrounds accept the new pluricentric conception of the French language represented by the new national dictionary for Standard Quebec French may not depend solely on corpus issues. As seen in the previous chapter, of paramount importance is the emotional attachment that Quebecers of non-French Canadian ethnicities have to the French language in particular, and to the new civic model of nation in general. These questions are examined in more detail in the next three chapters, which focus on the specific experiences of immigrants, Anglophones and Aboriginal peoples respectively.

Part III
Diverse Experiences

Part III focuses on the diverse experiences of Quebec's minorities. Chapter 7 examines specifically how immigrants themselves understand their relationship to Quebec society and explores the range of meanings that belonging can have for Quebecers of immigrant background, not least a sense of attachment to Montreal, rather than Quebec, and to multilingualism, rather than French alone.

Chapter 8 focuses on the extent to which Anglophone Quebecers can truly feel a sense of belonging to Quebec, and inversely whether the Francophone majority can fully accept Anglophones as 'true' Quebecers. The chapter also discusses the blurring of boundaries between the two groups, through growing bilingualism and mixing, particularly among the younger generation of Anglophones.

Chapter 9 examines how well official rhetoric on the linguistic rights of Aboriginal peoples in Quebec, as set out in policy documents and new agreements between the provincial and federal governments and various Aboriginal nations, squares with the vitality of Aboriginal languages within Aboriginal communities themselves.

7
Language, Immigration and Belonging

> *L'intensification de l'immigration lance au Québec le défi sans cesse renouvelé d'offrir aux nouveaux arrivants et à leurs enfants la chance de s'approprier pleinement la langue française. Pour se sentir chez eux au Québec, ils devront d'abord se sentir chez eux dans la langue française, l'outil indispensable de l'intégration, de l'accès aux savoirs, au travail, à la culture et à la citoyenneté.*
>
> The intensification of immigration is raising for Quebec the ongoing challenge of offering recent immigrants and their children the opportunity to make the French language fully their own. In order to feel at home in Quebec, they will have to first feel at home in French, the indispensable tool of integration and of access to knowledge, work, culture and citizenship. (Gouvernement du Québec 2001a: 71)

The Larose Commission understandably views French as crucial to the successful integration of immigrants, and considers that the 'ongoing challenge' of immigration for Quebec is to provide the conditions for the province's new arrivals to 'feel at home' – *se sentir chez eux* – in Quebec. This formulation says a great deal about how Quebec constructs itself in relation to the increasing cultural and linguistic diversity within its borders, and it is worthwhile examining its various meanings. Clearly, migration is about a spatial shift from home to host country, and with that shift comes unfamiliarity. One way for the host country to show migrants hospitality is to make them feel familiar with their new surroundings, to show them where things are and how they work, and to explain their rights and duties. 'Feeling at home' in this reading can be taken as a largely operational matter, as when a host shows his or her guests around the house when they first arrive.

However, the use of 'feeling at home' by the Larose Commission seems to be about something more than simply being hospitable and facilitating familiarity with a new place. Indeed, one could argue that the hospitality that host countries offer immigrants is often conditional: 'if a nation invites immigrants because they are valuable assets, because it needs them for an economic or demographic purpose, that country is not being hospitable. At least, not unconditionally, infinitely hospitable' (Rosello 2001: 12). In other words, within the metaphors of hospitality and the home there are obligations on the guests. In the case of Quebec, the immigrants are needed for economic and demolinguistic purposes, with the obligation on migrants 'to make the French language their own', as the Larose Commission puts it – to 'feel at home' in French. This is not just a question, it seems, of speaking enough French to get by or of using French as a simple *lingua franca*; rather, by invoking the metaphor of the home with its strong affective dimension, the report implies that there is some affective commitment required from immigrants towards the language. Indeed, French, Quebec's defining characteristic and the 'indispensable tool of integration', represents the path to Quebec as the new 'home/nation'. Chapter 5 examined the efforts of the Quebec authorities to generate such an affective attachment to French by means of the notion of *langue publique commune* (common public language). In so doing, it also noted the unproblematic relationship that is often assumed between acquiring French and developing a sense of belonging to Quebec society. As for the current chapter, the focus moves to the experiences of individuals themselves, both immigrant adults and young people of immigrant background. Before examining these experiences, however, it is worthwhile revisiting the efforts of the Quebec authorities, this time with particular focus on Quebec's role as a host for immigrants from an increasingly broad range of backgrounds.

7.1 Quebec's role as host

As elsewhere, immigration to Quebec has often tended to coincide with economic, political or social upheaval in countries of origin. Underlying this has been the changing nature of Canada's overall immigration policy in terms of which ethnic groups were considered 'acceptable', as well as Quebec's evolving role in immigrant selection. These three factors have combined to shape the various waves of immigration to the province. In the period 1901–31, for example, Jews from Eastern Europe and Italians in particular migrated to Quebec and Canada to escape economic and political turmoil in Europe (Larrivée 2003a: 167). In the post-war period to the 1960s, more than 90 per cent of immigrants who came to Quebec were of European origin, above all Italians and Greeks but also Poles, Germans and Portuguese. In the 1970s, there were fewer immigrants of European background, and a great number from India, Pakistan and Haiti, among other countries. More recent arrivals come from a wider variety of countries still, as will be seen below. Immigrants from France have been a fairly constant aspect of the migration picture in Quebec.

Immigrants, new Quebecers, Allophones (those whose mother tongue is neither French nor English), cultural communities, Quebecers of immigrant origin, minorities, ethnic groups – all these labels, and others, variously qualify the Quebecers who are the subject of this chapter. The civic approach, which is at the centre of this book's concerns, was precisely designed with Quebec's increasing immigrant population in mind. Quebec's policies on the integration of immigrants can in fact be viewed as embodying a mixture of civic and pluralist ideologies. Its policies are civic in the sense, of course, that French is promoted as the common public language and pluralist in that the Quebec state supports the maintenance of the linguistic and cultural heritage of minority groups, namely Anglophones and Aboriginal peoples, as well as ethnic minority groups of immigrant origin (Bourhis and Bougie 1998). Both these ideologies have two features in common: the state 'expects that immigrants will adopt the *public values* of the host country', but it 'has no right to interfere with the *private values* of its individual citizens' (Bourhis et al. 1997: 373, emphasis in original). Quebec as host is concerned with the common public language, and not with the language(s) of the private domain of the home (see Section 5.1). Feeling at home in Quebec and in French from this perspective is about the public as the 'collective' home, and the public language as that which unites the members of the collectivity.

So, how does Quebec acquit its hostly duties? First of all, Quebec has a say in choosing the majority of its own guests. Currently, immigrants mainly settle in Quebec as economic or independent migrants, family reunion migrants, or refugees. The 1991 Canada-Quebec Accord relating to Immigration and Temporary Admission of Aliens, which replaced the 1978 Couture-Cullen Agreement, provided Quebec with a greater say in who settles in the province. Quebec currently has the exclusive right to select economic migrants, Canada retaining responsibility for immigrant selection in the other two categories (Gouvernement du Québec 2004b). In 2004, Quebec welcomed a record number of 44,239 immigrants, selecting just over 60 per cent of its immigrant intake, with 19.5 per cent in the family reunion category, and just under 17 per cent who were refugees (Citizenship and Immigration Canada 2005a).

Quebec's control over the selection of economic migrants has meant that it can privilege knowledge of French as a key selection criterion for the majority of its immigrant intake, an essential strategy to maximise the number of French speakers. This has resulted in the percentage of immigrants knowing either French only or both French and English rising from 37 per cent in 1990 with some fluctuations to just over half of the total number of immigrants for the first time in 2003 (Institut de la Statistique Québec 2006). According to preliminary 2004 figures, two-thirds (66.6 per cent) of the economic migrants knew French on admission to Quebec, compared with around a third of those in the other two categories (38.7 per cent of family reunion migrants and 34.1 per cent of refugees), giving an overall figure of 55.3 per cent (Gouvernement du Québec 2005c: 10). Among the immigrants admitted in 2004, 12.9 per cent had French as their mother tongue (Ministère de l'Immigration et des Communautés Culturelles 2005: 13). The countries of origin of current immigrants to Quebec underline the importance of *la Francophonie*: among the top ten countries of origin in 2004 were member countries France, Morocco, Romania, Haiti and Lebanon. Algeria, where French continues to be widely used, is also in the top ten. Nevertheless, it is a challenge for Quebec to continue to attract French speakers, given global pressures on French as an international language, the limited number of French speakers in a number of countries currently part of *la Francophonie*, and the diversity in mastery of the French language. Spanish-speaking Colombia was also in the top ten, another plus for French: migrants from Spanish-speaking countries are considered to be 'Francophone friendly', given that their mother tongue is a related Romance language (e.g., Béland 1999; Carpentier 2004).

However, the three other top ten countries of origin in 2004 were China (in first place), Pakistan and India, all countries where English is an important second, or first, language. Knowledge of English is indeed strong among newly arrived immigrants: in 2004, among the three categories of immigrants, knowledge of English was lower than that of French only in the economic migrant group – the category that Quebec selects – but slightly higher in the other two categories. In addition, nearly half (47.5 per cent) of the economic migrants knew both French and English, compared to much lower levels in the other categories (14.4 per cent and 8.5 per cent respectively). To sum up, just over half (51.3 per cent) of the new arrivals in 2004 knew English, nearly as many as knew French. This widespread knowledge of English has repercussions on the linguistic allegiances of new Quebecers, as will be seen below. It is also the case that some immigrants to Quebec do not intend to settle there permanently, using the province as a stepping-stone to other parts of Canada or even North America. Those immigrants in this category who have little or no French thus resist acquiring the language (e.g., Laurier 2005: 576).

The vast majority of immigrants settle in Montreal, the economic centre of Quebec: for example, in 2004, nearly 86 per cent of new arrivals settled in the greater metropolitan region of Montreal (Citizenship and Immigration Canada 2005b),[1] where the mother tongue of just over 19 per cent of the population is a language other than English, this figure rising to just over 29 per cent on the island of Montreal. But Montreal is precisely the location in Quebec where the English language is at its most vital, and where it is in fact possible to live one's life entirely in English. In addition, English has an immense power of attraction as the major global language and as one of the two official languages of Canada (see Section 5.2). However, French also benefits from its role as official, common language of Quebec, and rates highly on a number of ethnolinguistic vitality indicators (Pagé 2005). Thus, 'the francisation of immigrants is carried out in a context of linguistic duality where both linguistic groups enjoy a high level of vitality' (Pagé 2005: 209). On the one hand, knowledge of French is increasing among the immigrant background population generally, both new and settled immigrants: from 1991 to 2001, for instance, the percentage of Quebecers of immigrant background who could speak French passed from 68.6 per cent in 1991 to 73.5 per cent in 2001; the figures for English show a shift from 67.5 per cent in 1991 to 69.1 per cent in 2001 (Office québécois de la langue française 2005: 29). On the other hand, the pull of English remains very strong, illustrated by language transfer in the home: in 2001, 54.3 per cent switched to English as the home language, against 45.7 per cent opting for French, although this represents an increase on the 1991 figures for French (35.8 per cent) (Office québécois de la langue française 2005). The dual linguistic nature of Montreal thus remains a challenge for French:

> [T]he specific linguistic situation in Quebec sends an ambiguous message to immigrants. This is particular to the metropolitan area, where French is the official language and where it is generally used, but where English is also a widely used language, even to the point – which is totally in keeping with the accepted sociopolitical consensus – that Quebecers can be born, be educated, work and live completely in English. In such a situation, it seems reasonable to believe that this ambiguity delays, or even prevents the very possibility for immigrants to develop a feeling of belonging and of basic allegiance to the political community of Quebec, which, in return, weakens the mobilisation to the cause of French in Quebec. (Georgeault 2006: 314)

In addition, the fact that Montreal is home to a unique sociolinguistic environment in which two dominant languages, English and French, are pulling in opposite directions opens up a 'clearly delimited socio-cultural space' that Montrealers who do not have an exclusive allegiance to the Francophone or Anglophone worlds have been able to occupy (Anctil 1984: 450). This sociocultural space is one in which ethnic markers such as language, religion and endogamy have been retained by ethnic minority groups at a much higher level than in other large North American cities (Meintel 1993, 1998). An analysis of 2001 survey data by the Association for Canadian Studies confirms the tendency for the greater retention in Montreal of languages of origin or heritage languages, and sets out three main reasons: (1) most children of immigrants attend Francophone school, but for those children whose parents have English as a second language and not French, the language of origin is the obvious choice of home language with their parents; (2) some ethnic minority groups in Montreal tend to live in more ethnically concentrated communities than in other cities; this concentration helps to maintain their language of origin, as it is more or less widely spoken in the neighbourhood; and (3) Quebecers of immigrant background have lower intermarriage rates than elsewhere in Canada, reinforcing the maintenance of the language of origin (Heinrich 2003).[2] Overall, the range of languages spoken other than French or English in the greater metropolitan region of Montreal is impressive: from French public school board figures, it can be estimated that there are more than 148 different mother tongues spoken in Montreal (Meilleur 2005) (see Section 7.3).

Taking up the Larose Commission's focus on making immigrants feel at home, Quebec has the 'hostly' duty to ensure that new Quebecers are provided with the opportunity to learn or perfect their knowledge of the French language. This duty is explicitly stated in Quebec's Action Plan on integration, *Des valeurs partagées, des intérêts communs*, mentioned in Section 5.2 as an illustration of official discourse on the seemingly unproblematic link between learning French and developing a sense of belonging to Quebec society. The Plan proposes a series of concrete objectives and actions under the pillar 'Learning French', with the focus on the instrumental goals of accelerating French learning and adapting francisation services to specific needs (Gouvernement du Québec 2004a: 68). Currently, the Ministère de l'Immigration et des Communautés Culturelles offers adult immigrants a range of full-time, part-time, and custom-made programmes through various public institutions and community organisations, as well as online courses to afford greater flexibility to learners (Ministère de l'Immigration et des Communautés Culturelles 2005). The Action Plan also makes clear that Quebec is not only acting in the best interests of its guests; it also, understandably, has its own best interests at heart, with an expectation that immigrants will use French as the common public language, in order to ensure 'the continuation of the French fact in Quebec' (Gouvernement du Québec 2004a: 68).

The Plan also announces the introduction of what it calls a 'roadmap' – *un carnet de route* – to signpost, one could say, the path to Quebec as home. According to the Plan, the roadmap 'will help immigrants pinpoint their needs, define their objectives and raise their awareness about the importance of *mapping out* their integration process, if possible before arriving in Quebec or very soon thereafter' (Gouvernement du Quebec 2004a: 5, emphasis added). The roadmap appeared in 2005 under the title *Apprendre le Québec. Guide pour réussir mon intégration*, and among other elements, it stresses the importance of learning or perfecting French before arriving in Quebec (Gouvernement du Québec 2005a: 21). The guide shows a similar approach to the Larose Commission's 'feeling at home', what could be called the 'showing around' model of hosting new arrivals. It is worth commenting on the title of the guide in French, *Apprendre le Québec* – literally 'Learning Quebec'. There is a conflation of space and language here, making Quebec itself a language to be learned, an element that is missing in the official

English and Spanish translations with their inclusion of 'about' (*Learning about Quebec* and *Aprender sobre Quebec*).

The new measures outlined in the Action Plan to accelerate French learning and to target specific needs are necessary among other reasons because of the fact that 'the more advanced educational qualifications of the clientele require the acquisition of a high level of written and spoken French, so that immigrants can make the fullest use of their professional skills' (Gouvernement du Québec 2004a: 67). In addition, certain groups of immigrants, in particular refugees and women who are admitted under family reunion status, do not tend to make use in francisation services and thus can find themselves isolated from mainstream society. Quebec is thus making additional efforts to be a more effective host, and improve on what have been rather low levels of uptake of its francisation programmes. A study of enrolments from 1994 to 1999, for example, showed that overall only 44 per cent of immigrants were enrolled (Paulin-Nteziryayo and Archambault 2000, reported in Laurier 2005). Geographically, lowest enrolments were recorded in Montreal – 40 per cent, compared with the regions at 72–80 per cent, thus reflecting the fact that 'immigrants who speak English tend to make less use of the services' (Laurier 2005: 575). There are other reasons for this lack of uptake, including the fact that some immigrants 'are able to gain rapid entry into the job market, without knowledge of French being considered a significant asset'; others have to wait some time before getting a place in a programme, sometimes up to six months; some get discouraged, in particular those with little education or whose mother tongue is very different from French; still others see their time in Quebec as temporary and are not prepared to learn French (Laurier 2005: 576).

School-aged immigrants need a different set of services from adults and Quebec has responded by setting up what are known as *classes d'accueil* ('welcoming classes') in many French public schools in Montreal. Since the advent of the Charter of the French language in 1977, children of immigrants must be schooled in French, and 95 per cent of new immigrants now do so (Mc Andrew 2003b: 59). In 2004–05, in the schools of the Francophone school board, the Commission scolaire de Montréal, 23.2 per cent of students on the island of Montreal – nearly 18,000 young people – were born outside Canada (Meilleur 2005: iv). The role of the *classes d'accueil* is to prepare these young people to join mainstream classes:

> [*Classes d'accueil*] consist of special full-time classes with reduced students/teacher ratios for immigrants who have been in the country for less than five years. Students are initiated to everyday life in Quebec and taught the basics of the French language and other school subjects until they are ready to integrate into regular classes, normally after one year, but sometimes longer. (Mc Andrew 2003b: 60)

The hospitality that Quebec's Ministry of Education extends to new young arrivals has, then, until recently, placed them in separate classes from their native-born classmates, to prepare their entry into regular classes. Over the years, the increasing cultural and linguistic diversity of school students, as well as greater socioeconomic divergence, has meant that it has become more of a challenge to turn young immigrants into competent French speakers. The Ministry of Education has responded by putting in place 'a linguistic support program that follows students during the first two years of their integration into regular classes [...] in schools where the proportion of allophone students exceeds 25 percent' (Mc Andrew 2003b: 60).

As with the adults above, Quebec as host to young immigrants seeks to be more effective, and there is growing awareness from researchers and others that the *classes d'accueil* are not necessarily appropriate as the 'first or foremost place for learning French' (Mc Andrew 2003a: 356). The need for separate classes is being questioned for preschool or primary students who are not in difficulty (Mc Andrew 2003a: 356), and the role of heritage languages in the acquisition of French is being raised again (Mc Andrew 2001: 57), important for those children who arrive in Quebec as adolescents and who were 'underschooled' in their country of origin (Mc Andrew 2001: 31).[3] The Francophone public school system in fact has a 'double mandate': not only 'hosting and integrating the children of the newly arrived immigrants' but also 'preparing all future citizens to live together in a pluralist society' (Mc Andrew 2003b: 60). This preparation is increasingly taking place through intercultural education programmes in Quebec schools, guided by the Ministry of Education's policy statement on educational integration and intercultural education, *Une école d'avenir* (A School for the Future) (Gouvernement du Québec 1998a). This statement is based on three basic principles: 'equal opportunity', 'proficiency in French, the language of public life', and 'education for citizenship in a democratic, pluralistic society' (Gouvernement du Québec n.d.). On the ground, however, intercultural education programmes face certain difficulties, such as the 'unsystematic nature of both initial and in-service teacher-training, on the one hand, and the persistence of ethnocentrism in the learning material, although revised, on the other' (Mc Andrew 2003b: 61). In addition, intercultural education objectives are not necessarily seen as a priority (Mc Andrew 2003b: 61).

So far, Quebec's qualities as a host have been discussed in terms of policy, where it has ambitions and good intentions, and the provision of services, which go a long way in providing the key of French, but which could be more effective. However, a host society is made up of individuals, and the 'moral contract' between immigrants and the host community, outlined in Quebec's 1991 immigration policy document *Au Québec pour bâtir ensemble*, emphasises the importance of 'being open to others as the host society and in developing harmonious intergroup relations' (Gouvernement du Québec 1991: 17; see also Section 2.1). Some consider that too much focus has been placed on how well, or not, immigrants themselves have been integrating, linguistically and otherwise, and not enough on the efforts of individual members of the host society in welcoming new arrivals. Quebec may provide intercultural education opportunities to the general school-age population, but it does not, for example, require of adults long established in Quebec to attend intercultural education classes on what shared social values might be or on how to live together harmoniously. Piché and Frenette's (2001) notion of 'social receptiveness', which refers 'to the attitudes and efforts of the Quebec population with respect to immigration and intercultural relations', is an innovative measure. It remains, however, focused on the successful acquisition of French, based as it is on 'the hypothesis that the linguistic choices of immigrants will be made all the easier if the host society is open and welcoming to them' (Piché and Frenette 2001: 25). In other words, if Francophone Quebecers wish to ensure that newcomers speak French and not English, thus making sure that French persists in North America, they must adopt some form of more unconditional hospitality.

The differences in the ways Quebec as host welcomes adult and young immigrants is echoed in the different attitudes that adult and young immigrants tend to have towards the host language, according to whether they emigrated as an adult or as a child, or whether they were born in Quebec of immigrant parents. In the following two sections, therefore, the discussion turns to the guests themselves.

7.2 Adult migrant experiences of language and belonging

How do the efforts that Quebec puts into making people feel at home in French translate in terms of their affective commitment to the language? In general terms, it seems that those immigrants who stay in Quebec end up settling in and integrating into Quebec society, at least according to a significant longitudinal study by Jean Renaud and a team of researchers of immigrant experiences during their first ten years in Montreal (Renaud *et al.* 2003).[4] The title of the study in French is worth commenting on: *Ils sont maintenant d'ici!* (Literally 'They are now from here!' but officially translated as *What a Difference Ten Years Can Make!*). The title affirms the fact that these particular immigrants belong to the 'here' of Quebec, but at the same time the very use of 'here' and 'now' serves as a reminder that this group of Quebecers came from a past 'elsewhere', and thus raises the ghost of their status as guests, not yet fully at home. In terms of language use, Renaud and his team found that after ten years participants used French as the predominant public language, defined as 'the language most frequently used outside the home with people who are neither relatives nor friends' (Renaud *et al.* 2003: 97). This was the case whether participants knew French or English before emigrating or not, with 61 per cent of the participants using French only in public, and under 20 per cent using English only. At home, after ten years, the mother tongue remained the predominant language, with just under half using it, and just over 37 per cent speaking French exclusively or with another language at home (Renaud *et al.* 2003: 98). Immigrants in the refugee class were more likely to use the mother tongue at home (80.5 per cent), compared with family migrants (50.6 per cent) and economic migrants (44.4 per cent). Over the ten-year period, participants' perceptions of the majority language in Quebec had changed, with a greater percentage (up from 4 per cent in 1990 to 21 per cent in 1999) viewing Quebec as a multilingual society (see Section 7.3).

In order to go more deeply into the question of the relationship between a sense of belonging and an affective commitment to French among new Quebecers, a particularly eloquent study is that of Helly and van Schendel (2001), and it is worth commenting on it in detail. The study is based on interviews with a group of 84 Montrealers undertaken in the months preceding the 1995 referendum. The timing of the study, at a period when attention was focused squarely on the possible separation of Quebec from Canada, may have influenced Helly and van Schendel's findings. However, the question of separation from Canada comes up periodically in the province – for example, in 2005 and 2006, sovereignty was again in the news – and it forms part of the backdrop to living in Quebec. It is reasonable to assume, then, that Helly and van Schendel's findings are still valid. The participants included 12 Montrealers of French settler background and 72 immigrants who had been in Quebec for roughly ten years, from six countries: France, Haiti, India, Morocco, El Salvador and Vietnam. Whereas Renaud and his team focused on the overall experience of integration into Quebec society, Helly and van Schendel were interested in examining the collective bonds linking immigrants to the state, the nation and civil society, both as regards Quebec and Canada. The whole question of collective bonds was of particular relevance given the debate on transnational and diasporic forms of belonging among immigrant populations, and what is perceived as their often weak attachment to their new society (Helly and van Schendel 2001: 22).

Three elements stand out from Helly and van Schendel's research. First, only a small minority of immigrants had not developed any sense of belonging at all to Quebec or Canadian society. The great majority of those surveyed 'show that they have a collective bond, do not display any deep alienation with regard to the Quebec or Canadian states, and show themselves to be strongly attached to the precepts of democracy and individual rights' (Helly and van Schendel 2001: 199).[5] In their analysis, Helly and van Schendel classified participants according to four types of 'civil bond': the first group had developed a sense of belonging to Quebec which was mainly exclusive to any other; a second group said they were doubly linked to Quebec and to the Canadian state. A third group considered their link to Quebec as 'basically mediated and conditioned by their status as Canadian citizens, and show[ed themselves to be attached] to Quebec society only because of the attractive conditions of settling in Montreal' (Helly and van Schendel 2001: 199). And the fourth group had a sense of belonging only to their country of origin or were unable to develop a sense of belonging to any society. Second, for the first three groups, Montreal was an important reference point for a sense of belonging and constituted 'the primary bond that they have developed with Quebec society' (Helly and van Schendel 2001: 23). Third, knowing French before migrating was a significant factor for the first two groups, who both expressed a strong attachment to Quebec and to French. Helly and van Schendel (2001: 227) indeed observe that 'there is in fact a strong correlation between knowing French and developing a sense of belonging through the appropriation of Franco-Quebecer traits, or through a spirit of conformity to the rules perceived as those of the linguistic majority.'

The first two groups included new Quebecers who 'feel at home' both in French and in Quebec, echoing the Larose Commission in the quotation that opened this chapter. The first group included seven French Canadians and 12 immigrants who demonstrated a strong sense of belonging to Quebec, which they considered their primary locus of identification, some identifying themselves exclusively as Quebecers, and most considering that they belonged first to Quebec and then to Canada (Helly and van Schendel 2001: 42). The immigrants in this group were amongst the best informed and prepared for emigration and were successfully integrated. All bar one knew French before their arrival, and all described themselves as bilingual: they chose Quebec because knowing French would help them settle in quickly. Montreal was an important element in their sense of attachment – as one immigrant put it: 'I feel at ease here, I feel at home here' (Helly and van Schendel 2001: 31). Integral to this 'feeling at home' was the fact that the French language allowed people who would otherwise be very different to 'come together around a common referent' (Helly and van Schendel 2001: 31). This group had what Helly and van Schendel (2001: 23) refer to as a republican conception of citizenship, such as that discussed in general in Section 1.6 and in the particular context of Quebec in Section 2.3.

The second group, which contained five French Canadians and 15 immigrants, also felt a 'strong attachment to Quebec civil society, to the way of living together and to the language' (Helly and van Schendel 2001: 85). Quebec is viewed as Canada's 'regional Francophone society', and Canada itself purely as the source of formal citizenship. In terms of the development of a sense of belonging, immigrants mentioned that 'the simple fact of having changed their way of life contributed to the development of their attachment to Quebec' (Helly and van Schendel 2001: 89), and that their children, socialised in Quebec, played a role in their acceptance of Quebec values and social norms. All of the 15 immigrants in this group except two knew French before they arrived, and most had at the end of ten years learned or perfected their English. The immigrants had in the main a deep attachment to the French language, and Montreal had become central to their migration project. A minority of them felt 'at home' in Quebec, but others did not have such a confident sense of being at home, and considered that there were 'social barriers between immigrants and a number of "French Canadians" ' (Helly and van Schendel 2001: 103).

The third group can be regarded as representing a majority immigrant view, in that it was made up solely of 37 immigrants. They viewed French from an instrumental perspective, although they recognised 'the special role of French in Quebec' (Helly and van Schendel 2001: 163), and a number of them stressed the importance of French–English bilingualism. Overall this group of immigrants had what Helly and van Schendel (2001: 163) describe as 'a remote form of belonging' to the province, and a Montreal identity was particularly strong. They had a formal liberal view of citizenship, that is, they viewed citizenship as protecting individual rights and freedoms, a conception of citizenship which is promoted by Canada as a whole (see Section 2.3).[6]

Finally, the fourth group, made up of eight immigrants, rejected all sense of belonging to Quebec or to Canada. This group was divided into two subgroups, four individuals in each. The first had 'an inalienable sense of belonging to their country of origin' (Helly and van Schendel 2001: 179): they remained attached to the political life in their home country and had not developed any particular allegiance to the Canadian state. Two members of this subgroup were from France, and considered the defense of French in Quebec simply as a way of maintaining 'the influence of France' (Helly and van Schendel 2001: 187). The second subgroup considered that they had 'no country, state or society as a point of reference, and they claim[ed] to ascribe to a status which signified their total exclusion from Canada and Quebec' (Helly and van Schendel 2001: 189). For them, racial belonging completely determined the place of an individual in Canadian and Quebec societies, and they had themselves experienced exclusion and racial discrimination. They were not favourable to the use of French or the debate on its protection, refusing its imposition.

Although these four groups and the distribution of participants across them do not represent the sum of migrant experience in Quebec, Helly and van Schendel's findings are echoed in other studies, in particular the place of Montreal, the importance of French–English bilingualism, and the obvious effects of racial discrimination and exclusion. Labelle and Salée (2001), for example, examined immigrants' perceptions of citizenship as constructed by the Canadian and Quebec states. They conducted a series of interviews in 1996–97 with a number of community activists of immigrant origin in Montreal.[7] Among their findings, in terms of a civic identity, of those participants who referred to Quebec or Canada to describe their own identity, more used the term *Québécois* than Canadian, whether alone or, as was more frequent, hyphenated with some element of their country or culture of origin. As we saw in Helly and van Schendel's study, an alternative identification proposed by some participants was that of being a Montrealer, which, according to Labelle and Salée (2001: 297), 'reveals the emergence of a new political identity associated with Montreal's cosmopolitanism and constitutive heterogeneity held as positive, in contrast to the narrow provincialism associated with the sovereignist vote and the rest of Quebec outside Montreal.'

Quebec's discourse on citizenship was endorsed by many, in principle, particularly by immigrants from Francophone countries or by those who were 'immersed in a Francophone cultural environment' (Labelle and Salée 2001: 304). However, a small number, all Anglophones, were of the view that 'the new emphasis of the Quebec government on civic relations risk[ed] losing the recognition of the minorities and failing to respond to their needs' (Labelle and Salée 2001: 304), a similar logic to that used to argue for interculturalism against multiculturalism, that is, the latter does not distinguish between national and ethnocultural minorities (see Section 2.3). In addition, 'Canada's bilingual status is often seen as a great gesture of social accommodation. Thus, in the minds of many, there should be no reason for Quebec to "impose" French as the official language when they live in a supposedly bilingual country' (Labelle and Salée 2001: 310). An affective commitment to French is limited, with divided loyalties between French and English, the latter considered as 'a pivotal language in public and private communication in Quebec, and a powerful instrument of socialization for immigrants, even those of French-speaking origin' (Labelle and Salée 2001: 310).

Overall, Labelle and Salée came to the following conclusion:

> there exists a gap between how the state envisions immigrant integration – particularly when it comes to unreservedly endorsing Canada's (or Quebec's) core values – and the terms by which immigrants and members of ethnocultural minorities understand their incorporation into Canadian and Quebec society. (Labelle and Salée 2001: 306)

They set out a series of persuasive reasons for this 'discursive divide'. First of all, the ways in which the state, whether Canada or Quebec, categorizes race and ethnicity – for example, in the Census data – can generate a feeling among Quebecers from ethnocultural minorities of being perpetually classified as 'other': '[a]s a result, within certain groups the emergence of a considerably adversarial attitude toward a sentiment of belonging to Canada or Quebec is inevitable' (Labelle and Salée 2001: 307). Second, racial discrimination and exclusion experienced by members of 'racialized minorities' is also clearly a deterrent to creating a sense of belonging to Quebec. Third, immigrants and Quebecers of immigrant origin may well have other, transnational affiliations and allegiances that cannot easily be replaced. Fourth, Canada's multiculturalism policy puts French Canadians on a par with other ethnic minorities (see Section 2.3), which means that 'the legitimacy of [the French Canadian] claim for a distinct but universal and inclusive Quebec citizenship is not strong among immigrants and members of ethnocultural minorities' (Labelle and Salée 2001: 310). Fifth, there is strong resistance to Quebec nationalism and sovereignty among some immigrants and their descendants.

The picture that Labelle and Salée paint is more negative than that of Helly and van Schendel, who consider that the majority of immigrants they interviewed had developed some sense of belonging to Quebec after several years in the province. However, for the group who represented the majority immigrant view, this belonging is described as remote, and French was regarded purely from an instrumental point of view, provoking no affective commitment. Quebec's efforts to make its adult guests feel at home in French have not necessarily had the desired outcome, but this is perhaps understandable:

> An immigrant who learns French as an adult may have already adopted deep cultural commitments. Learning French does not require her to abandon any of them, although it is likely to open her to new influences and to make her less tied to, because less dependent upon, her culture of origin. [...] An immigrant to Quebec who learns French as a child is likely to be much more profoundly affected by the experience than one who learns it as an adult. To learn a language as a child is normally to acquire a culture, at least to some extent, in part because one learns the language primarily in the course of learning other things. [...] Thus, it seems plausible to argue that a language acquired as a child is normally much more likely to have the intimate connection to one's most fundamental cultural commitments [...] than a language acquired as an adult. (Carens 2000: 128–9)

The experience of migration as an adult, then, can be distinct from that of a child or a young person in terms of integration into the host society. The following section examines the situation of young people of immigrant background in Quebec.

7.3 Les enfants de la loi 101

Les enfants de la loi 101 or *la génération 101* are expressions that refer to the children of immigrants who arrived after the introduction of the Charter of the French language in 1977 (see Section 5.1), and who were either born in another country or in Quebec of immigrant parents. In other settler societies, such as Australia and France for example, the usual term for designating this particular group is 'the second generation', those children who have been socialised, partially or wholly, in the host society. What these terms have in common is that they allow us 'to continue to think of "immigrants" as "guests" and of "us" as hosts. If we think of immigrants' children as "mediators" between "us" and "them" (rather than, for example, as part of "us"), the parents will continue to be seen as newcomers (even if they have been in the country for thirty years)' (Rosello 2001: 91). What the Quebec expression *génération 101* does in addition, of course, is to put the focus on the outcomes of Quebec's language legislation, marking this particular generation of young people as those with the potential to become fully at home in French, given their linguistic socialisation through school, gaining in most cases a Quebec French accent indistinguishable from that of young people of French Canadian background.

The linguistic diversity among young people of immigrant origin is striking. Overall, in the school year 2004–05, 43.5 per cent of students in the Francophone school system had a mother tongue other than French or English, with a total of 188 different places of birth, 148 mother tongues and 131 languages used at home (Meilleur 2005: 2). The two most popular mother tongues after French (52.7 per cent) were Spanish (9.1 per cent) and Arabic (6 per cent), followed by Creole (4.3 per cent), English (3.8 per cent) and Chinese (3.7 per cent) (Meilleur 2005: 5). It has been predicted that by perhaps as early as 2006 Arabic will be the most common mother tongue after French in the French-language school system, in part aided by immigration from Arabic-speaking countries such as Algeria and Morocco which have French as a second language (Heinrich 2005). The majority of schools are affected by this growing linguistic and cultural diversity, and 'over one-third of schools has more than 50 per cent of this clientele' (Mc Andrew 2003b: 59).

Greater retention of the ethnic marker of language (see Section 7.1), along with the status of French and English within the host society, create the conditions for trilingualism to flourish in Montreal. According to the Office québécois de la langue française (2005: 32–3), in 1996, 13.7 per cent of the population in the Montreal metropolitan region, and 19.5 per cent of those on the island of Montreal, knew at least three languages; by the 2001 census, these figures had risen to 15.5 per cent and 22.2 per cent respectively.[8] This gives Montreal the highest rate of trilingualism in Canada (see e.g., Termote 2000). In addition, the number of trilingual Montrealers whose mother tongue is a heritage language and who speak English and French rose between 1996 and 2001 from 48.1 per cent to 51.9 per cent in the Montreal metropolitan region, and from 46.6 per cent to 50.2 per cent on the island of Montreal. Again, this is a far higher proportion than anywhere else in Canada – compare only 4 per cent of Vancouver's immigrant background population (Lamarre and Dagenais 2004: 57).

Of interest to the discussion here is the extent to which the 101 generation has an affective commitment to the French language. A study undertaken in 2003 of over a thousand members of this generation showed that they were generally well integrated: 'the 101 generation has, on several points, values and expectations which are similar to those of most of the Quebec population. Distinctions made on the basis of immigrant origin are becoming less and less pertinent' (Beaulieu 2003: 261).[9] In terms of their identity, a little over a third (34 per cent) stated they were Canadian, just under a third (29 per cent) Montrealers, and just under another third (28 per cent) Quebecers. The strength of the Montreal identity echoes the importance of Montreal as a locus of identity for the 'first-generation' immigrants described in Section 7.2. The study also showed that the 101 generation is attached to the French language – 92 per cent considered that French is either a language they are proud to speak or a 'treasure which must be protected' (Beaulieu 2003: 264). As far as French as the language of use is concerned, over half (54 per cent) mainly used French with their friends, while 17 per cent used English, and 19 per cent both French and English, with a greater percentage using French with their parents (46 per cent) or their mother tongue (36 per cent), and only 8 per cent using English. At work, French was the most widely used language (59 per cent), followed by both French and English (21 per cent) and English alone (14 per cent). Finally, a large number of participants (86 per cent) considered that 'more must be invested into learning French in order to improve the integration of immigrants' (Beaulieu 2003: 265). This last point is significant for the focus of this chapter: the perception of these young people is that Quebec could do more to fulfil its duties as host.

The varied language practices of the 101 generation are underscored in a study undertaken in 2000 by the then Conseil de la langue française amongst 105 young people from the first and second generations (Conseil de la langue française 2002).[10] The study sought to examine the relationship between being schooled in French and the use of French as a public language. Among the study's conclusions was the following:

> The linguistic choices that the children of Bill 101 make regarding the two official languages are functional in nature to enable them to adapt to a foreign environment. They adapt to this environment in order to open as many doors as possible [...]. French and English thus represent two second languages [necessary] to function in a culture other than their culture of origin. (Conseil de la langue francaise 2002: 30)

According to the study, the adaptability of these young people to a variety of situations during their lives, and the functional attitude towards the use of language, result in a lack of affective commitment to French and to English, both of which are viewed as 'additional [tools] of communication', part and parcel of adapting to different contexts and interlocutors (Conseil de la langue française 2002: 29). This lack of attachment to French and English is contrasted to an attachment to their mother tongue, and 'a passion for multilingualism' (Conseil de la langue française 2002: 24). This finding contradicts that of the Beaulieu study cited above, which maintained that 'just like the general population, the 101 generation is attached to the French language and is concerned by its defence' (Beaulieu 2003: 264). This discrepancy may have something to do with the different methodologies employed (a telephone questionnaire for the Beaulieu study and focus group discussions for the Conseil study), the different questions asked, or perhaps different proportions of first and second generation participants. It could also point to the huge variability among young Quebecers of immigrant origin in terms of language choices and attitudes. Be that as it may, the Conseil study does note positive attitudes towards French: the participants generally considered that it was 'normal and respectful to speak French in Quebec' (Conseil de la langue française 2002: 30). In addition, the vast majority would choose to have their children educated in the Francophone school system. This shows that 'Allophones recognise the necessity of speaking French in Quebec, of having a solid basis [in the language] in order to communicate, and that the primary and secondary levels are indispensable to achieve this' (Conseil de la langue française 2002: 25).

The concern of much research on this generation has been to map the effects of the Charter of the French language on the francisation of immigrants through the schooling system and subsequent changes to the linguistic make-up of the population: '[q]uestions of language transfer and of the use of French in public interactions have largely dominated research on language practices' (Lamarre and Rossell Paredes 2003: 65). However, in recent work, particularly by Patricia Lamarre and colleagues, there has been a focus on multilingualism among young people of immigrant background (e.g., Lamarre 2001; Lamarre *et al.* 2002; Lamarre and Rossell Paredes 2003; Lamarre and Dagenais 2004). As Levine (2000: 374) points out, '[t]hese "children of Bill 101" are more and more trilingual: they keep their mother tongue, learn French at school and English on the television, in the street and through North American popular culture.' In addition, they are very aware of the worth of multilingualism: 'Young Allophones [...] are totally convinced of the value of multilingualism, are attached to their mother tongue, and are very aware of the national and international status of languages' (Mc Andrew *et al.* 1999: 121). Among young Quebecers of immigrant background, whether from the first or second generation, '[w]hile French was perceived as the most important language in Quebec, English/French bilingualism was perceived as the most valuable type of linguistic capital' and 'necessary for full participation in the life of the city' (Lamarre and Rossell Paredes 2003: 78).[11]

The Montreal that Lamarre and her colleagues give voice to is one in which young people are engaged in fluid, adaptive and varied bilingual or multilingual practices in a range of public spaces, from cafés and shopping centres to local health centres and public transport (Lamarre *et al.* 2002).[12] The traditional geo-linguistic division of Montreal into east-end Francophone and west-end Anglophone neighbourhoods still dictates to a certain extent the dominant language of interaction among young people, with multiethnic neighbourhoods and 'downtown' Montreal the areas where heritage languages are to be heard the most, in addition to bilingual and multilingual codeswitching. The 'downtown' space is in particular one where English–French bilingualism is predominant. However, generally many young people 'have the language skills needed to cross ethnic, linguistic, and geographic frontiers and are using languages to do just that in their daily activities' (Lamarre et al. 2002: 70). Particular institutional sites have a particular 'linguistic identity' which affects the choice of language: 'this linguistic identity does not appear to be necessarily linked to the overt language policies of institutions, but seems related to how speakers perceive ownership of a space and the stakes involved in the interactions that take place within that space' (Lamarre et al. 2002: 69). These institutional sites are contrasted to informal settings such as bars, restaurants, cafés, public transport and public events, which are considered to be ethnically and linguistically neutral, and which are, regardless of location, most likely to exhibit the most varied range of language practices.

In addition, Lamarre and her colleagues point out how young Montrealers who are bilingual and trilingual problematise the traditional categories of Francophone, Anglophone and Allophone (see e.g., Meintel and Fortin 2001). The crossing of 'traditional linguistic frontiers' that many of these young people practise results from speaking their parents' language in the home environment and within certain friendship circles, having been schooled in French, and then, for example, attending an Anglophone college (CEGEP) – nearly half of young Allophones who have received their secondary education in French decide to pursue their studies in an Anglophone institution. The consequence of such linguistic crossing is that 'homogenous linguistic and cultural identities make little sense' (Lamarre et al. 2002: 70).

Given the above discussion, and returning to the metaphor of hospitality, some members of the 101 generation could perhaps be described as unruly guests. They are at home in Montreal, but not necessarily in Quebec, and are at home in bilingual or multilingual language practices, but do not necessarily have any genuine affective commitment to French (or to English for that matter). The French–English bilingualism that Lamarre and her colleagues describe seems to be the inevitable result of Quebec's language policy which maintains the vitality of French, but in a context where English exerts huge attraction. The question that some in Quebec seek to answer now, in the bid to ensure the continuity of French in Quebec, is how to make French the predominant language in the linguistic repertoire of young bilinguals and trilinguals (Michel Pagé, personal communication, September 2005).

7.4 'Pure new wool' Quebecers?

On 25 January 2006, Télé-Québec, one of two public Francophone television stations in Quebec, broadcast the first two episodes of its new series,

Pure laine (Pure wool), the title a colloquial way of referring to members of the French Canadian majority. The series in fact portrays what one commentator has called an 'immigrant' family living in Montreal (Heinrich 2004): Dominique, originally from Haiti, long settled in Quebec; his partner Chantal, a French Canadian from the Îles-de-la-Madeleine, in effect an immigrant from the regions; and their daughter Ming, whom the couple adopted as a baby from China. In the promotional material, the series is described as 'a comedy which dares to tackle a subject rarely broached on the small screen: ethnic minorities and their point of view' (Télé-Québec 2006a). The 'nation' that *Pure laine* shows its audience is one of more or less integrated diversity – Télé-Québec describes the three main characters as 'an authentic Quebec family' – in which Quebec French is the language of the home as well as of public spaces for Quebecers of different origins. The innovative nature of the series is reflected in viewers' comments posted on the series' website, among which are several from Quebecers of immigrant background. One viewer says that she never watches Quebec television because 'as an immigrant I never feel targeted by programmes in French', but that *Pure laine* has changed this (Télé-Québec 2006b).

This television event goes to the heart of the issue identified by the Larose Commission and mentioned at the beginning of this chapter: immigrants 'feeling at home' in Quebec. The discussion above has partly focused on the practical aspects of Quebec's hospitality to new arrivals. Quebec as host has some say in choosing its guests, and it has ambitions and good intentions, not always fulfilled, to provide new arrivals with what could be called the 'key to the house' – the French language – so that they can make themselves totally at home. As for the guests themselves, there is a distinction to be made between adult and young immigrants. Although some adults do develop a sense of affective commitment both to French and to Quebec, a majority view French in instrumental terms, and have what Helly and van Schendel (2001: 163) have called 'a remote form of belonging' to Quebec. In addition, many adults share with young people of immigrant background a view of Montreal as the main locus of identification. For the so-called 101 generation, bilingual or multilingual language practices, rather than French alone, seem to hold a strong attraction. Rosello (2001: 176) argues that contained within the notion of hospitality is the risk that both the host and the guest run 'of being challenged, shaken, changed by the encounter'. New Quebecers are changed in that, in the main, they do successfully add French to their linguistic repertoires and they may well end up feeling at home, but not necessarily in the way that Quebec might envisage. Quebec in its turn is being challenged by the language practices of new Quebecers, practices in which French may not have a central place. The following chapter continues the exploration of the diverse experiences of minorities in Quebec, focusing this time on a group which has historical claims to special status in the province, namely Anglophone Quebecers.

8
Transformations of Anglophone Quebec

[L]*a communauté québécoise d'expression anglaise, dans son ensemble, se conçoit désormais partie prenante de l'affirmation du français comme langue de participation à la société québécoise et ses membres s'identifient comme citoyens du Québec selon nombre de témoignages entendus devant la Commission. Le rayonnement de sa culture, de ses institutions et de sa langue est perçu, de plus en plus, comme une composante de la culture québécoise plutôt qu'une source de concurrence à l'égard de la langue française. [...] Cette communauté peut représenter la meilleure interface entre le Québec et le reste de l'Amérique, puisque sa langue est la langue parlée par tous les voisins du Québec. Son apport à la culture québécoise doit être plus reconnu, mieux utilisé et davantage considéré comme une source de rayonnement du Québec dans toute l'Amérique.*

Quebec's English-speaking community, as a whole, now regards itself as a stakeholder in the confirmation of French as the language of participation in Quebec society and its members identify themselves as citizens of Quebec, according to numerous statements heard by the Commission. The influence of its culture, institutions and language is increasingly perceived as a facet of Quebec culture rather than as a source of competition in respect of the French language. [...] This community may be the best interface between Quebec and the rest of North America, since its language is spoken by all of Quebec's neighbours. Its contribution to Quebec culture must be more widely acknowledged, better used and considered more widely as a means of broadening Quebec's influence throughout North America. (Gouvernement du Québec 2001a: 17–18)

The Anglophone community in Quebec has undergone significant transformations since the Quiet Revolution in the 1960s, and much has been written on its subsequent evolution from majority to minority status within Quebec and on its changing relationship with the Francophone majority (see Caldwell and Waddell 1982d; Scowen 1991; Legault 1992; Stevenson 1999; among others). The Larose Commission claims a new shift in Anglophone–Francophone relations, with 'old French–English antagonisms having eased a little, if not substantially' (Gouvernement du Québec 2001a: 193). The report, cited above, considers that Anglophone Quebecers now regard themselves as Quebec citizens, that is, as fully participating members of Quebec society, with a sense of belonging or allegiance to Quebec. It presents a portrait of increasing integration within Quebec society of what it calls the 'Quebec English-speaking community', and in particular greater acceptance by the Francophone majority of the Anglophone community and its language. Far from being a threat, Quebec's Anglophones should now be seen as an asset or bridge in the development of the province's relationships with Anglophone North America.[1]

To what extent is this portrait of Anglophone Quebec an accurate one? Certainly, just after the publication of the Larose Commission's report, commentators were divided. On the Francophone side, some considered the report an act of reconciliation in general and between Francophones and Anglophones in particular: Boileau (2001) cited one of the two Anglophone commissioners of the Larose Commission, Dermod Travis – '[w]e are turning the page on the "two solitudes" '[2] – and Larose himself, who claimed that 'Anglophones are not our enemies but a constituent part of our reality'. Others applauded the report's audacity and vision for the future, but questioned the extent to which Anglophone Quebecers fundamentally considered themselves part of an inclusive, civic Quebec nation (Proulx 2001). Yet others contested the Commission's affirmation of the very existence of these 'new Anglophones' (Dubuc 2002). On the Anglophone side, divisions were more marked, some seeing the report as 'an opening up to diversity' while others viewed the proposal to introduce Quebec citizenship with the French language as the key element (see Section 2.2) as 'an attempt to prepare the ground for the separation of Quebec' (L.-J. Perreault 2001). In his (negative) reaction to the Larose Commission's report, Brent Tyler, an Anglophone rights lawyer and then president of the Anglophone advocacy group Alliance Quebec, insisted on the Canadian identity of Quebec's Anglophones: 'We self-identify with the Canadian people. We are English-speaking. We are Canadian citizens' (cited in Proulx 2001).

The issue of whether Anglophone Quebecers can truly feel a sense of belonging to Quebec, and inversely whether the Francophone majority can fully accept Anglophones as 'true' Quebecers, is extremely pertinent. In its naming, the minority Anglophone or English-speaking community is categorised along strictly linguistic lines, a constant reminder of its fundamental difference with respect to the majority Francophone community, in a society in which the new, inclusive civic order is Francophone first and foremost. The Anglophone community is thus in some sense 'always already', that is, in its very constitution, unable to transcend linguistic boundaries in order to integrate completely. This question of definition is taken up in the present chapter, which examines what is at stake in the various permutations of who counts as an Anglophone. It continues by exploring the theme of reconciliation or rapprochement between the 'two solitudes' in Quebec. The chapter concludes with a discussion of the blurring of boundaries between Anglophones and Francophones, through growing bilingualism and mixing among the younger generation.

8.1 Who is an Anglophone Quebecer?

An Anglophone or English Quebec identity only really came into being during the late 1960s and 1970s, the period during which *Québécois* came to replace 'French Canadian' to describe the collective identity of the Francophone majority (Caldwell and Waddell 1982b: 17; see also Section 2.1). Before then, the basic distinction of (English) Canadian and French Canadian separated the two main linguistic groups in Canada. With the advent of a new Francophone Quebec identity, however, Anglophones in Quebec found themselves for the first time in the position of a minority, forced to re-evaluate their role within Quebec society:

> By redefining their identity to reflect a demographic and geopolitical consolidation within Quebec, the French had conferred for the first time an unequivocal minority status on their English *concitoyens*. At the same time, the English, in continuing to characterize themselves as 'English Canadians', found themselves deprived of a culturally prescribed strategy to facilitate their political and social insertion in the new Quebec. (Caldwell and Waddell 1982b: 17)

That Quebec's Anglophones were unaware of their minority status before the rise of a Quebec identity, culminating in the election of the Parti Québécois in 1976, might at first glance seem difficult to believe: they were certainly numerically in the minority within Quebec. However, English Quebec can be considered an elite: its leaders 'played a decisive role in the exercise of power in the province, while the group as a whole, as an extension of English Canada, was omnipresent' (Waddell 1982: 29–30). The shift from majority to minority status took place in three stages following World War II: (1) 'a phase of self-confident "majority group" consciousness'; (2) 'a phase of majority–minority group image dissonance and defensiveness' and (3) 'a phase of minority group positive self-awareness and action' with the coming to power of the Parti Québécois in 1976 and the introduction of the Charter of the French language in 1977 (Stein 1982: 109). In other words, in the third phase in particular, as the dominant status of the Anglophone group was increasingly undermined by the rise in dominance of the Francophone group, Anglophones sought to regain at least part of their former status and regenerate a more positive social identity (see Section 1.2). It is this third phase of 'self-awareness and action' and its consequences that is the focus of the discussion here.

In this chapter, the terms 'Anglophone' and 'English-speaking' are used interchangeably, to refer to those Quebecers who prefer to use English in their everyday lives. In contrast, other authors and commentators have made explicit decisions about what they consider the meaning and use of the two terms. It is clear that in Quebec today, 'Anglophone' signifies particular things and raises particular problems depending on the focus and interests of those who name and define. Some dispute the very use of the term 'Anglophone Quebecer', arguing that it is a label for only those Quebecers whose mother tongue is English (Hook, cited in Bergeron 2004: 95). According to this definition, the term does not therefore include those for whom English is the usual language spoken but not necessarily the mother tongue, who represent a growing part of the 'Anglophone' population in Quebec. Others claim that members of the community generally feel uncomfortable with the term 'Anglophone' (e.g., Scowen 1991: 13). To counter such objections, the alternative 'English-speaking community' has been proposed and seems to be growing in popularity.

The more restricted definition of Anglophones as those whose mother tongue is English continues to be used to measure the Anglophone population, and has on occasion caused protests among Anglophones. An example is the case of Bills 170 and 171, adopted by Quebec's National Assembly in December 2000 (*Act to reform the municipal territorial organization of the metropolitan regions of Montréal, Québec and the Outaouais*, S.Q. 2000, c. 56 and *Act to amend the Charter of the French language*, S.Q. 2000, c. 57 respectively). The first of these acts amalgamated a number of municipalities to create five 'mega-cities' of Montreal, Quebec City, Gatineau-Hull, Longueuil and Lévis as well as other mergers, in an effort to reduce the very high number of municipalities in Quebec. For Montreal in particular, this meant the reduction of 28 municipalities into one 'mega-city' with a number of boroughs, as well as a formal declaration that French is the official language of the new city. The second act modified section 29.1 of the Charter of the French language relating to what constitutes a bilingual municipality, a status which grants the public's right to services in a language other than French – in reality English – and the use of that language within municipal bodies and in bilingual signs and posters (Office of the Commissioner of Official Languages 2003). Before the act, the definition of a bilingual municipality was based on a threshold of 50 per cent of 'users of a language other than French'; the act modified this threshold to 50 per cent of people *whose mother tongue was English* (Alliance Quebec 2001: 20), a much more restrictive definition. Both acts were vigorously opposed by the bilingual municipalities on the island of Montreal in particular, who feared the negative impact on their linguistic rights; 19 municipalities, 18 from the island of Montreal, challenged the first act in the courts for this reason. The Quebec Superior Court rejected the challenge, as did the Court of Appeal, which argued among other things that the second act in particular transferred the bilingual status of the former municipalities to the boroughs of which they became a part (see e.g., Office of the Commissioner of Official Languages 2003 for a discussion of the legal decisions on the challenges to both acts).

As for the Larose Commission, it defines the 'Quebec English-language community' as 'a community whose core, historically and currently, is formed of Anglo-Quebecers', including, one might assume, those of English, Irish and Scottish descent, among others (see e.g., Rudin 1985: 154–5 for the historical make-up of the Anglophone community). It also emphasises the community's growing diversity, as well as its institutional foundations: 'The members of this community benefit from certain rights in the areas of education, justice, health and social services' (Gouvernement du Québec 2001a: 224). Also of note is that this definition does not refer explicitly to language, in contrast to the report's definition of 'Anglophone', defined in purely linguistic terms: 'a person for whom English is the mother tongue or for whom English is the most often used language in their private life' (Gouvernement du Québec 2001a: 223).

This split between a definition which includes a cultural or institutional dimension and one that focuses purely on linguistic criteria is exemplified by various authors. For example, in answer to the question: 'What exactly is the civil society of anglophone Quebec?', Stevenson answers by referring to two opposing views, epitomised by Reed Scowen and Gary Caldwell, who are both passionate advocates of Anglophone Quebec (Stevenson 1999: 294–5). Caldwell, on the one hand, 'views anglophones not as a diverse collection of people who happen to share a language, but as an important cultural fragment in the Quebec mosaic' (Stevenson 1999: 295). The cultural heritage of Anglophones is made up of one half 'of British cultural tradition, one tenth Jewish, and four tenths of various European, Asiatic and central Caribbean and American cultural origins' (Caldwell 1998: 277).[3] Gretta Chambers, former chancellor of McGill University, argues for her part that what Anglophones share is not in fact ethnicity or cultural commonplaces, but 'the bonds of the language in which their institutions have been created in the service of their community' (Chambers 2000: 319). It seems that the English-speaking community is concerned about the vitality of its institutions and not the vitality of its language *per se*, which benefits from the strength of English elsewhere in Canada, in the US and in the rest of the world:

> Anglophones do not fear losing their language in a Francophone Quebec. When this phenomenon does occur, it is considered as the consequence of a deliberate choice and not of a cultural diktat. What they really fear, at the linguistic level, is the loss or weakening of their institutions. (Chambers 2000: 319)

These institutions traditionally include a well developed English-language education system from primary to university level, including McGill University, the oldest university in Montreal, and a health and social services network.[4] It is worth noting, in passing, that the education system plays a major role in reinforcing the existence of the Francophone and Anglophone communities, given that schools are 'major sites in language socialization, and play a very important role in the integration of newcomers into existing "official language communities"' (Lamarre and Rossell Paredes 2003: 68).

Scowen, for his part, defines an Anglophone linguistically, as 'anyone who speaks English, or at least anyone who uses English as his or her main language of communication' (Stevenson 1999: 295). Some have indeed gone as far as to claim that the Anglophone population is simply a 'disparate community of communities' with nothing in common besides speaking the same language (Lazar 2001: 22), the term Anglo-Quebecers 'a demographic construct created by relatively recent governments' (Lazar 2001: 17). The Quebec Community Groups Network (QCGN), an umbrella group set up in 1995 comprising 24 English-language groups across Quebec,[5] also applies a linguistic criterion – simply choosing to use English – but stresses the importance of identifying with the community thus defined: 'The English-speaking community of Quebec is made up of multiple communities that are diverse, multicultural and multiracial. These communities include citizens throughout Quebec who choose to use the English language and who identify with the English-speaking community' (QCGN 2005: 8).

The definition's wide scope is not surprising, given that the QCGN's mandate is to support and promote community vitality and the use of English in Quebec, and that maximising the number of Quebecers who count as Anglophones capitalises on federal funding (see e.g., Jedwab (2002: 190–1) on what he calls 'identity demographics'). The QCGN argues for a definition that is 'more open than closed, more descriptive than definitive', given the 'increasingly complex combination of race, culture, and religion', and that 'an increasing component of Quebec society does not see itself in the "either-or" framework of separate French-speaking and English-speaking communities' (QCGN 2005: 8; see also Section 8.3).

Table 8.1 shows the shifting size of the Anglophone community in Quebec based on the three categories used in the Census: mother tongue, language spoken at home, and first official language spoken, based on 1991 and 2001 Census data.[6] Considering the data in Table 8.1, it is understandable that one of the common descriptions of English-speaking Quebec is of a community in decline: for example, the Anglophone population defined by the criteria of English only mother tongue or English only home language is decreasing, with losses of 7.4 per cent and 2.1 per cent respectively over the ten-year period 1991–2001. Anglo-Quebecers have always been a mobile community, but significant out-migration and low rates of Anglophone in-migration

Table 8.1 Size of the English-speaking community, according to various criteria, 1991 and 2001 Census data

Census criteria	1991	2001
Mother tongue, English only	601,405	557,040
Mother tongue, English or English and other	738,640	622,140
Home language, English only	716,155	700,890
Home language, English or English and other	800,275	784,995
First official language spoken, English only	832,050	828,730
'Official language minority'*	904,305	918,955
First official language spoken, English only or English and French	976,560	1,009,180

* Defined formally as 'the number whose first official language spoken is the minority official language in the province, plus half of those whose first official language spoken is both English and French' (Stevenson 1999: 19).

Sources: 1991 Census: Stevenson (1999: 19); 2001 Census: Jedwab (2004a: 8).

towards the end of the 1970s contributed to a marked decline in numbers (Magnan 2005: 192), coupled with low fertility rates. Out-migration was the direct result of the election of the sovereignist Parti Québécois in 1976 and the introduction of the Charter of the French language in the following year, and the majority of those who left were of British descent. Based on Census figures, between 1971 and 1981 158,000 mother-tongue Anglophones left the province, a decline of 12 per cent (Bourhis and Lepicq 2004: 22).

Although the extent of out-migration by English-speaking Quebecers has slowed down more recently, there still continues to be a degree of movement, with 'a net loss of more than 29,000 Anglophones from interprovincial migration between 1996 and 2001, with 18,000 moving from the Montreal region' (Jedwab 2004: 3). The departure of young Anglophones in particular has been a cause of community concern: in the period 1996–2001, the rate of migration by young mother-tongue Anglophones aged 25–34 was 15.8 per cent. This compared to 6.1 per cent among mother-tongue Allophones and 1.6 per cent for mother-tongue Francophones (Magnan 2005: 3–4). Various reasons have been put forward to explain this out-migration by young Anglophones, as pointed out by Magnan in her review of studies on young Anglo-Quebecers and migration, including the following: they do not consider that their skills in French are necessarily good enough; they do not feel accepted by Francophone society; they do not agree with the language laws; they leave Quebec to study or to find work (Magnan 2005: 52–3). In a study published in 2006 by the Research Group on Youth Migration, however, it appears that the migration patterns of young Anglophones may be changing, with a majority of young Anglophones committed to the province (Magnan, Gauthier and Côté 2006).[7]

There are conflicting views about the future decline in the Anglophone population: Termote, for instance, argues that 'it is clear that we are witnessing an ongoing and significant erosion of the Anglophone group in Quebec' (2002: 24, cited in Magnan 2005: 16–17), whereas Castonguay (2002a) 'predicts a stabilization of the Anglo-Quebec population' (Magnan 2005: 19). Out-migration is compensated for by the substantial numbers of immigrants to Quebec who speak English as a second language mentioned above, with around 48,000 such immigrants during the 1990s (Jedwab 2004: 13). The criterion of first official language spoken, which includes immigrants, in fact depicts an English-speaking community on the increase: the figures in Table 8.1 for 'official language minority', for example, show a slight increase of 1.6 per cent over 1991–2001. In addition, the different criteria used to define the Anglophone population result in different figures for the proportion of Anglophones in Quebec: according to the criterion of mother tongue, English-speaking Quebecers make up 8.3 per cent of the total population; according to home language, the percentage is 11.6 per cent, and for first official language spoken, it rises to 12.9 per cent (Jedwab 2004: 10).

There are also striking differences between English-speaking communities in Montreal and those in Quebec's regions. Anglophones outside Montreal are more likely to have British ancestry than those in Montreal, and as they live in close proximity to the Francophone population, there tends to be 'a greater degree of mixing between the two communities' (Jedwab 2002: 196). This 'mixing' in the regions is reflected in the Census question on the language spoken most often at home, which was adapted in 2001 to include 'persons that "only, mostly, equally or regularly" spoke an official language at home'. If we include all these categories, the figure for those who speak some English at home rises to 1,190,435 (Jedwab 2004: 8). Mixing, which is not only linguistic but can also take the form of increasing exogamy, that is, mariages between Anglophones and non-Anglophones (Jedwab 2002: 193), takes different forms in Montreal and the regions, with integration between Anglophones and Allophones prominent in the former and between Anglophones and Francophones in the latter (Jedwab 2004: 9).

Are, then, Anglophone Quebecers more than a collection of individuals who simply use English in their daily lives? It certainly seems to be the case that the cultural and ethnic heterogeneity that characterises the population does not necessarily give rise to common values or customs. However, English language institutions can create shared commonplaces and a sense of community rootedness among Anglophones. Moreover, the recognition of the past and current contributions of Anglophones to Quebec, of the fundamental French character of Quebec society, and of a sense of belonging to the larger Quebec can serve as community anchors (Legault 1992: 197–8). The focus of the next section is on the sense of belonging among Anglophones to the new, civic Quebec nation, as well as the extent to which this evolving community of English speakers is accepted by the majority Francophone population.

8.2 Are Anglophone Quebecers *des citoyens à part entière* ('fully-fledged citizens')?

A June 2005 poll run by the polling company CROP and commissioned by the Francophone daily *La Presse* surveyed Quebecers on their attitudes towards electing a woman, a homosexual, a Black and an Anglophone as premier. The poll took place at a time when the sovereigntist Parti Québécois was deciding on a new leader following the resignation of Bernard Landry, and among the nine candidates for the position were a woman and an openly gay man. It is worth asking the question why *La Presse* included a Black and an Anglophone candidate on the list of possible premiers, given that no such candidates were standing. Was the paper being earnest, ironic or provocative? Certainly, the addition gives a well-rounded list of minority groups, identifiable as such according to various criteria. Anglophones, then, simply slip into this list of minorities. The editorial line of *La Presse* over the last twenty-five years or so has shown itself to be federalist in its leanings, although it could be argued that there is a range of political opinion among its journalists and columnists. This would lead us in the 'earnest' direction, especially given a 2005 conference presentation by chief editorial writer André Pratte in which he commended a new brand of consensual leadership within the Anglophone community in Quebec and expressed his hopes for a renewed dialogue between Francophones and Anglophones (Pratte 2005a; see also Pratte 2005b). There might well be a genuine desire to know whether pro-Anglophone sentiments are shared by the general public. Still, provocation sells newspapers and on the front page image of that edition, the various minority candidates are represented by young people in jeans and T-shirts – an indication that what is of interest too is the extent to which these minorities are accepted in general within Quebec society, rather than simply as candidates for premier.

The results of the poll, set out in Table 8.2, show that there was significant opposition to an Anglophone premier (35 per cent opposed) compared with other categories (between 4 per cent and 11 per cent). A partial breakdown of results shows that 52 per cent of Francophones were favourable to an Anglophone premier as opposed to 80 per cent of non-Francophones (Lessard 2005), the latter figure corresponding to the general percentage in favour of a woman, Black or homosexual premier. This lack of acceptance among some Francophone respondents of an Anglophone premier is linked to a lack of acceptance of Anglophones in general, as became clear in readers' responses to the poll, a selection of which were published in *La Presse* on 2 July 2005. In particular, *La Presse* had invited its readers to respond to the following questions: 'Are Anglophone Quebecers less *Québécois* than the rest? Might Quebecers be chauvinistic?'

What is striking in these responses, and in the *La Presse* articles and editorials accompanying the poll results and in the days afterwards, is what is 'sayable' in public about Anglophones. In the letters, as well as in contributions to various online forums which discussed the poll results, there is a polarised range of opinions about Anglophones, ranging from outright hostility, through more nuanced and inflected opinions to positions of support and inclusiveness. Overall, the answer to the first of *La Presse*'s questions is, yes, for some Francophones, Anglophone Quebecers are less *Québécois* than the rest. As Pratte concludes in his editorial on 4 July entitled 'Our master, the past', '[t]he poll reveals [...] that in the minds of many Francophones, Anglo-Quebecers are not yet fully-fledged Quebecers' (Pratte 2005c).

To follow up on the discussion of definitions of Quebec's Anglophone community in the previous section, how then do readers of *La Presse* and participants in internet forums understand the term 'Anglophone'? It seems that some Francophones do not entertain the idea that an Anglophone might speak French (see Section 8.3 on bilingualism). It is also the case that others make an unquestioned correspondence between Anglophone and *Anglais* (English), the so-called *méchants* or *maudits Anglais* (the damn English), conquerors of the French colony at the Battle of the Plains of Abraham in 1759, resulting in the colony coming under British rule in 1763 with the Treaty of Paris. The historical dimension to the refusal by some Francophones to accept an Anglophone premier is raised by André Pratte.

Table 8.2 Results of 2005 CROP-*La Presse* opinion poll: Quebecers and the choice of a premier*

Opinion poll question	Favourable (%)	Opposed (%)	Don't know/ Refusal/ Indifferent (%)
Personally, would you be favourable or opposed to a *woman* becoming premier of Quebec?	88	4	8
Personally, would you be favourable or opposed to a *Black* becoming premier of Quebec?	81	9	10
Personally, would you be favourable or opposed to a *homosexual* becoming premier of Quebec?	76	11	13
Personally, would you be favourable or opposed to an *Anglophone* becoming premier of Quebec?	57	35	8

* Based on 1001 telephone interviews over the period 16–27 June 2005; a sample of this size is accurate 19 times out of 20. The margin of error increases when the results relate to sub-groups of the sample.

Source: *La Presse*, 30 June 2005.

He argues that their negative reaction is understandable to a certain extent, 'given our history as a dominated people' (Pratte 2005c): dominated during the Conquest, subjugated to English rule, which nonetheless left French Canadians their language and their religion; dominated during the industrialisation of the nineteenth and twentieth centuries by the Anglophones who ran the businesses and factories in which Francophones toiled; and dominated more recently by Anglophone Canada which has refused to recognise Quebec's status as a distinct, Francophone society (see e.g., Rudin 1985 and Stevenson 1999 and 2004 for a detailed historical background to Anglophone–Francophone relations in Quebec).

A crucial element, too, in the Anglophobia expressed is the question of Quebec sovereignty or independence. Some political commentators see the poll results as reflecting 'the continuation of the constant division between federalists and sovereignists in Quebec' (Lessard 2005). Lessard surmises that most of the 35 per cent opposed to an Anglophone premier would be sovereigntists, supporters of the Parti Québécois. According to political scientist Réjean Pelletier, these sovereigntists 'feel that an Anglophone would inevitably be liberal and federalist. They have difficulty in distinguishing between their convictions on the national question and a candidate for the position of premier' (cited in Lessard 2005). The perception that Anglophones are federalists and not sovereigntists is borne out by a survey conducted by Léger Marketing in May 2005 based on 2,008 respondents, according to which support for sovereignty, understood as including economic and political partnership with the rest of Canada, was 62 per cent among Francophones, 31 per cent among Allophones, and only 13 per cent among Anglophones (Léger Marketing 2005).

It could be argued that the opinion poll run by *La Presse* cannot be taken as representative of attitudes within the population at large, and that the results cannot be used to talk about acceptance of Anglophones in general. However, the poll does indicate that in certain circles of public discourse in Quebec, Anglophones are legitimated targets of prejudice. Two of the *La Presse* journalists who commented on the poll results indeed maintain that Anglophones are not protected by the tenets of political correctness:

> Anglo-Quebecers are not a category of people protected by political correctness. You can express your hostility to Anglophones openly in Quebec, no-one, or very nearly, is going to denounce you in public, you won't have the human rights commission on your back [...]. There exists, in fact, in a marginal trend of Quebec opinion, a very palpable vein of Anglophobia, that is, a visceral hostility. (Boisvert 2005)

> There is no doubt that Quebecers are very open to minorities. But you just have to listen to the rumours, all the way to the corridors of the sovereigntist movement, to observe that reticence on the subject of

homosexuals in particular is quite a lot stronger than what is revealed in the polls. Quite simply, one cannot admit one's reticence, political correctness oblige. Whereas today, speaking ill of the 'English' is acceptable and accepted. (Pratte 2005c)

The Anglophobia remarked on above is not necessarily in evidence in daily interactions, where relations are generally viewed as cordial (see e.g., Larrivée 2003: 176–7). A shift towards more positive attitudes on the part of Francophones towards Anglophones is underlined by a telephone survey conducted by the Missisquoi Institute in 2000 of the views of 1,264 Francophones towards Anglophone Quebecers. The survey concluded that 'there are many signs that point to a reduction in the social distance between francophones and their anglophone neighbours. Bilingualism and social contact with anglophones are increasingly important hallmarks among francophone respondents' (Missisquoi Institute 2001b: 11). Chambers contrasts on the one hand these friendly social relations between the two populations in everyday interactions and on the other public discourse where prejudiced views of the other tend to be reinforced and become entrenched, resulting in rejection on both sides (Chambers 2000: 325). This point is also underlined by Tully who points to both the 'double belonging' of Quebec's Anglophones and the cyclical nature of their sense of belonging to Quebec, according to the political climate:

> Alongside their strong sense of belonging to Canada, the members of the English-speaking minority of Quebec have developed a strong sense of belonging to and identification with Quebec society over the last forty years by virtue of their participation in the public debate over Quebec's future. [...] The moment they are shut out of the discussions, however, as during and after the referendum of 1995, and their demands for recognition as a minority fall on deaf ears, this sense of Quebec-citizen belonging and identification dissipates, many leave the province, and the hard-line demands of those who remain increase, such as partition in the event of secession. (Tully 2001: 25–6)

It may well be the case that English-speaking Quebecers have a growing sense of 'citizen belonging' to Quebec. However, it seems that their attachment to Canada is still significantly stronger, understandable perhaps in that Canada represents a steady backdrop for a sense of national attachment and loyalty – for some out of an historical affiliation to English Canada, for others, especially immigrants, linked to their formal status as Canadian citizens. A 2003 survey undertaken by Statistics Canada on social engagement across the country found that the sense of belonging to Canada amongst Anglophone Quebecers was significantly higher than that of Francophone Quebecers (66.2 per cent of Anglophones describe it as very strong, compared to 29 per cent of Francophones) and was slightly higher than that of Anglophones in the rest of Canada (58.2 per cent) (Statistics Canada 2004).[8] As might be expected, the sense of belonging to Quebec amongst Anglophone Quebecers was clearly not as robust as that amongst Francophone Quebecers (69.6 per cent of the former described it as very strong or strong compared with 84.1 per cent of the latter); however, significantly it was also not as high as the sense of belonging of Anglophones in the rest of Canada to their province (76.7 per cent).

Despite the promotion by the Quebec authorities of a conception of citizenship which places great emphasis on its identity dimension (see Section 2.3), this does not necessarily translate into a sense of allegiance and belonging to a new civic Quebec nation (see Chapter 3). In his analysis of the Larose Commission's report, for instance, Jean-Pierre Proulx argued that

> while it is indisputable that a great number of Anglophone Quebecers participate in French in the life of society and that they consider themselves to be 'citizens of Quebec' [...], it is highly unlikely that the Anglophone community identifies itself with the 'Quebec nation', even when defined as a civic and inclusive nation. (Proulx 2001)

Thus, although Anglophones might not have any objections to participating in Quebec society, they may well feel a certain reticence to being part of the Quebec civic nation. Such reticence has various explanations, according to Seymour (2005: 61):

- some Anglophones believe that they would have to renounce their Canadian identity, or that allegiance to Quebec would have to take precedence over their allegiance to Canada;
- some 'are afraid to subscribe to the Quebec nation because they believe that this runs the risk of favouring the accession of Quebec to sovereignty';
- still others consider that Francophone Quebecers do not in fact perceive their nation as civic but as ethnocultural, and Anglophones do not feel they are included by Francophones;
- others 'believe that their rights are not sufficiently recognised'.

Seymour makes two recommendations for the establishment of a shared national identity: first, Anglophone rights must be recognised – whether formally by the government or informally by the population at large – if they are to feel fully-fledged members of the Quebec nation (Seymour 2005: 61–2). He explicitly defines these established rights as enshrined in English-language institutions such as schools, colleges, universities, hospitals and CLSCs,[9] institutions which Seymour regards as symbolising 'the [Anglophone] community's collective will to live together' (Seymour 2005: 60;

see also Chambers 1999: 255). Second, Anglo-Quebecers must themselves recognise that

> maintaining French as common public language in Quebec is a collective right for the Quebec people as a whole. Every Quebec citizen must accept that the rights and freedoms of individuals do not have absolute primacy over the right of peoples. (Seymour 2005: 63)

The question of the equality of rights between Anglophones and Francophones has been at the centre of the radical discourse of Anglophone advocacy groups such as Alliance Quebec and of Anglophone rights lawyers such as Brent Tyler, one-time president of Alliance Quebec. Quebec's signage laws, for instance, in radical Anglophone discourse, are viewed as an affront to the equality of English and French as Canada's two official languages (Larrivée 2003: 182). However, it must be remembered that English and French are not equal in Quebec:

> The difficulty of parity rests on a simple observation shared not only by a succession of Quebec governments, but also by the federal Supreme Court and by the Canadian diplomatic services in official circles such as UNESCO, for instance. Endowing English with an equal status would endanger the situation of French in Quebec. [...] With the continental pre-eminence of English and its international prestige, parity would only constitute an apparent version of equality, which would inevitably play to the disadvantage of French. (Larrivée 2003: 182–3)

Although the question of absolute parity between English and French is problematic, linguistic rights of Anglophone Quebecers are protected in law, although such protection has often been as a result of Anglophone protests. At the federal level, Anglophone linguistic rights were first enshrined in section 133 of the Constitution Act, 1867, the year Quebec entered the Confederation: the section stipulated that English could be used in parliament and in courts in Canada and Quebec. Replacing the original 1969 Act, the new Official Languages Act (R.S., 1985, c. 31 (4th Supp.)) conformed with the provisions in the Canadian Charter of Rights and Freedoms (*Constitution Act, 1982*, s. 33) and was a landmark in further establishing Anglophone – and Francophone – minority language rights. In particular, the Act underscores how the Government of Canada is committed to '(a) enhancing the vitality of the English and French linguistic minority communities in Canada and supporting and assisting their development; and (b) fostering the full recognition and use of both English and French in Canadian society' (*Official Languages Act*, R.S., 1985, c. 31 (4th Supp.), s. 41).

At a provincial level, Anglophones have been responsible for modifications to the Charter of the French language (see Section 5.1), often through

Anglophone advocacy groups. It was following the victory of the Parti Québécois in 1976 that various Anglophone organisations emerged to defend Anglophone interests, which included introducing bilingual signage, maintaining health and social services in English, gaining increased access to English-language schools, and turning the tide of out-migration by Quebec's Anglophones (Jedwab 2005: 8). Among the more significant of these organisations was Alliance Quebec, established in 1982, which became a conduit for Anglophone concerns. It intended 'to be a province-wide organization of moderate anglophones and [...] it hoped to enter into a constructive dialogue with the government' (Stevenson 1999: 171), which at that time was still the sovereigntist Parti Québécois. Alliance Quebec's first significant victory was the passing in 1983 of Bill 57 (*Act to amend the Charter of the French language*, S.Q. 1983, c. 56), which among other things amended the preamble to the Charter of the French language to include the statement that the 'National Assembly respected the institutions of the English-speaking community of Quebec' (Stevenson 1999: 172). During the period 1982–85, Alliance Quebec was seen as a successful organisation, supported by the Anglophone community and recognised as its legitimate representative by the Parti Québécois government (Stevenson 1999: 175).

Since 1985, however, Alliance Quebec has had a more rocky trajectory as defender of Anglophone rights. In particular, from the mid-1990s, the organisation has to some extent been prey to the personality of its president, becoming radicalised, for instance, under the direction of William Johnson, who was elected president in 1998, and 'advocated partition, official bilingualism and direct action through the courts and in the streets' (Seymour 2005: 52). By March 2005, the organisation was in the headlines because of financial difficulties: the federal body Canadian Heritage, which provides support to minority language groups, cut the organisation's annual grant in half to $200,000 because it had purportedly not fulfulled some of its funding requirements. This has been interpreted by some Anglophones as a deliberate attempt to silence the organisation, which has often been critical of federal responses to Anglophone concerns (e.g., Forester 2005).

On a more positive note, one of the foundation members of Alliance Quebec, John E. Trent, was appointed as a member of the Conseil de la langue française in late 2005. The presence of an Anglophone on the Conseil means that, in theory at least, a member of the Anglophone community is in a key position to put forward community concerns (*Le Devoir*, 12 October 2005). This is just one appointment, but a symbolic one. As Jedwab argues, '[s]eeing members of one's group reflected in government institutions and decision-making bodies is a critical issue for minority groups' (Jedwab 2004: 51). Indeed, there is a political component to the idea of belonging, and it could be argued that the reticence of some Anglophones to belong fully to Quebec is reflected in the fact that they are increasingly absent from political dialogue. However, this absence may well be in part a pragmatic move: André Pratte, for one, maintains that one of the reasons why relations between Anglophones and Francophones are more harmonious is precisely because Anglophones try to avoid raising issues of relevance to them in public, working quietly at a local level in order to avoid confrontation (Pratte 2005c). There are, nonetheless, problems of representation that are less to do with Anglophone reticence than with the seeming reluctance of Quebec institutions to take on Anglophone personnel: Anglophones (and Allophones) are underrepresented in Quebec's public service. For instance, figures for 1996 showed that Anglophones and Allophones, who represented 18 per cent of the population at the time, made up only 3 per cent of public servants (Bourhis and Lepicq 2004: 33).

Considered by some as more representative of the Anglophone community (e.g., Seymour 2005: 53), the QCGN (Quebec Community Groups Network) maintains that Anglophone invisibility is perpetuated by a variety of factors, including the following: (1) a leadership that is not sensitive to the new multicultural realities of English-speaking Quebec; (2) the lack of Anglophone representation in (Francophone) Quebec institutions, which means that the 'Francophone majority community is less aware of and responsive to English-speaking concerns'; (3) the problem of youth out-migration; and (4) a certain complacency among community members, who have other priorities (QCGN 2005: 14–15). This latter factor is a complex bundle of elements, including what some sense as the futility of trying to promote societal change, a withdrawal from the wider community into one's immediate social network, the feeling that one's French will never be good enough to fully participate in the larger society, and an identification with more than one linguistic group. Although the Network, and others, recognises the importance of Anglophone belonging to the wider Quebec society, this remains fragile. Back in 1991, Scowen claimed that 'a shared sense of belonging to a larger community' rested on bilingualism (Scowen 1991: 73). However, for Jedwab, increased *métissage* and rates of bilingualism have not necessarily led to a heightened sense of attachment to Quebec society (Jedwab 2004: 5). Clearly, the issue of bilingualism demands closer scrutiny.

8.3 Bilingualism: no problem(?)

In a society in which two groups speaking different languages have found themselves in cyclical periods of conflict, the other group's language can take on a huge symbolic load, standing for the perceived threat that the other group represents in terms of one's own survival. In Quebec, signs of a growing rapprochement between Francophones and Anglophones are to be found in an increasing awareness of the importance of learning and knowing the other's language. For a number of those Anglophones who stayed in Quebec, this awareness happened early on and has been accompanied by the recognition that staying and being part of an Anglophone minority necessarily means being able to participate in the new civic Quebec, through the acquisition of French. In contrast, for many Francophones, the realisation of the importance of acquiring English has been a more recent phenomenon, and has probably been less about 'knowing the other' than about coming to a realisation that English is no longer the language of the oppressor, but a global language the acquisition of which represents economic good sense for all kinds of reasons (see also Section 5.2).

The relative 'newness' of more or less widespread bilingualism for both groups is reflected in a project undertaken by two Quebec journalists, Jeff Heinrich from Montreal's Anglophone daily *The Gazette* and Matthieu Perreault from Francophone daily *La Presse*. In June 2002, at Heinrich's suggestion, they took part in a journalistic experiment which involved them swapping newspapers, press offices and languages, a first in the Quebec media landscape. Heinrich and Perreault chose to write a series of articles on the topic of bilingualism in Montreal and surrounding areas, personifying the progression of bilingualism in Quebec by writing in their 'other' language. The very fact that both newspapers agreed to the swap tells us something about the state of relations between the two communities. The presumption at each paper must have been that their readership would find it a thrill to read about the 'other', suggesting that Anglophones and Francophones are still to a greater or lesser extent closed-off communities, in spite of knowing each other's language. The two papers do their business in what is a polarised newspaper ecology, in which *The Gazette* as the sole local, paid English-language daily in Montreal is considered to play a major role in representing Anglophone interests (e.g., Jedwab 2005: 16). Although *The Gazette* and *La Presse* are not in open competition, at the time of the publication of these stories in 2002, the Gazette *was* actively seeking readers among the Francophone population in Montreal.[10]

The emphasis of the title of the series was slightly different in each newspaper, but both underscored the topic by using bilingual headlines. *The Gazette* settled on 'Bilingualism? Pas de problème', but *La Presse*, slightly more hesitant about affirming the unproblematic nature of bilingualism to its mainly Francophone readers across the province, shifted the question mark to the end of the phrase: 'Bilingualisme, No Problem?' (Heinrich 2002c). This suggests that Francophones may have residual fears about the domination of English. The series deals with a number of areas related to bilingualism. Of interest here are the following three themes: (1) bilingualism among Anglophones; (2) the Anglophone education system; and (3) biculturalism and mixing between the Francophone and Anglophone communities, which are discussed in turn.

It is well documented that Anglophones are increasingly bilingual in French, and many consider it to be an essential element: 'Not having a working knowledge of French is now very poorly thought of by any self-respecting

Table 8.3 Ability to speak both official languages in Quebec, by mother tongue and Census year

Mother tongue	1971	1991	1996	2001
English	36.7	58.4	61.7	67.2
Neither English nor French	33.1	46.5	46.7	50.5
French	25.7	31.3	33.7	36.9

Sources: 1971–96: Stevenson (1999: 305); 2001: calculated from Canadian Census data.

Anglophone' (Chambers 2000: 324). Table 8.3 illustrates the rising rates of bilingualism among mother-tongue Anglophones between 1971 and 2001.[11]

Within the metropolitan region of Montreal the number of mother-tongue Anglophone bilinguals has followed a similar, if amplified, progression in all groups: among Anglophones the number of bilinguals has risen from 35 per cent in 1971 to 68.6 per cent in 2001; among Allophones from 35 per cent to 52.6 per cent; and among Francophones, from 38 per cent to 50.4 per cent (Bourhis and Lepicq 2004: 37). The latter is the most striking difference between the overall figures in Table 8.3 and those for Montreal, a reflection of the proximity of Francophones in Montreal to English, which is much less the case in the regions. The relatively high number of Anglophones who are bilingual can be explained in part by the acquisition of French by Anglophones since the introduction of the Charter of the French language and 'the exodus of a substantial number of monolingual Anglophones' (Bourhis and Lepicq 2004: 22). The rate of bilingualism among Anglophones varies greatly between Montreal and regional populations, and '[i]n areas like the Eastern Townships, where the predominance of French is overwhelming, it probably approaches the level of bilingualism found among francophones in other provinces' (Stevenson 1999: 305).

The 'audioscape' of bilingualism is changing: in other words, within the bilingual landscape of Quebec, there is a shift in progress from a time when linguistic integration in the 'other' language passed through the ability to 'sound' authentically French or English to one in which an authentic accent is no longer as important:

> [t]he declining importance of accent underlines a fundamental change in the relationship between the two linguistic solitudes: both the Francophone and the Anglophone communities are slowly learning to disentangle language and emotion. For Anglophones, it seems an easier task. (M. Perreault 2002b)

Perreault says that he has 'not yet succeeded in disentangling language and emotions' himself, and he talks of feeling ambivalent and self-consciousness about speaking English (M. Perreault 2002a). He cites various experts who agree that in general 'Francophones have more ambivalence towards English' than Anglophones have towards French, whether this is manifested in lower tolerance of accents than Anglophones, an ambivalence towards teaching English in French schools, or the intergenerational transmission of negative attitudes towards English in the past, which has held up the acquisition of the language by Francophones (M. Perreault 2002b). Nonetheless, such ambivalence is decreasing in the younger generation of Francophones. As for the younger generation of Anglophones, 2001 Census data show that 83.4 per cent of those aged between 15 and 24 with English as their mother tongue consider themselves as bilingual. Moreover, young Anglophones use French more widely than do the older generations in a range of situations in the public domain, typically service encounter situations in shopping centres, small businesses, banks, CLSCs and verbal exchanges in government institutions (Béland 1999, cited in Jedwab 2002: 194–5). However, these young Anglophones still have English-language cultural habits, choosing overwhelmingly to read newspapers, watch television and see films in English.

The new generation of bilingual Anglophones has learned French in a variety of ways:

> Some have grown up in a bilingual context at home; others come from Anglophone families, but have chosen to attend a French-language school; yet others have learned French ... at an English-language school, thanks to French immersion programmes and other models of bilingual education. (Lamarre 2005: 554)

This raises the second aspect of particular relevance discussed by Heinrich and Perreault, namely the teaching of the 'other' language in the education system. In Quebec's 360 English-language schools in the public system, French is obligatory from the first year of primary school to the last year of secondary school (Lamarre 2005: 557). The importance of French was recognised by the Anglophone community in Quebec from the 1960s onwards, and it was in Montreal that French immersion was first introduced, a language acquisition model that was to become widespread in Canada and elsewhere, in which at least 50 per cent of the curriculum is taught in French to students learning French as a second language (see e.g., Genesee 1987: 1). The impetus for immersion came from a small number of 'liberal' parents who viewed proficiency in French as 'normal' for their children, and administrators subsequently came on board (Lamarre 2005: 564–5). Perreault noted the interest in French among Anglophones, epitomized in the continuing popularity of French immersion classes: for example, over 27 per cent of Anglophone students took French immersion classes in 1988 (26,000 out of a total of 95,000 students), rising to just over 39 per cent in 2002 (40,000 out of 102,000 students) (English School Boards Association, cited in M. Perreault 2002b).

Impetus from parents has shifted over the years, with from the 1980s some parents choosing to send their children to a French-language school, especially at primary level, and from the 1990s a greater concern with the acquisition of written as well as spoken skills (Lamarre 2005: 566). The Canadian Census question that seeks information on language proficiency in English and French in fact asks only about oral skills: 'Can this person speak English or French well enough to conduct a conversation?' This is a problematic measure of bilingualism, not only because writing and reading skills are not self-assessed, but also precisely because respondents are asked to self-evaluate their proficiency and the interpretation of 'well enough to conduct a conversation' is bound to vary among individuals (see e.g., Piché 2001; Magnan 2005: 10). The QCGN is aware of the difficulties of limited bilingualism among young English speakers: 'In spite of reports suggesting that English-speaking youth are becoming increasingly bilingual, it is unclear whether they are sufficiently bilingual to advance to higher employment levels (requiring good writing skills in the French language)' (QCGN 2005: 18; see also Magnan 2005: 52). Figures from 2000 on reading and writing proficiency confirm that writing skills lag behind, with only 32 per cent of young Anglophones between 18 and 24 claiming to write French very well, with a slightly higher 44 per cent claiming to read French very well (Missisquoi Institute 2001a: slide 10).[12] There does indeed seem to be a generalised feeling among some bilingual Anglophones that their French, particularly their written language, will never be quite good enough for them to fully participate in Quebec society or be fully accepted by the Francophone majority. This point is echoed by Lamarre, who notes that mastering oral and written skills 'is an issue that affects the future professional success of young Anglophones in Quebec, and also their integration in Quebec society' (Lamarre 2005: 566).[13]

Integration for Anglophones is not only about the well-rounded, functional bilingualism demanded of the workplace; it also consists of being able to participate fully in the cultural life of the larger society, which leads to the third point raised by the Heinrich and Perreault collaboration, the question of biculturalism and mixing. Cultural integration is more or less assured among young people growing up in a bilingual, bicultural home, a group who are becoming more and more numerous:

> Marriages between Anglophones and Francophones have increased to such an extent that the children of such unions, who are bilingual and profoundly bicultural, are in the process of outnumbering the traditional cohort of Anglophone children in Quebec brought up by parents who are both Anglophones. (Jedwab 2002: 195)

Indeed in 2001, the proportion of exogamous couples, that is, those that include an Anglophone and a Francophone or an Allophone, was 55 per cent. Of these, 44 per cent were Anglophone/Francophone couples and 11 per cent

Anglophone/Allophone couples. However, it is not always the case that children of Anglophone/Francophone couples end up bilingual or bicultural. In 2001, the rate of English transmission to children was 86 per cent overall, comprising 99 per cent in endogamous families, dropping to 65 per cent in exogamous families, and to 54 per cent when one parent was Francophone (Government of Canada 2003: 38).

It is clear that there are 'significant intergenerational differences in the ways in which Anglophones establish relations with the Francophone population' (Jedwab 2002: 182), and a number of Anglophones and Francophones still have little contact with the other's culture (M. Perreault 2002c). However, there is a new generation of young Anglophones who are increasingly integrated linguistically – and some even culturally – into Francophone Quebec society. As Heinrich notes, 'anglos feel increasingly part of the same family as francophones' (Heinrich 2002b). What is the impact of this new generation on what it means to be Anglophone? Lazar observes that 'as anglo-Quebecers become more comfortable speaking French, integrating into franco-Quebec culture, intermarrying and assimilating, there are artists charting the way' (Lazar 2001: 60). As an example, he mentions English theatre companies that are increasingly putting on bilingual or French productions, and he asks the question 'Is it still English theatre?' (2001: 70). Similar questions could be asked about the generation resulting from mixing between Anglophones and Francophones: Are they still Anglophones? Are they still Francophones? Jedwab underlines this conundrum from his personal experience: 'There are people like my children who are half Francophone and half Anglophone. Are they majorities or minorities, or do we have to invent another category?' (Jedwab, cited in Official Languages Support Programs Branch 2004: 148; see also Section 1.2). This blurring of boundaries is reflected in the study by Magnan, Gauthier and Côté (2006: xii) in which it was found that 41.3 per cent of the young Anglophones surveyed 'considered themselves as much members of the Francophone community as the Anglophone community'. Just 36.2 per cent considered themselves members of the Anglophone community, and 13.8 per cent members of the Francophone community (Magnan, Gauthier and Côté 2006).

8.4 A continuing rapprochement

In 2004–05, Justice John H. Gomery led the commission of inquiry into the *scandale des commandites* ('the sponsorship scandal'). His brief was to examine the federal government's role in the misuse of millions of dollars of funding in a sponsorship program intended to increase its visibility and Canadian patriotism in Quebec in the years after the 1995 Quebec referendum. Justice Gomery, a Quebec born and bred Anglophone judge whose accent in French straightaway reveals his mother tongue origins, quickly became a star and a hero amongst Francophones in Quebec – among other honours, he was elected 2005 Quebecer of the Year by the Francophone current affairs magazine *L'Actualité* (1 January 2006).[14] Justice Gomery is an interesting figure in evolving Francophone–Anglophone relations in Quebec, given his position as a prominent Anglophone working in the service of Francophone Quebec interests. His 'audible' Anglophone accent was no barrier at all to being taken to Quebec's (Francophone) heart (see e.g., Blue 2005), and illustrates the shifting perceptions of what it means both to 'sound' like a Francophone and to have enough French.

But it is not just being heard that is crucial for relations between Anglophones and Francophones in Quebec, it is also being seen and taking part. Josh Freed, a leading Anglophone satirist and regular column writer at *The Gazette*, in a piece entitled 'I'm just the anglo leader the PQ needs', argues for the visibility of Anglophones in high office and public posts – '[t]hat's the only way Quebecers will ever get to know anglos and stop being frightened of us' (Freed 2005). Stevenson, for his part, considers that collaboration between Anglophones and Francophones, particularly at municipal and local levels on issues other than those connected to language and federalism, is a significant element in the continuing rapprochement between the two communities, on condition that Anglophones have enough French. This kind of participation 'helps to persuade francophones that the anglophone community is a normal, useful, and permanent part of Quebec society, rather than a mysterious alien force or a collection of transients' (Stevenson 1999: 286). In spite of outstanding issues, including declining enrolments in English language schools, the underrepresentation of English-speaking Quebecers in the public service, and a lack of leadership, the Anglophone community is 'no longer beseiged' (Stevenson 2005). It may no longer be powerful, but it can continue for the foreseeable future, given its ties with Anglophone Canada and the US, and if Anglo Quebecers 'fully accept the society in which they live' (Stevenson 2005) – and perhaps if Francophone Quebecers can fully accept Anglophone Quebecers in their turn. As we have seen in this chapter, Anglophones may not yet be fully-fledged Quebecers, but there are some positive signs of increasing rapprochement between the two communities. It is also clear that factors such as increasing bilingualism among younger generations of Anglophones, as well as their growing multiethnic origins, are blurring the demarcation lines between the two groups. The next chapter examines another important minority, the Aboriginal peoples living within Quebec's boundaries, and the extent to which the civic approach is meaningful for them.

9
Linguistic Rights for Aboriginal Nations

> [L]a commission considère comme essentiel de continuer à reconnaître que les nations amérindiennes et inuite ont contribué à façonner l'âme québécoise et que leurs membres sont citoyens du Québec à part entière. Le Québec ne peut prétendre mettre en valeur son américanité sans refonder ses rapports culturels avec les nations autochtones, premiers occupants du territoire. Il ne peut non plus militer en faveur de la diversité culturelle et linguistique mondiale et ne pas valoriser l'intégralité de l'héritage linguistique et culturel présent sur son territoire.
>
> [T]he Commission considers it essential to continue to recognise that the Amerindian and Inuit nations have helped fashion the Quebec soul and that their members are fully-fledged citizens of Quebec. Quebec cannot claim to emphasise its North American character without restructuring its cultural relations with the Aboriginal nations who are the territory's first occupants. Neither can it fight for world cultural and linguistic diversity and not value the totality of the cultural and linguistic heritage that exists on its territory. (Gouvernement du Québec 2001a: 16)

As seen in Chapter 4, Quebec is indeed engaged in the fight for 'world cultural and linguistic diversity' to which the Larose Commission refers above, one that has most recently taken the form of supporting UNESCO's Convention on the Protection and Promotion of the Diversity of Cultural Expressions, with a view to protecting its own (Francophone) cultural heritage in the world order. In reality, the UNESCO Convention is more attuned to the protection of endangered indigenous cultures such those of Quebec's Aboriginal peoples, and the Larose Commission cited above is right to underline the global importance of protecting Quebec's indigenous cultural and linguistic heritage. But while this part of the quotation is unambiguous, the assertion that 'it is essential to continue to recognise that the Amerindian and Inuit nations have helped fashion the Quebec soul and that their members are fully-fledged citizens of Quebec' is less clear. This is not a simple declaration that Aboriginal people are recognised by the state as 'fully-fledged citizens'. The value judgement in 'it is essential', combined with the fact that recognition has to be reiterated or continually affirmed, points to the Commission's awareness of the complications involved in including Aboriginal people within the civic model of citizenship that it is promoting. More precisely, the Commission's position has to be understood in terms of the racism of past neglect and discrimination with regard to Aboriginal people that is the legacy of Quebec and Western settler states in general. The continuing marginalisation and exclusion that still needs to be addressed is alluded to obliquely, it could be argued, in the report's reference to 'restructuring its cultural relations with the Aboriginal nations'.

Where does this understanding leave the basic position of the Larose Commission, and of official government discourse, which affirms a civic republican definition of citizenship that stresses the identity dimension, that is, a sense of belonging to Quebec? There are two elements worth raising in this regard. First, there is a general view that, in order for Aboriginal peoples to feel a sense of civic integration into and belonging to the national political community, some kind of 'differentiated citizenship' is required, 'in which many aboriginal people would have a self-governing aboriginal community as their primary locus of political identity and participation', at the same time as being national citizens (Carens 2000: 177). This differentiated citizenship is at odds with a notion of citizenship that expects a high degree of identification with the state (see Section 1.6). Second, given the last 30 years or so of Aboriginal politics, the twenty-first century nation-state has to make gestures towards the cultural survival of Aboriginal peoples, at the same time as presenting a range of citizenship benefits that do not always favour cultural survival. In other words, the dilemma facing settler states is to offer citizenship without it turning into some form of cultural genocide, by taking the 'privilege' of citizenship to its most monocultural extreme. This complicated scenario is facing quasi nation-state Quebec, which, at the same time as offering its own non-formalised citizenship which takes place through French, must ensure that it recognises, respects and gives equal opportunity to Aboriginal languages and cultures.

The position of the Larose Commission on Aboriginal cultures and languages can be understood generally as one that seeks to 'say the right thing' in respect of Aboriginal peoples. However, within this position are embedded the two conflicting imperatives referred to above – the first which endeavours to promote Quebec as a Francophone civic polity with French as the language of citizen-belonging, and the second which affirms 'fully-fledged' citizenship for Aboriginal peoples and the central importance of Aboriginal languages and cultures. This chapter seeks to examine how well each of these imperatives, as expressed in official rhetoric, squares with what is actually happening on the ground. The chapter opens with a portrait of Aboriginal Quebec, focusing on questions of demography and language, and the linguistic rights of Aboriginal nations as recognised by Quebec. It continues by taking up recent territorial agreements between the Quebec government and Aboriginal nations, examining whether such agreements are shifting the parameters of citizenship for Aboriginal peoples, and the extent to which they give a place to Aboriginal languages. The chapter then focuses on language survival in practice for three Aboriginal peoples in Quebec: the Inuits, the Crees and the Innus.[1]

9.1 Aboriginal nations and linguistic rights in Quebec

The question 'who are they?' was asked about Anglophones in Chapter 8; in the case of Aboriginal peoples, it is a much more complex question to answer, and it is worthwhile responding in some detail. As will be seen below, the blanket term 'Aboriginal peoples' covers considerable ethnic diversity. The picture is further complicated by the fact that both federal and provincial governments have responsibilities towards Aboriginal peoples in Quebec, with the federal government having the main jurisdiction until relatively recently.[2] Terminology is also an issue: the federal government, for example, officially categorises the 'Aboriginal peoples of Canada' into three groupings – Indian, Inuit, and Métis – following the Constitution Act, 1982 (s. 35). The term 'Indian' is not accepted among the peoples so designated, their preferred term being First Nation, which is the expression used in this chapter when referring to this specific grouping.[3] Quebec official discourse, for its part, tends to use other words, in French, such as *Amérindien* ('Amerindian') as in the quotation from the Larose Commission above, or *autochtones* ('Aboriginal people') as in the name of Quebec's Secrétariat aux affaires autochtones (Secretariat for indigenous affairs).

The Quebec government also uses the term 'nation', and its National Assembly officially recognises eleven Aboriginal nations: the Abenaki, Algonquin, Attikamek, Cree, Huron-Wendat, Innu,[4] Inuit, Malecite, Micmac, Mohawk and Naskapi nations. Their members are identified as those Aboriginal people who are 'registered Indians' according to the federal Indian Act (R.S. 1985, c. 1–5), and Crees, Inuits and Naskapis who are registered as 'beneficiaries' of the James Bay and Northern Quebec Agreement (JBNQA) and the Northeastern Quebec Agreement (NEQA).[5] According to these criteria, in 2004/2005 the population of the ten First Nations was 72,770 and the Inuits numbered 10,054 (Secrétariat aux affaires autochtones 2005). The Aboriginal population thus defined makes up just over 1 per cent of Quebec's inhabitants, and represents 10 per cent of Aboriginal people in Canada.

It is possible, too, to assert some kind of Aboriginal affiliation and not necessarily belong officially to one of the eleven nations above as a 'registered Indian' or a 'beneficiary'. The Canadian Census, for example, asks questions about Aboriginal identity and origins, using the same three categories as in the Constitution Act: North American Indian, Inuit and Métis.

Linguistic Rights for Aboriginal Nations 175

According to 2001 Census figures, among the population 15 years and over, a total of 51,125 and 130,170 people in Quebec declared a 'North American Indian' identity and origins respectively; similarly, a total of 9,530 and 10,745 people declared an Inuit identity and origins respectively (figures include both single and multiple responses).

The third main Aboriginal group that the federal government recognises is the Métis, who are descendants of European trappers, traders and fishermen and Indian or Inuit women and who 'established distinct communities, cultures, and ways of life in the west of Canada during the eighteenth and nineteenth centuries' (Carens 2000: 182). They were recognised only very recently as an Aboriginal people at the federal level, in the Constitution Act, 1982. However, the Métis in Quebec, whose origins are similar to those of the western Métis, are not officially recognised as an Aboriginal nation by the provincial government, nor are they recognised by the Métis National Council, an umbrella group of five administrative regions in the western provinces (Manitoba, Alberta, Saskatchewan, Ontario and British Columbia) established in 1983, representing the Métis nation (Métis National Council n.d.; Corbeil 2005; Métis Corporation of Québec 2004). In the 2001 Canadian Census, those who self-identified as Métis in Quebec numbered 15,855, and 21,755 people declared Métis origins (both single and multiple responses).

So, the portrait that is developing is one of a high number of ethnic identifiers, particularly given the small numbers of people involved: the 'who' of our initial question has become linked with 'how many'. Indeed, the current official demographic portrait published annually by Quebec's Secrétariat des affaires autochtones, which gives information on the number of communities within each nation – according to the Secrétariat's figures, there are a total of 57 communities – and the number of people living within and outside the communities, highlights further the complexity of this small population base. Aboriginal nations range in size from the smallest, the Malecite nation, who number 759, to the Innus – 15,385 people – and the Mohawk nation – 16,211 people (see Table 9.1). They also vary in their geographical location and the number of communities, from the 15 Inuit villages of the far north region of Quebec known as Nunavik to the three Mohawk communities near Montreal, to the nine Innu settlements principally on the North Shore of the Saint Lawrence River (see map at Figure 9.1). In addition, just over a quarter (25.4 per cent) live outside an Aboriginal community, in a rural or urban environment.

The languages of these 11 nations belong to one of three linguistic families: Algonquian (the Abenaki, Algonquin, Attikamek, Cree, Innu, Malecite, Micmac and Naskapi languages), Iroquoian (Huron-Wendat and Mohawk) and Eskimo-Aleut (Inuttitut – the variety of Inuktitut spoken in Quebec).[6] However, not all these languages are still spoken in Quebec: four nations no longer have their mother tongue as language of use (see Table 9.1).

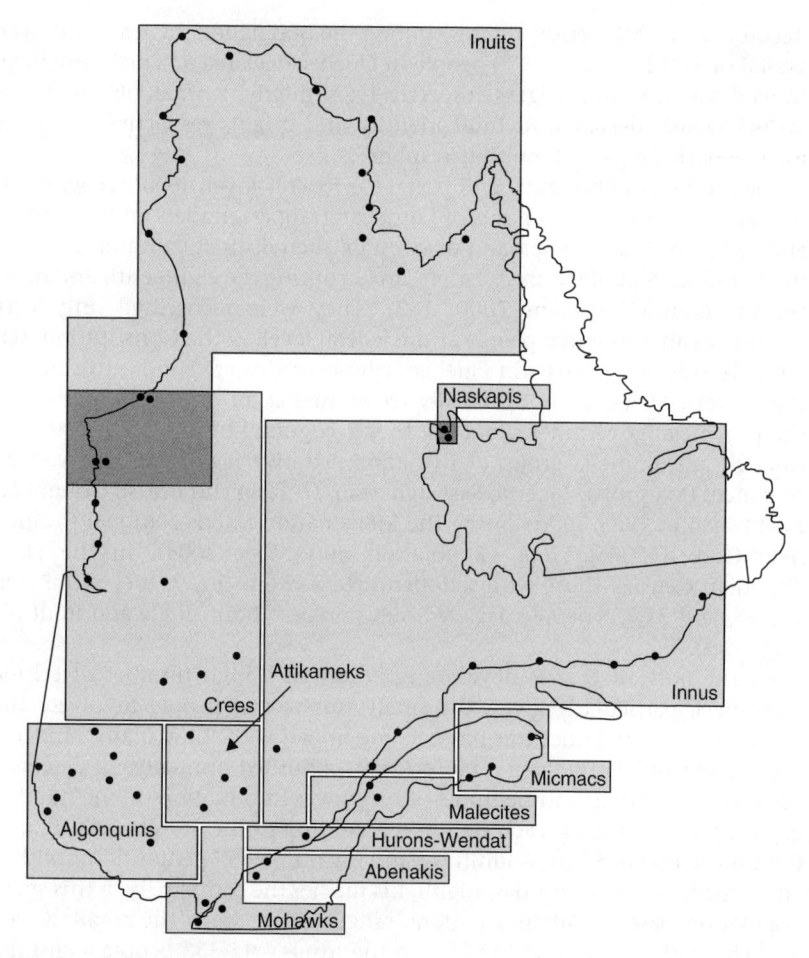

Figure 9.1 Aboriginal nations in Quebec

Source: Adapted from Ministère des Ressources naturelles map (http://www.mrn.gouv.qc.ca/autochtones/images/english/trnation.gif).

For historical reasons, in the various communities, only the Innus and Attikameks have French as sole second language, with Crees, Inuits, Malecites and Naskapis having English as their main second language, and Algonquins and Micmacs using both French and English according to the community. English has considerable social importance as a *lingua franca* for those Aboriginal nations whose populations cross Quebec's borders into English-speaking Canada and the United States, such as the Cree, Mohawk and Inuit nations (Cleary and Dorais 2005: 245). It is also increasingly common for the younger generation to speak both official languages; this is particularly the case, for example, for the Crees and the Inuits.

Table 9.1 Aboriginal nations in Quebec: demolinguistic background*

Nation	Total population	Linguistic family	Language of use	Second language
Abenaki	2,048	Algonquian	French (Abenaki)	Abenaki
Algonquin	9,111	Algonquian	Algonquin	French or English (according to community)
Attikamek	5,868	Algonquian	Attikamek	French
Cree	14,632	Algonquian	Cree	English (and French)
Huron-Wendat	2,988	Iroquoian	French	English
Innu	15,385	Algonquian	Innu	French
Inuit	10,054	Eskimo-Aleut	Inuttitut	English (and French)
Malecite	759	Algonquian	French	English
Micmac	4,865	Algonquian	Micmac	French or English (according to community)
Mohawk	16,211	Iroquoian	English	Mohawk
Naskapi	834	Algonquian	Naskapi	English

* These figures are from the Secrétariat des affaires autochtones and date from December 2004 (First Nations) and January 2005 (Crees, Inuits and Naskapis). The number of communities and their members varies according to the information source (e.g., Indian and Northern Affairs Canada 2003, which does not include the Mohawk community of Akwesasne).

Sources: Beaulieu (2000); Dorais (1996: 56–8); Leclerc (2005c); Secrétariat aux affaires autochtones (2005).

Norris and Jantzen (2002: 23), who classify the Aboriginal languages of Canada according to whether they are viable or endangered, observe that Cree, Inuktitut – both spoken in Quebec – and Ojibway are 'the only viable languages with large population bases' across Canada. However, some consider that even these seemingly robust languages are at risk (e.g., Nunavik Commission 2001 for Inuttitut in Quebec). Some of the smaller languages are also considered viable – in Quebec these include Attikamek, Innu, Micmac and Naskapi – but others, in particular most of those in British Columbia, are endangered or close to disappearing. Figures on language retention and transmission show that Aboriginal languages are in better health in Quebec than in the rest of Canada (e.g., Hamers and Hummel 1998: 385; Norris and Jantzen 2002: 18). For example, in Canada as a whole, only 19.8 per cent of those who declared an Aboriginal identity in the 2001 Census had an Aboriginal language as their mother tongue, whereas in Quebec this percentage was 46.5 per cent (Cleary and Dorais 2005: 235). This distinction is also reflected in the percentage of Aboriginal mother tongue speakers who speak that language at home, either solely or primarily: 60.7 per cent overall in Canada according to the 2001 Census, in contrast to 89.3 per cent in Quebec (Dorais 2003).[7]

Nevertheless, the grave situation of a significant number of Canada's Aboriginal languages has only recently become a matter of concern to the Canadian and Quebec governments (Trudel 1996: 122), coming '[a]fter a century of almost total neglect and following numerous representations from [Aboriginal people]' (Trudel 1996: 110). Given in part that 'Aboriginal affairs' were a federal domain, the Quebec government showed little desire to play any role in Aboriginal issues until the early 1960s, when it became interested in the far north of the province and its resources. It gradually introduced administrative services such as health and schooling and thus French as an administrative language (Trudel 1996: 107). In terms of both provincial and federal language policy, the JBNQA signed with the Crees and the Inuits in 1975 and the NEQA signed with the Naskapis in 1978 (see above) mark a significant shift. These two agreements came about as a result of Cree and Inuit protests against Quebec's proposed hydro-electric project at James Bay, planned without consulting local Aboriginal populations. These agreements, among other things, devolved the administration of education and cultural matters to the Crees, Inuits and Naskapis, resulting in the establishment of the Cree School Board and the Kativik School Board (for the Inuits) in 1978, as well as a special school for the Naskapis.

At around the same time on the political front, significant change was, of course, taking place in Quebec, with the sovereigntist Parti Québécois coming to power in 1976, and in the following year the passing of the Charter of the French language (see Section 5.1). Although primarily about the protection and promotion of French, the Charter also includes provisions for Aboriginal languages. The Charter states that 'the National Assembly of Québec recognises the right of the Amerinds and the Inuits of Québec, the first inhabitants of this land, to preserve and develop their original language and culture' (*Charter*, preamble). It also stipulates that 'nothing *prevents* the use' of Aboriginal languages as languages of instruction for First Nation and Inuit peoples (*Charter*, s. 87, emphasis added), and affirms that Cree, Inuktitut and Naskapi are languages of teaching (*Charter*, s. 88), following the two agreements mentioned above (see Section 9.2).

The Constitution Act, 1982 adopted at the federal level, which resulted in the recognition of Aboriginal rights, was also the source of gains for Aboriginal people in Quebec. During constitutional discussions (which ended with Quebec refusing to sign the new Constitution for reasons of separatist politics), 'the Aboriginal people of Quebec asked the government [of Quebec] to recognise their rights in an official document' (Leclerc 2005c). In response, in 1983 Quebec's cabinet adopted a series of 15 principles 'to guide its relations with the Aboriginal peoples of Quebec', two of which refer explicitly to Aboriginal languages (Trudel 1996: 115). Quebec thus became the first province in Canada to recognise 'Aboriginal peoples as distinct nations who have a right to their own culture, to their own *language*, and to their own customs and traditions, just as they have the right to guide the development of their own identity themselves' (Maurais 2000: 284, emphasis added). In 1985, Quebec's National Assembly enshrined these principles in a resolution on the recognition of Aboriginal rights.

Policy statements specifically on Aboriginal languages have followed, including the 1989 *Maintien et développement des langues autochtones du Québec* (Maintenance and development of the Aboriginal languages of Quebec), which among other things sets out 12 objectives which recognise 'the legitimacy and the value of these languages', and the importance of safeguarding the heritage of Aboriginal language and culture, and establishing language maintenance and development programmes (Trudel 1996: 116). More recently, other statements have appeared, although not in official policy documents. In 1992, for example, the then Conseil de la langue française published a volume dedicated to Aboriginal languages in Quebec (Maurais 1992; published in English as Maurais 1996). As seen above, the Larose Commission underlined the world heritage of Aboriginal languages and cultures, and also put the case for the Quebec government to prioritise and financially support Aboriginal languages (Gouvernement du Québec 2001a: 17). In addition, it recommended that Aboriginal languages be considered as public languages along with English: 'English, Inuktitut and Aboriginal languages all have their own place in public life and spaces, in harmony with the official and common language' (Gouvernement du Québec 2001a: 230), although French retains its predominance as 'official common language'.

In addition, in 2005 the Conseil supérieur de la langue française published an edited volume, *Le français au Québec. Les nouveaux défis*, which proposes 'a new programme of reflection' on the situation of the French language in Quebec at the beginning of the twenty-first century (Rocher 2005: 17). A whole chapter is devoted to Aboriginal languages, proposing an Aboriginal component to Quebec's (French) language legislation in order to concretise the government's good intentions. This echoes the call in 2004 from Innu Ghislain Picard, Regional Chief of the Assembly of First Nations of Quebec and Labrador, for a charter of Aboriginal languages (Doyon 2004). Cleary and Dorais (2005: 247) suggest that the component on Aboriginal languages could include the recognition of 'the languages of the First Peoples as the first languages of Quebec' and as 'official languages in the territories where they are spoken'. They also point out 'the need for the most advanced education possible in Aboriginal languages' and the importance of financial resources, which should be dedicated as a matter of priority 'to education in ancestral languages and to the creation of an institute for Aboriginal languages for linguistic and educational purposes'. Georgeault (2006: 316) also proposes that the use of Aboriginal languages be made official on territories under Aboriginal jurisdiction, and that French have the status of 'official language of codevelopment'.

There are echoes here of current initiatives at the federal level.[8] In June 2005, the federal department Canadian Heritage received the report of the Task Force on Aboriginal Languages and Cultures. In response to its mandate, the Task Force duly recommended how to set up a national Aboriginal Languages and Cultures Council and set out a series of other recommendations, including federal legislation to recognise First Nation, Inuit and Métis languages as 'the First Languages of Canada' and the provision of 'financial resources for their preservation, revitalization, promotion and protection' (TFALC 2005: ix–x). It now finally looks likely, some 18 or so years after it was suggested by the Assembly of First Nations, that a national organisation devoted to Aboriginal languages and cultures will see the light of day. It remains to be seen, however, how the recommendations of the Task Force will be put into practice, and whether any initiatives will be put in place at the provincial level, especially given looming federal involvement.

Nevertheless, Quebec's provisions overall as they stand may be seen to *recognise* basic Aboriginal linguistic rights. In other words, they are an example of Quebec 'saying the right thing'. However, it has been argued that, as for translating words into actions, provisions on Aboriginal languages remain vague, with no clear guidelines as to how they will be put into practice or how they will be funded (Trudel 1996: 122); they are arrived at with little or no consultation with Aboriginal people themselves (Larrivée 2003: 190); and they transfer responsibility for implementation to the community level (Drapeau and Corbeil 1996: 293; see also Sections 9.2 and 9.3).

As has already been indicated, the Cree, Inuttitut and Naskapi languages have benefited from the JBNQA and the NEQA, which have provided locally run educational structures within which to anchor the teaching of Aboriginal languages. Cleary and Dorais (2005) suggest that the issues of language and education be explicitly included in any new territorial agreements. The next section examines the changing status of new treaties and the place they assign to language.

9.2 Aboriginal citizenship, new agreements and language

The position expressed by the Larose Commission concerning the importance of recognising 'fully-fledged' citizenship for Aboriginal peoples needs to be set in the historical context of evolving relations between the Canadian state and Aboriginal peoples, given that this is the overall legacy with which Aboriginal peoples are coming to terms. It is a legacy of exclusion and marginalisation – of non-citizenship, to adopt the terms of the current discussion. From 'a time of *coexistence* between Aboriginal societies and the European colonial powers that fought for control over the land' (Papillon 2005: 7) in which relations have been described as 'nation to nation' (RCAP 1996), there was a shift to 'a period of *colonial domination* that saw the assertion of British, then Canadian, sovereignty on the land' (Papillon 2005: 7). During this period, Aboriginal people became excluded from 'the benefits of citizenship' under the Indian Act adopted in 1876. This loss of political status also involved cultural loss in various ways, including the development of a residential schooling system from the mid-nineteenth century that took Aboriginal children out of family and community life, and within which Aboriginal languages and cultures were generally forbidden (Fettes 1998). The postwar period saw 'the formal *incorporation* [of Aboriginal people] in the citizenship regime', justified in that 'equality of status and the principle of universality [were seen as] the best guarantees against discrimination and exclusion' (Papillon 2005: 8). This is exemplified in the federal government's 1969 White Paper on Indian Policy in which 'becoming full citizens' for Aboriginal peoples was equated with becoming 'citizens like any other' (see Section 2.3). More recently, there has been increasing *recognition* of Aboriginal rights, including the right to self-government, 'with a shift from a language of equal rights to one of differentiated rights'; however, such rights remain limited in interpretation to traditional Aboriginal customs and traditions, and 'must be reconciled with the Canadian constitution and federal and provincial jurisdiction' (Papillon 2005: 10).

The current debate in Canada on the relationship between citizenship and Aboriginal rights is too complex and wide-ranging to go into here (but see Kymlicka 1995; Tully 1995, 2000; Cairns 2000; Carens 2000; Macklem 2001; Kernerman and Resnick 2005; Murphy 2005; among many others). However, one central element to take from this debate is the importance of thinking through how citizenship might not only accommodate but be transformed by the self-autonomy within the Canadian polity that many Aboriginal nations consider to be the key to their cultural and economic survival. How might this accommodation or transformation be playing out in the Quebec context?

Current relations between Aboriginal peoples and the Quebec state have evolved considerably over the last 30 years or so since what was the ground-breaking JBNQA in 1975, thanks in no small part to the continued mobilisation of many Aboriginal individuals and organisations (Salée 2005: 57–8). An important step in this process came from the Quebec government in 1998, in its policy document *Partnership, Development, Achievement* (Gouvernement du Québec 1998b).[9] The introduction to the present chapter pointed out the difficulty that settler states face in offering citizenship – understood here as *recognition, respect* and *equality of opportunity* – to Aboriginal peoples without it resulting in cultural loss or diminishment. This difficulty is subtly acknowledged in *Partnership, Development, Achievement*:

> The approach is one that seeks overall fairness: aboriginal and non-aboriginal people must both have access to the same living conditions, the same general development conditions and a fair share of the collective

wealth, while enabling aboriginal people to maintain and develop their identity. (Gouvernement du Québec 1998b: 8)

It is in the faint ambition of 'overall fairness' that the document acknowledges both that Aboriginal people do not necessarily benefit from the same 'citizenship' conditions as non-Aboriginal people in the province (i.e., *equality of opportunity*), that to benefit from the same opportunities is their right, and also that this right should not impinge on their cultural survival – 'while enabling aboriginal people to maintain and develop their identity' – 'identity' here understood to mean linguistic and cultural specificity (it is, incidentally, surprising that there is no overt discussion of language or cultural issues in the document, given their centrality to Quebec's own nation-building purposes).

Furthermore, there is an emphasis on partnership, and the importance of 'harmonious relations based on *respect* and mutual trust between aboriginal and non-aboriginal people' (Gouvernement du Québec 1998b: 23, emphasis added). The document recognises that the question of self-government is central, and that Quebec itself has an important role to play, given that 'the powers claimed by aboriginal people generally concern provincial jurisdiction' (Gouvernement du Québec 1998b: 12). At the same time, it is made clear that three elements of what could be called Quebec's statehood – 'territorial integrity, sovereignty of the National Assembly, legislative and regulatory effectivity' – are 'fundamental reference points' (Gouvernement du Québec 1998b: 12). In other words, they form the bedrock of future agreements, and are non-negotiable.

The main preoccupation of this chapter is to examine the tension between Quebec's focus on citizenship through French and its affirmation of the central importance of Aboriginal languages and cultures. This tension has its parallels in the scholarly perception of current Aboriginal–state relations in Quebec, epitomised here by Salée (e.g., 2005) who argues that in spite of new treaties focusing on partnership and openness, the structure of authority remains firmly within the hands of the Quebec state; and Papillon (e.g., 2005) who, views current developments in Aboriginal–state relations in Quebec as a promising sign of movement towards new political configurations.

In essence, Papillon views Aboriginal peoples as 'embedded nations', that is, not 'nations' in the traditional sense of the term (see Section 1.4), given the 'profoundly relational and interdependent nature' of their relationship with the state (Papillon 2005: 18). He points to a new stage in Aboriginal–state relations, arguing that the existence of a parallel regime of citizenship in Quebec – considered as such through Quebec's distinct social policy, 'strong symbols and identity markers' (Papillon 2005: 6), and distinct responsibilities in certain domains such as immigration, among other elements – creates distinct opportunities for Aboriginal peoples in the province to shape their own citizenship regimes:

> the particular context in Quebec, where in effect two citizenship regimes are already competing for legitimacy – the pan-Canadian and Quebec regimes – has opened opportunities for Aboriginal peoples to significantly alter their relation to both the Canadian and Quebec states and develop what in many ways can be defined as their own citizenship regime, not completely separated [from] nor simply congruent with Canada's. (Papillon 2005: 3)

The tension between Canada's and Quebec's citizenship regimes is comparable to the tension between English and French in Quebec, which has created the conditions for other languages – those of immigrants and Aboriginal peoples – to persist (see Sections 7.1 and 9.1). It is precisely the existence in Quebec of 'a discursive environment where assumptions about political membership, identities and state sovereignty are constantly challenged and debated' (Papillon 2005: 7) that has allowed Aboriginal nationalism to challenge 'the orthodoxy of state sovereignty', at both the Canadian and Quebec levels. Quebec can in effect be seen as an example of the 'rescaling' of citizenship regimes, through its actions both beyond and below the provincial level (Papillon 2005: 5; see also Chapter 4). This is equally the case for Aboriginal peoples, who have created transnational alliances and networks to promote their interests, as well as more locally based arrangements (Papillon 2005: 5–6). To illustrate his point, Papillon uses the *Paix des braves* signed between the then Grand Chief of the Crees Ted Moses and Quebec Premier Bernard Landry in February 2002. He argues that this agreement marks a new dynamic in Quebec–Cree relations in that it represents 'a reconfiguration of power relations', with Quebec recognising 'the existence of the Cree nation and the necessity to take it seriously as a political partner' (Papillon 2005: 15). With the *Paix des braves*, the Crees also agreed to put an end to an extended period of contestation, although not all members of the Cree nation supported the agreement (see e.g., Richer 2005).

As far as Salée is concerned, he argues that, although the 1998 Quebec policy 'demonstrates a real desire for forgiveness and atonement' (reported in Tremblay 2004), and that the Quebec state is indeed offering citizenship benefits, for example in its support of 'socio-economic development', there is nonetheless a fundamental sense in which Aboriginal people are not treated as equals in the process:[10]

> [E]ven if the latest incarnation of the Québec state policy towards Indigenous peoples can appear to be imbued with open-mindedness, generosity, and a genuine desire to support their socio-economic development,

many within Indigenous communities see it as problematic. They deplore the fact that the policy remains within the confines of a structure of authority and administrative jurisdiction over which Indigenous peoples have no control and that rests within the exclusive domain of the Québec state. They point out that the policy was not devised in collaboration or in consultation with Indigenous peoples and that it did not receive the benefit of a negotiated agreement between equals. (Salée 2004: 107)

For Salée and others, the solution to the persistence of marginalisation and exclusion of Aboriginal peoples can be none other than to '*autochtoniser l'État*' ('indigenise the state') (Green 2004: 27; see also Green 2005). In other words, they argue for the transformation of current state structures and policies by ensuring that 'every fibre of the Aboriginal imaginary is directly involved in the dynamics of such a transformation' (Green 2004: 28, cited in Salée 2005: 71). Salée maintains that the future health of democracy in Quebec and Canada is at stake and 'largely depends on the nature of the social and institutional space that will be arranged for Aboriginal peoples [...] in agreement with them and according to procedures which they will have helped to establish' (Salée 2005: 72). The challenge is precisely not to construct the best way to include Aboriginal people within the 'national space' but rather 'to ensure that they define by themselves, and for themselves, the conditions of this inclusion – indeed, if they so wish, of their non-inclusion – and to accept the terms thereof' (Salée 2005: 69).

But what of language in the 'reconfiguration of power relations' or the 'indigenisation of the state'? In the latter, although language is not explicitly mentioned, it is implicit in the phrase 'every fibre of the Aboriginal imaginary', the imaginary as defined and shaped by language. Indeed, there are echoes of Tully's (1995) formulation of an intercultural approach to the 'politics of cultural recognition', in which the dominant group's imposition of 'European-derived traditions and institutions' (Tully 1995: 54) is transposed into a dialogue in which listening to others involves 'listening not only to what they say, but also to the way or *language* in which it is said' (Tully 1995: 57, emphasis added). Within Tully's model, 'the mutual recognition of cultures' creates a sense of belonging to the association precisely because one has a *voice* in the shaping of that association and because one's own culture is publicly affirmed as an intrinsic part of the whole (Tully 1995: 197–8).

Language is not an element taken into account in Papillon's understanding of the emergence of Aboriginal citizenship regimes. It is absent, too, in the text of the *Paix des braves* and in the similarly structured *Sanarrutik* agreement between the Quebec government and the Inuits signed in April 2002. Both of these agreements focus on the increasing autonomy that each Aboriginal people will gain via economic development of local resources. This lack of focus on language is not surprising in a sense, as Aboriginal concerns about territorial rights and self-governance have tended to take precedence over language (e.g., Trudel 1996). Linguistic and cultural survival, however, can be predicated on greater Aboriginal autonomy through economic development and partnership with the Quebec state. The *Sanarrutik* agreement, for example, has been beneficial for language through a flow of funding to the Avataq Cultural Institute (Makivik Corporation 2005: 5), enabling it to operate more effectively. As a non-profit organisation outside the JBNQA, the Institute was set up in 1980 'in response to concerns from Nunavik elders that Inuktitut and Inuit culture were in jeopardy' (Makivik Corporation 2005: 3) and is currently involved in various language development and promotion activities including language workshops and an Inuttitut terminology database (Makivik Corporation 2005: 5–6). The JBNQA, too, has had a considerable impact on the maintenance of Cree and Inuttitut, through the creation of the Cree School Board and the Kativik School Board, as has been noted.[11]

The most recent land claim development in Quebec is the Agreement-in-principle signed in March 2004 between four Innu communities – the Conseil Tribal Mamuitun (Betsiamites, Essipit and Mashteuiatsh) and Nutashkuan – and the federal and provincial governments (see http://www.ainc-inac.gc.ca/pr/agr/mamu/index_e.html). Land claim negotiations between the Innus and the Quebec and Canadian governments have been ongoing since 1980, and currently negotiations are at a less advanced stage with other Innu communities. The Agreement-in-principle is considered part of a new generation of treaties between the state and Aboriginal peoples in that, unlike previous agreements, it does not extinguish Aboriginal rights (Grammond 2005). Section 3.3.9 of the Agreement states that '[t]he culture of the Innus as well as their language, Innu Aimun, shall be protected by the Treaty. The Treaty shall facilitate the adoption of protection and promotion measures for the Innu culture and Innu Aimun'; Section 3.5.1 states that the 'Treaty shall be drafted in the Innu, French and English languages'. Finally, it is noted in Section 8.4.4.1 that Innu laws have precedence in '[t]he protection and diffusion of the Innu language, heritage, culture, identity and […] in the traditional lifestyle of the Innus', among other areas. The Agreement-in-principle thus sets up the future elaboration of specific language measures.

In spite of the complex relationship between 'linguistic and political self-determination', Fettes (1998: 122) observes that 'many of the Aboriginal groups who have gained the greatest control over their own lives have also gone the furthest in developing language policies to suit their needs'. In this context, it is instructive to examine the current moves by the Inuits towards greater overall autonomy with the proposed establishment of a Nunavik government, a further innovation in Aboriginal–state relations in Quebec and in Canada. An explicit language policy is a central element within proposed governance structures. In its 2001 report *Mapping the Road Toward a Government for Nunavik*, the Nunavik Commission (2001) presents what could be called a 'language policy roadmap' for other Aboriginal nations by underlining the importance of including strong language support and protection provisions in self-government policy documents. In this roadmap, the official languages of Nunavik would be Inuttitut, French and English. However, Inuttitut would be 'the predominant language of work in the operation of the Nunavik institutions' (Nunavik Commission 2001: ii).[12]

In its recommendation on language and culture, the Commission proposes, among other elements, that Inuit language and culture come directly under the jurisdiction of the proposed Nunavik Assembly, with the Avataq Cultural Institute playing a major role, and that a 'Charter of the Inuit language and culture' be drawn up (Nunavik Commission 2001: 31). The language policy model that the Nunavik Commission is proposing thus has elements in common with Quebec's own, including a language Charter and the role of Inuttitut as a 'public' language. This Charter will have similar aims to the Charter of the French language in that they both seek to keep a dominant language or languages at bay – for Quebec it is English, for Nunavik, it is both English and French.[13]

The Nunavik Commission stresses the fact that Inuttitut is 'still the predominant and strongest language in all Nunavik communities' (Nunavik Commission 2001: 30). However, it takes on board the assessment of the Kativik School Board (KSB) that the status of Inuttitut 'is under threat from English, especially among the youngest group of Inuit where the fluency in English (or French) seems to make gains at the expense of ability in Inuttitut' (KSB cited in Nunavik Commission 2001: 30), and that language erosion has begun, with interference particularly from English. Indeed, there is evidence of a change of position within the Commission as it went through the process of carrying out its mandate: it became increasingly aware of the need to protect and promote Inuit language and culture, the most often heard concerns at the Commission's public hearings:

> In carrying out its mandate and in developing its recommendations, the future of the Inuit language and culture *has become* a major consideration for the Commission, and *it has come to accept, with conviction*, that Inuttitut is indeed *fighting for its very survival*. (Nunavik Commission 2001: 30, emphasis added)

The following section examines language survival in practice, with particular focus on the Inuit, Cree and Innu nations.

9.3 Language survival in practice

Previous sections of this chapter have discussed the provisions for Aboriginal languages – or lack of them – in policy documents, both those developed by the Quebec state and those by Aboriginal nations at the level of treaty making and self-government policy. The current state of policy provides a framework within which to situate actual language practices for three Aboriginal peoples – the Inuits, the Crees and the Innus – who are considered to have viable languages. The great majority of Inuits and Crees live in geographically remote communities and share their language with Aboriginal populations outside Quebec. Both have English as the second language, although French is gaining ground, and, as seen in Section 9.2, they have benefited from thirty years or so of treaty making. The Innus are based mainly in Quebec, with just under three quarters of the population living in Innu communities, in a region that they share to a greater extent with non-Aboriginal populations (see map at Figure 9.1). Their language is one of the smaller ones to be considered viable, they have French as their second language,[14] and they have yet to finalise a land claims treaty (see Section 9.2). This section concentrates on language in education, an area crucial for language maintenance and promotion, and examines the initiatives taken by each nation.

Education in Canada in the past was an area which explicitly excluded Aboriginal languages and cultures. This exclusion has been referred to as a policy of 'linguicide' (Fettes 1998):

> For several generations, beginning in the mid-19th century, Aboriginal languages were systematically excluded from Canadian schools and public life; especial havoc was wreaked by Aboriginal boarding schools, where children were separated from their families for 6 months or more per year and forced to use English even among themselves [...]. In the 1960s, this policy of linguicide was abandoned for the practice of neglect, leaving children, parents and grandparents to cope as best they could with psychological scars, linguistic handicaps, and an institutional framework built on French and English. The result has been continued language loss in most communities, but also the slow development of effective language programs, largely through trial and error. (Fettes 1998: 118–19)

The residential schooling system was in place over a much longer period in Canada than in Quebec. For this and other reasons, language and culture loss was greater outside the province (Sarrasin 1998: 109). Nevertheless, the legacy in Quebec of the marginalisation and exclusion of Aboriginal languages and cultures is evident in the great variation both between Aboriginal nations in terms of the extent to which the mother tongue has been maintained, if at all (see Section 9.1), and within nations in relation to the level of mother tongue use in the various communities.

Since the 1970s, the federal government has progressively devolved its responsibilities for First Nation education to the band councils in First Nation communities across the country. This sweeping change took place in response to the 1972 declaration of the Indian Brotherhood of Canada (later to become the Assembly of First Nations) in its policy document *Indian*

Control of Indian Education (Trudel 1996: 105). By 1998, the process of devolving education to First Nation communities was complete, with a school run by each community, funded by the federal government (Hudon, Dorman and Moore 2004: 5–6), the exceptions to this process of course being the Cree, Inuit and Naskapi nations. Aboriginal nations in Quebec have thus established their own ancestral language programmes (Cleary and Dorais 2005: 240).[15] As was noted in Section 9.1, the Charter of the French language allows all Aboriginal communities to use their mother tongue as a language of instruction (*Charter*, s. 87). Many programmes concentrate on teaching in the Aboriginal language during the first years of schooling from kindergarten, in some cases up to the 2nd, 3rd or 4th year of primary school (Cleary and Dorais 2005: 240). This follows a generally accepted model for the teaching of minority languages, which has demonstrated that those children from a minority-language background whose early schooling is in their first language do better at acquiring the second, dominant language – as well as their mother tongue – than if they began straight away in second language immersion (e.g., Cummins 1991; see also UNESCO 1968).

In Quebec, the Ministère de l'Éducation provides the overall school curriculum framework which is used in Aboriginal community schools, although the JBNQA has given the Crees and the Inuits a substantial amount of freedom. As Burnaby and MacKenzie (2001: 198) note for the Crees, '[t]he new Cree School Board was given considerable latitude [...] to create a curriculum based on local language and cultural interests within the basic curriculum framework for Québec schools.' The Crees themselves took the basic decision in 1975 to 'work within established mainstream frameworks for education' as they believed 'in the importance of a formal, Western-style education for their children' (Burnaby and MacKenzie 2001: 201).[16]

The complexities of Aboriginal language survival and promotion within Aboriginal communities are underlined by Burnaby and MacKenzie (2001), who take as a case study the Cree Language of Instruction Program in Quebec.[17] They argue that because of the complexities of each language situation, it is not possible to provide a straightforward model of language maintenance that fits all Aboriginal languages. However, they isolate three main factors that can contribute to programme success:

> [I]t [...] seems worth speculating that the success of Aboriginal language medium of instruction programmes is at least in part related to three factors: the human resources in the community which can be rallied in direct support of the programme; the extent of relevant external support (e.g. specialised teacher training, orthography development, curriculum expertise); as well as the level of local control over the administration of education. (Burnaby and MacKenzie 2001: 204)

These elements have come together for Cree and Inuttitut. At present, Inuttitut is the sole language of instruction from kindergarten to grade 2 of primary school. In grade 3, students choose between the English stream or the French stream of instruction, and classes in that year consist of 50 per cent of teaching in Inuttitut, and 50 per cent in English or French (Makivik Corporation 2004: 12). In subsequent years, Inuttitut is taught as a subject of instruction. Provisions for Cree language instruction are similar. Cree is the main language of instruction up to and including grade 3 in the majority of communities, depending on staffing, with English Tribal or French 'subjects of instruction and the medium of one or two subjects (such as art and physical education) starting in grade two' (Burnaby and MacKenzie 2001: 191), and a focus on learning the Cree writing system in syllabics. In grade 4, the main language of instruction becomes either English or French, with Cree as a subject of instruction throughout primary and secondary schooling. Mandatory instruction in Inuttitut or Cree at school is combined with other initiatives. An example is the Cree Literacy Program, developed by the Cree School Board in conjunction with the Office of First Nation and Inuit Education at McGill University, for school instructors and officials within the Cree community, with the end goal of a Certificate in Aboriginal (Cree) Literacy Education (Canadian Heritage 2003). In a survey undertaken by the federal government's Aboriginal Languages Initiative, which provided a small amount of funding to the Literacy Program, respondents said that 'they have witnessed a remarkable change in attitude in their own Cree communities about their language', and '[w]here once they felt the language dying, [...] they felt much more confident of its survival today' (Canadian Heritage 2003).

Nevertheless, for both Inuits and Crees, the signing of agreements with the Quebec government, as well as providing opportunities for their languages – unintentionally, as Burnaby and MacKenzie (2001: 207) put it – has also complicated the linguistic landscape, which is increasingly marked by the prestige of French as it becomes a language of employment opportunities. In Nunavik, for instance, 'the new political and economic reality [...] is situated within the larger French-speaking Quebec State, and [...] there are forms of French dominance in government agencies and French symbolic domination in institutional practices' (Patrick 2003: 174). This French dominance is reflected in the fact that currently the number of Inuit children enrolled in the French primary school stream is greater than those enrolled in the English stream (Makivik Corporation 2004: 12–13). For the Crees, too, 'the value of French, in addition to English, as a language of economic activity and government, has been rising' (Burnaby, MacKenzie and Bobbish Salt 1999: 1). It is clear that, despite enjoying favourable conditions relative to other Aboriginal languages in Quebec, both Inuttitut and Cree are in serious competition with English and increasingly with French.

For the Innu language, the situation is slightly different. At the level of treaty making, as seen earlier, language does not figure greatly in the current Agreement-in-principle, although there are provisions to create language 'protection and promotion measures'. The Conseil Tribal Mamuitun recognises both the importance of language and the similarity of the Innus' fight to that of Quebec's: 'just like the Innus, French Canadians too have become aware throughout their history of the importance of defending their rights, their culture and their *language*, and of taking their destiny back into their own hands. Our fight is the same' (Conseil Tribal Mamuitun 2004, emphasis added). Crucially, the Innus have not benefited from the treaty framework over the past two or three decades in the way that the Inuits and the Crees have been able to, particularly with the creation of autonomous school boards.[18] As Burnaby and MacKenzie (2001: 204) note, 'the amount of local control of education in Aboriginal communities has increased a great deal over the past decade or so, but [...] many of the communities are very small and not always affiliated in significant ways (as through a school board or otherwise) with other communities with which they can share resources'.

In terms of the two other areas that Burnaby and Mackenzie highlight – external support and the community's human resources – Innu communities are faring well on several fronts. First, the dynamism and commitment of Innu educators, linguists and others, combined with external support from linguists such as Drapeau (1985), Mailhot (1985, 1996, 1999 [1997]) and Baraby (1999, 2002), has contributed to the successful standardisation of the written language. Standardisation of Innu has followed a similar path to that of many other indigenous languages, including Inuttitut and Cree, which are traditionally oral languages, with a standard orthography a crucial element in encouraging literacy in the language through the schooling system, and thus the maintenance of the language itself (Drapeau 1996: 152). There are two main dialects of Innu, with some sub-dialects, and after 25 years of negotiation and dialogue on how to represent various morphological, phonological and lexical differences between the dialects, 'an officially recognized common spelling system for the Innu language' came into existence in 1997 (Baraby 2002: 198). This has been accompanied by the publication of dictionaries (e.g., Drapeau 1994b) and the imminent publication of a comprehensive Innu grammar (Baraby and Drapeau, forthcoming).

An important element of local community support and human resources is the Institut culturel et éducatif montagnais (ICEM, *Innu-aitun mak innu-tshishkutamatun*, Montagnais Institute for Culture and Education), set up in its initial incarnation in 1978 and based at Sept-Îles. The Institute has been closely involved in the development and implementation of the standard spelling system, sponsoring workshops on the question in 1989 and again in 1997, with the participation of linguists and teachers and resource people from various Innu communities (Mailhot 1999 [1997]). The ICEM has responsibility for ensuring that all publications in Innu, both new and old, follow the standardised spelling system.[19] The Institute receives the majority of its funding from the federal Department of Indian Affairs and Northern Canada, as part of the Education/Cultural Centres Program, and provides services for eight of the nine Innu communities in Quebec. Its four principal dossiers are general education and special education, which take up the major part of its budget and activities, and the Innu language and culture (ICEM n.d.).

ICEM activities to promote and develop the Innu language, which necessarily touch on the educational domain, include (1) the development and publication of teaching materials for the kindergarten and primary levels; (2) the publication of literary works in Innu; (3) a specialised linguistic consultation service on the new spelling system and on translations from French to Innu; and (4) the promotion of the language and its use, including teacher training activities (ICEM n.d.). Within Innu schools generally, the language of instruction is Innu during the two-year kindergarten programme.[20] The kindergarten programme is not compulsory, but the great majority of eligible children attend. Most Innu children then attend the community primary school(s), but they are also able to attend local provincially administered schools, and a small minority do this. At the community primary schools, classes are taught in French, following the programme laid out by Quebec's Ministry of Education, and few if any allowances are made for students who have French as a second language. During primary schooling within Innu communities, Innu is offered as a subject of instruction, usually on a weekly basis, and this is generally continued into secondary school, although this varies from school to school.[21] The Innu language, then, is more restricted in its use within the education system than Inuttitut and Cree.

The concern within the Inuit and Cree communities about erosion of their mother tongue by the dominant majority language(s) has already been signalled. This is equally a concern within the Innu community. Bilingualism – and for a minority trilingualism – is typical of all Aboriginal nations in Quebec 'in which the Aboriginal language is still transmitted within the family' (Drapeau and Corbeil 1996: 290) and represents a classic diglossic relationship:

> Wherever the ancestral language is still spoken, a state of diglossia between the vernacular (Aboriginal) language and the majority language has gradually come into being while the number of unilinguals has decreased with the passing of generations. This diglossia is characterised by the use of the majority language in the domain of education, in white collar work, and almost anywhere where writing is used. The vernacular is used in private life and in social relations in the community, in manual or unskilled labour, and, recently and in a limited way, in teaching. (Drapeau and Corbeil 1996: 290)

The balance between the languages is a delicate one, and 'generalized bilingualism presents the danger of bringing about rapid assimilation to the majority language among ethnolinguistic minorities' (Drapeau and Corbeil 1996: 290; see also Fishman 1991, 2001, Nettle and Romaine 2000, among others, on endangered languages).

This delicate balance is evident among Innu speakers, in particular among the current generation of parents whose role in the transmission of Innu is complicated by the widespread use of code-switching, that is, switching between Innu and French, either between sentences or between clauses within a sentence – code-switching proper – or within the sentence itself, known as code-mixing (Drapeau 1995: 159). Drapeau, who undertook research in the Betsiamites community in the early 1990s, describes the community as one in which Innu was the regular language used within the family and the 'normal language of daily interactions in the village' (Drapeau 1995: 158). French had fairly restricted use, mainly within the school environment and in the media. It was clear that Innu was being transmitted normally to the next generation of young children, with no language shift underway (Drapeau 1994a: 364).

However, when Drapeau tested the lexical abilities of preschool children, who in principle would have been exposed to little or no French, it was clear that they were using a mixed Innu-French code (Drapeau 1995: 162). The explanation was that the language used by parents with their children was the same mixed code. Drapeau describes a 'proficiency continuum' in which bilingual adults were proficient in Innu (which they used in formal speech situations), the mixed code and French, and young people were inclined to be proficient in the mixed code and French only (Drapeau 1995: 160,162). Such code-mixing has been reported more recently in Innu communities to the east which have long been considered as more protected from French language influence, such as Unaman-shipu (Groupe de travail, école Olamen 2000), and in other Aboriginal languages such as Inuktitut (Dorais and Collis 1987, reported in Drapeau and Corbeil 1996: 306). Drapeau goes as far as to argue that 'language mixing might actually be an inevitable component of language maintenance in Fourth World settings' (Drapeau 1995: 162).

9.4 Shared interests, shared concerns

In March 2002, Ted Moses, then Grand Chief of the Crees, made a presentation to a symposium on 'Quebec society and Aboriginal people' held in Quebec City (Moses 2002). His topic was the recently concluded *Paix des braves*, and he pointed out that the shared sensitivities of the Crees and Quebec create 'enormous potential for us to work together'. To illustrate such shared sensitivities he took the example of language. It is worthwhile quoting Moses in some detail:

> As a Cree, I understand in a very deep and personal way why Québec takes such insistent pride in the application and promotion of the French language. The language of the Cree nation is Cree. I speak to my mother in Cree. Our people speak Cree. Cree is the first language in our schools. But as everyone here knows, we were punished as children for speaking in our own language when we went to school.
>
> We had to fight for the recognition of our language – one of the basic attributes of our Cree nationhood – and one of the essential attributes of

nationhood in general. We enshrined our right to use Cree in the James Bay and Northern Québec Agreement, and this is reflected in Québec legislation concerning the protection of the French language.

Language is one of our sensitivities, and we guard it jealously, as an attribute of our nationhood, as a right, and as a part of our culture and our identity as a people.

Language has the potential to divide us – to create a gulf between the Crees and Québec society – and perhaps it has done this in the past. I would argue, however, that our common experience of our need to maintain the viability of our languages creates a common ground and field for cooperation between the Crees and Québec society. (Moses 2002)

Moses' speech underscores the difficulty in resolving the inherent tension between promoting French on the one hand and Aboriginal languages on the other. As seen above, it is clear that even those Aboriginal languages in Quebec that are considered the strongest and the most viable such as Inuttitut and Cree, and that have the best treaty protection, are under considerable threat from the dominant French and English languages. The 'common ground and field for cooperation' of language politics that Moses identifies is thus surely worth building on to ensure the survival not only of French but just as importantly the Aboriginal languages spoken in Quebec.

A fundamental question is how to move away from negative perceptions within the Aboriginal population of French (and English). At worst, Quebec's insistence on French as the civic language is viewed as 'the utmost ethnocentric manifestation of Québec nationalism, which [...] is seen as being focused on the preservation of the French language and culture over all others' (Salée 2004: 109). In this view, such privileging of French leaves little space for Aboriginal languages, precisely tipping the balance towards cultural diminishment or loss. At best, the role of French as the 'common public language', as the language of belonging to the Quebec civic nation, might be rather meaningless for Aboriginal communities whose own languages and cultures are central to their identity affirmation (Cleary and Dorais 2005: 245).

In the end, the citizenship framework that Quebec favours remains problematic for many Aboriginal people. The framework, which has been designed with mostly immigrants, and to a lesser extent Anglophones, in mind, needs to be transformed, in concertation with Aboriginal nations. Whether the future of Aboriginal and Quebec state relations lies in Papillon's 'reconfiguration of power relations' or in Salée and Green's 'indigenisation of the state', or another model, it is clear that some kind of differentiated citizenship is the best hope for the future strength of at least some Aboriginal languages, complemented by greater community involvement. In addition, the Quebec state could pass language legislation to protect and promote Aboriginal languages, supported by the requisite funding, as well as grant Aboriginal languages and French equal status on lands under Aboriginal jurisdiction.

10
Conclusion

In this first decade of the twenty-first century, Quebec faces the challenges of a globalising world in which boundary crossings and transnational movements of goods and people are increasingly the norm, and where English is the global *lingua franca*. This book has sought to explore the relationship between language, citizenship and identity in Quebec in such a global context. Three questions were raised in the Introduction that have guided this exploration, corresponding to the three parts of the book:

- In its effort to maintain a distinct national identity, how is Quebec dealing with the new realities of ethnic diversity and globalisation?
- What is Quebec doing to forge a sense of common identity through language?
- To what extent is official policy concerning these issues compatible with the diverse experiences of minorities in Quebec?

In response to the first question, Chapters 2, 3 and 4 examined the ways in which Quebec is responding both to increasing ethnic diversity within its borders and to the possibilities and challenges of globalisation. Chapter 2 focused on the evolution of a distinctive, collective identity in Quebec, and the province's recent attempts to construct a common identity in inclusive, civic and territorial terms in order to provide an anchor point and a locus of belonging for new Quebecers, as well as to unite Quebecers of all ethnic origins. Quebec's model of intercultural citizenship provides a third way between a civic republican notion of citizenship and the liberal model espoused by Canada together with its policy of multiculturalism. This third way privileges a common identity constructed through dialogue between groups – a dialogue that takes place in French, at the same time as accommodating and respecting pluralism. Faced with increasing immigration, Quebec's dilemma, as expressed in both Chapters 2 and 3, has been to reconcile its collective ethnic past with a collective civic present and future. Chapter 3 specifically addressed the theoretical debate on the model of nation suitable for contemporary Quebec. It was argued that the most appropriate models represent a balance between the recognition of the pluralism of present-day Quebec on the one hand and of the continuity of French language and culture on the other. Such a balance is necessary given that a purely civic national model, which might seem a reasonable choice given Quebec's growing ethnic pluralism, would evacuate French Canadian ethnicity and would thus risk alienating the majority group.

Chapter 4 looked beyond Quebec's borders to discuss the ways in which Quebec is responding to the opportunities that globalisation offers in terms of acting locally through global cooperation. Quebec's use of various official and informal transnational forums provides a model for other sub-national units who seek to further their own agendas, but who do not have the legitimation and independence that come from being a nation-state. Quebec is in fact in a unique position, given that it operates in two 'global' arenas: that of *la Francophonie* and the 'semi-global' arena of the Americas. The challenge of the Americas comes in the form of creating a multilingual space in which French has equal status with English, Spanish and Portuguese. Within *la Francophonie*, most recently Quebec has managed to harness matching interests, particularly with France, on the importance of an international convention on cultural diversity. However, it remains to be seen how the UNESCO Convention, adopted in October 2005, will serve Quebec's interests in protecting its culture and language.

The second part of the book explored how Quebec is forging a sense of common identity through language. Chapter 5 examined the effect of the new approach on status planning, in particular efforts to ensure the status of French as the 'common public language' of Quebec. Given the growing reliance of Quebec on immigrants, it is essential that these new Quebecers develop an integrative attachment to French in order to ensure the future of the language. A crucial issue that this Chapter raised was to what extent language can be 'de-ethnicised'. On the one hand, in order to encourage immigrants to feel a sense of affective commitment to French, it is important for them not to view the language as too intimately and narrowly connected to the French Canadian majority. However, at the same time, the French language cannot be completely dissociated from French Canadian ethnicity, as no language is ethnoculturally neutral. Moreover, ethnicity represents a major source of motivation for maintaining French in North America.

The question of what kind of French Quebec is seeking to maintain was raised in Chapter 6. In its promotion of an inclusive, civic identity, Quebec needs to reflect on the variety of French that is the most appropriate to its goals. This choice is embedded in an historical context in which French Canadians have traditionally experienced a degree of linguistic insecurity towards their own variety of French *vis-à-vis* the standard French of France. In present-day Quebec, such insecurity is waning, with Francophones generally expressing positive attitudes towards Quebec French. Furthermore, the view of French as a pluricentric language, made up of a series of national, regional and local varieties, is taking hold. However, those new immigrants who already speak French often arrive with a monocentric, France-based view of the language, and are not necessarily open to the variety of French that they discover in Quebec. One way forward is the promotion of a socially acceptable, locally-defined standard for Quebec French, as embodied in the forthcoming dictionary being compiled by the FRANQUS team at the Université de Sherbrooke.

The third part of the book focused on the diverse experiences of three groups: immigrants, Anglophones and Aboriginal people, labels that, it was shown, mask considerable heterogeneity. It became clear that Quebec's official policy, aimed mainly at constructing a sense of belonging and identification among immigrants, was more problematic for the Anglophone population, and not relevant for many Aboriginal people whose primary locus of identification remains their own language and culture. In Chapter 7, it was argued that, if Quebec as host seeks to engender an affective commitment to French among new arrivals, it must provide them with every opportunity to master the language. At present, francisation services, through adult language learning programmes and welcoming classes in schools, are adequate, but could be made more effective. The experiences of adult and young immigrants and their attitudes to French varied. Some adult immigrants do develop an integrative attachment to French accompanied by a sense of belonging to Quebec, but for a number of them French is viewed from an instrumental point of view, coupled with a remote sense of belonging to Quebec. Montreal is a locus of identification for many, rather than Quebec as a whole, and this is often accompanied by a preference for French–English bilingualism. Among young immigrants, the process of language socialisation at school means that the French language is much more deeply anchored. However, it was shown that for a number of these young people, not only is Montreal an important element in how they situate themselves in Quebec, they also have a sense of attachment to bilingualism and multilingualism, rather than to French alone.

Chapter 8 described the growing heterogeneity of the Anglophone community as well as continuing issues such as youth out-migration, under-representation in the Quebec public service, and the Anglophone withdrawal from wider social participation. In addition, there is a sentiment among some bilingual Anglophones that their French is not quite good enough to be fully accepted by Francophone Quebecers. The question of acceptance, of Anglophone Quebecers by Francophones and vice versa, remains a crucial one. For example, Anglophobia can still be expressed openly by parts of the French Canadian population, and there is a reticence on the part of Anglophones towards Francophone Quebec's sovereigntist aspirations. It is thus to be expected that Anglophones do not necessarily feel a sense of allegiance and belonging to the new civic Quebec nation.

However, there are signs of a growing rapprochement between the two groups, as well as a blurring of boundaries between them, with increasing bilingualism and growing multiethnic origins among younger generations of Anglophones.

Finally, Chapter 9 examined the difficulty of including Aboriginal people within the civic model of citizenship favoured by the Larose Commission. As is the case of other Western settler states, Quebec has somehow to balance offering the benefits of citizenship, including equality of opportunity which takes place through the public language, and ensuring that Aboriginal cultures and languages are not disadvantaged or diminished. The Chapter pointed to the importance of some kind of differentiated citizenship for Aboriginal peoples, in which Aboriginal self-government has a central place. This could have positive outcomes in terms of creating the conditions for Aboriginal people to feel a sense of civic integration into the Quebec political community. At present, it is clear that those communities which have well-established agreements with Quebec and Canada are in a better position to maintain and promote their languages and cultures. Quebec has gone some way to recognising the importance of Aboriginal languages in legislation and policy, but it needs to go further still. Increased government support and recognition, through legislation and financial aid, alongside community initiatives both as a result of specific treaty arrangements and growing community involvement, are crucial for the survival of Aboriginal languages in Quebec.

It is of course hard to predict how the three questions that have guided the discussion in this book will play out during the next decade. However, it seems clear that present global conditions will continue in the foreseeable future, and that Quebec will continue to be faced with the challenge of new arrivals from an increasingly wide range of countries of origin. Quebec's model of intercultural citizenship, which allows the affirmation of a distinct culture predicated on the French language, the accommodation and respect of pluralism, and the construction of a common identity by Quebecers of all ethnic origins, is thus worth pursuing.

However, Quebec needs to reflect on a number of issues. First, its inclusive, civic model finds no echo among a number of immigrants, for whom French remains a simple language of communication to which they feel no affective commitment. The authorities are already doing a great deal to ensure that new arrivals feel welcome in their new society. Creating a sense of citizen-belonging through French among a greater number of new Quebecers might, in purely practical terms, involve further improving francisation services, as well as reflecting more deeply on the welcome extended to immigrants by members of the host society itself. A second issue concerns the importance of the continued reflection on the variety of French to promote as the civic language and the asssociated question of the quality of language. The aim is to describe and promote a variety which can be shared by all members of the collectivity, whatever their origins, but which at the same time expresses local specificities and the fundamental link to the French Canadian majority. Third, and a related issue, it is crucial to recognise ethnicity, both of the majority French Canadian group and, just as importantly, of minorities. Not only is it disingenuous not to recognise the ethnic identity of the majority group, but the promotion of a strictly civic model risks alienating French Canadians from the civic project, which can only cut across the efforts of successive governments. In addition, the civic model needs to be adapted or transformed for and by Aboriginal nations and the English-speaking community. These minority groups within Quebec's borders have historical claims to special status which need be taken into consideration. The success of Quebec's civic model will partly rest on developing mechanisms to ensure that each minority's voice is clearly heard in the shaping of its own and the collective present and future.

In the strength of its reflection on issues of language and nation, Quebec is a model for other sub-state units such as Catalonia, which also seeks to ensure the use of its language in the public sphere in a context of increasing immigration. But Quebec has something to offer nation-states as well. Its continual reflection on the status and future of the French language within its borders puts it at the forefront of what it means to construct a modern, inclusive, liberal democracy. For the question that Quebec constantly asks itself is how to create the conditions to generate a genuine sense of attachment to the collectivity amongst all its members, surely the fundamental question that all liberal democracies should be asking themselves in the present global conjuncture.

Appendix

Recent Quebec Premiers

Maurice Duplessis	Union nationale	1944–59
Paul Sauvé	Union nationale	1959–60
Antonio Barrette	Union nationale	1960
Jean Lesage	Parti libéral du Québec (PLQ)	1960–66
Daniel Johnson (senior)	Union nationale	1966–68
Jean-Jacques Bertrand	Union nationale	1966–70
Robert Bourassa	Parti libéral du Québec (PLQ)	1970–76
René Lévesque	Parti québécois (PQ)	1976–85
Pierre Marc Johnson	Parti québécois (PQ)	1985
Robert Bourassa	Parti libéral du Québec (PLQ)	1985–94
Daniel Johnson (junior)	Parti libéral du Québec (PLQ)	1994
Jacques Parizeau	Parti québécois (PQ)	1994–96
Lucien Bouchard	Parti québécois (PQ)	1996–01
Bernard Landry	Parti québécois (PQ)	2001–03
Jean Charest	Parti libéral du Québec (PLQ)	2003–

Recent Canadian Prime Ministers

William Lyon Mackenzie King	Liberal	1935–48
Louis Stephen Saint-Laurent	Liberal	1948–53
John George Diefenbaker	Conservative	1957–63
Lester Bowles Pearson	Liberal	1963–68
Pierre Elliott Trudeau	Liberal	1968–79
Joe Clark	Conservative	1979–80
Pierre Elliott Trudeau	Liberal	1980–84
John Turner	Liberal	1984
Brian Mulroney	Conservative	1984–93
Kim Campbell	Conservative	1993
Jean Chrétien	Liberal	1993–2003
Paul Martin	Liberal	2003–2006
Stephen Harper	Conservative	2006–

Notes

Introduction

1. The nine commissioners were Josée Bouchard, Hélène Cajolet-Laganière, Stéphane Éthier, Patricia Lemay, Norm Lopez-Therrien, Stanley Péan, Gary Richards, Marie-Claude Sarrazin and Dermod Travis. The secretary was Jean-Claude Corbeil. While the official website for the Commission no longer exists, the submissions of the national public hearings can be consulted on the website of the Secrétariat à la politique linguistique (http://www.spl.gouv.qc.ca/langue/index.html). In addition, the 'Commission des États généraux sur la langue française' corpus available on the website of the Centre d'analyse et traitement informatique du français québécois at the Université de Sherbrooke (http://www.usherbrooke.ca/catifq/corpus) contains all of the submissions presented during both the regional and national hearings, the presentations given at the themed conference sessions and the international conference, as well as articles appearing in the French-language press during the period of operation of the Commission.
2. Like all those that follow, the translation of this citation from the final report of the Larose Commission draws on the English summary: *French, a Language for Everyone: A New Strategic Approach Centred on the Citizen in Society*. With regard to citations from other documents, published English translations have been used where possible; otherwise the translations are those of the authors.
3. The fact that Barth claims that some cultural factors are ignored implies that they nonetheless exist. This is presumably one of the reasons why he has been accused by A. Cohen (1974a: xii–xv) of promoting not a situational but rather a primordial view of ethnicity (see Eriksen 1993: 54–5).
4. The term 'nationalism' is used with a variety of meanings by both academics and the public in general. Some commentators reserve it for a language and symbolism of the nation, a sociopolitical movement, or an ideology, rather than for national consciousness or a sentiment (A. D. Smith 1991: 72–3, 2001: 5–9). Others make a distinction between the official *nationalism* of the authorities on the one hand, and the everyday *national sentiment* of the population at large on the other (Canet 2003: 149–50). Contrary to the claims of many of its detractors, nationalism need not be associated with violence, but is also expressed in less pernicious forms, as 'banal nationalism' (Billig 1995). Nor is it necessarily linked to right-wing ideologies: 'Through an emphasis on equality between citizens, it may be an ideology of the left' (Eriksen 1993: 107).
5. With its origins in Meinecke's (1970 [1907]) opposition between *Kulturnation* and *Staatsnation* and especially Kohn's (1944) distinction between 'Eastern' and 'Western' nationalisms, the ethnic/civic dichotomy has now spawned a whole series of terminological variations: cultural versus political, emotional versus rational, voluntarist versus organic, etc. (see Brown 2000: 53–4; Spencer and Wollman 2002: 96–7).
6. For example, Robertson (1992, 1995) considers that the phenomenon has existed since the mid-fifteenth century, a time which saw the crystallisation of conceptions

of international relations and the beginning of international exhibitions (Robertson 1992: 49, 58). The same scholar does in fact distinguish between different *stages* of globalisation, the most recent – 'the uncertainty phase' – having begun in the late 1960s (Robertson 1992: 59). Held *et al.* (1999: 424) regard 'contemporary globalisation' as beginning even earlier, namely in the immediate years following the Second World War.
7. 'Nationality' also has other meanings; for example, it is also used to refer to an ethnic minority within a state, to national sentiment or nationalism, to national character, even to the attainment of statehood (see Varouxakis 2001).

2 From French Canadian to Quebecer

1. Other commentators maintain that the division between French speakers inside and outside Quebec began even earlier: 'Contrary to what is generally accepted, this break does not date back to the 1960s, for historians have reported strong opposition between different groupings within French Canada itself well before the rise of Quebec neo-nationalism, an opposition which reflects the objective differences between the national minorities in English-speaking environments and the French-speaking majority in Quebec from the 1930s to the 1960s' (Langlois 2003: 173).
2. According to the *Charter of the French language* (R.S.Q. c. C-11, s. 14; see Section 5.1), '[t]he Government, the government departments, the other agencies of the civil administration and the services thereof shall be designated by their French names alone.' The English names given in this book are thus the translations of the authors and provided purely for the benefit of English-speaking readers.
3. The Conseil des relations interculturelles is the new name given to the Conseil des communautés culturelles et de l'immigration (Council for cultural communities and immigration), a permanent and autonomous body founded in 1984 with the function of advising the Minister on issues related to the integration of immigrants and intercultural relations (Juteau 2002: 444).
4. While the term citizenship now appears to be eschewed, reference is still made, perhaps contradictorily, to *'citoyens du Québec'* (Quebec citizens), implying that these are somehow distinct from *'citoyens canadiens'* (Canadian citizens). (see e.g., http://www.micc.gouv.qc.ca and http://www.gouv.qc.ca).
5. We are grateful to David Marrani for clarification on the constitutional arrangements of New Caledonia, French Polynesia and Corsica.
6. In fact, it is no surprise that Canada's commitment to multiculturalism is superficial. With its preference for group rights over individual ones, true multiculturalism poses a major challenge to classic liberalism that can only be alleviated if multiculturalism remains largely a symbolic concession that works to the ultimate benefit of individual rights (Gagnon and Iacovino 2002).
7. HLMs (*habitations à loyer modéré*) are the French equivalent of council flats or public sector housing.

3 Redefining the Quebec Nation

1. The difference between broad and narrow definitions of ethnicity is, no doubt, also at the root of the criticisms of Bouchard's interpretation of Dumont, such as that of Cantin (2001a): 'Not only did Fernand Dumont never defend the theory that Bouchard associates him with, he categorically came out against any ethnic

conception of the nation. Thus, in an interview he gave a year before his death to Michel Vastel, he declared: "We must forget the word 'ethnic' because the nation is essentially a cultural reality." Four years earlier, before the parliamentary commission on the sovereignty of Quebec, Dumont was even clearer about his reasons for rejecting the word "ethnic": "For a long time," he said, "there have been no nations in the organic sense of the term, that is of a strictly ethnic nature. What exists nowadays are cultural nations" '.
2. The point in the past that Derriennic refers to is 1931, when the British Parliament could have included Quebec in the Statute of Westminster, which allowed for various dominions to declare independence (Derriennic 1995: 25).
3. See also Oakes (2001) on Sweden, a country often cited for the same purpose and which shares many characteristics with Denmark in this respect.
4. While these are the three ethnic nations most frequently identified, Bouchard recognises that there are variants of this theory: 'some distinguish several nations within the Aboriginal population, while others are tempted to elevate to the rank of nations what are commonly called the cultural communities' (G. Bouchard 1999: 44).
5. Bouchard clearly distinguishes between ethnicity and ethnicism/ethnocentrism, the latter being when 'the superiority of one ethnicity or ethnic group over another is affirmed and used to justify acts of discrimination, exclusion and the like' (Bouchard 2001a: 199).
6. Seymour is referring especially to new Quebecers and the English-speaking minority. His view on Quebec's indigenous populations is more nuanced and seems to have changed slightly over time. In 1999, he claimed that '[t]he 74,000 individuals that make up the eleven Aboriginal communities are in fact Quebec citizens, but they do not *only* belong to the Quebec nation' (Seymour 1999a: 74, emphasis added). However in later publications, he agrees with Dumont that, because the Aboriginal nations do not on the whole identify with Quebec, '[t]heir members are citizens of Quebec and are part of the Quebec state, but *not* of the Quebec nation' (Seymour 2001a: 151, emphasis added).
7. Seymour decides not to make a distinction between multiculturalism and interculturalism (see Sections 2.1 and 2.3), preferring instead to argue that multiculturalism *per se* is not intrinsically bad, as long as it does not deny other conceptions of nation (Seymour 1999a: 45–59). In other words, multiculturalism can function well in Seymour's sociopolitical nation, which can exist alongside other definitions of the nation, such as the Canadian civic nation.
8. Because his defence of culture is in fact a defence of ethnic culture, Kymlicka has even been accused of defending a position of ethnic hegemony, which seeks to promote the rights of ethnic groups over those of other cultural groups (e.g., women, gays and lesbians, urban neighbourhoods, labour movements, fishing communities, etc.) (Walker 1999).

4 Quebec in a Globalising World

1. Quebec is represented in 28 foreign locations: 6 general delegations (Brussels, London, Mexico City, New York, Paris and Tokyo); 4 delegations (Boston, Buenos Aires, Chicago and Los Angeles); 9 government bureaux (Barcelona, Beijing, Damascus, Hong Kong, Miami, Munich, Shanghai, Vienna and Washington); 6 trade branches (Atlanta, Berlin, Rome, Santiago, Seoul and Taipei); and 3 business agents (Lima, Hanoi and Milan).

2. The strategy of 'multilateral cooperation' was already mooted by Labrie (1995) in his discussion of the linguistic issues surrounding NAFTA by creating a North American forum and the drawing up of a Charter of North American languages and cultures. He also proposed the promotion of plurilingualism at the local level, another area taken up by the Fréchette 2001 report, and the development of a North American conception of lingustic diversity.
3. The Quebec City seminar adopted a series of resolutions which mirror to a certain extent those of the 2001 opinion, but which include 'linguistic policies regarding creoles and native languages'. The question of native languages is a more salient one outside Quebec, and indeed outside the US and Canada overall. Mexico, for example, has taken what can be described as an indigenous approach, 'aimed at developing a Mexican identity which differentiates itself from its colonialist past and which contributes to the integration of Amerindian culture into the identity of the new authentic "Mexican" ' (Labrie 1995).
4. Lamonde (see e.g., 2001: 8, 29–30) points to the importance of US cultural influence in his graphic formula representing what he considers to be the main historical factors contributing to Quebec's identity: $Q = - (F) + (GB) + (USA)^2 - (R) + (C)$. He argues that France (F) is less important than we think; Great Britain (GB), on the other hand, has played a decisive role, as has Canada (C); the cultural influence of the USA is the most underestimated; and the influence of Rome (R), i.e. the Catholic religion, has played a different role from that commonly assumed.
5. G. Bouchard (2001b: 12–13) defines 'new collectivities' as 'collectivities formed since the sixteenth century from the movements of intercontinental migration from Europe towards *new* territories, or rather, those considererd as such by the new arrivals' (G. Bouchard 2001b: 12, emphasis in original). 'A new collectivity' is distinguished from a simple colonial enclave in that: (1) its members consider themselves to form a separate society, both geographically and socially, from that of the mother country; (2) they share 'a distinct collective consciousness'; (3) they 'formulate utopias for *their* society'; and (4) it is the descendents of Europeans who 'sever colonial ties', and not the indigenous population.
6. See, for example, the work by the Groupe de recherche sur l'américanité (GRAM), illustrated in Cuccioletta (2001), which conducted a survey of Quebecers on the questions of identity, values and attitudes, and political culture, as they related to *américanité*.
7. Already in the 1950s, there was an interest in Quebec in creating some kind of non-governmental international organisation that would regroup all French-speaking countries 'for the purposes of dialogue, all kinds of exchanges, mutual support and the defence and promotion of the common language' (Léger 1987: 82). In the 1950s and 1960s, Quebecers were key players in forming various non-governmental organisations regrouping Francophones, such as the Association des universités entièrement ou partiellement de langue française (AUPELF; now l'Agence universitaire de la francophonie) (Léger 2000: 335).
8. Two countries voted against the Convention (US and Israel) and there were four abstentions, including Australia. The Convention will come into force three months after a minimum of 30 states have ratified it.
9. These measures, which number five, include the following: 'measures which in an appropriate manner reserve a certain space for domestic cultural goods and services among all those available within the national territory, in order to ensure opportunities for their production, distribution, dissemination and consumption, and include, where appropriate, provisions relating to the *language* used for the

above-mentioned goods and services' (UNESCO 2004: 5, emphasis added). In Annex 2, the draft Convention noted, amongst other things, that cultural policies are aimed at 'promoting pluralism, cultural and *linguistic* diversity in and for the information society' (UNESCO 2004: 19, emphasis added).
10. Aside from the question of linguistic diversity, the scope of the Convention also raised concerns before its adoption, in particular whether the Convention should have equal status with other international agreements (Bernier in Dutrisac 2004) or whether it should have the potential to overrule international trade agreements (Beaudoin in C. Rioux 2004). The final Convention states that it is not subordinate to other treaties (UNESCO 2005a: 11).
11. Yet again, there is some tension between Quebec and Canada, this time over who is inviting *la Francophonie* to the Summit. Jacques Saada, Canada's Minister of *la Francophonie*, made it clear that, in accordance with *Francophonie* policy, the summit would be 'co-presided by the "inviting power" and by the participating government', the former referring to Canada and the latter to Quebec (Saada 2004). This has been interpreted by some as 'Ottawa's relentless determination to confine Quebec to the role of second fiddle' (Léger 2004).

5 French: A language for All Quebecers

1. At the end of the 1960s, the ethnolinguistic breakdown of Saint-Léonard was 60 per cent Francophone, 30 per cent Italian and 10 per cent from various communities, including Anglophones (Levine 1997: 117; Robert 2000: 244).
2. In October 1970, a small group of radicals forming the Front de libération du Québec (FLQ) kidnapped the British diplomat James Cross and the Quebec Minister of Work, Pierre Laporte, who was subsequently assassinated. Federal Prime Minister Pierre Trudeau responded by enacting the War Measures Act, which resulted in the Canadian army being sent to the streets of Quebec and the arrest of hundreds of supposed FLQ sympathisers.
3. Indeed in his capacity as Deputy Minister for Cultural Development, the main architect of the *culture de convergence* policy, the sociologist Fernand Dumont (see also Section 3.1), was one of the co-signatories of the 1977 White Paper (Mathieu 2001: 18–19).
4. In 1970, the average income of a monolingual Anglophone was 59 per cent greater than that of a monolingual Francophone. By 1995, monolingual Anglophones earned on average 19 per cent more than monolingual Francophones, but 12 per cent less than bilingual Francophones (Levine 2000: 366).
5. Indeed, such is the extent to which integrative and instrumental motivations are often mutually reinforcing that many researchers in the field of second language acquisition (e.g., Muchnick and Wolfe 1982) have pointed out the difficulty in separating the two in many cases.
6. CEGEPs are post-secondary schools that prepare students for university (2 years) and provide technical and other diplomas (3 years).
7. In fact, the Commission of Inquiry on Bilingualism and Biculturalism also favoured the principle of personality for Canadian language policy. However, as Edwards (1994: 66–7) notes, this preference was 'motivated largely by political considerations' and the Commission nonetheless 'recognized the advantages of territorialism.'

8. In a similar manner, the French exclude themselves from the term Francophone, which they tend to reserve for French speakers from countries other than France (Pöll 2001: 21–2).
9. Graddol (1998: 29) estimates the former to be 1.1 billion, as opposed to the 'mere' 375 million represented by the latter.
10. Pennycook (1998: 216) argues that the colonial discourses that are associated with English can in fact only be confronted effectively through English, the language in which they were constructed. This is not a view shared by all, however. For example, the Kenyan writer Ngũgĩ wa Thiong'o (1986) advocates an outright rejection of English, claiming that the use of English in his home country is a form of neo-colonialism that serves to maintain the dominance of a small elite and their foreign allies. The different strategies used to combat colonialist discourse aside, most commentators nonetheless agree that English is never ethno-culturally neutral.

6 Whose French? Language Attitudes, Linguistic Insecurity and Standardisation

1. These and other similar citations from this period are listed in Dulong (1966) and discussed further in Gendron (2000).
2. While 'French Canadian Patois' was by far the most common term, a whole gamut of derogatory expressions were in fact used with the purpose of denigrating the local variety of French: *Canadian French, Quebec French, Quebec Patois, patois canadien/canayen, Patois canadien-français, langue canayenne, parler canadien, Canayen habitant, Indian jargon, Beastly horrible French, méprisable patois, misérable patois, jargon, petit-nègre, langage incompréhensible, patois vulgaire* (C. Bouchard 2002: 150–1).
3. Many of these language columns can be searched and consulted in their entirety on the ChroQué website (http://www.lexique.ulaval.ca). Extracts from more general comments about the quality of language spoken in Quebec can be found in the 'Perception de la qualité de la langue au Québec' corpus at the Centre d'analyse et traitement informatique du français québécois at the Université de Sherbrooke (http://www.usherbrooke.ca/catifq/corpus).
4. For an in-depth discussion of the history of the concept of *bon usage*, see D. Trudeau (1992).
5. In the beginning, the term 'regional French' was used mostly to refer to the French-speaking regions bordering France, especially Belgium. Only later did it come to be used for standard varieties of French (as opposed to 'popular French' or dialects) in France itself (Valdman 1983: 681).
6. It should, however, be noted that the Académie française represents an extreme prescriptive view that is not shared by many others in France, including the governments of Laurent Fabius and Lionel Jospin who pushed for the feminisation of profession titles in their own country in 1986 and 1997–98 respectively (Conrick 2002b: 210–13).
7. However, this is not the view of all commentators: 'One is [...] led to conclude that if, as some have believed, the prescriptive norm of *bon usage* is, or has been, in Quebec an external norm, imposed from outside, this imposition is a success and that not only is it widely internalised and accepted, but large numbers of speakers also wish for it to be reproduced' (Paquot 1988).

8. These *faux amis* and *calques* are listed in the 'Répertoire d'emprunts critiqués à l'anglais' corpus at the Centre d'analyse et traitement informatique du français québécois at the Université de Sherbrooke (http://www.usherbrooke.ca/catifq/corpus).
9. This general or global approach was in fact first used by Louis-Alexandre Bélisle in his *Dictionnaire général de la langue française au Canada* (Bélisle 1954). However, unlike the *Dictionnaire du français plus* and the *Dictionnaire québécois d'aujourd'hui*, the latter still adopted a corrective approach which sanctioned only a limited number of Canadianisms. Moreover, 'it completely separated the Quebec usages from those of general French. The Bélisle dictionary is a hybrid work, made up of a Québécois glossary and a French dictionary, the entries of the first having been, so to speak, cut and pasted into the second' (Poirier 1990: 342). As such, it cannot be considered as being completely committed to a pluricentric conception of the French language.
10. The *Multidictionnaire de la langue française*, at least in its latest edition (Villers 2003), goes some way to meeting the need for a description of Standard Quebec French. However, this is not a general dictionary so much as a list of difficulties of the French language with a corrective agenda. In addition, it has been criticised for its numerous omissions, errors and dubious decisions regarding the acceptability and register of certain Quebecisms, the slowness with which several Quebec usages have been accepted by the various editions, and the fact that it is inconsistent with some recommendations made by the Office de la langue française in its online *Grand dictionnaire terminologique* (see J. Auger 2005: 70–1).
11. In fact, the two principal researchers of the FRANQUS project are largely responsible for linking the national dictionary project to the new civic approach to Quebec national identity: Pierre Martel was president of the Conseil de la langue française at the time of the opinion presented to the Minister in 1991; he was also responsible for organising the day devoted to questions of quality of language for the Larose Commission, of which Hélène Cajolet-Laganière was a commissioner.
12. As a further assessment of the civic credentials of the FRANQUS project, it would be useful to know if the database being used also includes texts written by Quebecers of non-French Canadian backgrounds. Unfortunately, no such information could be obtained.

7 Language, Immigration and Belonging

1. Montreal can be delimited geographically in two main ways: first the greater metropolitan area, which comprises the island of Montreal and surrounding regions both to the north and south of the island; and the island of Montreal itself.
2. The study used 2001 Census data and compared mother tongue and language used regularly or most often at home, among young people aged 24 years and under. The languages with the highest retention were: Yiddish (95 per cent), Vietnamese (89 per cent), Punjabi (85 per cent), Russian (90 per cent), Armenian (83 per cent), Cantonese (81 per cent), Spanish (80 per cent) and Polish (76 per cent). The study also found that students of immigrant background in Francophone schools retained their mother tongue to a greater extent than those in Anglophone schools (Heinrich 2003).
3. At its origins in 1977, Quebec's Heritage Language Programme (*Projet d'enseignement en langue d'origine*, PELO) had as the main objective the educational integration

of children of immigrant origin. From a promising start, PELO stagnated for various reasons (see Mc Andrew 2001: 52–4 for details). PELO is now in some sense a shadow of its former self, running heritage language programmes at primary level only for two and a half hours a week generally outside normal class hours, with just 13 heritage languages being taught in 2002–03 (Mc Andrew 2001: 53, 2003b: 60). More than 80 per cent of students are Italian background speakers from the second or third generation.

4. One thousand immigrants took part in the first round of interviews, a year into their migration experience, followed by 729 of the original 1,000 at the end of the second year, 508 at the end of the third year, and finally 429 in the tenth year of immigration. The most common countries of birth of participants over the four rounds of interviews were Lebanon, France, Vietnam, Haiti, Morocco, Egypt, Syria, Portugal, China and the Philippines (Renaud *et al.* 2003: 10). The areas focused on included 'residence, employment, education and training, non-employment, the household and its make-up, and citizenship' (Renaud *et al.* 2003: 1).

5. This finding is supported by the results of a survey undertaken by Statistics Canada in 2003 in which Canadians across the country were asked to describe their sense of belonging to Canada, their province and their community (Statistics Canada 2004; see Section 8.2 for Anglophone responses to the survey). Overall, Quebecers of immigrant background, identified as such through speaking a language other than English or French at home, had a greater sense of belonging to Canada than their counterparts in the rest of Canada (66.3 per cent and 49.8 per cent respectively expressed a very strong sense of belonging). However, when asked to describe their sense of belonging to their province, a greater proportion of Quebec Allophones expressed a very strong sense of provincial belonging (36.4 per cent) than did Allophones overall in the rest of Canada (27.1 per cent), approaching the percentage of Francophone Quebecers who also described a very strong sense of belonging to Quebec (38.2 per cent). Overall, similar proportions of Allophones in Quebec and in the rest of Canada reported very strong or somewhat strong feelings of belonging to their province (74.9 per cent and 75.8 per cent respectively).

6. Eighteen members of the group were bilingual French–English, with some having learned French on arriving in Quebec, and others knowing the language before emigrating. Their interest in French was essentially an instrumental one and not about cultural affinities. French–English bilingualism was also important to their social integration, as they worked or lived in an Anglophone or a bilingual environment. They would like to see more acceptance of English, bilingual signage and the abolition of compulsory Francophone schooling (Helly and van Schendel 2001: 143). A small minority (seven) refused a sense of belonging to Quebec and had total allegiance to the Canadian state. This was not just about having experienced discrimination or non-acceptance, but also about the French language, which they saw as rather useless and not influential (Helly and van Schendel 2001: 172).

7. Labelle and Salée undertook forty interviews and a focus group with Francophone and Anglophone immigrant community activists in Montreal 'involved in promoting immigrant integration in Quebec society' (Labelle and Salée 2001: 289). Five of the participants were born in Canada, with the rest from a variety of continents and regions: North Africa, the Middle East, the Caribbean, Latin America, Asia, Africa and Europe (Labelle and Salée 2001: 312–13).

8. The Office notes that the changes between 1991, 1996 and 2001 could be affected by the changes made to the wording of question and responses in the 2001 Census (Office québécois de la langue française 2005: 33).
9. The study was undertaken by Léger Marketing as a series of telephone interviews with 1,025 young people from the greater Montreal metropolitan region aged between 18 and 35 who were born outside Canada or whose parents were born in another country, and who had attended Francophone primary and/or secondary school in Quebec for at least two years (Beaulieu 2003).
10. The study is based on discussions which took place in a series of focus groups. The ethnolinguistic background of participants, who were aged between 18 and 30, is indicated as follows: Asian (35 per cent), Hispanic (19 per cent), Eastern European (12 per cent), Western European (12 per cent), Arab (9 per cent), Indian (5 per cent), African (5 per cent) and Creole (3 per cent). Seventy per cent were born outside Canada, 22 per cent in Quebec and 8 per cent elsewhere in Canada (Conseil de la langue française 2002: 4).
11. Lamarre and Rossell Paredes (2003) report on a preliminary phase of a major research project on multilingualism in Montreal, based on interviews conducted in 2000 with ten multilingual college students aged between 18 and 24, from a range of ethnolinguistic backgrounds: mother tongues included Tagalog, Portuguese, Fanti, Italian, Spanish, Punjabi, Cantonese and Arabic; five were born in and five outside Canada.
12. The data for the study reported on here were based on a series of 190 observations of the language practices of young Montrealers aged between 18 and 35 years. The observations, lasting from 15 to 60 minutes, were made over eight months in various parts of the city of Montreal in a variety of social contexts (Lamarre *et al.* 2002: 51–2).

8 Transformations of Anglophone Quebec

1. The idea of English Quebec as a 'linguistic bridge' between Quebec and North America is not a new one, having already been mooted in the late 1970s–early 1980s (e.g., Scowen 1979, cited in Caldwell and Waddell 1982a: 429–30; see also Stein 1982: 122). More recently, it has been argued that the Anglophone community should be seen as an asset to Quebec (e.g., Scowen 1991: 129; Alliance Quebec 2001: 3).
2. The notion of two solitudes to describe the separation and non-dialogue between the Anglophone and Francophone communities in Canada comes from the book *Two Solitudes* (MacLennan 1945).
3. Caldwell himself seems to have shifted somewhat in his delimitation of the Anglophone community. In a 1998 chapter (based on Caldwell 1994), his definition of the community was based on two criteria: being born in Canada and having English as one's mother tongue, 'a reasonably valid and reliable indicator of early socialization', such socialisation being primarily in 'the English/French dynamic in Canada' (Caldwell 1998: 276). By 2002, however, in a chapter on Anglophone reactions to Charter of the French language, Caldwell chose to extend the boundaries of the Anglophone population by including those Quebecers who used English at home (Caldwell 2002: 27).
4. In addition, a municipality as a whole can be an 'Anglophone institution', or at least that is what the Mayor of Anglophone Westmount, Peter Trent, maintained around the time of the Montreal fusions issue. Westmount, according to Trent, has its own unique 'institutional' elements, including the lawn bowling club, the

Westmount library, and the Royal Montreal Regiment, among others (Winer 2001: 155).
5. The Network includes a diverse range of organisations, some of which are regional, and some of which are sector-based groups, ranging from the Quebec Farmers Association and the Townshippers' Association to the Community Health and Social Services Network and Youth Employment Services, and receives financial support from Canadian Heritage.
6. The Canadian Census questions on language have evolved to mirror Canada's growing diversity: mother tongue was first used as a Census category in 1921, language spoken at home in 1971, and first official language spoken in 1991 (Stevenson 2004: 330). The federal government uses the 'first official language spoken' criterion to determine its responsibilities as far as the provision of public services in the two official languages is concerned (Magnan 2005: 9). It is also the variable which captures Anglophone Quebec's heterogeneity, taking in as it does those minority groups for whom English is not the mother tongue and those who use English in the public domain.
7. The study was based on a telephone survey of 1,237 Anglophone participants, which took place from spring 2004 to winter 2005. 33.1 per cent were from the Montreal region and 66.9 per cent from other Quebec regions. 60 per cent were born in Quebec, 12 per cent in another Canadian province, and 27.9 per cent outside Canada (Magnan, Gauthier and Côté 2006).
8. The survey did not provide a definition of belonging, and participants 'based their responses on their own understanding of the term' (Statistics Canada 2004: 5). It distinguished between Francophones and Anglophones using the criterion of language spoken at home. There is no indication of when in 2003 the survey took place, that is, whether it was before or after the election of the Quebec Liberals to power in the province. Presumably, the election of the Liberals would have had a positive effect on the extent to which the English-speaking community, in the majority federalist, felt comfortable in Quebec.
9. CLSCs, *centres locaux de services communautaires* (local community service centres), are free health clinics run by the Quebec government.
10. *The Gazette* does have English-language competition from two free local weeklies (*Hour* and the *Montreal Mirror*), two free dailies (*Metro* and *24 Hours*) as well as Canadian dailies the *National Post* and *The Globe and Mail*, the latter two actively pursuing Anglophone readers in Montreal. Current policy at *The Gazette* on targetting readers prioritises Anglophones, both 'old' and 'new', with Francophone Montrealers in third place.
11. Changes to the 2001 Census questions may have affected results upwards (see Castonguay 2003).
12. This lagging behind of writing skills is echoed in Magnan, Gauthier and Côté (2006: 18) who found that 82.2 per cent, 85.5 per cent and 81.5 per cent respectively of their sample of young Anglophones could read, understand and speak French, whereas only 66.9 per cent could write French.
13. A recent, related phenomenon is taking place on the Francophone side, with increasing numbers of eligible Francophone students attending Anglophone schools. Heinrich takes the example of an English-language school in Hudson, a primarily Anglophone town to the west of Montreal island, where there were 15 Francophones out of 700 pupils in 2002, and a prediction that figures would double over the following two years (Heinrich 2002a). Overall, in the period 1991–2003, the number of mother-tongue Francophones enrolled in public and private English-language schools in Montreal increased by around 35 per cent,

whereas outside Montreal the number increased by nearly 115 per cent (Jedwab 2004: 33). It is this increase in numbers of Francophone students that has maintained the viability of some English-language schools, particularly outside Montreal (Jedwab 2004: 35). The keenness of Francophone parents for their children to learn English has also led some to prefer enrolling their children in French-language schools that offer English immersion classes (Heinrich 2002b).
14. Justice Gomery was equally appreciated at the national level: he was chosen as *Time* magazine's 2005 Canadian Newsmaker of the Year.

9 Linguistic Rights for Aboriginal Nations

1. The plural nouns referring to specific Aboriginal nations have been marked here by 's' for the sake of uniformity in English. This differs from some current usage; for example, in Louis-Jacques Dorais' work in English, the noun 'Inuit' is invariable, following Inuit grammatical conventions.
2. The Quebec government recognises the three-way nature of the Aboriginal–state relationship: 'Under the current constitutional framework, Québec offers its own Québec–Aboriginal dynamic in which the federal government will be invited to participate when necessary. This applies, for instance, in matters in which the federal government is already involved and in tripartite agreements' (Gouvernement du Québec 1998b: 15).
3. The term 'First Nations' was coined in the 1970s as a political statement by Aboriginal peoples of their right to self-autonomy. 'First Nation' has also been adopted by some communities or bands within an Aboriginal nation (NAHO 2003).
4. The term 'Innu', which is used in this chapter for the nation and the language, has been increasingly used by the Innus themselves since the 1980s, instead of 'Montagnais', the French term meaning 'mountain people', first used by the early missionaries (Tanner 1999) and still used in some quarters.
5. Under the Indian Act, registered or status Indians are included on the federal Indian Register, and have certain legal rights and benefits; non-status Indians self-identify as members of a First Nation but are not recognized as Indians under the Indian Act and do not have the rights and benefits granted to status Indians (NAHO 2003). The Quebec government has a particular role to play with regard to the Inuits, Crees and Naskapis within Quebec, following the James Bay and Northern Quebec Agreement signed between the governments of Canada and Quebec, Hydro-Québec and the Cree and Inuit peoples in 1975 and the Northeastern Quebec Agreement signed with the Naskapi in 1978. The signing of these agreements means that the Crees and Naskapis are no longer subject to the Indian Act, but rather to the Cree-Naskapi (of Quebec) Act (1984, c. 18), which gives them 'a different legal framework' (Secrétariat aux affaires autochtones 2001: 7). The Inuits also have a particular arrangement, in that they 'choose to be governed by Québec, rather than be subject to a federal statute' (Secrétariat aux affaires autochtones 2001: 7). A proportion of First Nation members in Canada live on 'reserves' or 'communities' – the latter being the commonly accepted term in Quebec (Lévesque 2003: 33) – which were set aside for the use of First Nations and are under federal jurisdiction; Inuits live mainly in villages in the far north which are entirely under Quebec jurisdiction (Secrétariat aux affaires autochtones 2001: 9).

6. Cleary and Dorais (2005: 235) observe that 'from a strictly linguistic point of view, some Algonquian idioms [...] (Cree, Naskapi, Innu-Montagnais and Attikamek), all very closely related, belong to the same language, East Cree [...]. However, we consider them as separate languages since their speakers consider them as such'. In addition, it has proved difficult in some cases to decide on the spelling and/or the naming of the various languages and there is some variation as a consequence. Additional information on the languages of the various Aboriginal nations in Quebec is as follows: the Mohawk language is also known as Kanienkeha; Micmac is also spelled Mi'kmaq, and the dialect spoken in Quebec is called Restigouche or Listuguj.
7. It has been suggested that the higher retention of Aboriginal languages in Quebec is 'perhaps due to the fact that the coexistence of two majority languages – French and English – reduces the impact of external linguistic domination' (Cleary and Dorais 2005: 235), the same argument put forward to explain the higher retention of heritage languages in Quebec than elsewhere in Canada (see Section 7.1). It is also the case that 'the Aboriginal languages of Northern Quebec [were] protected from linguistic assimilation by their geographic isolation, by the continuation of their traditional activities of subsistence hunting and by a low rate of schooling', although these conditions are changing dramatically (Drapeau and Corbeil 1996: 289).
8. Indeed, initiatives from the federal government, as well as from Aboriginal groups, provide a context for Quebec's own policy, but space precludes their examination here. See Trudel (1996) for a detailed discussion of the history of federal as well as Aboriginal directions on Aboriginal languages; see for example, AFN (n.d.) for a chronology of First Nation language policy and initiatives.
9. Events that took place in 1990 – the defeat of the Meech Lake Accord, which would have recognised Quebec as a 'distinct society' (Cree politician Elijah Harper opposed the Accord because it did not grant rights to Canada's Aboriginal peoples), and the Oka crisis, a land dispute between the municipality of Oka and the Mohawk community of Kanesatake which resulted in one death and the blockade of a major bridge into Montreal which lasted for several weeks – had hardened attitudes of non-Aboriginal Francophones towards Aboriginal people in Quebec at the beginning of the 1990s (Gidengil *et al.* 2004), and served as a 'trigger for the realisation by the state of the need to establish measures which would favour a more egalitarian and more just relationship between Aboriginal and non-Aboriginal people' (Salée 2005: 59).
10. However, Salée has admitted more recently that his position has become more nuanced: 'I realise that it is perhaps not as clear as all that [...]. Certain Aboriginal leaders like Ted Moses and Roméo Saganash, who are both behind the *Paix des braves* agreement, are prepared to admit that the state has taken a step, that a new interface is currently being created' (Salée cited in Tremblay 2004).
11. In sections 16 and 17 on Cree and Inuit education respectively, the JBNQA specifically mentions that the languages of instruction are Cree and Inuttitut, in concertation with French (s. 16.0.10 and 17.0.59), and that the School Boards have the power to develop course materials in Cree and Inuttitut (s. 16.0.9 and 17.0.64).
12. The Nunavik government itself will be 'non-ethnic', that is, it will comprise representatives from the region, regardless of their ethnic identity. Alacie Nalukturak, of the Avataq Cultural Institute, proffers a word of caution, viewing

the protection of Inuttitut within the framework of a non-ethnic government as a huge challenge (see George 2005).
13. However, by making French and English official languages alongside Inuttitut, as opposed to Quebec's sole official language, French, there are potential dangers for the health of Inuttitut. Daveluy (2004) points out that what she calls the 'negotiated linguistic peace' in Nunavik over the past 30 years through the JBNQA has been beneficial to Inuttitut, whereas there is less certainty regarding the position of Inuktitut as one of the three official languages in Nunavuk, the Canadian territory created in 1999 in the north-west of the country dominated by the Inuit population.
14. Part of the Pakua Shipu community, which is near the Labrador border, has English as a second language (Anne-Marie Baraby, personal communication, July 2006).
15. Even those languages that are no longer spoken such as Huron can sometimes be taken as a subject of study at school (Cleary and Dorais 2005: 240).
16. Under section 88 of the Charter of the French language, Crees and Inuits have the right 'to determine the rate of introduction of French and English as languages of instruction'. However, the same section requires that '[t]he Cree School Board and the Kativik School Board shall pursue as an objective the use of French as a language of instruction so that pupils graduating from their schools will in future be capable of continuing their studies in a French school, college or university elsewhere in Québec, if they so desire'.
17. Efforts to maintain and promote Aboriginal languages are of necessity focused on language use within Aboriginal communities. Those Aboriginal people who live permanently or for extended periods of time in rural or urban environments outside their communities are inevitably less able to benefit from the sustained collective contact with native speakers of their language that is a strong support for language maintenance, and thus they are more likely to become linguistically and culturally integrated into the wider society. While the links between the urban Aboriginal population in Quebec and their communities of origin remain strong, with 90 per cent of 'Quebec's urban Aboriginal population [...] still from the communities' (Lévesque 2003: 26), it is clear that Aboriginal languages fare less well outside the community environment.
18. However, the Institut culturel et éducatif montagnais (ICEM) is undertaking a project, starting in 2006, to create a uniform programme for the teaching of Innu over the six years of primary school, integrating community elders (Yvette Mollen, personal communication, September 2005).
19. There are also other important, federally funded Innu language initiatives: for example, in 2005, the government funded a five-year project run by Marguerite MacKenzie of Memorial University entitled 'Knowledge and human resources for Innu language development' which focuses on the Labrador Innu dialects. The project includes the continued development of the *Innu-aimun* (Innu language) website (http://www.innu-aimun.ca), the completion of a trilingual Innu–French–English dictionary, the creation of teaching materials, and the running of workshops and language promotion activities; the ICEM is involved as a community partner. Also in 2005, Lynn Drapeau received federal funding to work collaboratively with the ICEM on a three-year project on the Innu language (Rice 2005).
20. The situation is slightly different in Mashteuiatsh, where 25 per cent of the community speak Innu: formerly, a two-year kindergarten programme in Innu was offered, but was not well received by parents who were concerned about their

children's academic progress. Since 2003, the programme has been open only to those children who have at least one parent who speaks Innu, thus providing support for language acquisition. Those children in primary school who followed the kindergarten programme in Innu have an hour of Innu at school daily, whereas those who have followed the regular kindergarten programme have an hour of Innu every nine days (Boucher 2005: 135–6).

21. There have been moves to extend Innu as language of instruction into the first years of primary school. This was the case at Betsiamites from 1982 to 1987 (Drapeau 1994c). However, there was a certain resistance to the programme from parents, and it was discontinued after the first cohort had completed the programme. There was a similar programme at Uashat/Maliotenam at the end of the 1980s, but this ended in 1991, for the same reasons (Anne-Marie Baraby, personal communication, July 2006).

Bibliography

Achebe, C. (1988). *The African Trilogy*. London: Picador.
Adelman, H. (1995). Quebec: the morality of secession. In J. H. Carens (ed.) *Is Quebec Nationalism Just? Perspectives from Anglophone Canada*. Montréal/Kingston: McGill-Queen's University Press, 160–92.
AFN (Assembly of First Nations) (n.d.). Chronology of language and culture activities and events. <http://www.afn.ca/article/asp?id=833> Accessed 9 January 2006.
Ager, D. E. (2001). *Motivation in Language Planning and Language Policy*. Clevedon: Multilingual Matters.
Ajzenstat, J. (1995). Decline of procedural liberalism: the slippery slope to secession. In J. H. Carens (ed.) *Is Quebec Nationalism Just? Perspectives from Anglophone Canada*. Montréal/Kingston: McGill-Queen's University Press, 120–36.
d'Aleyrac, J.-B. (1935). *Aventures militaires du XVIIIe siècle d'après les mémoires de Jean-Baptiste d'Aleyrac*. (Edited by C. Coste). Paris: Éditions Berger-Levrault.
Allegritti, I. (2003). Exploring intercultural citizenship in Australia. (Paper presented for the Department of Political Studies' Colloquiumat, Queen's University, Kingston, Ontario, Canada, 26 March 2003).
Alliance Quebec (2001). La communauté d'expression anglaise du Québec. (Mémoire presented to the États généraux sur la situation et l'avenir de la langue française au Québec, 2 March 2001).
Ammon, U. (1989). Towards a descriptive framework for the status/function/social position of a language within a country. In U. Ammon (ed.) *Status and Function of Language and Language Varieties*. Berlin: de Gruyter, 21–106.
Anctil, P. (1984). Double majorité et multiplicité ethnoculturelle à Montréal. *Recherches sociographiques* 25(3): 441–56.
Anctil, P. (1996). La trajectoire interculturelle du Québec: la société distincte vue à travers le prisme de l'immigration. In A. Lapierre, P. Smart and P. Savard (eds) *Language, Culture and Values in Canada at the Dawn of the 21st Century/Langues, cultures et valeurs au Canada à l'aube du XXIe siècle*. Ottawa: International Council for Canadian Studies/Carleton University Press, 133–54.
Anderson, B. (1983). *Imagined Communities: Reflections on the Origin and Growth of Nationalism*. London: Verso.
d'Anglejan, A. and Tucker, R. (1973). Sociolinguistic correlates of speech style in Quebec. In R. Shuy and R. Fasold (eds) *Language Attitudes: Current Trends and Prospects*. Washington: Georgetown University Press, 1–27.
Appadurai, A. (1990). Disjuncture and difference in the global cultural economy. In M. Featherstone (ed.) *Global Culture: Nationalism, Globalization and Modernity*. London: Sage, 295–310.
Appadurai, A. (1996). *Modernity at Large: Cultural Dimensions of Globalization*. Minneapolis: University of Minnesota Press.
Ardagh, J. (1999). *France in the New Century: Portrait of a Changing Society*. London: Viking.
Arel, D. (2001). Political stability in multinational democracies: comparing language dynamics in Brussels, Montreal and Barcelona. In A.-G. Gagnon and J. Tully (eds) *Multinational Democracies*. Cambridge: Cambridge University Press, 65–89.

Asselin, C. and McLaughlin, A. (1994). Les immigrants en Nouvelle-France au XVIIe siècle parlaient-ils français? In R. Mougeon and E. Beniak (eds) *Les origines du français québécois*. Sainte-Foy: Presses de l'Université Laval, 101–30.
Association québécoise des professeurs de français (1977). Le congrès du dixième anniversaire. Les résolutions de l'Assemblée générale. *Québec français* 28: 10–12.
Auger, J. (2005). Un bastion francophone en Amérique du Nord: le Québec. In A. Valdman, J. Auger and D. Piston-Hatlen (eds) *Le français en Amérique du Nord. État présent*. Sainte-Foy: Les Presses de l'Université Laval, 39–79.
Auger, P. (1988). Identification linguistique des Québécois et dictionnaire général d'usage ou le comment du sentiment linguistique des Québécois en 1986. *Revue québécoise de linguistique théorique et appliquée* 7(1): 55–69.
Bacqueville de la Potherie, C.-C. Le Roy dit (1753). *Histoire de l'Amérique septentrionale. Tome 1*. Paris: Brocas.
Baillargeon, S. (2001). Canada, Québec, même combat: protéger la diversité culturelle. In R. Côté (ed.) *L'annuaire du Québec 2002*. [Montréal]: Fides, 23–31.
Balthazar, L. (1988). Quebec's triangular situation in North America: a prototype? In I. D. Duchacek, D. Latouche and G. Stevenson (eds) *Perforated Sovereignties and International Relations*. New York: Greenwood Press, 83–9.
Balthazar, L. and Hero A. O. Jr. (1999). *Le Québec dans l'espace américain*. Montréal: Québec Amérique.
Baraby, A.-M. (1999). *Guide de conjugaisons en langue innue*. Sept-Îles: ICEM.
Baraby, A.-M. (2002). The process of spelling standardization of Innu-aimun (Montagnais). In B. Burnaby and J. Reyhner (eds) *Indigenous Languages across the Community*. Flagstaff, AZ: College of Education, Northern Arizona University. <http://jan.ucc.nau.edu/~jar/ILAC/ILAC_21.pdf> Accessed 15 July 2005.
Baraby, A.-M. and Drapeau, L. (forthcoming). *Grammaire de la langue innue*.
Barbaud, P. (1984). *Le choc des patois en Nouvelle-France*. Sillery: Presses de l'Université du Québec.
Bariteau, C. (1996). Pour une conception civique du Québec. *L'Action nationale* 86(9): 105–63.
Bariteau, C. (1998). *Québec 18 septembre 2001. Le monde pour horizon*. Montréal: Quebec Amérique.
Bariteau, C. (2000). La citoyenneté québécoise en devenir: des pratiques vers un projet. In Y. Boisvert, J. Hamel and M. Molgat (eds), with the collaboration of B. Ellefsen, *Vivre la citoyenneté. Identité, appartenance et participation*. Montréal: Éditions Liber, 135–41.
Bariteau, C. (2001). Quebec as a political, democratic and sovereign nation. In M. Venne (ed.) *Vive Quebec! New Thinking and New Approaches to the Quebec Nation*. (Translated by R. Chodos and L. Blair). Toronto: James Lorimer and Company, 137–45.
Barth, F. (1969). Introduction. In F. Barth (ed.) *Ethnic Groups and Boundaries: The Social Organisation of Cultural Difference*. Oslo: Universitetsforlaget, 9–38.
Barth, F. (1981). *Process and Form in Social Life: Selected Essays of Frederik Barth. Volume 1*. London: Routledge and Kegan Paul.
Baum, G. (2001). Nationals and social movements against market hegemony. In M. Venne (ed.) *Vive Quebec! New Thinking and New Approaches to the Quebec Nation*. (Translated by R. Chodos and L. Blair). Toronto: James Lorimer and Company, 80–6.
Beauchamp, L. (2004). Le français standard en usage au Québec. (Speech made by the ministre de la Culture et des Communications, Madame Line Beauchamp, 17 February). <http://www.spl.gouv.qc.ca/secretariat/d_subvention_Franqus.html> Accessed 15 February 2005.

Beauchemin, J. (2001). Defence and illustration of a nation torn. In M. Venne (ed.) *Vive Quebec! New Thinking and New Approaches to the Quebec Nation*. (Translated by R. Chodos and L. Blair). Toronto: James Lorimer and Company, 155–68.

Beauchemin, J. (2002). *L'histoire en trop. La mauvaise conscience des souverainistes québécois*. Montréal: VLB éditeur.

Beauchemin, N. (1976). Joual et français au Québec. In E. Snyder and A. Valdman (eds) *Identité culturelle et francophonie dans les Amériques (1). Colloque tenu à l'Université d'Indiana, Bloomington du 28 au 30 mars 1974*. Québec: Les Presses de l'Université Laval, 6–15.

Beaudoin, L. (2001). Québec in the Americas. (Address at the Summit of the Americas, Québec, 9 April 2001). <http://www.csis.org/americas/2001summit_beaudoin.htm> Accessed 27 July 2004.

Beaudoin, L. (2004a). Marchandisation et diversité culturelle. *Le Devoir*, 16 March.

Beaudoin, L. (2004b). Vue d'Afrique, à quoi sert la Francophonie? *Le Devoir*, 24 November.

Beaulieu, A. (2000). *Les autochtones du Québec. Des premières alliances aux revendications contemporaines*. Québec: Musée de la Civilisation/Fides.

Beaulieu, I. (2003). Le premier portrait des enfants de la loi 101. Sondage auprès des jeunes Québécois issus de l'immigration récente. In M. Venne (ed.) *L'annuaire du Québec 2004*. [Montréal]: Fides, 260–73.

Beiner, R. (2003). *Liberalism, Nationalism and Citizenship: Essays on the Problem of Political Community*. Vancouver: UBC Press.

Béland, P. (1999). *Le français, langue d'usage public au Québec en 1997. Rapport de recherche*. [Québec]: Conseil de la langue française.

Bélanger, H. (1972). *Place à l'homme. Éloge du français québécois*. Montréal: HMH.

Bélisle, L.-A. (1954). *Dictionnaire général de la langue française au Canada*. Québec: Bélisle éditeur.

Bellay, J. du (1549). *Défense et illustration de la langue françoise*. Paris: Langelier.

Bergeron, J. (2004). Where is bilingualism between identities and generations? In E. Floch and Y. Frenette (eds) *Community Vitality, Community Confidence: Analysis and Discussion on GPC International Survey on Attitudes and Perceptions of Official Languages*. Gatineau: Canadian Heritage, 71–98.

Bergeron, L. (1980). *Dictionnaire de la langue québécoise*. Montréal: VLB éditeur.

Bergeron, L. (1981). *La charte de la langue québécoise*. Montréal: VLB éditeur.

Bernier, I. (2001). La préservation de la diversité linguistique à l'heure de la mondialisation. *Cahiers de droit de l'Université Laval* 42(4): 930–60. <http://www.mcc.gouv.qc.ca/international/diversite-culturelle/pdf/diversite-linguistique.pdf> Accessed 27 July 2004.

Bernier, I. and Ruiz Fabri, H. (2002). *Évaluation de la faisabilité juridique d'un instrument international sur la diversité culturelle*. Québec: Groupe de travail franco-québécois sur la diversité culturelle. <http://www.mcc.gouv.ca/international/diversite-culturelle/pdf/106145-faisabilite.pdf> Accessed 27 July 2004.

Berrendonner, A. (1982). *L'éternel grammairien. Étude du discours normatif*. Bern/Frankfurt: Lang.

Bienvenue, J. (1990). La norme contre l'usage: 'office' et 'bureau' devant le tribunal du Québec. In N. Corbett (ed.) *Langue et identité. Le français et les francophones d'Amérique du Nord*. Sainte-Foy: Les Presses de l'Université Laval, 353–68.

Billig, M. (1995). *Banal Nationalism*. London: Sage Publications.

Birnbaum, P. (2004). Between universalism and multiculturalism: The French model in contemporary political theory. In A. Dieckhoff (ed.) *The Politics of Belonging: Nationalism, Liberalism, and Pluralism*. Lanham: Lexington Books, 177–93.

Bissoondath, N. (2002). *Selling Illusions: The Cult of Multiculturalism in Canada.* (Revised and updated edition). Toronto: Penguin.

Bloc Québécois (1999). Chantier de réflexion sur la citoyenneté et la démocratie. (Presented at the Conseil Général du Bloc Québécois held at Rivière-du Loup, 17–18 April).

Blue, R. (2005). Let's hear it for an audible Anglo star. *Log Cabin Chronicles*, 11 June 2005. <http://www.tomifobia.com/ricky-blue/audible_anglo.shtml> Accessed 15 June 2005.

Boileau, J. (2001). Commission des États généraux sur la langue française: Larose prêche la réconciliation. *Le Devoir*, 21 August.

Boileau, J. (2005). L'anglais à six ans. *Le Devoir*, 14 February.

Boisvert, Y. (2005). On va les avoir, les Anglais! *La Presse*, 30 June.

Bouchard, C. (2000). Anglicisation et autodépréciation In M. Plourde (ed.), with the collaboration of H. Duval and P. Georgeault, *Le français au Québec. 400 ans d'histoire et de vie*. [Montréal/Québec]: Fides/Publications du Québec, 197–205.

Bouchard, C. (2002). *La langue et le nombril. Une histoire sociolinguistique du Québec*. (2nd edition). [Montréal]: Fides.

Bouchard, C. (2005). La question de la qualité de la langue aujourd'hui. In A. Stefanescu and P. Georgeault (eds) *Le français au Québec. Les nouveaux défis.* [Montréal]: Fides, 387–97.

Bouchard, G. (1997). Ouvrir le cercle de la nation. Activer la cohésion sociale. Réflexion sur le Québec et sa diversité. *L'Action nationale* 87(4): 107–37.

Bouchard, G. (1999). *La nation québécoise au futur et au passé*. Montréal: VLB éditeur.

Bouchard, G. (2001a). Building the Quebec nation: manifesto for a national coalition. In M. Venne (ed.) *Vive Quebec! New Thinking and New Approaches to the Quebec Nation.* (Translated by R. Chodos and L. Blair). Toronto: James Lorimer and Company, 27–38.

Bouchard, G. (2001b). *Genèse des nations et cultures du Nouveau Monde*. (Boréal compact 126). Montréal: Boréal.

Bouchard, G. (2002). Un monde à repenser: la crise des imaginaires, la mondialisation et les petites nations. (Presentation at the *Colloque Panaméricain. Industries culturelles et dialogue des civilisations dans les Amériques*). <http://www.er.uqam.ca/nobel/gricis/even/collpan/cp_ps_a.htm> Accessed 27 July 2004.

Bouchard, G., Rocher, F. and Rocher, G. (1991). *Les francophones québécois*. Montréal: Conseil scolaire de l'île de Montréal.

Bouchard, P. and Maurais, J. (1999). La norme et l'école. L'opinion des Québécois. *Terminogramme* 91/92: 91–116.

Boucher, G. (2004) Une « convention presque aussi importante que celle des droits de l'homme ». *Le Devoir*, 20–21 November.

Boucher, N. (2005). La transmission intergénérationnelle des savoirs dans la communauté innue de Mashteuiatsh. Les savoir-faire et les savoir-être au coeur des relations entre les Pekuakamiulnuatsh. Unpublished Masters thesis, Université Laval.

Bourdieu, P. (1982). *Ce que parler veut dire. L'économie des échanges linguistiques*. Paris: Fayard.

Bourhis, R. Y. (1984). *Conflict and Language Planning in Québec*. Clevedon: Multilingual Matters.

Bourhis, R. Y. (1997). Language policies and language attitudes: le monde de la francophonie. In N. Coupland and A. Jaworski (eds) *Sociolinguistics: A Reader and Coursebook*. Basingstoke: Macmillan, 306–22.

Bourhis, R. Y. and Bougie, E. (1998). Le modèle d'acculturation interactif: une étude exploratoire. *Revue québécoise de psychologie* 19(3): 75–114.

Bourhis, R. Y. and Lepicq, D. (1993). Québécois French and language issues in Québec. In R. Posner and J. N. Green (eds) *Trends in Romance Linguistics and Philology. Volume 5. Bilingualism and Linguistic Conflict in Romance.* Berlin/New York: Mouton de Gruyter, 345–81.

Bourhis, R. Y. and Lepicq, D. (2004). *La vitalité des communautés francophone et anglophone du Québec. Bilan et perspectives depuis la loi 101.* (Cahier de recherche no. 11). Montréal: Chaire Concordia-UQÀM en études ethniques.

Bourhis, R. Y., Moïse, L. C., Perreault, S. and Sénécal, S. (1997). Towards an interactive acculturation model: a social psychological approach. *International Journal of Psychology* 32(6): 369–86.

Bourque, G. (2001). Between nations and society. In M. Venne (ed.) *Vive Quebec! New Thinking and New Approaches to the Quebec Nation.* (Translated by R. Chodos and L. Blair). Toronto: James Lorimer and Company, 98–112.

Bourque, G. and Duchastel, J. (2000). Multiculturalisme, pluralisme et communauté politique: le Canada et le Québec. In M. Elbaz and D. Helly (eds) *Mondialisation, citoyenneté et multicultutalisme.* Paris/Sainte-Foy: L'Harmattan/Les Presses de l'Université Laval, 147–69.

Bouthillier, G. (1997). *L'obsession ethnique.* Outremont: Lanctôt éditeur.

Bouthillier, G. and Meynaud, J. (1972). *Le choc des langues au Québec, 1760–1970.* Montréal: Presses de l'Université du Québec.

Brass, P. R. (1991). *Ethnicity and Nationalism.* Newbury Park: Sage.

Breton, R. (1986). Multiculturalism and Canadian nation-building. In A. Cairns and C. Williams (eds) *The Politics of Gender, Ethnicity and Language in Canada.* Toronto: University of Toronto Press, 27–66.

Breton, R. (1988). From ethnic to civic nationalism: English Canada and Quebec. *Ethnic and Racial Studies* 11(1): 85–102.

Brière, M. (2002). Nation civique ou nation ethnique. *L'Action nationale* 92(3). <http://www.action-nationale.qc.ca/02-3/briere.html> Accessed 15 April 2002.

Brochu, A. (2000). L'éveil de la parole. In M. Plourde (ed.), with the collaboration of H. Duval and P. Georgeault, *Le français au Québec. 400 ans d'histoire et de vie.* [Montréal/Québec]: Fides/Publications du Québec, 260–71.

Brown, D. (2000). *Contemporary Nationalism: Civic, Ethnocultural and Multicultural Politics.* London/New York: Routledge.

Bulmer, M. (2001). Ethnicity. In A. S. Leoussi (ed.) *Encyclopaedia of Nationalism.* New Brunswick/London: Transaction, 69–73.

Burnaby, B. and Mackenzie, M. (2001). Cree decision making concerning language: a case study. *Journal of Multilingual and Multicultural Development* 22(3): 191–209.

Burnaby, B., Mackenzie, M. and Bobbish Salt, L. (1999). Native language for every subject: the Cree Language of Instruction Project. In J. Reyhner, G. Cantoni, R. N. St. Clair and E. Parsons Yazzie (eds) *Revitalizing Indigenous Languages.* Flagstaff, AZ: Northern Arizona University. <jan.ucc.nau.edu/~jar/Burnaby.html> Accessed 31 December 2005.

Cairns, A. (2000). *Citizens Plus: Aboriginal Peoples and the Canadian State.* Vancouver/Toronto: UBC Press.

Cajolet-Laganière, H. and Martel, P. (1995). *La qualité de la langue au Québec.* (Diagnostic 18). Québec: Institut québécois de recherche sur la culture.

Caldwell, G. (1988). Immigration et la nécessité d'une culture publique commune. *L'Action nationale* 78(8): 705–11.

Caldwell, G. (1994). *La question du Québec anglais.* Québec: Institut québécois de recherche sur la culture.

Caldwell, G. (1998). English Quebec. In J. Edwards (ed.) *Language in Canada*. Cambridge: Cambridge University Press, 273–92.
Caldwell, G. (2001). *La culture publique commune. Les règles du jeu de la vie publique au Québec et les fondements de ces règles*. Québec: Éditions Nota bene.
Caldwell, G. (2002). La Charte de la langue française vue par les anglophones. In P. Bouchard and R. Y. Bourhis (eds) *L'aménagement linguistique au Québec: 25 ans d'application de la Charte de la langue française*. (*Revue d'aménagement linguistique*, hors série), 27–36.
Caldwell, G. and Harvey, J. (1994). Le prérequis à l'intégration des immigrants: une culture publique commune au Québec. *L'Action nationale* 84(6): 786–94.
Caldwell, G. and Waddell, E. (1982a). Conclusion: looking to the future. In G. Caldwell and E. Waddell (eds) *The English of Quebec: From Majority to Minority Status*. Québec: Institut québécois de recherche sur la culture, 414–49.
Caldwell, G. and Waddell, E. (1982b). Introduction: taking stock and confronting the future. In G. Caldwell and E. Waddell (eds) *The English of Quebec: From Majority to Minority Status*. Québec: Institut québécois de recherche sur la culture, 15–23.
Caldwell, G. and Waddell, E. (1982c). Preface to Part III: the many faces of English Quebec. In G. Caldwell and E. Waddell (eds) *The English of Quebec: From Majority to Minority Status*. Québec: Institut québécois de recherche sur la culture, 155–8.
Caldwell, Gary and Waddell, E. (eds) (1982d). *The English of Quebec: From Majority to Minority Status*. Québec: Institut québécois de recherche sur la culture.
Canadian Heritage (2003). Site visit – Waskaganish (Cree Literacy Program). *Aboriginal Languages Initiative (ALI) Evaluation*. <http://www.pch.gc.ca/progs/em-cr/eval/2003/2003_01/15_e.cfm> Accessed 31 December 2005.
Canet, R. (2003). De la conception allemande à la conception française de la nation: réflexion sur le déterminisme historico-social de la pensée. In R. Canet and J. Duchastel (eds) *La nation en débat. Entre modernité et postmodernité*. Outremont: Athéna éditions, 135–51.
Cantin, S. (2001a). Cinq ans de Bouchardisme. *Le Devoir*, 20 January. <http://www.vigile.net/01–1/demission-cantin.html> Accessed 25 October 2002.
Cantin, S. (2001b). Emerging from survival mode. In M. Venne (ed.) *Vive Quebec! New Thinking and New Approaches to the Quebec Nation*. (Translated by R. Chodos and L. Blair). Toronto: James Lorimer and Company, 49–58.
Carens, J. H. (1995a). Immigration, political community, and the transformation of identity: Quebec's immigration policies in critical perspective. In J. H. Carens (ed.) *Is Quebec Nationalism Just? Perspectives from Anglophone Canada*. Montréal/Kingston: McGill-Queen's University Press, 20–81.
Carens, J. H. (ed.) (1995b). *Is Quebec Nationalism Just? Perspectives from Anglophone Canada*. Montréal/Kingston: McGill-Queen's University Press.
Carens, J. H. (2000). *Culture, Citizenship and Community. A Contextual Exploration of Justice as Evenhandedness*. New York: Oxford University Press.
Carpentier, A. (2004). *Tout est-il joué avant l'arrivée? Étude de facteurs associés à un usage prédominant du français ou de l'anglais chez les immigrants allophones arrivés au Québec adultes*. [Québec]: Conseil supérieur de la langue française.
Castells, M. (1997). *The Power of Identity*. Oxford: Blackwell Publishers.
Castonguay, C. (2002a). Assimilation linguistique et remplacement des générations: francophones et anglophones au Québec et au Canada. *Recherches sociographiques* 43(1): 149–82.
Castonguay, C. (2002b). Et la langue de travail, monsieur Larose? In C. Castonguay, P. Dubuc and J.-C. Germain *Larose n'est pas Larousse. Regards critiques – La*

Commission des États généraux sur la situation et l'avenir de la langue française au Québec. Paroisse Notre-Dame-des-Neiges/Montréal: Éditions Trois-Pistoles/Éditions du Renouveau québécois, 11–15.

Castonguay, C. (2003). La vraie question linguistique: quelle est la force d'attraction réelle du français au Québec? In M. Venne (ed.) *L'annuaire du Québec 2004*. [Montréal]: Fides, 232–53.

Certeau, M. de, Julia, D. and Revel, J. (1975). *Une politique de la langue. La Révolution française et les patois*. Paris: Gallimard.

Chambers, G. (1999). La communauté des anglophones d'hier et d'aujourd'hui. In R. Lahaise (ed.) *Québec 2000. Multiples visages d'une culture*. Montréal: Hurtubise HMH, 255–65.

Chambers, G. (2000). Les relations entre anglophones et francophones. In M. Plourde (ed.), with the collaboration of H. Duval and P. Georgeault, *Le français au Québec. 400 ans d'histoire et de vie*. [Montréal/Québec]: Fides/Publications du Québec, 319–25.

Charlevoix, P.-F.-X. de (1744). *Histoire et description générale de la Nouvelle-France avec le Journal historique d'un voyage fait par ordre du Roi dans l'Amérique Septentrionale. Volume 3*. Paris: Giffart.

Chatton, P.-F. and Bapst, J. M. (1991). *Le défi francophone*. Brussels/Paris: Bruylant/LGDJ.

Chevrier, M. (1997). *Laws and Languages in Québec: The Principles and Means of Québec's Language Policy*. [Québec]: Ministère des Relations internationales.

Chevrier, M. (2003). Language policy for a language in exile. In P. Larrivée (ed.) *Linguistic Conflict and Language Laws: Understanding the Quebec Question*. Houndmills, Basingstoke/New York: Palgrave Macmillan, 118–62.

Citizenship and Immigration Canada (2005a). Canada – Permanent residents by provincial/territorial region and category. *Facts and Figures 2004. Immigration Overview: Permanent and Temporary Residents*. <http://www.cic.gc.ca/english/pub/facts2004/permanent/19.html> Accessed 12 February 2006.

Citizenship and Immigration Canada (2005b). Canada – Permanent residents by provincial or territorial and urban area. *Facts and Figures 2004. Immigration Overview: Permanent and Temporary Residents*. <http://www.cic.gc.ca/english/pub/facts2004/permanent/18.html> Accessed 12 February 2006.

Citron, S. (1991). *Le mythe national*. (2nd edition). Paris: Les Éditions Ouvrières/Études et Documentation Internationales.

Clapin, S. (1894). *Dictionnaire canadien-français ou Lexique-glossaire des mots, expressions et locutions ne se trouvant pas dans les dictionnaires courants et dont l'usage appartient surtout aux Canadiens français*. Montréal: Beauchemin et fils.

Cleary, B. and Dorais, L.-J. (2005). Le défi des langues autochtones au Québec. In A. Stefanescu and P. Georgeault (eds) *Le français au Québec. Les nouveaux défis*. [Montréal]: Fides, 233–51.

Clyne, M. (1992). Epilogue. In M. Clyne (ed.) *Pluricentric Languages: Differing Norms in Different Nations*. Berlin: Mouton de Gruyter, 455–65.

Cohen, A. (1974a). Introduction: the lesson of ethnicity. In A. Cohen (ed.) *Urban Ethnicity*. London: Tavistock, ix–xxii.

Cohen, A. (1974b). *Two-Dimensional Man: An Essay on the Anthropology of Power and Symbolism in Complex Society*. London: Tavistock.

Cohen, J. A. (2001). Value judgements and political assessments about national models of citizenship: the U.S. and French cases. In C. C. Gould and P. Pasquino (eds) *Cultural Identity and the Nation-State*. Lanham: Rowman and Littlefield Publishers, 109–30.

Comité constitutionnel du Parti libéral du Québec (1991). *Un Québec libre de ses choix.* Montréal/Québec: Parti libéral du Québec.
Commission sur l'avenir politique et constitutionnel du Québec (1991). *L'avenir politique et constitutionnel du Québec.* [Québec]: Les Publications du Québec.
Connor, W. (1993). Beyond reason: the nature of the ethnonational bond. *Ethnic and Racial Studies* 16(3): 373–89.
Conrick, M. (2002a). French in the Americas. In K. Salhi (ed.) *French in and out of France: Language Policies, Intercultural Antagonisms and Dialogue.* (Modern French Identities 18). Bern: Peter Lang, 237–63.
Conrick, M. (2002b). Language policy and gender issues. In K. Salhi (ed.) *French in and out of France: Language Policies, Intercultural Antagonisms and Dialogue.* (Modern French Identities 18). Bern: Peter Lang, 205–35.
Conseil de la langue française (ed.) (1990a). *Actes du colloque sur l'aménagement de la langue au Québec. Communications et synthèse, Mont-Gabriel, 7 et 8 décembre 1989.* [Québec]: Conseil de la langue française. <http://www.cslf.gouv.qc.ca> Accessed 7 March 2005.
Conseil de la langue française (ed.) (1990b). *Dix études portant sur l'aménagement de la langue au Québec.* [Québec]: Conseil de la langue française. <http://www.cslf.gouv.qc.ca> Accessed 7 March 2005.
Conseil de la langue française (1991). *L'aménagement de la langue. Pour une description du français québécois. Rapport et avis au ministre responsable de la Charte de la langue française.* [Québec]: Conseil de la langue française. <http://www.cslf.gouv.qc.ca> Accessed 24 March 2005.
Conseil de la langue française (2002). *Les enfants de la loi 101. Groupes de discussion exploratoires, novembre 2000.* [Québec]: Conseil de la langue française.
Conseil Tribal Mamuitun (2004). Signature de l'entente de principe d'ordre général entre les premières nations de Mamuitun et Nutashkuan et les gouvernements du Québec et du Canada. Une nouvelle page de notre histoire commune. *Conseil Tribal Mamuitun. Secteur Négociations.* <http://www.mamuitun.com/signature-discours.asp> Accessed 18 January 2006.
Cooper, R. L. (1989). *Language Planning and Social Change.* Cambridge: Cambridge University Press.
Corbeil, J.-C. (1979). Essai sur l'origine historique de la situation linguistique du Québec. In A. Valdman (ed.), with the collaboration of R. Chaudenson and G. Manessy, *Le français hors de France.* Paris: Honoré Champion, 21–32.
Corbeil, J.-C. (1986). Le régionalisme lexical: un cas privilégié de variation linguistique. In L. Boisvert, C. Poirier and C. Verreault (eds) *La lexicographie québécoise: bilan et perspectives.* Québec: Les Presses de l'Université Laval, 55–61.
Corbeil, J.-C. (1988). Assumer ou taire les usages lexicaux du Québec. *Revue québécoise de linguistique théorique et appliquée* 7(1): 69–79.
Corbeil, M. (2005). Première rencontre sur le statut de Métis. *Le Soleil,* 18 September.
Council of Europe (2004). *Education for Democratic Citizenship.* Strasbourg: Council of Europe, Division for Citizenship and Human Rights Education. <http://www.coe.int/T/E/Cultural_Co-operation/education/E.D.C/> Accessed 19 January 2005.
Croucher, S. L. (2004). *Globalization and Belonging. The Politics of Identity in a Changing World.* Lanham: Rowman & Littlefield Publishers.
CRI (Conseil des relations interculturelles) (1997). *Un Québec pour tous les citoyens. Les défis actuels d'une démocratie pluraliste.* Québec: Conseil des relations interculturelles.
Cuccioletta, D. (ed.) (2001). *L'américanité et les Amériques.* Sainte-Foy: Les Presses de l'Université Laval.

Cummins, J. (1991). Interdependence of first- and second-language proficiency in bilingual children. In E. Bialystok (ed.) *Language Processing in Bilingual Children*. Cambridge: Cambridge University Press, 70–89.

Dagger, R. (1997). *Civic Virtues: Rights, Citizenship and Republican Liberalism*. New York: Oxford University Press.

Daveluy, M. (2004). Self-governance vs linguistic peace among the Canadian Inuit. (Presentation at the Fòrum Universal de les Cultures, Barcelona 2004). <http://www.barcelona2004.org/esp/banco_del_conocimiento/docs/PO_35_EN_D AVELOUY.pdf> Accessed 25 September 2005.

Derriennic, J.-P. (1995). *Nationalisme et démocratie. Réflexion sur les illusions des indépendantistes québécois*. Montréal: Éditions du Boréal.

Desbiens, J.-P. (1960). *Les insolences du frère Untel*. Montréal: Les Éditions de l'Homme.

Deshaies, D. (1984). Une norme, des normes ou pourquoi pas autre chose? In M. Amyot (ed.) *Le statut culturel du français au Québec. Actes du congrès Langue et société au Québec. Volume 2*. Québec: Éditeur officiel du Québec. <http://www.cslf.gouv.qc.ca> Accessed 18 July 2005.

Dictionnaire du français plus à l'usage des francophones d'Amérique (1988). (Edition established under the responsibility of A. E. Shiaty, with the collaboration of P. Auger and N. Beauchemin; principal editor: C. Poirier, with the assistance of L. Mercier and C. Verreault). Montréal: Centre Éducatif et Culturel inc.

Dictionnaire québécois d'aujourd'hui (1992). (Edited by J.-C. Boulanger; supervised by A. Rey). Saint Laurent: Dicorobert inc.

Dieckhoff, A. (2000). *La nation dans tous ses états. Les identités nationales en mouvement*. Paris: Flammarion.

Dion, S. (1991). Le nationalisme dans la convergence culturelle: le Québec contemporain et le paradoxe de Tocqueville. In R. Hudon and R. Pelletier (eds) *L'engagement de l'intellectuel. Mélanges en l'honneur de Léon Dion*. Sainte-Foy: Les Presses de l'Université Laval, 291–311.

Dor, G. (1996). *Anna braillé ène shot (Elle a beaucoup pleuré). Essai sur le langage parlé des Québécois*. Outremont: Lanctôt éditeur.

Dor, G. (1997). *Ta mé tu là? (Ta mère est-elle là?). Un autre essai sur le langage parlé des Québécois*. Outremont: Lanctôt éditeur.

Dor, G. (1998). *Les qui qui et les que que, ou le français torturé à la télé. Troisième et dernier essai sur le langage parlé des Québécois*. Outremont: Lanctôt éditeur.

Dorais, L.-J. (1996). The Aboriginal languages of Quebec, past and present. In J. Maurais (ed.) *Quebec's Aboriginal Languages. History, Planning, Development*. Clevedon: Multilingual Matters, 43–100.

Dorais, L.-J. (2003) Les langues autochtones en 2003. (Presentation at the 14th GETIC-CIERA conference, 27 March 2003). <http://www.getic.ulaval.ca/publications/langues2003.htm> Accessed 11 February 2003.

Dorais, L.-J. and Collis, D. R. F. (1987). *Inuit Bilingualism and Diglossia*. Sainte-Foy: Centre international de recherche sur le bilinguisme, Université Laval.

Doyon, F. (2004). S.O.S. langues autochtones – vers une loi 101 des Premières Nations?, *Le Devoir*, 25 October.

Drapeau, L. (1985). Decision making on a standard orthography: the Betsiamites case. In B. Burnaby (ed.) *Promoting Native Writing Systems in Canada*. Toronto: OISE Press, 27–48.

Drapeau, L. (1994a). Bilinguisme et érosion lexicale dans une communauté montagnaise. In P. Martel and J. Maurais (eds) *Langues et sociétés en contact. Mélanges en l'honneur de J.-C. Corbeil*. Tübingen: Niemeyer, 363–76.

Drapeau, L. (1994b). *Dictionnaire montagnais-français*. (2nd edition). Sainte-Foy: Presses de l'Université du Québec.

Drapeau, L. (1994c). L'utilisation des langues autochtones en milieu scolaire. *Vie pédagogique* 87: 15–18.
Drapeau, L. (1995). Code-switching in caretaker speech and bilingual competence in a native village of northern Quebec. *International Journal of the Sociology of Language* 113: 157–64.
Drapeau, L. (1996). The state of the art in linguistic research, standardisation and modernisation in Quebec Aboriginal languages. In J. Maurais (ed.) *Quebec's Aboriginal Languages: History, Planning, Development*. Clevedon: Multilingual Matters, 129–58.
Drapeau, L. and Corbeil, J.-C. (1996). The Aboriginal languages in the perspective of language planning. In J. Maurais (ed.) *Quebec's Aboriginal Languages: History, Planning, Development*. Clevedon: Multilingual Matters, 288–307.
Dubuc, P. (2002). Y a-t-il un « *anglo rose* » ? In C. Castonguay, P. Dubuc and J.-C. Germain *Larose n'est pas Larousse. Regards critiques – La Commission des États généraux sur la situation et l'avenir de la langue française au Québec*. Paroisse Notre-Dame-des-Neiges/ Montréal: Éditions Trois-Pistoles/Éditions du Renouveau québécois, 91–4.
Duchacek, I. D. (1988). Multicommunal and bicommunal polities and their international relations. In I. D. Duchacek, D. Latouche and G. Stevenson (eds) *Perforated Sovereignties and International Relations*. New York: Greenwood Press, 3–28.
Duchastel, J. (2000). De l'universel au particulier. De l'individu citoyen au citoyen incorporé. In Y. Boisvert, J. Hamel and M. Molgat (eds), with the collaboration of B. Ellefsen, *Vivre la citoyenneté. Identité, appartenance et participation*. Montréal: Éditions Liber, 37–52.
Dufour, F.-G. (2001). *Patriotisme constitutionnel et nationalisme. Sur Jürgen Habermas*. Montréal: Liber.
Dulong, G. (1966). *Bibliographie linguistique du Canada français*. Québec/Paris: Les Presses de l'Université Laval/Klincksieck.
Dumas, D. (1987). *Nos façons de parler. Les prononciations en français québécois*. Presses de l'Université du Québec.
Dumas, D. (2001). Tendances récentes dans la prononciation du français québécois. In M.-A. Hintze, T. Pooley and A. Judge (eds) *French Accents: Phonological and Sociolinguistic Perspectives*. London: AFLS/CILT, 240–50.
Dumas, G. (2004). La mondialisation et la diversité linguistique: le nécessaire dialogue. (Address at the Congrès mondial des professeurs de français, *Le français: le défi de la diversité*, Atlanta, 20 July 2004). <http://www.spl.gouv.qc.ca/secretariat/ d_atlanta.html> Accessed 28 February 2005.
Dumont, F. (1996). *Genèse de la société québécoise*. (Boréal compact 74). Montréal: Boréal.
Dumont, F. (1997). *Raisons communes*. (Boréal compact 80). Montréal: Boréal.
Dunn, O. (1880). *Glossaire franco-canadien et vocabulaire de locutions vicieuses usitées au Canada*. Québec: A. Côté et Cie.
Dutrisac, R. (2002). Mondialisation tous azimuts à Québec. In R. Côté and M. Venne (eds) *L'annuaire du Québec 2003*. [Montréal]: Fides, 664–9.
Dutrisac, R. (2004). Louise Beaudoin placerait la barre trop haut. *Le Devoir*, 27 September.
Edwards, J. (1994). Ethnolinguistic pluralism and its discontents: a Canadian study, and some general observations. *International Journal of the Sociology of Language* 110: 5–85.
Edwards, J. (2003). Language and the future: choices and constraints. In H. Tonkin and T. Reagan (eds) *Language in the Twenty-First Century*. Amsterdam/Philadelphia: John Benjamins, 35–45.
Eriksen, T. H. (1993). *Ethnicity and Nationalism*. London: Pluto Press.

Facal, J. (2001). Identité québécoise: trop tôt pour une commission sur la citoyenneté. *Le Devoir*, 26 June. <http://www.ledevoir.com> Accessed 14 February 2005.
Featherstone, M. (ed.) (1990). *Global Culture: Nationalism, Globalization and Modernity*. London: Sage.
Feldman, E. J. and Feldman, L. G. (1988). Quebec's internationalization of North American federalism. In I. D. Duchacek, D. Latouche and G. Stevenson (eds) *Perforated Sovereignties and International Relations*. New York: Greenwood Press, 69–80.
Feldstein, P. (2003). Translator's preface. In J. Maclure *Quebec Identity: The Challenge of Pluralism*. Montréal/Kingston: McGill-Queen's University Press, xvii–xviii.
Ferguson, M. (1992). The mythology about globalization. *European Journal of Communication* 7: 69–93.
Fettes, M. (1998). Life on the edge: Canada's Aboriginal languages under official bilingualism. In T. Ricento and B. Burnaby (eds) *Language and Politics in the United States and Canada*. Mahwah, NJ/London: Lawrence Earlbaum Associates, 117–49.
Fieschi, C. and Varouxakis, G. (2001). Citizenship and nationality. In A. S. Leoussi (ed.) *Encyclopaedia of Nationalism*. New Brunswick/London: Transaction, 21–5.
Fishman, J. A. (1977). The spread of English as a new perspective for the study of 'language maintenance and language shift'. In J. A. Fishman, R. L. Cooper and A. W. Conrad (eds) *The Spread of English: The Sociology of English as an Additional Language*. Rowley: Newbury House, 109–33.
Fishman, J. A. (1991). *Reversing Language Shift: Theoretical and Empirical Foundations of Assistance to Threatened Languages*. Clevedon: Multilingual Matters.
Fishman, J. A. (ed.) (2001). *Can Threatened Languages be Saved? Reversing Language Shift, Revisited: A 21st Century Perspective*. Clevedon: Multilingual Matters.
Flosse, G. (2001). The concept of Polynesian citizenship. *Revue juridique polynésienne* Hors série 1. <http://www.upf.pf/recherche/IRIDIP/RJP/RJP.htm> Accessed 22 January 2006.
Forester, H. (2005). Alliance Quebec deserves support. *The Gazette*, 24 May.
Fournier, M., Rosenberg, M. and White, D. (1997). *Quebec Society: Critical Issues*. Scarborough: Prentice Hall Canada.
Francard, M. (1998). La légitimité passe-t-elle par la reconnaissance d'une variété 'nationale'? Le cas de la communauté française de Wallonie-Bruxelles. In C. Verreault and L. Mercier (eds), with the participation of D. Dumas, *Représentation de la langue et légitimité linguistique: le français et ses variétés nationales*. (*Revue québécoise de linguistique* 26 (2)). Montréal: Université du Québec à Montréal, 13–23.
FRANQUS (Français standard en usage au Québec) (n.d.). Problématique. <http://franqus.usherbrooke.ca/problematique.html> Accessed 5 April 2005.
Fréchette, C. (2001). *Language Issues in the Integration of the Americas*. Québec: Conseil de la langue française.
Fréchette, C. (2005). Pour un changement du chapitre linguistique. In A. Stefanescu and P. Georgeault (eds) *Le français au Québec. Les nouveaux défis*. [Montréal]: Fides, 31–89.
Freed, J. (2005). I'm just the anglo leader the PQ needs. *The Gazette*, 2 July.
Frenette, Y. (2000). Les relations entre le Québec et les francophones hors Québec. In M. Plourde (ed.), with the collaboration of H. Duval and P. Georgeault, *Le français au Québec. 400 ans d'histoire et de vie*. [Montréal/Québec]: Fides/Publications du Québec, 326–9.
Friedman, J. (1990). Being in the world: globalization and localization. In M. Featherstone (ed.) *Global Culture: Nationalism, Globalization and Modernity*. London: Sage, 311–28.

Fry, E. (2003a). Le Québec tire profit de sa relation économique avec les États-Unis. In M. Venne (ed.) *L'annuaire du Québec 2004*. [Montréal]: Fides, 952–64.
Fry, E. (2003b). Les relations internationales du Québec. In A.-G. Gagnon (ed.) *Québec: État et société. Tome 2*. Montréal: Québec Amérique, 505–35.
Gadet, F. (2001). Préface. In B. Pöll, *Francophonies périphériques. Histoire, statut et profil des principales variétés du français hors de France*. Paris: L'Harmattan, 7–10.
Gagné, G. (1979). Quelques aspects 'sociolinguistiques' du français au Canada et au Québec. In A. Valdman (ed.), with the collaboration of R. Chaudenson and G. Manessy, *Le français hors de France*. Paris: Honoré Champion, 33–59.
Gagné, G. (1983). Norme et enseignement de la langue maternelle. In É. Bédard and J. Maurais (eds) *La norme linguistique*. [Québec]: Conseil de la langue française, 463–509.
Gagnon, A.-G. (2000). Plaidoyer pour l'interculturalisme. *Possibles* 24(4): 11–25.
Gagnon, A.-G. (2001). Plaidoyer pour une commission nationale sur la citoyenneté québécoise. *Le Devoir*, 15 June. <http://www.vigile.net/dossier-nation/1-6/15-gagnon.html> Accessed 20 June 2001.
Gagnon, A.-G. and Iacovino, R. (2002). Framing citizenship status in an age of polyethnicity: Quebec's model of interculturalism. In H. Telford and H. Lazar (eds) *Canada: The State of the Federation 2001. Canadian Political Culture(s) in Transition*. Montréal/Kingston: McGill-Queen's University Press, 313–42. <http://www.iigr.ca/pdf/publications/163_Canada_The_State_of_the_.pdf> Accessed 11 February 2005.
Gagnon, A.-G. and Iacovino, R. (2004). Interculturalism: expanding the boundaries of citizenship. In A.-G. Gagnon (ed.), *Québec: State and Society*. (3rd edition). Peterborough,CA: Broadview Press, 369–88.
Gagnon, A.-G. and Jézéquel, M. (2004). Pour une reconnaissance mutuelle et un accommodement raisonnable – le modèle québécois d'intégration culturelle est à préserver. *Le Devoir*, 17 May. <http://www.ledevoir.com> Accessed on 5 February 2005.
Gagnon, E. (1916[1802]). Notre langue. *Le Devoir*, 12 February.
Gandhi, M. (1965). *Our Language Problem*. (Edited by A. T. Hingorani). Bombay: Bhartiya Vidya Bhavan.
Gardner, R. C. and Lambert, W. E. (1972). *Attitudes and Motivation in Second-Language Learning*. Rowley: Newbury House.
Garmadi, J. (1981). *La sociolinguistique*. Paris: Presses Universitaires de France.
Geertz, C. (1973). *The Interpretation of Cultures*. London: Fontana.
Gellner, E. (1983). *Nations and Nationalism*. Oxford: Basil Blackwood.
Gendron, J.-D. (1986). Existe-t-il un usage lexical prédominant à l'heure actuelle au Québec? In L. Boisvert, C. Poirier and C. Verreault (eds) *La lexicographie québécoise: bilan et perspectives*. Québec: Les Presses de l'Université Laval, 198–209.
Gendron, J.-D. (1990a). Les arguments pour ou contre un projet de dictionnaire décrivant les usages du français au Québec. In Conseil de la langue française (ed.) *Actes du colloque sur l'aménagement de la langue au Québec. Communications et syntèse, Mont-Gabriel, 7 et 8 décembre 1989*. [Québec]: Conseil de la langue française. <http://www.cslf.gouv.qc.ca> Accessed 7 March 2005.
Gendron, J.-D. (1990b). La conscience linguistique des Franco-Québécois depuis la Révolution tranquille. In N. Corbett (ed.) *Langue et identité. Le français et les francophones d'Amérique du Nord*. Sainte-Foy: Les Presses de l'Université Laval, 53–62.
Gendron, J.-D. (1990c). Modèles linguistiques, évolution sociale et normalisation du langage. In N. Corbett (ed.) *Langue et identité. Le français et les francophones d'Amérique du Nord*. Sainte-Foy: Les Presses de l'Université Laval, 369–88.
Gendron, J.-D. (2000). Remarques sur la prononciation du français parlé au Canada sous le régime français (1608–1760). In M.-R. Simoni-Aurembou (ed.) *Français du*

Canada – *français de France. Actes du cinquième Colloque international de Bellême du 5 au 7 juin 1997.* Tübingen: Max Niemeyer Verlag, 9–23.
Genesee, F. (1987) *Learning through Two Languages: Studies in Immersion and Bilingual Education.* Cambridge, MA: Newbury House.
George, J. (2005). Like Quebec's language law, but more complicated. *Nunatsiaq News,* 25 November. <http://www.nunatsiaq.com/archives/51125/news/nunavik/51125_01html> Accessed 1 February 2006.
Georgeault, P. (2003). Le français dans les Amériques. Pour une politique d'aménagement de l'usage des langues. (Presentation at the Colloque du Réseau francophone du français dans le monde (RIFRAM), Paris, 4–5 November 2003).
Georgeault, P. (2006). Langue et diversité: un défi à relever. In P. Georgeault and M. Pagé (eds) *Le français, langue de la diversité québécoise. Une réflexion pluridisciplinaire.* (Débats). Montréal: Québec Amérique, 283–325.
Gervais, S. (2001). Les trois partis et la question de la langue. In R. Côté (ed.) *Québec 2002. Annuaire politique, social, économique et culturel.* [Montréal]: Fides, 538–47.
Giddens, A. (1985). *The Nation-State and Violence.* Cambridge: Polity Press.
Giddens, A. (1990). *The Consequences of Modernity.* Cambridge: Polity Press.
Giddens, A. (1998). *The Third Way: The Renewal of Social Democracy.* Cambridge: Polity Press.
Gidengil, E., Blais, A., Nadeau, R. and Nevitte, N. (2004). Language and cultural insecurity. In A.-G. Gagnon (ed.) *Quebec: State and Society.* (3rd edition). Peterborough, CA: Broadview, 345–67.
Giles, H. (1979). Ethnicity markers in speech. In K. R. Scherer and H. Giles (eds) *Social Markers in Speech.* Cambridge: Cambridge University Press, 251–89.
Giles, H. and Coupland, N. (1991). *Language: Contexts and Consequences.* Milton Keynes: Open University Press.
Giles, H., Bourhis, R. Y. and Taylor, D. M. (1977). Towards a theory of language in ethnic group relations. In H. Giles (ed.) *Language, Ethnicity and Intergroup Relations.* London: Academic Press, 307–48.
Giles, H., Mulac, A., Bradac, J. J. and Johnson, P. (1987). Speech accommodation theory: the next decade and beyond. In *Communication Yearbook. Volume 10.* Newbury Park: Sage, 13–48.
Gouvernement du Québec (n.d.). *Reach for Your Dreams. The Policy on Educational Integration and Intercultural Education.* [Montréal]: Ministère de l'Éducation.
Gouvernement du Québec (1965). *Livre blanc sur la politique culturelle.* [Québec]: Ministère des Affaires culturelles.
Gouvernement du Québec (1972). *La situation de la langue française au Québec. Rapport de la commission d'enquête sur la situation de la langue française et sur les droits linguistiques au Québec. Livre I. La langue de travail. La situation du français dans les activités de travail et de consommation des Québécois.* [Québec]: Gouvernement du Québec.
Gouvernement du Québec (1977). *La politique québécoise de la langue française.* [Québec]: Gouvernement du Québec.
Gouvernement du Québec (1978). *La politique québécoise du développement culturel.* [Québec]: Gouvernement du Québec.
Gouvernement du Québec (1981). *Autant de façons d'être québécois. Plan d'action à l'intention des communautés culturelles.* [Québec]: Ministère des Communautés culturelles et de l'Immigration.
Gouvernement du Québec (1991). *Au Québec, pour bâtir ensemble. Énoncé de politique en matière d'immigration et d'intégration.* (Reprint of 1990 edition). [Québec]: Ministère des Communautés culturelles et de l'Immigration.

<http://www.mrci.gouv.qc.ca/publications/pdf/Enonce_politique_immigration_int egration_Quebec1991.pdf> Accessed 19 January 2005.

Gouvernement du Québec (1996). *Le français langue commune. Enjeu de la société québécoise*. (Rapport du Comité interministériel sur la situation de la langue française). [Québec]: Gouvernement du Québec.

Gouvernement du Québec (1998a). *Une école d'avenir. Intégration scolaire et éducation interculturelle*. [Québec]: Ministère de l'Éducation.

Gouvernement du Québec (1998b). *Partnership, Development, Achievement*. [Québec]: Secrétariat aux affaires autochtones.

Gouvernement du Québec (2000). *La citoyenneté québécoise. Document de consultation pour le forum national sur la citoyenneté et l'intégration*. [Québec]: Ministère des Relations avec les citoyens et de l'Immigration.

Gouvernement du Québec (2001a). *Le français, une langue pour tout le monde*. (Rapport de la Commission des États généraux sur la situation et l'avenir de la langue française au Québec). [Québec]: Gouvernement du Québec.

Gouvernement du Québec (2001b). *Le Québec dans un ensemble international en mutation. Plan stratégique 2001–2004*. [Québec]: Ministère des Relations internationales.

Gouvernement du Québec (2004a). *Des valeurs partagées, des intérêts communs. Pour assurer la pleine participation des Québécois des communautés culturelles au développement du Québec*. [Québec]: Ministère des Relations avec les citoyens et de l'Immigration. <http://www.mrci.gouv.qc.ca> Accessed 13 June 2005.

Gouvernement du Québec (2004b). *L'immigration au Québec*. [Québec]: Ministère des Relations avec les citoyens et Immigration.

Gouvernement du Québec (2004c). *2004 Québec Awards for Citizenship*. [Québec]: Ministère des Relations avec les citoyens et de l'Immigration. <http://www.mrci.gouv.qc.ca/publications/pdf/PQCBrochureFormulaires2004_anglais.pdf> Accessed 19 January 2005.

Gouvernement du Québec (2005a). *Apprendre le Québec. Guide pour réussir mon intégration*. [Québec]: Ministère de l'Immigration et des Communautés culturelles.

Gouvernement du Québec (2005b). *Plan stratégique en matière de politique linguistique 2005–2008*. [Québec]: Gouvernement du Québec.

Gouvernement du Québec (2005c). *Tableaux sur l'immigration au Québec, 2000–2004*. [Québec]: Ministère de l'Immigration et des Communautés culturelles.

Government of Canada (2003). *The Next Act: New Momentum for Canada's Linguistic Duality*. <http://www.pco-bcp.gc.ca/olo/default.asp?Language=E&Page=Action&doc=cover_e.htm> Accessed 6 January 2006.

Graddol, D. (1997). *The Future of English?* London: The British Council.

Graddol, D. (1998). Will English be enough? In A. Moys (ed.) *Where Are We Going with Languages?* London: Nuffield Foundation, 24–32.

Grammond, S. (2005). L'accord Nisga'a et l'entente avec les Innus: vers une nouvelle génération de traités? In G. Otis (ed.) *Droit, territoire et gouvernance des peuples autochtones*. Sainte-Foy: Les Presses de l'Université Laval, 83–98.

Green, J. (2004). Autodétermination, citoyenneté et fédéralisme: pour une relecture autochtone du palimpseste canadien. *Politique et sociétés* 23(1): 9–32.

Green, J. (2005). Self-determination, citizenship, and federalism: indigenous and Canadian palimpsest. In M. Murphy (ed.) *Reconfiguring Aboriginal-State Relations. Canada: The State of the Federation 2003*. Montréal/Kingston: McGill-Queen's University Press, 329–52.

Groupe de travail, école Olamen (2000). *Rapport d'enquête: État de la langue innue à La Romaine*. La Romaine: École Olamen/ICEM.

Habermas, J. (1994). Struggles for recognition in the democratic constitutional state. In A. Gutmann (ed.) *Multiculturalism*. Princeton: Princeton University Press, 107–48.
Habermas, J. (1996). *Between Facts and Norms: Contributions to a Discourse Theory of Law and Democracy*. (Translated by W. Rehg). Cambridge: Polity Press.
Hall, S. (1990). Cultural identity and diaspora. In J. Rutherford (ed.) *Identity: Community, Culture and Difference*. London: Lawrence and Wishart, 222–37.
Hall, S. (1991). The local and the global: globalization and ethnicity. In A. D. King (ed.) *Culture, Globalization and the World-System: Contemporary Conditions for the Representation of Identity*. Basingstoke: Macmillan, 19–40.
Hall, S. (1996). Introduction: who needs identity? In S. Hall and P. DuGay (eds) *Questions of Cultural Identity*. London: Sage, 1–17.
Hamelink, C. (1983). *Cultural Autonomy in Global Communications*. New York: Longman.
Hamers, J. F. and Hummel, K. M. (1998). Language in Quebec: aboriginal and heritage varieties. In J. Edwards (ed.) *Language in Canada*. Cambridge: Cambridge University Press, 385–99.
Hannerz, U. (1990). Cosmopolitans and locals in world culture. In M. Featherstone (ed.) *Global Culture: Nationalism, Globalization and Modernity*. London: Sage, 237–51.
Hannerz, U. (1991). Scenarios for peripheral cultures. In A. D. King (ed.) *Culture, Globalization and the World System*. London: Macmillan, 107–28.
Hausmann, F. J. (1986). Les dictionnaires du français hors de France. In L. Boisvert, C. Poirier and C. Verreault (eds) *La lexicographie québécoise: bilan et perspectives*. Québec: Les Presses de l'Université Laval, 3–19.
Heater, D. (1999). *What Is Citizenship?* Cambridge: Polity Press.
Heinrich, J. (2002a). Le nombre d'élèves francophones en hausse dans les écoles anglaises. *La Presse*, 17 June.
Heinrich, J. (2002b). L'exode des petits cerveaux. *La Presse*, 18 June.
Heinrich, J. (2002c). Dans la peau d'un franco. *Le 30*, September: 6–8.
Heinrich, J. (2003). Mother tongues spoken most in Montreal: study. *The Gazette*, 12 December.
Heinrich, J. (2004). Revisiting Quebec culture: Pure Laine, a new television series written by Martin Forget, takes a humorous look at the province's new reality: its increasingly hybrid culture of immigrants. *The Gazette*, 13 September.
Heinrich, J. (2005). Arabic overtaking English as Quebec schools' second language. *The Gazette*, 31 March.
Held, D., Mcgrew, A., Goldblatt, D. and Perraton, J. (1999). *Global Transformations: Politics, Economics and Culture*. Cambridge: Polity Press.
Helly, D. (2000). La nouvelle citoyenneté, active et responsable. In Y. Boisvert, J. Hamel and M. Molgat (eds), with the collaboration of B. Ellefsen, *Vivre la citoyenneté. Identité, appartenance et participation*. Montréal: Éditions Liber, 119–31.
Helly, D. and van Schendel, N. (2001). *Appartenir au Québec. Citoyenneté, nation et société civile. Enquête à Montréal, 1995*. Sainte-Foy: L'institut québécois de recherche sur la culture/Les Presses de l'Université Laval.
Hirst, P. and Thompson, G. (1996). *Globalization in Question: The International Economy and the Possibilities of Governance*. Cambridge: Polity Press.
Hobsbawm, E. (1992). *Nations and Nationalism since 1780*. (2nd edition). Cambridge: Cambridge University Press.
Hoffmann, C. (2000). Balancing language planning and language rights: Catalonia's uneasy juggling act. *Journal of Multilingual and Multicultural Development* 21(5): 425–41.
Holborow, M. (1999). *The Politics of English: A Marxist View of Language*. Thousand Oaks, CA/London: Sage.

Houdebine, A.-M. (1982). Norme, imaginaire linguistique et phonologie du français contemporain. *Le français moderne* 50(1): 42–51.

Houdebine, A.-M. (1993). De l'imaginaire des locuteurs et de la dynamique linguistique: aspects théoriques et méthodologiques. In M. Francard (ed.), with the collaboration of G. Geron and R. Wilmet, *L'insécurité linguistique dans les communautés francophones périphériques. Actes du colloque de Louvain-la-Neuve, 10–12 novembre 1993. Volume 1. (Cahiers de l'institut de linguistique de Louvain-la-Neuve* 19 (3–4)), 31–40.

Houdebine, M.-A. (1995). L'unes langue. In J.-M. Eloy (ed.) *La qualité de la langue? Le cas du français*. Paris: Champion, 95–121.

Hudon, S., Dorman, J. and Moore, M. (2004). Statistical portrait of school-age populations in Aboriginal communities in Québec. *Education Statistics Bulletin/Bulletin statistique de l'Éducation* 30: 1–27.

ICEM (Institut culturel et éducatif montagnais) (n.d.). *Institut culturel et éducatif montagnais. Innu utshissenitamun, uitshiueu anite tshishkutamatunit/Le savoir innu au service de l'éducation*. Sept-Îles: ICEM.

Institut de la Statistique Québec (2006). Série 600. Les migrations. *La situation démographique au Québec. Bilan 2005*. <http://www.stat.gouv.qc.ca/publications/demograp/sit_demo_pdf_an.htm> Accessed 7 March 2006.

Jefferys, T. (1761). *The Natural and Civil History of the French Dominions in North and South America, etc.* London: Charing Cross.

Jedwab, J. (2002). La Révolution « tranquille » des Anglo-Québécois. In D. Lemieux (ed.) *Traité de la culture*. Sainte-Foy: Les Presses de L'Université Laval, 181–99.

Jedwab, J. (2004). *Going Forward: The Evolution of Quebec's English-Speaking Community*. Ottawa: Commissariat aux langues officielles/Office of the Commissioner of Official Languages.

Jedwab, J. (2005). *What Do Québec Anglophones Want? Governance, Leadership and Involvement in an Evolving Community*. Moncton: Institut canadien de recherche sur les minorités linguistiques/The Canadian Institute for Research on Linguistic Minorities.

Joseph, J. (2004). *Language and Identity: National, Ethnic, Religious*. Houndmills, Basingstoke/New York: Palgrave Macmillan.

Jucquois, G. (1995). L'unification européenne et la question des langues. In Conseil de la langue française (ed.) *Langue nationale et mondialisation: enjeux et défis pour le français. Actes du Séminaire*. [Québec]: Conseil de la langue française, 67–109.

Judge, A. (1996). La francophonie: mythes, masques et réalités. In B. Jones, A. Miguet and P. Corcoran (eds) *Francophonie. Mythes, masques et réalités*. Paris: Publisud, 19–43.

Juteau, D. (1999). *L'ethnicité et ses frontières*. Montréal: Les Presses de l'Université de Montréal.

Juteau, D. (2001). The challenge of the pluralist option. In M. Venne (ed.) *Vive Quebec! New Thinking and New Approaches to the Quebec Nation*. (Translated by R. Chodos and L. Blair). Toronto: James Lorimer and Company, 119–26.

Juteau, D. (2002). The citizen makes an entrée: redefining the national community in Quebec. *Citizenship Studies* 6(4), 441–58.

Juteau, D. (2004). 'Pures laines' Québécois: the concealed ethnicity of dominant majorities. In E. Kaufmann (ed.) *The Challenge of Ethnicity: Majority Groups and Dominant Minorities*. London/New York: Routledge, 84–101.

Kachru, B. (1986). *The Alchemy of English: The Spread, Functions, and Models of Non-Native Englishes*. Urbana/Chicago: University of Illinois Press.

Kachru, B. (ed.) (1992). *The Other Tongue: English across Cultures*. Urbana/Chicago: University of Illinois Press.

Karmis, D. (2004). Pluralism and national identity(ies) in contemporary Québec. In A.-G. Gagnon (ed.) *Québec: State and Society*. (3rd edition). Peterborough,CA: Broadview Press, 69–96.

Keating, M. (2001a). *Nations against the State: The New Politics of Nationalism in Quebec, Catalonia and Scotland*. (2nd edition). Houndmills, Basingstoke: Palgrave.

Keating, M. (2001b). Par-delà de la souveraineté: la démocratie plurinationale dans un monde postsouverain. In J. Maclure and A.-G. Gagnon (eds) *Repères en mutation. Identité et citoyenneté dans le Québec contemporain*. Montréal: Québec Amérique, 67–103.

Kelman, H. C. (1972). Language as aid and barrier to involvement in the national system. In J. A. Fishman (ed.) *Advances in the Sociology of Language. Volume 2: Selected Studies and Applications*. The Hague/Paris: Mouton, 185–212.

Kernerman, G. and Resnick, P. (eds) (2005). *Insiders and Outsiders: Alan Cairns and the Reshaping of Canadian Citizenship*. Vancouver/Toronto: UBC Press.

Kloss, H. (1969). *Research Possibilities on Group Bilingualism: A Report*. Sainte-Foy: Centre international de recherche sur le bilinguisme, Université Laval.

Kohn, H. (1944). *The Idea of Nationalism: A Study of its Origins and Background*. New York: Collier-Macmillan.

Koubi, G. (2004). The management of cultural diversity in France. In A. Dieckhoff (ed.) *The Politics of Belonging: Nationalism, Liberalism, and Pluralism*. Lanham: Lexington Books, 195–220.

Kristeva, J. (1988). *Étrangers à nous-mêmes*. Paris: Fayard.

Kymlicka, W. (1995). *Multicultural Citizenship*. Oxford: Clarendon Press.

Kymlicka, W. (1998). *Finding Our Way. Rethinking Ethnocultural Relations in Canada*. Toronto: Oxford University Press.

Kymlicka, W. (1999). Misunderstanding nationalism. In R. Beiner (ed.) *Theorizing Nationalism*. Albany: State University of New York Press, 131–40.

Kymlicka, W. (2001). *Politics in the Vernacular: Nationalism, Multiculturalism and Citizenship*. Oxford: Oxford University Press.

Labelle, M. and Rocher, F. (2001). People who live in a glass house ... Citizenship and national identity in Canada and Quebec. In J. MacInnes and D. McCrone (eds) *Stateless Nations in the 21st Century: Scotland, Catalonia and Quebec*. (Special issue of *Scottish Affairs*). Edinburgh: Unit for the Study of Government in Scotland, Edinburgh University, 65–77.

Labelle, M. and Salée, D. (2001). Immigrant and minority representations of citizenship in Quebec. In T. A. Aleinikoff and D. Klusmeyer (eds) *Citizenship Today. Global Perspectives and Practices*. Washington: Carnegie Endowment for International Peace, 278–315.

Labov. W. (1972). *Sociolinguistic Patterns*. Philadelphia: University of Pennsylvania Press.

Labrie, N. (1995). Les enjeux linguistiques nord-américains de l'Accord de libre-échange entre le Canada, le Mexique et les États-Unis: quelles stratégies mettre au point face à l'anglais *lingua franca* de fait? In Conseil de la langue française (ed.) *Langue nationale et mondialisation. Enjeux et défis pour le français. Actes du Séminaire*. [Québec]: Conseil de la langue française, 111–39.

Lacroix, A. (2000). Solidarité et citoyenneté. In Y. Boisvert, J. Hamel and M. Molgat (eds), with the collaboration of B. Ellefsen, *Vivre la citoyenneté. Identité, appartenance et participation*. Montréal: Éditions Liber, 53–62.

Laforest, G. (1995). *De l'urgence. Textes politiques, 1994–1995*. Montréal: Boréal.

Laforest, M., in collaboration with Caouette, C., Drolet, J.-F., Marais, S., Ménard, L., Ouellet, M., Tardif, B., Thibault, L., Vézina, R. and Vincent, D. (1997). *États d'âme, états de langue*. Québec: Nuit blanche éditeur.

Laforest, M. (2002). Attitudes, préjugés et opinions sur la langue. In G. Verreault, L. Mercier and T. Lavoie (eds) *Le français, une langue à apprivoiser. Textes de conférences prononcées au Musée de la civilisation (Québec, 2000–2001) dans le cadre de l'exposition Une grande langue: le français dans tous ses états.* Sainte-Foy: Les Presses de l'Université Laval, 81–91.

Lajoie, A. (2004). The Clarity Act in its context. In A.-G. Gagnon (ed.) *Québec: State and Society.* (3rd edition). Peterborough,CA: Broadview Press, 151–64.

Lalonde, M. (1973). La deffence and illustration de la langue québecquoyse. *Maintenant* 125, April: 15–25.

Lamarre, P. (2001). Le multilinguisme des jeunes allophones québécois: ressource sociétale et défi éducatif. (Mémoire presented to the Commission des États généraux sur la situation et l'avenir de la langue française au Québec, 26 January).

Lamarre, P. (2005). L'enseignement du français dans le réseau scolaire anglophone: à la recherche du bilinguisme. In A. Stefanescu and P. Georgeault (eds) *Le français au Québec. Les nouveaux défis.* [Montréal]: Fides, 553–68.

Lamarre, P. and Rossell Paredes, J. (2003). Growing up trilingual in Montreal: perceptions of college students. In R. Bayley and S. R. Schecter (eds) *Language Socialization in Bilingual and Multilingual Societies.* Clevedon: Multilingual Matters, 62–80.

Lamarre, P. and Dagenais, D. (2004). Language practices of trilingual youth in two Canadian cities. In C. Hoffmann and J. Ytsma (eds) *Trilingualism in Family, School and Community.* Clevedon: Multilingual Matters, 53–74.

Lamarre, P., Paquette, J., Kahn, E. and Ambrosi, S. (2002). Multilingual Montreal: listening in on the language practices of young Montrealers. *Canadian Ethnic studies/Études ethniques au Canada* 34(3): 47–75.

Lambert, J. (1814). *Travels through Canada and the United States of North America in the years 1806, 1807 and 1808. Volume 1.* (2nd edition, corrected and improved). London: printed for C. Cradock and W. Joy.

Lamonde, D. (1998). *Le maquignon et son joual. L'aménagement du français québécois.* Saint-Laurent: Liber.

Lamonde, D. (2004). *Anatomie d'un joual de parade. Le bon français d'ici par l'exemple.* Montréal: Les Éditions Varia.

Lamonde, Y. (1996). *Ni avec eux ni sans eux. Le Québec et les États-Unis.* Montréal: Nuit blanche.

Lamonde, Y. (2001). *Allégeances et dépendances. L'histoire d'une ambivalence identitaire.* Montréal: Editions Nota bene.

Lamoureux, D. (1995a). L'autodétermination comme condition du multiculturalisme québécois. *Politique et sociétés* 28, automne: 53–69.

Lamoureux, D. (1995b). Le patriotisme constitutionnel et les États multinationaux. In F. Blais, G. Laforest and D. Lamoureux (eds) *Libéralismes et nationalismes. Philosophie et politique.* Sainte-Foy: Les Presses de l'Université Laval, 131–44.

Langlois, S. (2003). Briser les solitudes entre francophones. In S. Langlois and J.-L. Roy (eds) *Briser les solitudes. Les francophonies canadiennes et québécoises.* Québec: Éditions Nota bene.

Lapierre Vincent, N. (2005). *Le français, langue normale et habituelle du travail dans une économie ouverte.* [Québec]: Conseil supérieur de la langue française.

Laporte, P.-É. (1984). L'attitude des Québécois francophones à l'égard du français au Québec: idées pour une problématique de recherche. In M. Amyot (ed.) *Le statut culturel du français au Québec. Actes du congrès Langue et société au Québec. Volume 2.* Québec: Éditeur officiel du Québec. <http://www.cslf.gouv.qc.ca> Accessed 18 July 2005.

Larrivée, P. (2003a). Anglophones and allophones in Quebec. In P. Larrivée (ed.) *Linguistic Conflict and Language Laws: Understanding the Quebec Question*. Houndmills, Basingstoke/New York: Palgrave Macmillan, 163–87.
Larrivée, P. (2003b). A final note on culture, Quebec native languages and the Quebec question. In P. Larrivée (ed.) *Linguistic Conflict and Language Laws: Understanding the Quebec Question*. Houndmills, Basingstoke: Palgrave Macmillan, 188–98.
Lash, S. and Urry, J. (1994). *Economies of Signs and Spaces*. London/Thousand Oaks, CA: Sage.
Latouche, D. (1988). State building and foreign policy at the subnational level. In I. D. Duchacek, D. Latouche and G. Stevenson (eds) *Perforated Sovereignties and International Relations*. New York: Greenwood Press, 29–42.
Latouche, D. (1995). Quebec in the emerging North American configuration. In R. Earle and J. Wirth (eds) *Identities in North America: The Search for Community*. Stanford: Stanford University Press, 117–39.
Laurier, M. (2005). La maîtrise du français dans la formation des immigrants adultes. In A. Stefanescu and P. Georgeault (eds) *Le français au Québec. Les nouveaux défis*. [Montréal]: Fides, 569–87.
Lazar, B. (2001). *Underestimated Importance: la culture anglo-québécoise*. Montréal: INRS Urbanisation, Culture et Société.
Leclerc, J. (2005a). Corse. In *L'aménagement linguistique dans le monde*. Québec: Trésor de la langue française au Québec (TLFQ), Université Laval, 4 October. <http://www.tlfq.ulaval.ca/axl/europe/corsefra.htm> Accessed 17 October 2005.
Leclerc, J. (2005b). Le défi de l'immigration. In *L'aménagement linguistique dans le monde*. Québec: Trésor de la langue française au Québec (TLFQ), Université Laval, 20 August. <http://www.tlfq.ulaval.ca/axl/amnord/quebecdefi.htm> Accessed 24 September 2005.
Leclerc, J. (2005c). Les droits linguistiques des autochtones. In *L'aménagement linguistique dans le monde*. Québec: Trésor de la langue française au Québec (TLFQ), Université Laval, 20 August. <http://www.tlfq.ulaval.ca/AXL/amnord/quebecautocht.htm> Accessed 30 December 2005.
Leclerc, J. (2005d). Nouvelle-Calédonie. (4) Les fluctuations politiques. In *L'aménagement linguistique dans le monde*. Québec: Trésor de la langue française au Québec (TLFQ), Université Laval, 6 October. <http://www.tlfq.ulaval.ca/axl/pacifique/ncal4fluc_pol.htm> Accessed 17 October 2005.
Leclerc, J. (2005e). Polynésie française. In *L'aménagement linguistique dans le monde*. Québec: Trésor de la langue française au Québec (TLFQ), Université Laval, 6 October. <http://www.tlfq.ulaval.ca/axl/pacifique/polfr.htm> Accessed 17 October 2005.
Lefebvre, C. (1984). Une ou plusieurs normes. In M. Amyot (ed.) *Le statut culturel du français au Québec. Actes du congrès Langue et société au Québec. Volume 2*. Québec: Éditeur officiel du Québec. <http://www.cslf.gouv.qc.ca> Accessed 18 July 2005.
Lefebvre, G.-R. (1984). Le problème de la norme linguistique au Québec, à la lumière des idéologies socioculturelles. In M. Amyot (ed.) *Le statut culturel du français au Québec. Actes du congrès Langue et société au Québec. Volume 2*. Québec: Éditeur officiel du Québec. <http://www.cslf.gouv.qc.ca> Accessed 18 July 2005.
Legaré, A. (2003). *Le Québec, otage de ses alliés. Les relations du Québec avec la France et les États-Unis*. Montréal: VLB éditeur.
Legault, J. (1992). *L'invention d'une minorité. Les Anglo-Québécois*. Montréal: Boréal.
Léger, J.-M. (1987). *La francophonie. Grand dessein, grande ambiguïté*. LaSalle: Hurtubise.
Léger, J.-M. (2000). Le Québec et la Francophonie. In M. Plourde (ed.), with the collaboration of H. Duval and P. Georgeault, *Le français au Québec. 400 ans d'histoire et de vie*. [Montréal/Québec]: Fides/Publications du Québec, 335–9.

Léger, J.-M. (2001). Le rapport de la Commission Larose laisse entiers les problèmes de fond. *L'Action nationale* 91(8). <http://www.actionnationale.qc.ca/01–10/edito.html> Accessed 10 July 2003.

Léger, J.-M. (2004). Le prochain Sommet de la Francophonie à Québec – Le Québec encore roulé par Ottawa. *Le Devoir*, 2 December.

Léger Marketing (2005). Québec Poll for *The Globe and Mail* and *Le Devoir*, 27 April. <www.legermarketing.com/documents/spclm/050427ENG.pdf> Accessed 27 December 2005.

Lessard, D. (2005). Un anglophone? Euh! *La Presse*, 30 June.

Létourneau, J. (1998). La nation des jeunes. In B. Jewsiewicki and J. Létourneau (eds) *Les Jeunes à l'ère de la mondialisation. Quête identitaire et conscience historique*. Sillery: Septentrion, 411–30.

Létourneau, J. (2001). Rethinking Quebec (in the Canadian Landscape). In M. Venne (ed.) *Vive Quebec! New Thinking and New Approaches to the Quebec Nation*. (Translated by R. Chodos and L. Blair). Toronto: James Lorimer and Company, 59–69.

Létourneau, J. (2002). Langue et identité au Québec aujourd'hui. Enjeux, défis, possibilités. *Globe. Revue internationale d'études québécoises* 5(2): 79–110.

Lévesque, C. (2003). The presence of Aboriginal peoples in Quebec's cities: multiple movements, diverse issues. In D. Newhouse and E. Peters (eds) *Not Strangers in These Parts. Urban Aboriginal Peoples*. Ottawa: Policy Research Initiative, 23–34. <http://www.recherchepolitique.gc.ca/doclib/AboriginalBook_e.pdf> Accessed 6 January 2006.

Levine, M. (1997). *La reconquête de Montréal*. Montréal: VLB éditeur.

Levine, M. (2000). L'usage du français, langue commune. In M. Plourde (ed.), with the collaboration of H. Duval and P. Georgeault, *Le français au Québec. 400 ans d'histoire et de vie*. [Montréal/Québec]: Fides/Publications du Québec: 366–76.

Levine, M. (2002). La question 'démographique', un quart de siècle après la Charte de la langue française. In P. Bouchard and R. Y. Bourhis (eds) *L'aménagement linguistique au Québec: 25 ans d'application de la Charte de la langue française*. (*Revue d'aménagement linguistique*, hors série), 165–82.

Levinson. S. (1995). Is liberal nationalism an oxymoron? *Ethics* 103(3): 626–45.

Leydet, D. (1995). Intégration et pluralisme: le concept de culture politique. In F. Blais, G. Laforest and D. Lamoureux (eds) *Libéralismes et nationalismes. Philosophie et politique*. Sainte-Foy: Les Presses de l'Université Laval, 117–30.

Lisée, J.-F. (2001). Citoyenneté: réparer le passé et préparer l'avenir. *La Presse*, 14 October. <http://www.cyberpresse.ca/reseau/editorial/0110/edi_101100024307.html> Accessed 29 October 2001.

Lockerbie, I. (2005). The debate on l'aménagement du français au Québec. In *French as the Common Language in Québec: History, Debates and Positions*. (New Perspectives in Québec Studies). Montréal: Nota bene, 15–65.

Lodge, A. R. (1993). *French: From Dialect to Standard*. London/New York: Routledge.

Lortie, M. (2002). Le multilinguisme dans les organisations interaméricains. (Presentation at the Inter-American Languages Management Seminar, Québec, 28–30 August 2002.) <www.cslf.gouv.qc.ca/Seminaire/Conferences/MLortie.doc> Accessed 24 August 2004.

Lüdi, G. (1992). French as a pluricentric language. In M. Clyne (ed.) *Pluricentric Languages: Differing Norms in Different Nations*. Berlin: Mouton de Gruyter, 149–78.

Maalouf, A. (1998). *Les identités meurtrières*. Paris: Grasset et Fasquelle.

Mc Andrew, M. (2001). *Intégration des immigrants et diversité ethnoculturelle à l'école de demain. Le débat québécois dans une perspective comparative*. Montréal: Presses de l'Université de Montréal.

Mc Andrew, M. (2003a). Immigration, pluralisme et éducation. In A.-G. Gagnon (ed.) *Québec: État et société. Tome 2*. Montréal: Québec Amérique, 345–68.
Mc Andrew, M. (2003b). Immigration and diversity: some policy issues confronting the Quebec schooling system. *Policy Options/Options politiques* October: 59–62.
Mc Andrew, M., Veltman, C., Lemire, F. and Rossell, J. (1999). *Concentration ethnique et usages linguistiques en milieu scolaire*. (Research report). Montréal: Immigration et métropoles.
Macklem, P. (2001). *Indigenous Difference and the Constitution of Canada*. Toronto: University of Toronto Press.
MacLennan, H. (1945). *Two Solitudes*. New York: Duell, Sloan and Pearce.
McLuhan, M. (1962). *The Gutenberg Galaxy*. Toronto: University of Toronto Press.
Maclure, J. (2001). Commission nationale sur la citoyenneté: pour une politique des relations civiques. *Le Devoir*, 8 August. <http://www.ledevoir.com/public/client-old/news-webview.jsp?newsid=3597> Accessed 16 August 2001.
Maclure, J. (2003). *Quebec Identity: The Challenge of Pluralism*. Montréal/Kingston: McGill-Queen's University Press.
Maclure, J. (2004). Des leçons à tirer. *La Presse*, 8 February. <http://www.vigile.net/ds-actu/docs4/2-10.html#lpjm> Accessed 5 February 2005.
Magnan, M.-O. (2005). *'To Stay or Not to Stay': Migration of Young Anglo-Quebecers*. Montréal: INRS Urbanisation, Culture et Société.
Magnan, M.-O., Gauthier, M. and Côté, S. (2006). *La migration des jeunes au Québec. Résultats d'un sondage auprès des anglophones de 20–34 ans*. Montréal: INRS Urbanisation, Culture et Société.
Maguire, T. (1841). *Manuel des difficultés les plus communes de la langue française, adapté au jeune âge, et suivi d'un recueil de locutions vicieuses*. Québec: Fréchette et Cie.
Mailhot, J. (1985). Implementation of mother-tongue literacy among the Montagnais: myth or reality? In B. Burnaby (ed.) *Promoting Native Writing Systems in Canada*. Toronto: OISE Press, 17–26.
Mailhot, J. (1996). L'écrit comme facteur d'épanouissement de la langue innue. *Recherches amérindiennes au Québec* 26(3–4): 21–54.
Mailhot, J. (1999[1997]). *Towards a Common Spelling System for the Innu Language (Pour une orthographie unique pour la langue innue)*. (Translated by J. Bannister and M. MacKenzie). Sept-Îles: ICEM. <http://www.innu-aimun.ca/modules/spelling/files/common%20spelling.pdf> Accessed 6 January 2006.
Makivik Corporation (2004). *Nunavik: Infrastructure*. (*Nunavik Newsletter* 4). <http://www.nunavikgovernment.ca/en/documents/Nunavik_4.pdf> Accessed 1 February 2006.
Makivik Corporation (2005). *Nunavik: The Road to the AIP*. (*Nunavik Newsletter* 5). <http://www.nunavikgovernment.ca/en/documents/NUNAVIK5.pdf> Accessed 1 February 2006.
Marcel, J. (1973). *Joual de Troie*. Montréal: Éditions du jour.
Marshall, T. H. and Bottomore, T. (1992). *Citizenship and Social Class*. London/Concord, MA: Pluto Press.
Martel, P. (1990). Les préoccupations du Conseil de la langue française en matière de qualité et d'aménagement de la langue. In *Actes du colloque sur l'aménagement de la langue au Québec. Communications et synthèse, Mont-Gabriel, 7 et 8 décembre 1989*. [Québec]: Conseil de la langue française. <http://www.cslf.gouv.qc.ca> Accessed 7 March 2005.
Martel, P. and Cajolet-Laganière, H. (1996). *Le français québécois. Usages, standard et aménagement*. (Diagnostic 22). Québec: Institut québécois de recherche sur la culture.

Martel, P., Vincent, N. and Cajolet-Laganière, H. (1998). Le français québécois et la légitimité de sa description. In C. Verreault, and L. Mercier (eds), with the participation of D. Dumas, *Représentation de la langue et légitimité linguistique: le français et ses variétés nationales*. (*Revue québécoise de linguistique* 26(2)). Montréal: Université du Québec à Montréal, 95–106.

Mathieu, G. (2001). *Qui est Québécois? Synthèse du débat sur la redéfinition de la nation*. Montréal: VLB éditeur.

Maurais, J. (1985a). *Aspects de l'aménagement linguistique du Québec*. [Québec]: Conseil de la langue française.

Maurais, J. (1985b). La crise du français au Québec. In J. Maurais (ed.) *La crise des langues*. [Québec]: Conseil de la langue française, 37–83.

Maurais, J. (ed.) (1985c). *La crise des langues*. [Québec]: Conseil de la langue française.

Maurais, J. (1986). Régionalisme et langue standard. In L. Boisvert, C. Poirier and C. Verreault (eds) *La lexicographie québécoise: bilan et perspectives*. Québec: Presses de l'Université Laval, 79–88.

Maurais, J. (ed.) (1992). *Les langues autochtones du Québec*. [Québec]: Conseil de la langue française. <http://www.cslf.gouv.qc.ca/publications/pubb133/b133ch1.html> Accessed 25 September 2005.

Maurais, J. (ed.) (1996). *Quebec's Aboriginal Languages: History, Planning and Development*. Clevedon: Multilingual Matters.

Maurais, J. (2000). Les langues autochtones et le Québec. In M. Plourde (ed.), with the collaboration of H. Duval and P. Georgeault, *Le français au Québec. 400 ans d'histoire et de vie*. [Montréal/Québec]: Fides/Publications du Québec, 284.

Maurais, J. (2003). Towards a new global linguistic order? In J. Maurais and M. A. Morris (eds) *Languages in a Globalising World*. Cambridge: Cambridge University Press, 13–36.

May, S. (2001). *Language and Minority Rights: Ethnicity, Nationalism and the Politics of Language*. Harlow: Longman.

May, S. (2003). Misconceiving minority language rights: implications for liberal political theory. In W. Kymlicka and A. Patten (eds) *Language Rights and Political Theory*. Oxford: Oxford University Press, 123–52.

Meilleur, N. (2005). *Profil sociolinguistique des élèves du secteur des jeunes de la Commission scolaire de Montréal – Année scolaire 2004–2005*. Montréal: Commission scolaire de Montréal.

Meinecke, F. (1970[1907]). *Cosmopolitanism and the National State*. (Translated by R. B. Kimber; introduction by F. Gilbert). Princeton: Princeton University Press.

Meintel, D. (1993). Transnationalité et transethnicité chez des jeunes issus de milieux immigrés à Montréal. *Revue européenne des migrations internationales* 9(3): 63–79.

Meintel, D. (1998). Les comportements linguistiques et la nouvelle pluriethnicité montréalaise. *Études Canadiennes/Canadian Studies* 45: 83–93.

Meintel, D. and Fortin, S. (2001). Identités et langues. (Mémoire presented to the États généraux sur la situation et l'avenir de la langue française au Québec, 26 January).

Meney, L. (1999). *Dictionnaire québécois-français*. Montréal: Guérin.

Meney, L. (2003a). La qualité de la langue française au Québec: 'le français ne se dégrade pas, il change !' *Le Soleil*, 6 December.

Meney, L. (2003b). Qualité de la langue: réaffirmer que la langue du Québec est bien le francais. *Le Soleil*, 8 December.

Meney, L. (2004a). Parler français comme un vrai Québécois? *Le Devoir*, 7 January.

Meney, L. (2004b). La qualité de la langue et la norme (1). *Le Droit*, 26 January.

Meney, L. (2004c). La qualité de la langue et la norme (2). *Le Droit*, 27 January.

Meney, L. (2004d). Lettre ouverte au premier ministre. 18 November.
Meney, L. (2005a). Un autre dictionaire québécois, pourquoi? *Le Devoir*, 7 January.
Meney, L. (2005b). Décrire le français québécois ou en faire une norme? *Le Devoir*, 20 January.
Meney, L. (2005c). L'inquiétante hostilité québécoise au français. *Le Monde*, 19 March.
Mercier, L. (2002a). Le français, une langue qui varie selon les contextes. In C. Verreault, L. Mercier and T. Lavoie (eds) *Le français, une langue à apprivoiser. Textes de conférences prononcées au Musée de la civilisation (Québec, 2000–2001) dans le cadre de l'exposition* Une grande langue: le français dans tous ses états. Sainte-Foy: Les Presses de l'Université Laval, 41–60.
Mercier, L. (2002b). *La Société du parler français au Canada et la mise en valeur du patrimoine linguistique québécois (1920–1962). Histoire de son enquête et genèse de son glossaire*. Sainte-Foy: Les Presses de l'Université Laval.
Mercier, L. and Verreault, C. (2002). Opposer français 'standard' et français québécois pour mieux se comprendre entre francophones? Le cas du Dictionnaire québécois français. *Le français moderne* 70(1): 87–108.
Métis Corporation of Québec (2004). The Congress of Aboriginal Peoples and the Métis National Council do not recognize the Métis of eastern Canada. *E-Journal of the Métis of Québec and of Eastern Canada* 1(1). <http://www.metisduquebec.ca/en/communique6juin04.htm> Accessed 28 December 2005.
Métis National Council (n.d.). *Métis Governments*. <http://www.metisnation.ca/gov> Accessed 30 December 2005.
Meyer, B. and Geschiere, P. (1999). Introduction. In B. Meyer and P. Geschiere (eds) *Globalization and Identity: Dialectics of Flow and Closure*. Oxford: Blackwell, 1–15.
Michaud, N. (2003). Des relations internationales à la politique étrangère du Québec. In M. Venne (ed.) *L'annuaire du Québec 2004*. [Montréal]: Fides, 944–52.
Miller, D. (1993). In defence of nationality. *Journal of Applied Philosophy* 10(1): 3–16.
Miller, D. (1995). *On Nationality*. Oxford: Clarendon Press.
Milroy, J. and Milroy, L. (1999). *Authority in Language: Investigating Standard English*. (3rd edition). London/New York: Routledge.
Ministère de la Culture et des Communications (2004). Coalition pour la diversité culturelle. *Diversité culturelle*. <http://www.mcc.gouv.qc.ca/international/diversite-culturelle/coalition.html> Accessed 28 February 2005.
Ministère de l'Immigration et des Communautés culturelles (2005). À votre arrivée. Cours de français. <http://www.immigration quebec.gouv.qc.ca/francais/installation/cours-francais.html> Accessed 24 February 2006.
Ministère des Relations internationales (2003a). Le gouvernement du Québec adopte une position officielle en matière de diversité culturelle. Communiqué, 19 September 2003. <http://www.mri.gouv.qc.ca/fr/ministere/communiques/textes/2003/2003_09_19.asp> Accessed 12 July 2004.
Ministère des Relations internationales (2003b). Diversité culturelle. <http://www.mri.gouv.qc.ca/fr/politique_internationale/dossiers/diversite.asp> Accessed 12 July 2004.
Missisquoi Institute (2001a). *The Anglophone Community of Quebec in the Year 2000*. <http://www.chssn.org/en/missisquoi.html> Accessed 6 October 2005.
Missisquoi Institute (2001b). *How Do Francophones Regard Quebec Anglophones and Their Issues of Concern?* <http://www.chssn.org/en/missisquoi.html> Accessed 6 October 2005.
Molinaro, I. (2005). Context and integration: the allophone communities in Québec. In *French as the Common Language in Québec: History, Debates and Positions*. (New Perspectives in Québec Studies). Montréal: Nota bene, 67–115.

Monette, P. (2002). La langue de chez eux. *Voir* 16(36), 12 September.
Monière, D. (2003). La lutte des langues au Canada. *L'Action nationale* 93(2): 17–25.
Montcalm, Marquis de (1895). *Journal du Marquis de Montcalm durant ses campagnes en Canada 1756 à 1759*. (Edited by l'Abbé H.-R. Casgrain). Québec: L.-J. Demers & frère.
Moreau, M.-L. (1999). Pluralité des normes et des appartenances. Convergences et diveregences en situation pédagogique. In C. Ouellon (ed.) *La norme du français au Québec. Perspectives pédagogiques*. (*Terminogramme* 92–92). Québec: Les Publications du Québec, 41–63.
Morris, M. A. (2003). Effects of North American integration on linguistic diversity. In J. Maurais and M. A. Morris (eds) *Languages in a Globalising World*. Cambridge: Cambridge University Press, 143–56.
Moses, T. (2002). Notes for a statement. (Presentation at the symposium La société québécoise et les Autochtones. Comprendre les différences, construire le rapprochement, 26–27 March 2002, Québec City, Archives of the Grand Council of the Cree). <http://www.gcc.ca/archive/article.php?id=94> Accessed 4 February 2006.
Muchnick, A. G. and Wolfe, D. E. (1982). Attitudes and motivations of American students of Spanish. *The Canadian Modern Language Review* 38: 262–81.
Murphy, M. (ed.) (2005). *Reconfiguring Aboriginal-State Relations. Canada: The State of the Federation 2003*. Montréal/Kingston: McGill-Queen's University Press.
NAHO (National Aboriginal Health Organization) (2003). *Terminology Guide*. <http://16016.vws.magma.ca/english/pdf/terminology_guidelines.pdf> Accessed 28 December 2005.
Neathery-Castro, J. and Rousseau, M. (2001/2002). Quebec, *Francophonie*, and globalization. *Québec Studies* 32: 17–35.
Nederveen Pieterse, J. (1995). Globalization as hybridization. In M. Featherstone, S. Lash and R. Robertson (eds) *Global Modernities*. London: Sage, 45–68.
Nederveen Pieterse, J. (2004). *Globalization and Culture: Global Mélange*. Lanham, MD: Rowman and Littlefield.
Nemni, M. (1993). Le dictionnaire québécois d'aujourd'hui ou la description de deux chimères. *Cité libre* 2(21): 30–4.
Nemni, M. (1998). Le français au Québec: représentation et conséquences pédagogiques. In C. Verreault, and L. Mercier (eds), with the participation of D. Dumas, *Représentation de la langue et légitimité linguistique: le français et ses variétés nationales*. (*Revue québécoise de linguistique* 26(2)). Montréal: Université du Québec à Montréal, 151–75.
Nettle, D. and Romaine, S. (2000). *Vanishing Voices: The Extinction of the World's Languages*. Oxford: Oxford University Press.
Ngũgĩ wa Thiong'o (1986). *Decolonising the Mind: The Politics of Language in African Literature*. London: James Currey.
Nguyen, E. (1998). *Les nationalismes en Europe. Quête d'identité ou tentation de repli?* Paris: Le Monde/Éditions Marabout.
Nguyên-Duy, V. (1999). Le téléroman et la volonté d'une télévision originale. In F. Sauvageau (ed.) *Variations sur l'influence culturelle américaine*. Sainte-Foy: Les Presses de l'Université Laval, 131–57.
Nielsen, K. (1998). Un nationalisme culturel, ni ethnique ni civique. In M. Sarra-Bournet (ed.), assisted by P. Gendron, *Le pays de tous les Québécois. Diversité culturelle et souveraineté*. Montréal: VLB éditeur, 143–59.
Nielsen, K. (1999). Cultural nationalism, neither ethnic nor civic. In R. Beiner (ed.) *Theorizing Nationalism*. Albany: State University of New York Press, 119–30.
Norman, W. (1995). The ideology of shared values: a myopic vision of unity in the multi-nation state. In J. H. Carens (ed.) *Is Quebec Nationalism Just? Perspectives from Anglophone Canada*. Montréal/Kingston: McGill-Queen's University Press, 137–59.

Norris, M. J. and Jantzen, L. (2002). *From Generation to Generation: Survival and Maintenance of Canada's Aboriginal Languages within Families, Communities and Cities.* Ottawa: Minister of Indian Affairs and Northern Development.

Nunavik Commission (2001). *Amiqqaaluta – Let Us Share. Mapping the Road Toward a Government for Nunavik.* <http://www.ainc-inac.gc.ca/pr/agr/nunavik/lus_e.html> Accessed 26 January 2006.

Nunberg, G. (1997). Lingo jingo: English only and the new nativism. *The American Prospect* 8(33). <http://www.prospect.org> Accessed 17 April 2000.

Oakes, L. (2001). *Language and National Identity: Comparing France and Sweden.* Amsterdam/Philadelphia: John Benjamins.

Oakes, L. (2005). From internationalisation to globalisation: language and the nationalist revival in Sweden. *Language Problems and Language Planning* 29(2): 151–76.

Office de la langue française (1965). *Norme du français parlé et écrit au Québec.* (Cahiers de l'Office de la langue française 1). [Québec]: Ministère des affaires culturelles.

Office de la langue française (1969). *Canadianismes de bon aloi.* (Cahiers de l'Office de la langue française 4). [Québec]: Ministère des affaires culturelles.

Office québécois de la langue française (2005). *Les caractéristiques linguistiques de la population du Québec: profil et tendances 1991–2001.* [Québec]: Gouvernement du Québec.

Office of the Commissioner of Official Languages (2003). *Language Rights 2001–2002* <http://www.ocol-clo.gc.ca/archives/lr_dl/2001-2002/2001_e.htm> Accessed 27 December 2005.

Official Languages Support Programs Branch (Research Team) (2004). Methodological issues and use of the survey in developing linguistic policies in Canada. In W. Floch and Y. Frenette (eds) *Community Vitality, Community Confidence: Analysis and Discussion on GPC International Survey on Attitudes and Perceptions of Official Languages.* Gatineau: Canadian Heritage, 127–53.

Ohmae, K. (1995). *The End of the Nation-State.* New York: Free Press.

Ostiguy, L. and Tousignant, C. (1993). *Le français québécois. Normes et usages.* Montréal: Guérin universitaire.

Pagé, M. (2005). La francisation des immigrants au Québec en 2005 et après. In A. Stefanescu and P. Georgeault (eds) *Le français au Québec. Les nouveaux défis.* [Montréal]: Fides, 191–231.

Pagé, M. (2006). Propositions pour une approche dynamique de la situation du français dans l'espace linguistique québécois. In P. Georgeault and M. Pagé (eds) *Le français, langue de la diversité québécoise. Une réflexion pluridisciplinaire.* (Débats). Montréal: Québec Amérique, 27–76.

Papen, R. A. (1998). French: Canadian varieties. In J. Edwards (ed.) *Language in Canada.* Cambridge: Cambridge University Press, 160–76.

Papillon, M. (2005). Embedded nations? Changing dynamics of Aboriginal governance in Quebec. (Paper presented at the conference Claiming Citizenship in the Americas, University of Montreal, 27 May 2005). <http://www.cccg.umontreal.ca/pdf/papillon.pdf> Accessed 6 January 2006.

Paquot, A. (1988). *Les Québécois et leurs mots.* Québec: Conseil de la langue française/Les Presses de l'Université Laval. <http://www.cslf.gouv.qc.ca> Accessed 25 April 2005.

Paquot, A. (1990). Architecture de la langue, connotations et régionalismes. *Langues et linguistique* 16: 177–89.

Paré, J. (1993). Une langue juste pour rire. *L'Actualité,* 15 March.

Pastor, R. A. and Fréchette, C. (2003). Quand le libre-échange ne suffit pas. In M. Venne (ed.) *L'annuaire du Québec 2004.* [Montréal]: Fides, 975–86.

Patrick, D. (2003). Language socialisation and second language acquisition in a multilingual Arctic Quebec community. In R. Bayley and S. R. Schecter (eds) *Language Socialisation in Bilingual and Multilingual Societies.* Clevedon: Multilingual Matters, 165–81.

Patten, A. (2003). Liberal neutrality and language policy. *Philosophy and Public Affairs* 3(4): 356–86.

Paulin-Nteziryayo, F. and Archambault, Y. (2000). *Comparaison entre la clientèle rejointe et la clientèle potentielle des services de francisation du MRCI.* [Québec]: Ministère des Relations avec les citoyens et l'Immigration.

Pennycook, A. (1998). *English and the Discourses of Colonialism.* London: Routledge.

Perreault, L. J. (2001). Les anglophones partagés. *La Presse,* 21 August.

Perreault, M. (2002a). Times have changed. *The Gazette,* 17 June.

Perreault, M. (2002b). Accent's now on communicating. *The Gazette,* 17 June.

Perreault, M. (2002c). Bilingual? Yes, but separate cultures. *The Gazette,* 19 June.

Piché, V. (2001). Immigration et intégration: une crise qui n'a pas eu lieu. In R. Côté (ed.) *Québec 2002. Annuaire politique, social, économique et culturel.*[Montréal]: Fides, 43–50.

Piché, V. and Frenette, L. (2001). Intégration et langue française. Une affaire de réciprocité pour la société québécoise. (Mémoire presented to the États généraux sur la situation et l'avenir de la langue française au Québec, 12 March 2001, for the Conseil des relations interculturelles).

Pipes, R. (1975). Nationality problems in the Soviet Union. In N. Glaser and D. Moynihan (eds) *Ethnicity: Theory and Experience.* Cambridge, MA: Harvard University Press, 453–65.

Plourde, M. (1993). *La politique linguistique du Québec, 1977–1987.* (Diagnostic 6). Québec: Institut québécois de recherche sur la culture.

Poirier, C. (1987). Le français 'régional': méthodologies et terminologies. In H.-J. Niederehe and L. Wolf (eds) *Français du Canada – français de France. Actes du colloque de Trèves du 26 au 28 septembre 1985. (Canadania Romania* 1). Tübingen: Niemeyer, 139–76.

Poirier, C. (1990). Un dictionnaire général du français québécois: produit original ou produit adapté? In N. Corbett (ed.) *Langue et identité. Le français et les francophones d'Amérique du Nord.* Sainte-Foy: Les Presses de l'Université Laval, 339–51.

Poirier, C. (1994). La langue parlée en Nouvelle-France: vers une convergence des explications. In R. Mougeon and E. Beniak (eds) *Les origines du français québécois.* Sainte-Foy: Les Presses de l'Université Laval, 237–73.

Poirier, C. (1998). De la défense à la codification du français québécois: plaidoyer pour une action concertée. In C. Verreault, and L. Mercier (eds), with the participation of D. Dumas, *Représentation de la langue et légitimité linguistique: le français et ses variétés nationales. (Revue québécoise de linguistique* 26 (2)). Montréal: Université du Québec à Montréal, 129–50.

Poisson, E. (2002). Français en usage au Québec et dictionnaires. In C. Verreault, L. Mercier and T. Lavoie (eds) *Le français, une langue à apprivoiser. Textes de conférences prononcées au Musée de la civilisation (Québec, 2000–2001) dans le cadre de l'exposition Une grande langue: le français dans tous ses états.* Sainte-Foy: Les Presses de l'Université Laval, 93–111.

Pöll, B. (2001). *Francophonies périphériques. Histoire, statut et profil des principales variétés du français hors de France.* Paris: L'Harmattan.

Poole, R. (1999). *Nation and Identity.* London: Routledge.

Pratte, A. (2005a). Québec Anglophones: a new leadership for a renewed dialogue. (Presentation at the Conférence de recherche sur les communautés anglophones du Québec, Université du Québec à Montréal, 25–26 February 2005).

Pratte, A. (2005b). Un nouveau dialogue. *La Presse*, 29 March.
Pratte, A. (2005c). Notre maître, le passé. *La Presse*, 4 July.
Proulx, J.-P. (2001). Le rapport Larose s'accroche à un but plus grand que lui. *Le Devoir*, 28 August.
Prujiner, A. (2005). L'impact des conventions internationales sur les politiques linguistiques. In A. Stefanescu and P. Georgeault (eds) *Le français au Québec. Les nouveaux défis*. [Montréal]: Fides, 357–84.
QCGN (Quebec Community Groups Network) (2005). *Community Development Plan for the English-Speaking Communities of Quebec: 2005–2010*. <http://www.qcgn.ca> Accessed 6 January 2006.
Rawls, J. (1999). *A Theory of Justice*. (Revised edition). Cambridge, MA: Belknap Press.
RCAP (Royal Commission on Aboriginal Peoples) (1996). *Highlights from the Report of the Royal Commission on Aboriginal Peoples*. <http://www.ainc-inac.gc.ca/ch/rcap/rpt/lk_e.html> Accessed 2 February 2006.
Reich, R. B. (1992). *The Work of Nations*. New York: Vintage.
Renan, E. (1990). What is a nation? (Translated and annotated by M. Thom). In H. K. Bhabha (ed.) *Nation and Narration*. London: Routledge, 1–22.
Renaud, J., Gingras, L., Vachon, S., Blaser, C., Godin, J. F. and Gagné, B. (2003). *What a Difference Ten Years Can Make! The Settlement Experience of Immigrants Admitted to Québec in 1989*. Sainte-Foy: Les Publications du Québec.
Rice, K. (2005). The linguist's responsibilities to the community of speakers. (Paper presented at the Conference on Language Documentation: Theory, Practice, and Values, 2005 LSA Linguistic Institute, Harvard University, 9–10 July 2005). <http://www.chass.utoronto.ca/lingfieldwork/pdf/1.pdf> Accessed 6 January 2006.
Richer, J. (2005). Hydro-Québec aura maille à partir avec le nouveau chef des Cris. *Le Devoir*, 17–18 December.
Rioux, C. (2004). « Au moins, livrons bataille! » Si Québec ne fait rien, la convention sur la diversité culturelle sera sans effet, dit Louise Beaudoin. *Le Devoir*, 23 September.
Rioux, M. (1990). Se différencier, se définir et s'affirmer. In N. Corbett (ed.) *Langue et identité. Le français et les francophones d'Amérique du Nord*. Sainte-Foy: Les Presses de l'Université Laval, 7–10.
Ritzer, G. (1997). *The McDonaldization Thesis: Explorations and Extensions*. London: Sage.
Robert, J.-C. (2000). Luttes pour la primauté du français (1960–1976). In M. Plourde (ed.), with the collaboration of H. Duval and P. Georgeault, *Le français au Québec. 400 ans d'histoire et de vie*. [Montréal/Québec]: Fides/Publications du Québec, 239–46.
Robertson, R. (1992). *Globalization. Social Theory and Global Culture*. London: Sage.
Robertson, R. (1995). Glocalization: time-space and homogeneity-heterogeneity. In M. Featherstone, S. Lash and R. Robertson (eds) *Global Modernities*. London: Sage, 25–44.
Rocher, G. (2005). Introduction. In A. Stefanescu and P. Georgeault (eds) *Le français au Québec. Les nouveaux défis*. [Montréal]: Fides, 13–28.
Roosens, E. (1989). *Creating Ethnicity*. London: Sage.
Rosello, M. (2001). *Postcolonial Hospitality. The Immigrant as Guest*. Stanford: Stanford University Press.
Rosenberg, M. and Simmons, R. (1972). *Black and White Self-Esteem: The Urban Schoolchild*. Washington: American Sociological Association.
Roy, C. (2001). L'usage des langues dans la sphère publique au Québec. *Bulletin d'histoire politique* 10(1): 151–60.

Rudin, R. (1985). *The Forgotten Quebecers: A History of English-Speaking Québec, 1759–1980*. Québec: Institut québécois de recherche sur la culture.
Saada, J. (2004). Libre opinion: sommet de la francophonie, Québec et Ottawa sur la même longueur d'onde. *Le Devoir*, 7 December.
Sachdev, I. and Bourhis, R. Y. (1990). Language and social identification. In D. Abrams and M. Hogg (eds) *Social Identity Theory: Constructive and Critical Advances*. New York: Harvester Wheatsheaf, 211–29.
Saint-Jacques, B. (1990). Le français québécois: langue de communication et symbole d'identité. In N. Corbett (ed.) *Langue et identité. Le français et les francophones d'Amérique du Nord*. Sainte-Foy: Les Presses de l'Université Laval, 229–44.
Saint Robert, M. J. de (2000). *La politique de la langue française*. (Que sais-je? 3572). Paris: Presses Universitaires de France.
Salée, D. (1997). NAFTA, Quebec and the boundaries of cultural sovereignty: the challenge of identity in the era of globalization. In D. G. Dallmeyer (ed.) *Joining Together, Standing Apart: National Identities after NAFTA*. Netherlands: Kluwer Law International, 73–89.
Salée, D. (2004). The Québec state and indigenous peoples. In A.-G. Gagnon (ed.) *Québec: State and Society*. (3rd edition). Peterborough, CA: Broadview Press, 97–124.
Salée, D. (2005). Peuples autochtones, racisme et pouvoir d'État en contextes canadien et québécois. Éléments pour une ré-analyse. *Nouvelles pratiques sociales* 17(2): 54–74. <http://www.erudit.org/revue/nps/2005/v17/n2/011226ar.pdf> Accessed 24 September 2005.
Sarrasin, R. (1998). L'enseignement du français et en français en milieu amérindien au Québec: une problématique ethnopédagogique. *Revue canadienne de linguistique appliquée/Canadian Journal of Applied Linguistics* 1: 107–25.
Schiller, H. I. (1985). Transnational media and national development. In K. Nordenstreng and H. I. Schiller (eds) *National Sovereignty and International Communication*. Norwood, NJ: Ablex, 21–32.
Schmid, C. L. (2001). *The Politics of Language. Conflict, Identity, and Cultural Pluralism in Comparative Perspective*. New York: Oxford University Press.
Schnapper, D. (1994). *La communauté des citoyens. Sur l'idée de nation*. Paris: Gallimard.
Schnapper, D. (1996). Beyond the opposition: civic nation versus ethnic nation. In J. Couture, K. Nielsen and M. Seymour (eds) *Rethinking Nationalism*. (*Canadian Journal of Philosophy*, supplementary volume 22), 219–34.
Scholte, J. (2000). *Globalization: A Critical Introduction*. New York: St Martin's Press.
Scowen, R. (1979). Reflections on the future of the English language in Quebec. Montréal, May 1979. Unpublished paper.
Scowen, R. (1991). *A Different Vision: The English in Quebec in the 1990s*. Don Mills, ON: Maxwell Macmillan.
Secrétariat aux affaires autochtones (2001). *The Amerindians and Inuit of Québec. Eleven Contemporary Nations*. [Québec]: Gouvernement du Québec. <http://www.autochtones.gouv.qc.ca/publications_documentation/publications/onze_nations_en.pdf> Accessed 6 January 2006.
Secrétariat aux affaires autochtones (2005). Aboriginal population in Québec. <http://www.autochtones.gouv.qc.ca/nations/population_en.htm> Accessed 28 November 2005.
Séguin, R. (2004). Charest praises Ottawa over trip. *The Globe and Mail*, 18 November 2004.
Seymour, M. (1998). Une conception sociopolitique de la nation. *Dialogue* 37(3): 435–71.

Seymour, M. (1999a). *La nation en question*. Montréal: l'Hexagone.
Seymour, M. (1999b). Plaidoyer pour la nation sociopolitique. In M. Seymour (ed.) *Nationalité, citoyenneté et solidarité*. Montréal: Liber, 153–67.
Seymour, M. (1999c). Les stratégies fédérales pour ethniciser le Québec. <http://www.vigile.net/998/seymourethniciser.html> Accessed 11 July 2002.
Seymour, M. (2000). Le libéralisme, la politique de la reconnaissance, et le cas du Québec. In W. Kymlicka (ed.) *Comprendre* 1(1). <http://mapageweb.umontreal.ca/lepagef/dept/cahiers/Seymour_liberalisme.pdf> Accessed 11 July 2002.
Seymour, M. (2001). An inclusive nation that does not deny its origins. In M. Venne (ed.) *Vive Quebec! New Thinking and New Approaches to the Quebec Nation*. (Translated by R. Chodos and L. Blair). Toronto: James Lorimer and Company, 146–54.
Seymour, M. (2005). Le français comme langue publique commune. In J. Boucher and J.-Y. Thériault (eds) *Petites sociétés et minorités nationales. Enjeux politiques et perspectives comparées*. Sainte-Foy: Presses de l'Université du Québec, 49–66.
Seymour, M. with Couture, J. and Nielsen, K. (1996). Introduction: questioning the ethnic/civic dichotomy. In J. Couture, K. Nielsen and M. Seymour (eds) *Rethinking Nationalism*. (*Canadian Journal of Philosophy*, supplementary volume 22), 1–61.
Shils, E. (1957). Primordial, personal, sacred and civil ties. *British Journal of Sociology* 7: 13–45.
Simard, C. (1990). Les besoins lexicographiques du milieu de l'enseignement du Québec. In Conseil de la langue française (ed.) *Dix études portant sur l'aménagement de la langue au Québec*. [Québec]: Conseil de la langue française. <http://www.cslf.gouv.qc.ca> Accessed 7 March 2005.
Slattery, K. (1998). *Chinua Achebe and the Language of the Colonizer*. <http://www.qub.ac.uk/en/imperial/nigeria/language.htm> Accessed 4 October 2005.
Smith, A. D. (1986). *The Ethnic Origins of Nations*. Oxford: Blackwell.
Smith, A. D. (1991). *National Identity*. Harmondsworth: Penguin.
Smith, A. D. (1996/1997). Civic and ethnic nationalism revisited: analysis and ideology. *ASEN Bulletin* 12: 9–11.
Smith, A. D. (2001). *Nationalism: Theory, Ideology, History*. Cambridge: Polity Press.
Smith, D. (1990). Pour l'établissement d'une norme québécoise dans l'enseignement du français. In N. Corbett (ed.) *Langue et identité. Le français et les francophones d'Amérique du Nord*. Sainte-Foy: Les Presses de l'Université Laval, 47–51.
Société du parler français au Canada (1930). *Glossaire du parler français au Canada*. Québec: l'Action sociale limitée.
Sonntag, S. K. (2003). *The Local Politics of Global English*. Lanham, MD: Lexington Books.
Spencer, P. and Wollman, H. (2002). *Nationalism: A Critical Introduction*. London: Sage.
Spolsky, B. (2004). *Language Policy*. Cambridge: Cambridge University Press.
Statistics Canada (2004). *2003 General Social Survey on Social Engagement, Cycle 17: An Overview of Findings*. <http://www.statcan.ca:80/english/freepub/89-598-XIE/2003001/pdf/89-598-XIE2003001.pdf> Accessed 27 December 2005.
Stefanescu, A. and Georgeault, P. (2005). Conclusion. In A. Stefanescu and P. Georgeault (eds) *Le français au Québec. Les nouveaux défis*. [Montréal]: Fides, 589–608.
Stein, M. (1982). Changing Anglo-Quebecer counciousness [*sic.*]. In G. Caldwell and E. Waddell (eds) *The English of Quebec: From Majority to Minority Status*. Québec: Institut québécois de recherche sur la culture, 107–25.
Stevenson, G. (1999). *Community Besieged: The Anglophone Minority and the Politics of Québec*. Montréal/Kingston: McGill-Queen's University Press.

Stevenson, G. (2004). English-Speaking Québec: a political history. In A.-G. Gagnon (ed.) *Québec: State and Society*. (3rd edition). Peterborough, CA: Broadview Press. 329–44.
Stevenson, G. (2005). No longer besieged? An update on the Anglophone community and the politics of Quebec. (Paper presented at the Conférence de recherche sur les communautés anglophones du Québec, Université du Québec à Montréal, 25–26 February 2005).
Tajfel, H. (1974). Social identity and intergroup behaviour. *Social Science Information* 13: 65–93.
Tajfel, H. (1978). *The Social Psychology of Minorities*. (Minority Rights Group Report 38). London: Minority Rights Group.
Tajfel, H. and Turner, J. C. (1986). The social identity theory of intergroup behaviour. In S. Worchel and W. G. Austin (eds) *Psychology of Intergroup Relations*. (Revised edition of *The Social Psychology of Intergroup Relations*, 1979). Chicago: Nelson-Hall Publishers, 7–24.
Tamir, Y. (1993). *Liberal Nationalism*. Princeton: Princeton University Press.
Tanner, A. (1999). *Innu Culture*. St. John's: Memorial University of Newfoundland. <http://www.heritage.nf.ca/aboriginal/innu_culture.html> Accessed 30 December 2005.
Tardivel, J.-P. (1880). *L'anglicisme, voilà l'ennemi*. Québec: Imprimerie du Canadien.
Taylor, C. (1992). *Rapprocher les solitudes*. (Introduced by G. Laforest). Sainte-Foy: Les Presses de l'Université Laval.
Taylor, C. (1994). The politics of recognition. In C. Taylor et al. (Edited and introduced by A. Gutman). *Multiculturalism: Examining the Politics of Recognition*. Princeton: Princeton University Press, 25–73.
Taylor, C. (1996). Les sources de l'identité moderne. In M. Elbaz, A. Fortin and G. Laforest (eds) *Les frontières de l'identité. Modernité et postmodernisme au Québec*. Sainte-Foy/Paris: Les Presses de l'Université Laval/L'Harmattan, 347–64.
Taylor, C. (2001). Cultural nation, political nation. In M. Venne (ed.) *Vive Quebec! New Thinking and New Approaches to the Quebec Nation*. (Translated by R. Chodos and L. Blair). Toronto: James Lorimer and Company, 19–26.
Télé-Québec (2006a). À propos de l'émission *Pure laine*. <http://www.telequebec.qc.ca/purelaine/index.aspx?sec=propos> Accessed 10 February 2006.
Télé-Québec (2006b). *Pure laine*. Vos réactions et commentaires à cet épisode. <http://www.telequebec.tv/purelaine/commentaires.aspx?id=2> Accessed 17 February 2006.
Termote, M. (2000). Le poids de l'immigration. In M. Plourde (ed.), with the collaboration of H. Duval and P. Georgeault, *Le français au Québec. 400 ans d'histoire et de vie*. [Montréal/Québec]: Fides/Publications du Québec, 348–51.
Termote, M. (2002). L'évolution démolinguistique du Québec et du Canada. In *La mise à jour des études originairement préparées pour la Commission sur l'avenir politique et constitutionnel du Québec*. (Rapport soumis au ministre délégué aux affaires intergouvernementales canadiennes, volume 2, livre 2). Québec: Bureau de coordination des études, ministère du Conseil exécutif, 161–244.
TFALC (Task Force on Aboriginal Languages and Cultures) (2005). *Towards a New Beginning. A Foundational Report for a Strategy to Revitalize First Nation, Inuit and Métis Languages and Cultures*. <http://www.aboriginallanguagestaskforce.ca/foundreport_e.html> Accessed 31 December 2005.
Thériault, J.-Y. (2000). La langue, symbole de l'identité québécoise. In M. Plourde (ed.), with the collaboration of H. Duval and P. Georgeault, *Le français au Québec. 400 ans d'histoire et de vie*. [Montréal/Québec]: Fides/Publications du Québec, 254–9.

Thériault, J.-Y. (2002a). *Critique de l'américanité. Mémoire et démocratie au Québec.* Montréal: Québec Amérique.

Thériault, J.-Y. (2002b). Le projet d'une citoyenneté québécoise: un décollage difficile. In R. Côté and M. Venne (eds) *L'annuaire du Québec 2003*. [Montréal]: Fides, 27–32.

Thibault, A. (1998). Légitimité linguistique des français nationaux hors de France: le cas du français de Suisse romande. In C. Verreault and L. Mercier (eds), with the participation of D. Dumas, *Représentation de la langue et légitimité linguistique: le français et ses variétés nationales*. (*Revue québécoise de linguistique* 26(2)). Montréal: Université du Québec à Montréal, 25–42.

Tomlinson, J. (1999). *Globalization and Culture*. Cambridge: Polity Press.

Tremblay, M. (2004). Le Québec et les autochtones – une réconciliation en cours. *Le Devoir*, 2–3 October.

Trudeau, D. (1992). *Les inventeurs du bon usage (1529–1647)*. Paris: Les Éditions de Minuit.

Trudeau, P. E. (1977). *Federalism and the French Canadians*. (Laurentian Library 48). Toronto: Macmillan.

Trudel, F. (1996). Aboriginal language policies of the Canadian and Quebec governments. In J. Maurais (ed.) *Quebec's Aboriginal Languages: History, Planning, Development*. Clevedon: Multilingual Matters, 101–28.

Tully, J. (1995). *Strange Multiplicity: Constitutionalism in an Age of Diversity*. Cambridge: Cambridge University Press.

Tully, J. (2000). A just relationship between Aboriginal and non-Aboriginal peoples of Canada. In C. Cook and J. Lindau (eds) *Aboriginal Rights and Self-Government: The Canadian and Mexican Experience in North American Perspective*. Montréal/Kingston: McGill-Queen's University Press, 39–71.

Tully, J. (2001). Introduction. In A.-G Gagnon and J. Tully (eds) *Multinational Democracies*. Cambridge: Cambridge University Press, 1–33.

Turi, G. (1971). *Une culture appelée québécoise*. Montréal: Les Éditions de l'Homme.

Turner, J. C. (1985). Social categorization and the self-concept: a social-cognitive theory of group behaviour. In E. J. Lawler (ed.) *Advances in Group Processes: Theory and Research. Volume 2*. Greenwich, CT: JAI Press, 77–121.

Turner, J. C. and Oakes, P. J. (1989). Self-categorization theory and social influence. In P. B. Paulus (ed.) *Psychology of Group Influence*. (2nd edition). Hillsdale, NJ: Erlbaum, 223–75.

Turner, J. C. with Hogg, M. A., Oakes, P. J., Reicher, S. D. and Wetherell, M. (1987). *Rediscovering the Social Group: A Self-Categorization Theory*. Oxford: Blackwell.

UNESCO (1968). The use of vernacular language in education: the report of the UNESCO Meeting of Specialists, 1951. In J. A. Fishman (ed.) *Readings in the Sociology of Language*. The Hague/Paris: Mouton, 688–716.

UNESCO (2002). *UNESCO Universal Declaration on Cultural Diversity*. <http://unesdoc.unesco.org/images/0012/001271/127160m.pdf> Accessed 23 November 2004.

UNESCO (2004). *Preliminary Draft of a Convention on the Protection of the Diversity of Cultural Contents and Artistic Expressions*. <http://portal.unesco.org/culture/en/ev.php-URL_ID=21972&URL_DO=DO_TOPIC&URL_SECTION=201.html> Accessed 24 August 2004.

UNESCO (2005a). *Convention on the Protection and Promotion of the Diversity of Cultural Expressions*. <http://unesdoc.unesco.org/images/0014/001429/142919e.pdf> Accessed 11 December 2005.

UNESCO (2005b). *General Conference Adopts Convention on the Protection and Promotion of the Diversity of Cultural Expressions*. <http://portal.unesco.org/culture/en/

ev.php-URL_ID=29078&URL_DO=DO_TOPIC&URL_SECTION=201.html> Accessed 11 December 2005.
Valdman, A. (1983). Normes locales et francophonie. In É. Bédard and J. Maurais (eds) *La norme linguistique*. [Québec]: Conseil de la langue française, 667–706.
Varouxakis, G. (2001). Nationality. In A. S. Leoussi (ed.) *Encyclopaedia of Nationalism*. New Brunswick/London: Transaction, 232–4.
Vassberg, L. M. (1993). *Alsatian Acts of Identity: Language Use and Language Attitudes in Alsace*. Clevedon: Multilingual Matters.
Venne, M. (2000a). Citoyen ou loyal sujet? *Le Devoir*, 22 September.
Venne, M. (2000b) La fin d'un faux débat entre nationalisme civique et ethnique. *Le Devoir*, 14 April. <http://www.ledevoir.com> Accessed 12 January 2001.
Venne, M. (ed). (2000c). *Penser la nation québécoise*. Montréal: Le Devoir/Québec Amérique.
Venne, M. (2001a). La citoyenneté sans la souveraineté? Impossible. *Le Devoir*, 10 November.
Venne, M. (2001b). Rethinking the nation, or how to live together. In M. Venne (ed.) *Vive Quebec! New Thinking and New Approaches to the Quebec Nation*. (Translated by R. Chodos and L. Blair). Toronto: James Lorimer and Company, 3–16.
Venne, M. (ed.) (2001c). *Vive Quebec! New Thinking and New Approaches to the Quebec Nation*. (Translated by R. Chodos and L. Blair). Toronto: James Lorimer and Company.
Verreault, C. (1999a). De *La deffence et illustration de la langue françoyse* de Joachim du Bellay (1549) à *La deffence & illustration de la langue quebecquoyse* de Michèle Lalonde (1973): qu'est donc le français devenu par-delà les mers? In *Actes des Journées de la langue française. 1549–1999, 450ème anniversaire de « Deffence et illustration de la langue françoyse » de Joachim du Bellay, 23–24 octobre 1999, Liré*. Liré: Musée Joachim du Bellay, 97–105.
Verreault, C. (1999b). L'enseignement du français en contexte québécois: de quelle langue est-il question? In C. Ouellon (ed.) *La norme du français au Québec. Perspectives pédagogiques*. (*Terminogramme* 92–92). Québec: Les Publications du Québec, 21–40.
Verreault, C. and Mercier, L., with the participation of Dumas, D. (1998). *Représentation de la langue et légitimité linguistique: le français et ses variétés nationales*. (*Revue québécoise de linguistique* 26(2)). Montréal: Université du Québec à Montréal.
Villers, M.-É. de (2003). *Multidictionnaire de la langue française*. (4th edition). Montréal: Québec Amérique.
Villers, M.-É. de (2005). La norme réelle du français. In A. Stefanescu and P. Georgeault (eds) *Le français au Québec. Les nouveaux défis*. [Montréal]: Fides, 399–420.
Waddell, E. (1982). Place and people. In G. Caldwell and E. Waddell (eds) *The English of Quebec: From Majority to Minority Status*. Québec: Institut québécois de recherche sur la culture, 27–55.
Walker, B. (1999). Modernity and cultural vulnerability: should ethnicity be privileged? In R. Beiner (ed.) *Theorizing Nationalism*. Albany: State University of New York Press, 141–65.
Weinstock, D. (2000). La citoyenneté en mutation. In Y. Boisvert, J. Hamel and M. Molgat (eds), with the collaboration of B. Ellefsen, *Vivre la citoyenneté. Identité, appartenance et participation*. Montréal: Éditions Liber, 15–26.
Winer, L. (2001). Les Anglo-Québécois voient d'un mauvais oeil les fusions municipales. In R. Côté (ed.) *L'annuaire du Québec 2002*. [Montréal]: Fides, 153–7.
Woehrling, J. (2000). La Charte de la langue française: les ajustements juridiques. In M. Plourde (ed.), with the collaboration of H. Duval and P. Georgeault, *Le français au*

Québec. 400 ans d'histoire et de vie. [Montréal/Québec]: Fides/Publications du Québec, 285–91.

Woehrling, J. (2005). L'évolution du cadre juridique et conceptuel de la législation linguistique au Québec. In A. Stefanescu and P. Georgeault (eds) *Le français au Québec. Les nouveaux défis*. [Montréal]: Fides, 253–356.

Wright S. (2004). *Language Policy and Language Planning: From Nationalism to Globalisation*. Houndmills, Basingstoke: Palgrave Macmillan.

Yack, B. (1999). The myth of the civic nation. In R. Beiner (ed.) *Theorizing Nationalism*. Albany: State University of New York Press, 103–30.

Zølner, M. (2000). *Re-imagining the Nation: Debates on Immigrants, Identities and Memories*. Bruxelles/Bern/Berlin/Frankfurt/Oxford/New York/Vienna: Peter Lang.

Index

NOTE: Names of official organisations are given in the language used in the text, usually French. Organisations and legislation are for Quebec unless otherwise specified.

Abenaki people and language 174, 175, 176, 177
Aboriginal Languages and Cultures Council (Canada) 180
Aboriginal Languages Initiative (Canada) 189
Aboriginal peoples and languages 4, 172–93, 196; assimilationist policies 37, 181; borrowings in Quebec French 120; and citizenship debate 172–3, 180–6, 197; constitution of Aboriginal nations 174–80; demographics 175–7; and education 178, 180, 181, 185, 187–92, 211*n*.11, 212*n*.16; endangered languages and language survival 177–8, 185, 186–93, 211*n*.7, 212*n*.17; and English 176–7, 186, 187; and ethnic theory of nation 54, 202*n*.6; federal and provincial responsibility 174, 210*n*.2; and French 176–7, 186, 187, 189, 191–2, 193, 212*n*.16; linguistic rights 6, 178–86; and national identity 53, 180–6, 202*n*.6; and self-autonomy in Canada 181, 184–6, 197; and sovereignty referenda 31; territorial agreements 174, 185, 210*n*.5
Académie française 117
accommodement raisonnable 41
Achebe, C. 102
acquisition of French as second language 123, 134, 142; and education 92–3, 135–8, 146–7; and *langue publique commune* 94, 104, 132, 133, 136, 146; motivation for 91–7, 104, 136, 144, 146–7, 204*n*.5; and policy 84, 85, 91, 92, 93, 94, 104, 136–7; *see also* francisation programmes

Action démocratique du Québec (ADQ) 4
Ager, D. E. 92
Algonquin people and language 174, 175, 176, 177
Allaire Report 30
Alliance Quebec 151, 163, 164
Allophone Quebecers 59, 89, 94–5, 133, 147, 148, 156, 157, 160, 165, 167, 169–70; and national dictionary project 123; and quality of Quebec French 118; and sense of belonging 207*n*.5; *see also* cultural communities; *enfants de la loi 101*; immigrants
américanisation 73, 74
américanité 55, 73–4
Americas: Decade of the Americas 74; economic integration 68–9; Quebec's integration in 63, 67–75, 79, 80, 195; and language issues 69–72, 79–80; *see also* Canada; United States
Anderson, B. 83–4, 101
anglicisms 109, 110, 111, 120–1
Anglophobia 160–1, 196
Anglophone Quebecers 4, 58, 118, 150–71, 196–7; attitudes of Francophone majority towards 6, 151–2, 158–61, 170–1, 196; attitudes towards Francophone majority 151–2, 196; bilingualism as way forward 165–70; and citizenship debate 158–65, 196–7; definitions of 153–5; demographic decline 155–7; and education 85, 87–8, 155, 168–9; French language proficiency 169, 171, 196, 209*n*.12; and language policies 85–6, 163–4; as linguistic bridge with North America

Anglophone Quebecers – *continued*
  151, 208*n*.1; linguistic rights
  163–4; in Montreal 134–5, 157;
  and national dictionary project
  123–4; and Quebec national identity
  46, 57–9, 151–2, 161–2; out-
  migration 155–7, 164, 167, 196;
  representation issues 164–5, 171,
  196; self-awareness as minority
  group 152–3; *see also* English
  Canadians; English language
*Apprendre le Quebec. Guide pour réussir
  mon intégration* (policy document)
  136–7
Arabic language 145
archaisms in Quebec French 110, 120
Ardagh, J. 40–1
Arel, D. 38
Assembly of First Nations 180, 187
assimilation policies 26–7, 28, 37,
  88–9; *see also* integration policies
Association québécoise des professeurs
  de français 119
Attikamek people and language 174,
  175, 176, 177, 211*n*.6
*Au Québec, pour bâtir ensemble. Énoncé de
  politique en matière d'immigration et
  d'intégration* (policy document)
  29–30, 50, 89, 93, 94, 138–9
Autant de façons d'être Québécois (policy
  document) 28, 29

Baraby, A.-M. 190
Barbaud, P. 108
Bariteau, C. 32; civic model of nation
  52–4, 103–4
Barth, F. 11–12
Beauchamp, L. 66, 125
Beauchemin, J. 55
Beauchemin, N. 111
Beaudoin, L. 71, 79
Beaulieu, I. 145–7
Beiner, R. 40, 42
Bélanger, H. 112
Bélanger-Campeau Commission 30
Bélisle, L.-A. 206*n*.9
Bellay, J. du 112
Bergeron, L. 121
Bernier, I. 77, 78
Bertrand, J.-J. 85

Bibaud, M. 109
biculturalism 98, 169–70
bilingualism: and Aboriginal peoples
  191–2; and Anglophone and
  Francophone communities 165–70;
  bilingual municipalities 153–4; and
  federal language policy 97–8, 143;
  increase in 6, 166–8; language
  policy in schools 85, 86, 87–8; in
  Montreal 142, 147–8, 167, 196
Bills: 1 86; 22 85; 52 66; 57 164;
  63 85; 86 87; 99 31, 66; 101
  86; 104 88; 170 153; 171 153;
  178 87 *see also* Charter of the
  French language
Bloc Québécois 15
B'Nai Brith 42
Boileau, J. 151
Boisvert, Y. 160
bon usage 114–15, 123, 205*n*.7
borrowings in Quebec French 120–1;
  see also anglicisms
Bouchard, C. 107, 109, 112–13
Bouchard, G. 47, 75; and *américanité*
  55, 73–4; on Americas as
  community of interests 69, 70;
  civic model of nation 54–7, 61, 94;
  on ethnicity 11, 40, 100; French
  language and cultural heritage
  103; new collectivities 73–4
Bouchard, L. 4, 42–3
Bouchard, P. 118–19
Bourassa, R. 85
Bourhis, R. Y. 12, 133, 167
Bourque, G. 14
Bouthillier, G. 31, 98
Breton, R. 43, 98
Brunet, M. 27
Buies, A. 109–10
Burnaby, B. 188–9, 190

Cajolet-Laganière, H. 114, 206*n*.11
Caldwell, G. 152, 154; civic model of
  nation 51–2
calques 109, 120
Canada: and Aboriginal peoples 174,
  180–1, 185–6, 187–8, 189, 210*n*.5;
  allegiance of Anglophone
  community 161–2; Canadian
  citizenship and Quebec citizenship

Canada – *continued*
  26, 32–6, 43, 94, 201*n*.4; and cultural diversity debate 76, 77; *la Francophonie* and Quebec's participation 76, 204*n*.11; and liberal citizenship model 36, 37–8; multiculturalism 28–9, 37–8, 53, 54, 98, 143–4, 194; and Quebec's international relations 63, 64–6, 79, 80, 204*n*.11; *see also* Americas; French Canadians
Canada–Quebec Accord on Immigration and Temporary Admission of Aliens (1991) 133
Canada–United States Free Trade Agreement (1988) 67
Canadian Census data 95, 145, 155–6, 157, 167, 168, 169, 174–5, 177–8, 206*n*.2, 209*n*.6
Canadian Charter of Rights and Freedoms (1982) *see* Charter of Rights and Freedoms
Canadian French: historical development 107–12; *see also* Quebec French
Canadian Heritage 164, 180, 189, 209*n*.5
canadianismes de bon aloi 112, 120; *see also québécismes*
Cantin, S. 48, 201–2*n*.1
Carens, J. H. 92, 173, 175
Castells, M. 83
Castonguay, C. 90, 157
Catalonia 97, 198
Chamberland, P. 111
Chambers, G. 154, 161, 166–7
Charest, J. 34–5, 64–5, 66, 72
Charlottetown Accord (1992) 30
Charter of Human Rights and Freedoms (1975) 27, 87
Charter of Rights and Freedoms (1982) (Canada) 37, 87, 88, 163
Charter of the French language (1977) 34, 118, 121, 201*n*.2; and Aboriginal languages 178, 188; amendments 87, 88, 153, 163–4; and Anglophone community 87–8, 152, 156, 163–4, 167; anniversary celebration 126; policy development 86–9; and French language instruction 87–8, 92–3, 137, 147; *see also enfants de la loi* 101
Cité libre (journal) 36
citizenship 18–21, 25–43; democratic citizenship 35; immigrant perceptions of 141–3; and liberalism in Canada and Quebec 36–42; models of 19–21; and national identity 5, 15, 25–6, 39–40, 43; and nationality 18, 32–3, 36; *see also* civic republican citizenship model; intercultural citizenship; liberal citizenship model; Quebec citizenship
civic nationalism 2, 13–14, 194; and Aboriginal peoples 172–3, 193, 198; and Anglophone community 151–2, 198; and de-ethnicisation of language 101, 103–4, 105, 195; and immigration 29–31, 133, 197; and language policy 83, 91–7, 104–5, 113, 123, 126–7; and models of nation 26, 38, 46, 47–54, 194–5, 198; and national dictionary project 123, 125, 126–7; and Quebec citizenship 34
civic republican citizenship model 19, 20–1, 30, 36, 38–41; in France 26, 40–1, 48–9; immigrant integration 141; in Quebec 38–9, 41–2, 43, 194–5
Clapin, S. 110
Clarity Act (2000) 31
classes d'accueil 137–8, 196
Cleary, B. 179, 180, 211*n*.6&7
Coalition for Cultural Diversity 77
Cohen, A. 10, 11, 200*n*.3
Cohen, J. A. 18
colonialism: and Aboriginal peoples 180–1; and attitudes towards Anglophone community 159–60; and development of French in Canada 107–12; new collectivities 73–4; and use of English language 102
Comité interministériel sur la situation de la langue française 89–90, 93
Commission de protection de la langue française 121
Commission d'enquête sur la situation de la langue française et sur les droits linguistiques au Québec *see* Gendron Commission

Commission d'enquête sur le bilinguisme et le biculturalisme *see* Laurendeau-Dunton Commission
Commission des États généraux sur la situation et l'avenir de la langue française au Québec *see* Larose Commission
Commission on the Political and Constitutional Future of Quebec *see* Bélanger-Campeau Commission
common language *see langue commune*
common public culture *see culture publique commune*
common public language *see langue publique commune*
communitarianism 41, 51
Conseil de la langue française (1977–2002) 70, 164, 179; *enfants de la loi 101* 146–7; and national dictionary project 122–3; study on *langue d'usage public* 89–90; *see also* Conseil supérieur de la langue française
Conseil des communautés culturelles et de l'immigration (1984–96) 201*n*.3; *see also* Conseil des relations interculturelles
Conseil des relations interculturelles (CRI) (1996–) 32, 39–40; *see also* Conseil des communautés culturelles et de l'immigration
Conseil supérieur de la langue française (2002–) 71, 88, 91, 179; *see also* Conseil de la langue française
Conseil Tribal Mamuitun 185, 189–90
Constitution Act (1867) 88, 163
Constitution Act (1982) 88, 163, 174, 175, 178–9
constitutional patriotism 52–3, 58, 103–4
convergence culturelle see culture de convergence
Corbeil, J.-C. 191, 211*n*.7
Corsica 35–6
Côté, S. 156, 170, 209*n*.12
Coupland, N. 101
Cree people and language 174, 175, 176, 177, 178, 180, 210*n*.5, 211*n*.6, 211*n*.11, 212*n*.16; Cree Language of Instruction Programme 188–9; Cree Literacy Programme 189;

Cree School Board 178, 185, 188, 189, 211*n*.11, 212*n*.16; language survival 186–7, 188–9, 190, 191, 192–3; *Paix des braves* 183, 184–5, 192, 211*n*.10
Cree-Naskapi (of Quebec) Act (1984) 210*n*.5
CROP-*La Presse* poll 158–61
Cross, J. 204*n*.2
Croucher, S. L. 65
cultural communities 28, 29, 133; and concept of nation 46, 53, 59; and Quebec citizenship 32, 34–5; *see also* Allophone Quebecers; immigrants
cultural diversity: and globalisation 62–3, 66, 72, 79, 195; and *la Francophonie* 75–9; and linguistic diversity 62, 77–9; *see also* interculturalism; multiculturalism
cultural nation 13, 47, 59, 60, 202*n*.1
culture: *américanité* and *américanisation* 73–4; and economic integration 69, 74–5; and ethnicity 11–12, 60–1; exogamy and cultural integration 169–70; French Canadian culture and *survivance* 45–6; and globalisation 16–17; and models of nation 45–7, 51–3; *see also culture publique commune*
culture de convergence policy 27–8, 47, 51, 89
culture publique commune 13, 26, 32; and concepts of nation 44, 47, 49, 50, 51–3, 56

Dagger, R. 41
Daveluy, M. 212*n*.13
de-ethnicisation 27, 39–40, 52, 56; of language 84, 97–104, 105, 195
Derriennic, J.-P.: model of nation 47–9, 53–4
Desbiens, J.-P. 111
Des valeurs partagées, des intérêts communs (policy document) 35, 94, 136–7
Devoir, Le 3, 33, 44, 120
dictionaries: Canadian French 110, 111, 206*n*.9; national dictionary project 122–7, 196; Quebec French 121–2, 206*n*.9&10

Dictionnaire de la langue québécoise 121
Dictionnaire du français plus 121–2
Dictionnaire du québécois-français 125
Dictionnaire général de la langue française au Canada 206*n*.9
Dictionnaire québécois d'aujourd'hui 121–2
Dieckhoff, A. 17
discrimination: ethnic minorities in France 40–1, 100; immigrants and sense of belonging 142; and language 100–1
Dor, G. 122
Dorais, L. J. 179, 180, 210*n*.1, 211*n*.6&7
Drapeau, L. 190, 191, 192, 211*n*.7, 212*n*.19
Dubuc, P. 151
Duchacek, I. D. 64
Duchastel, J. 32
Dufour, F.-G. 44, 103–4
Dumas, G. 71
Dumont, F. 102, 204*n*.3; ethnic model of nation 45–7, 53, 54, 57, 59, 201–2*n*.1, 202*n*.6
Dunn, O. 110
Duplessis, M. 36
Durham, Lord 26–7

education: and Aboriginal peoples and languages 178, 179, 180, 181, 185, 187–92, 211*n*.11, 212*n*.16; and Anglophone community 85, 87–8, 155, 168–9; *classes d'accueil* 137–8, 196; Francophones attending English-language schools 209–10*n*.13; Quebecers of immigrant origin and second language acquisition 92–3, 135–6, 146–7, 148; and language policy 85, 86, 87–8, 168–9; linguistic diversity in schools 136, 137, 145; and Standard Quebec French 119
Edwards, J. 38, 96, 204*n*.7
enfants de la loi 101 55, 92, 144–8, 149
English Canadians 54, 152–3; *see also* Anglophone Quebecers
English language: and Aboriginal peoples 176–7, 186, 187; in Americas 69, 70, 71, 72; attitudes of Francophone community towards 62–3, 67–8, 69, 72, 161, 166, 167–8, 209–10*n*.13; as global *lingua franca* 5, 62–3, 92, 96–7, 102, 194; historical impact on French language 109, 110–11, 120–1; linguistic rights of Anglophone Quebecers 163–4; motivation for second language acquisition 91, 92, 95, 96; as official language of United States 101; and Quebecers of immigrant origin 134–5, 141, 143, 146, 147, 157; vitality in Montreal 134–5, 147, 148, 167; world Englishes 113; *see also* Anglophone Quebecers
English-medium schools 85, 86, 87–8, 93, 155, 168; Francophone students in 209–10*n*.13
English-speaking Quebecers: *see* Anglophone Quebecers
Eriksen, T. H. 10, 11
États généraux du Canada français (1967) 27
ethnic identity *see* ethnicity/ethnic identity
ethnic minority groups 5–6, 129–93; assimilationist policies 37, 181; citizenship models and ethnic majority 39–41, 49–50; and concept of nation 13, 45–7, 53–4, 56, 58–9, 60–1; *culture de convergence* policy 27–8, 47, 51, 89; ethnic discrimination 27, 40–1, 100–1, 142, 143, 173, 202*n*.5; and integration policy 28–9, 41–2, 52–3; and language diversity in Montreal 135–6, 137, 145; and Bouchard's model of nation 54–5; CROP-*La Presse* poll 158–61; and Seymour's sociopolitical nation model 57–9; *see also* Aboriginal peoples; Allophone Quebecers; Anglophone Quebecers; cultural communities; ethnicity/ethnic identity; French Canadians; immigrants; interculturalism; multiculturalism
ethnic nationalism 13, 26–7, 37, 48–9, 53, 60; and models of nation 45–7, 54, 58

ethnicism/ethnocentrism 56, 100, 101, 202*n*.5
ethnicity/ethnic identity 10–12; challenges of ethnic diversity 4, 5, 198; and culture 11–12, 60–1; ethnic groups and nations 13, 45–7, 53–4, 56, 58–9; federal policy and Quebec 31; and language 1, 84, 101, 97–104, 105; need for recognition of 60–1, 105, 198; primordialism and instrumentalism 10, 200*n*.3; *see also* de-ethnicisation; immigrants; interculturalism
European Union: European citizenship 35; language issue 102

Fabius, L. 205*n*.6
Facal, J. 34
faux amis 120
Fettes, M. 185, 187
First Nation peoples 174; and education policy 187–8; official languages 179–80; *see also* Aboriginal peoples and languages
Forum national sur la citoyenneté et l'intégration 32–3, 38–9
Fournier, M. 28–9
français d'ici see Quebec French
français international see international French
français populaire 122; *see also* joual
français standard 5, 107
français standard d'ici see Standard Quebec French
France: Canadian settlement and early language 107–9; citizenship and ethnic minorities 40–1; citizenship and overseas territories 35–6; civic republicanism model 26, 40–1, 48–9; discrimination against ethnic minorities 40–1, 100; French as common public language 101; immigrants from 132, 142; international relations with 63, 64, 75, 76–7, 195; *la Francophonie* and cultural diversity 76–7; and linguistic variation 116–17; trade mission with Quebec 66; use of term Francophone 205*n*.8; *see also* French language

francisation programmes 94, 96–7, 135, 136, 137, 196, 197; in schools 92–3, 147, 168; and workplace 86, 88
francismes 121
Franco-Quebec Working Group on Cultural Diversity 77
Franco-Québécois (Franco-Quebecers) 12, 99; *see also* French Canadians
Francophone Quebecers: attitudes towards Anglophone community 6, 151–2, 158–61, 170–1, 196; attitudes towards speaking English 167–8, 209–10*n*.13; attitudes towards standard of Quebec French 118–19; and data on language 89–90; definitions of Francophone 99; and interculturalism 139; language as primary attribute of culture 12, 98; linguistic insecurity 117, 119, 124, 126, 195; and national identity 57–9, 60–1, 99–100; use of term 12; *see also* French Canadians; Quebec French
francophones de souche (old stock Francophones) 99; *see also* French Canadians
francophones hors de Québec 27
Francophonie: as global linguistic network 5, 63, 75–9, 80; immigration from 134, 143; international relations with 64, 79, 80, 195; Quebec as North American *francophonie* 56
FRANQUS project 123–5, 196, 206*n*.12
Fréchette, C. 67, 70–1
Fréchette, L. 109–10
Free Trade Area of the Americas (FTAA) 67, 70, 71
Freed, J. 171
Frégault, G. 27
French Canada: decline of concept 12, 57; as a nation 54, 59–60; *see also* French nation in America model
French Canadian patois 5, 108, 109–12
French Canadians 41, 53, 54, 56, 58, 60–1, 141–2, 143–4, 149, 160, 190, 195, 196; attitudes towards ethnic minorities 30–1; and

French Canadians – *continued*
de-ethnicisation of language 97–100, 102–4, 105, 113, 195; definition of and use of terms 12, 15, 27, 99–100, 152; and ethnicity 44, 45–7, 51, 52, 54, 55, 56, 57, 59–60, 198; historical context of ethnic nationalism 26–7; and income discrepancies 9; language development 107–12; and language policy 104–5, 126; linguistic insecurity 110–11, 117–19, 195; as a nation 54, 59–60; policy towards ethnic minorities 27–9; Trudeau's federalism 36–7; *see also* Francophone Quebecers

French language 76, 81–127; and Aboriginal peoples 176–7, 186, 187, 189, 191–2, 193, 212*n*.16; accent and spoken French 100–1, 170–1; and Anglophone Quebecers 165–70, 171, 196, 209*n*.12; as used in France 5, 107, 110, 114–15, 117–18, 205*n*.7; *bon usage* 114–15, 205*n*.7; and Bouchard's model of nation 55, 56; and civic model of nation 50–1; and ethnic model of nation 46, 47; and French Canadian identity 103, 104–5; historical development in Quebec 107–12; immersion programmes in schools 168; and immigrants' sense of belonging 131–49, 196; importance of protecting linguistic diversity 70–2, 75, 79–80; and integration policies 29–30, 91, 92, 93, 95–6, 104, 136–7; and international relations 67–8, 69–72, 79–80; monocentric ideology 114–15, 118, 196; vitality in Montreal 90, 93, 95, 134–5, 137, 147, 148; motivation for learning as second language 91–7; Parisian French 109, 112, 114, 115, 117–18, 119, 122; pluricentric approach 114, 115–17, 118, 121, 126, 196; quality of Quebec French 4, 5, 106, 107, 111–12, 113, 118, 197–8; and Quebec citizenship 34, 36, 151–2; standardisation 119–25, 196; status in Americas 70–2, 92; varieties found in Quebec 5, 106–27, 195–6, 197–8; *see also* acquisition of French as second language; *Francophonie*; international French; language policy and planning; *langue commune*; *langue publique commune*; Quebec French

French nation in America model 45–7; *see also* Dumont, F.
French people 35, 36, 99
French Polynesia 35, 36
French-speaking *see* Francophone
Frenette, L. 139
Friedman, J. 16–17
Front de libération du Québec (FLQ) 204*n*.2
Frulla, L. 66

Gadet, F. 117
Gagnon, A.-G. 41, 43, 98
Gagnon, E. 110
Gagnon-Tremblay, M. 79
Gandhi, M. 102
Gardner, R. C. 91
Garmadi, J. 114–15
Gauthier, M. 156, 170, 209*n*.12
Gazette, The 3, 57, 166, 171, 209*n*.10
Gendron Commission 84–5, 113
Gendron, J.-D. 118
génération 101 see enfants de la loi 101
Georgeault, P. 2, 78–9, 91, 97, 135, 179–80
Gérin-Lajoie doctrine 65–6
Gervais, S. 4
Giddens, A. 15–16, 17
Giles, H. 67, 101
Girouard, L. 111
globalisation 4, 5, 15–18, 62–80, 194, 195; and citizenship 18, 26; and internationalisation 15–16, 17; and the local 16–17, 63, 79, 80; and national identity 17–18, 37
Glossaire du parler français au Canada 111
Godin, G. 111
Gomery, J. H. 170–1
Grand dictionnaire terminologique 206*n*.10
Grégoire, Abbé 109

Habermas, J. 52, 53, 103
Harper, E. 211n.9
Harvey, J. 51–2
Heater, D. 20, 21, 33
Heinrich, J. 166, 168, 169, 170, 209–10n.13
Held, D. 201n.6
Helly, D. 140–2, 143, 144, 149
Herder, J. G. 83
heritage languages (languages of origin) 89, 138, 211n.7; in Montreal 135–6, 145, 148
Hoffmann, C. 97
Holborow, M. 63
home languages *see* language spoken at home
Huron-Wendat people and language 8, 174, 175, 176, 177, 212n.15

Iacovino, R. 98
identity 6–10; and citizenship 18, 19, 20; multiple identities 9–10, 54–5; *see also* ethnicity/ethnic identity; national identity; social identity theory
identity nationalism 48–9; *see also* ethnic nationalism
immigrants 4, 5–6, 131–49, 196, 197; adult migrant experiences 139–44, 149; countries of origin and Quebec as host nation 132–9; English as first official language 157; existing knowledge of French language 133–4, 141; experiences of language and belonging 131, 139–49, 196; French language learning *see* acquisition of French as second language; as future of French language 84, 104, 107, 118, 126–7, 195; language spoken at home 88, 133, 135, 139–40, 155–6, 157; moral contract 29, 41, 138–9; and national dictionary project 123; second generation 144–5 *see also enfants de la loi 101*; selection of economic migrants on language criterion 133–4; *see also* Allophone Quebecers; integration policies; interculturalism; multiculturalism
India 102
Indian Act (1876) (Canada) 181

Indian Act (1985) (Canada) 174
Indian Brotherhood of Canada 187–8
Indians *see* First Nation peoples
indigenous peoples *see* Aboriginal peoples and languages
Innu people and language 174, 175, 176, 177, 210n.4, 211n.6, 212n.18, 212n.19, 212–13n.20, 213n.21; Agreement-in-principle 185, 189–90; Betsiamites community 192, 213n.21; language survival 186–7, 189–92, 212n.17
Institut culturel et éducatif montagnais (ICEM) 190–1, 212n.18
Institut de diction française au Québec 113
instrumentalism: and Aboriginal use of French language 189; and ethnicity 10, 13; and second language acquisition 91–2, 93, 95, 136, 144, 146–7
integration policies 27–30, 38–9; and *culture publique commune* 52–3; *Des valeurs partagées, des intérêts communs* 35, 94, 136; moral contract 29, 41, 138–9; and motivation for second language acquisition 91, 92, 93, 95–6, 104, 136–7; roadmap for immigrants 136–7; *see also* immigrants; interculturalism
intercultural citizenship 42–3, 194, 197
interculturalism 28–30, 32, 138–9, 197; *see also* cultural diversity; integration policies; multiculturalism
international French 5, 107, 112–19, 124
Inuit people 174, 175, 176, 177, 178, 210n.1, 210n.5; Avataq Cultural Institute 185, 186, 211–12n.12; Kativik School Board (KSB) 178, 185, 186, 212n.16; language survival 186–7, 188–9, 191; Nunavik government 185–6; *Sanarrutik* agreement 184–5
Inuktitut language 175, 177, 178, 179, 185, 192, 212n.13
Inuttitut language 175, 177, 180, 185, 186, 188–9, 190, 193, 211n.11, 211–12n.12, 212n.13

James Bay and Northern Quebec Agreement (JBNQA) (1975)   174, 178, 180, 185, 188, 193
Jantzen, L.   177
Jedwab, J.   156, 157, 164, 165, 169, 170
Jewish community   42
Jézéquel, M.   41, 43
Johnson, W.   164
Joseph, J.   93
Jospin, L.   205*n*.6
joual   111–12, 113, 119, 122, 124, 126
Juteau, D.   12, 38, 39–40, 60–1

Kohn, H.   200*n*.5
Koubi, G.   40
Kristeva, J.   100
Kymlicka, W.   42, 43, 60, 101

Labelle, M.   142–4
Labov, W.   117
Labrie, N.   203*n*.2, 203*n*.3
Lacroix, A.   26, 43
Laforest, M.   122
Lalonde, M.   112
Lamarre, P.   145, 147, 148, 155, 168, 169
Lambert, J.   109
Lambert, W. E.   91
Lamonde, D.   124
Lamonde, Y.   73, 74
Lamoureux, D.   52
Landry, B.   34, 158, 183
Langlois, S.   201*n*.1
language policy and planning   1–2, 83–105; and Aboriginal languages   6, 178–9, 184–6, 193, 197; acquisition planning   81, 104; and common identity for Quebec   4; corpus planning   81, 106, 114, 117, 119–27; de-ethnicisation of language   84, 97–104, 105, 195; and education system   85, 86, 87–8, 146, 168–9; indicator of the languages of public use   89–90; integration policies   29–30, 91, 92, 93, 95–6, 104; interparty political similarities   4; and *lingua franca*   96; linguicide   187; principles of personality and territoriality   98; public signage in French   87, 121, 153, 163; status planning   81, 83–105, 106, 114, 195; *see also* Charter of the French language; francisation programmes; French language; Larose Commission
language spoken at home (*langue d'usage*)   89, 90; Aboriginal peoples   177–8, 191–2; Anglophone community   90, 155–6, 157; Allophone communities   88–9, 90, 133, 135, 139–40, 149; *see also* mother tongue
languages of origin: *see* heritage languages
langue commune   1, 29–30, 84–9, 93, 95–6; *see also langue publique commune*
langue d'usage public   89–90, 105
langue identitaire   56
langue publique commune   50–1, 52, 56, 84, 86–91, 195; and Aboriginal languages   179, 193; immigrants and second language acquisition   94, 104, 132, 133, 136–7, 146
Laporte, P.   204*n*.2
Larose Commission: and Aboriginal peoples and languages   172, 179–80, 197; and Anglophone community   150–1, 154; and Charter of the French language   88; definition of citizenship   39; definition of Francophone   99; on dictionaries   123; foundation and findings   1–2; and French Canadian identity   104; on French language and national identity   83; on French language quality and status   106; on globalisation and diversity   62; on immigration and French language   131–2, 149; and international French   113; and national identity   44; on outside perceptions   3; and Quebec citizenship   25, 33–4, 36, 94; and second language acquisition   93–4
Larrivée, P.   163
Latouche, D.   64, 75
Laurendeau-Dunton Commission   98
Laurin, C.   86, 106
Lazar, B.   155, 170
Leclerc, J.   178
Legaré, A.   69

Léger, J.-M.   34, 76
Léger Marketing   160
Lemieux, D.   34
Lepage, R.   73
Lepicq, D.   167
Lessard, D.   160
Létourneau, J.   100, 103
Lévesque, R.   27
Levine, M.   85–6, 89, 92, 147
Leydet, D.   37, 49–51
liberal citizenship model   19–20, 21, 26, 142; and Canada   36, 37–8, 194
liberal nationalism   41–2, 43
Liberal Party *see* Parti Libéral du Québec (PLQ)
liberalism: and citizenship issues   18, 26, 36–42; liberal paradox   38; and nationalism   41–2, 43, 49
linguicide   187
linguistic diversity: and cultural diversity   62, 77–9; immigrant community   135–6, 137, 145; promotion of French in the Americas   70–2, 75, 79–80
linguistic norms *see* norms
linguistic separatism   124–5, 126
Lisée, J.-F.   34
Livre blanc sur la politique culturelle (policy document)   84
loi 101 see Charter of the French language
Lortie, S.   110–11
Lüdi, G.   115

Maalouf, A.   9
Mc Andrew, M.   137, 138, 147
McGill University   154, 155, 189
MacKenzie, M.   188–9, 190, 212*n*.19
Magnan, M.-O.   156, 157, 170, 209*n*.12
Maguire, T.   109
Mailhot, J.   190
Maintien et développement des langues autochtones du Québec (policy document)   179
Major, A.   111
Malecite people and language   174, 175, 176, 177
Manseau, J.-A.   109–10
Marcel, J.   112
Marshall, T. H.   20, 39

Martel, P.   114, 206*n*.11
Mathieu, G.   47, 59
Maurais, J.   71–2, 118–19, 120, 179
Meech Lake Accord (1987)   30, 211*n*.9
Meinecke, F.   200*n*.5
Meney, L.   124–5
Métis National Council   175
Métis people   174, 175
Mexico   69, 203*n*.3
Michaud, Y.   42–3
Micmac people and language   174, 175, 176, 177, 211*n*.6
Miller, D.   50
Ministère de l'Éducation   90, 122, 138, 188, 191
Ministère de l'Immigration (1968–81)   28
Ministère de l'Immigration et des Communautés culturelles (2005–)   35, 136
Ministère des Communautés culturelles et de l'immigration (1981–96)   31, 32; *Autant de façons d'être Québécois*   28, 29
Ministère des Relations avec les citoyens et de l'immigration (1996–2005)   32, 35
Ministère des Relations internationales   65, 76
Ministry of Cultural Affairs   84
Ministry of Education *see* Ministère de l'Éducation
minority groups *see* ethnic minority groups
Missisquoi Institute   161
Mohawk people and language   174, 175, 176, 177, 211*n*.6, 211*n*.9
Monde, Le   120
Monière, D.   92–3, 94
Montagnais *see* Innu people and language
Montreal: Anglophones in   134–5, 156, 157, 167, 208–9*n*.4; bilingual municipalities   153–4; French-English bilingualism in   86, 142, 148, 166–7, 196; heritage languages (languages of origin)   135–6, 145, 148; immigrant population   134–6, 137; immigrant sense of belonging and language   139–42, 143, 145–6,

Montreal – *continued*
  147–8, 149, 196; trilingualism in 145, 146, 147, 148; and *visage linguistique* 102; vitality of English in 134–5, 147, 148, 167; vitality of French in 90, 93, 95, 134–5, 137, 147, 148
Montreal School 27
moral contract 29, 41, 138–9
Morris, M. A. 72
Moses, T. 183, 192–3, 211*n*.10
mother tongue 89, 90, 95; Aboriginal peoples 175, 177–8, 187, 191; adult immigrants survey 134, 139–40; census data 155–6, 157, 169; in Montreal 135–6, 145
motivation and language acquisition: instrumental and integrative/sentimental motivations 91–5; *see also* acquisition of French as a second language; instrumentalism
multiculturalism: in Canada 28–9, 37–8, 53, 54, 98, 143–4, 194; and Seymour's model of nation 58; *see also* interculturalism
Multidictionnaire de la langue française 206*n*.10
multilingualism 6, 70–2, 98, 102–3, 145, 146–8; *see also* bilingualism; plurlingualism

Nalukturak, A. 211–12*n*.12
Naskapi people and language 174, 175, 176, 177, 178, 180, 210*n*.5, 211*n*.6
national identity 13–15; and Aboriginal peoples 53, 133, 180–6, 202*n*.6; and Anglophone Quebecers 6, 53, 58–9, 133, 151–2, 161–2; and citizenship 5, 15, 18, 26, 37, 39–40; and ethnic majority in France 40; and Francophone Quebecers 57–9, 60–1, 99–100; and globalisation 17–18, 37; immigrants and sense of belonging 140–3; and language 2–3, 4, 91–2, 93, 99–103, 112–13, 116, 117–18; *see also* civic approach to national identity
nationalism: ethnic/civic dichotomy 13–15, 18, 34, 38, 43, 44, 47–8; federal attitudes towards 31–2, 36–7; historical evolution in Quebec 26–32; and liberalism 41–2, 43, 49
nationality: and citizenship 18, 26, 32–3, 43
nations: characteristics 13; and ethnic groups 13; and ethnic/civic dichotomy 14–15, 47–61, 194–5; and globalisation 17, 37, 65; models of nation for Quebec 44–61; primordialism and instrumentalism 13
Nederveen Pieterse, J. 63, 70
neo-nationalism 27
New Caledonia 35, 36
new collectivities 73–4
new Quebecers 59, 96, 104, 118, 133; *see also* Allophone Quebecers; immigrants
Ngũgĩ wa Thiong'o 205*n*.10
Nigeria 102
norms: and language 107, 114–15, 119, 125
Norris, M. J. 177
North American Forum on Integration 67, 69
North American Free Trade Agreement (NAFTA) 67, 69, 72
Northeastern Quebec Agreement (NEQA) (1978) 174, 178, 180, 193
Nunavik 185–6, 189
Nunavik Commission 177; *Amiqqaaluta – Let Us Share. Mapping the Road Toward a Government for Nunavik* (policy document) 185–6

October crisis (1970) 85
Office de la langue française (1961–2002) 84, 90, 112, 120; *see also* Office québécois de la langue française
Office québécois de la langue française (2002–) 88, 145; *see also* Office de la langue française
Official Language Act (1974) 85–6, 163
Oka crisis (1990) 211*n*.9
old stock Quebecers (*Québécois de souche*) 15, 30–1, 54; *see also* French Canadians
Organisation internationale de la Francophonie (OIF) 65, 76, 77, 79

Organization of American States (OAS) 69, 72

Pagé, M. 95, 96, 99
Paix des braves (2002) 183, 184–5, 192
Papillon, M. 180–1, 182–3
Paquot, A. 205*n*.7
Parent Commission 112
Parizeau, J. 30–1
Parti Libéral du Québec (PLQ) 4, 30, 34–5, 64–5, 72, 85–6, 94
Parti pris (journal) 27, 111
Parti Québécois (PQ) 1–2, 4, 34, 86–9, 118; and Aboriginal peoples 178; and Anglophone community 152, 156, 158, 160, 164; *culture de convergence* policy 27–8; *peuple québécois* definition 31; and sovereignty referendum (1995) 30–1, 42–3
Partnership, Development, Achievement (policy document) 181–2
patois 5, 108, 109–12; *see also* joual
Patrick, D. 189
Patriot revolt (1837–38) 26–7, 46, 102
Pelletier, R. 160
Pennycook, A. 205*n*.10
Perreault, L.-J. 151
Perreault, M. 166, 167–8, 169
Perreault, R. 33
Petit Robert, Le (dictionary) 121
Pettigrew, P. 17
peuple québécois definition 31
Picard, G. 179
Piché, V. 139
Pipes, R. 10
Plan stratégique en matière de politique linguistique 2005–2008 (policy document) 90–1
pluralism: citizenship and de-ethnicisation 39–40; and civic model of nation 50, 195; education and integration policies 138; in immigration policy 29, 30, 133; and Quebec citizenship debate 43; *see also* cultural diversity; interculturalism; multiculturalism
plurilingualism 71, 203*n*.2; *see also* bilingualism; multilingualism
Poirier, C. 206*n*.9
Poisson, E. 124–5
politics of recognition 53, 59

politique québécoise de la langue française, La (white paper) 86, 88
politique québécoise du développement culturel, La (white paper) 27–8
Portuguese language 70, 71–2
Pratte, A. 158, 159–60, 160–1, 165
Presse, La 3, 120, 158–61, 166
primordialism 10, 13, 200*n*.3
Projet d'enseignement en langue d'origine (PELO) 206–7*n*.3
Proulx, J.-P. 162
public language *see langue publique commune*
Pure laine (TV series) 148–9

Quebec Association of French Teachers 119
Quebec citizenship 4, 32–6, 94, 143; Aboriginal peoples and conflicting imperatives 173, 180–6, 193; and Anglophone community 158–65, 196–7; civic republicanism model 38–9, 41–2, 43, 194–5; and French language 34, 36, 151–2; immigrants and sense of belonging 141–2, 143, 196; *see also* civic approach to national identity
Quebec Community Groups Network (QCGN) 155, 165, 169
Quebec French (*français d'ici*) 106–27, 149, 195–6; attitudes of Francophone Quebecers towards 118–19; dictionaries and usage 121–5; dictionary corpuses 107, 123–5; distinguishing features 119–21; linguistic separatism accusations 124–5; historical development 107–12; and international French 112–19; *joual* 111–12, 113, 122, 124; language attitudes survey 118–19; as national variety of French 116–17; and pluricentric model 115–17, 118, 121, 126, 196; quality of language 4, 5, 106, 107, 111–12, 113, 118, 197–8; Standard Quebec French 107, 119–25, 196
Quebecers of French-Canadian background 12; *see also* French Canadians

québécismes 120 *see also* canadianismes de bon aloi
Québécois: definition of and use of term 12, 27, 28, 142–3, 152, 158–9; *see also* French Canadian
Québécois de souche (old stock Quebecers) 15, 30–1, 54; *see also* French Canadians
Québécois pure laine 30–1; *Pure laine* TV series 148–9; *see also* French Canadians
Quiet Revolution 4–5, 7, 12, 27, 42, 57; and French language in Canada 111–12

Radio-Canada French 119; *see also* Standard Quebec French
Raffarin, J.-P. 66
Rawls, J. 20
referenda on sovereignty 28, 30–1, 42–3, 140
Régie de la langue française (1974–77) 86
regionalisms in Quebec French 120
Renan, E. 47
Renaud, J. 111, 139, 140
Répertoire d'emprunts critiqués à l'anglais 120
republican liberalism 41
republicanism *see* civic republican citizenship model
Rioux, M. 27
Rivard, A. 110–11
Robertson, R. 17, 63, 200–1n.6
Robillard, L. 66
Roosens, E. 8
Rosello, M. 131–2, 144–5, 149
Rosenberg, M. 8, 28–9
Rossell Paredes, J. 147, 155
Roy, C. 111
Royal Commission of Inquiry on Education in the Province of Quebec *see* Parent Commission
Ruiz Fabri, H. 77

Saada, J. 204n.11
Sachdev, I. 12
Saganash, R. 211n.10
Saint-Jacques, B. 117–18
Saint-Léonard crisis (1967–68) 85

Salée, D. 142–4, 182, 183–4, 193, 211n.9&10
Sanarrutik agreement (2002) 184–5
scandale des commandites 170–1
Schnapper, D. 14
Scowen, R. 154, 155, 165
second language acquisition *see* acquisition of French as second language
Secrétariat à la politique linguistique 90
Secrétariat aux affaires autochtones 174, 175, 177
secularisation 4–5, 26
Séguin, Maurice 27
self-categorisation theory 9, 12, 95
semi-endonormativity 119, 125
Seymour, M. 14, 15, 31, 40, 45; Anglophones and Quebec nation 162–3; and ethnic model of nation 47, 49, 57; sociopolitical nation model 57–9, 61
Simmons, R. 8
situationalism 10, 11–12
Smith, A. D. 10
social identity theory 6–10, 27; and ethnic identity 10–12; and language 95, 98, 99–100; national identity and globalisation 17–18
Société du parler français du Canada 110–11
sociopolitical nation model 57–9
Soleil, Le 120
Sonntag, S. K. 63
sovereignty project: and Anglophobia 160–1, 196; and citizenship issues 33, 34, 94; and concept of nation 53–4, 94; immigrant view of 144; referenda 28, 30–1, 42–3, 140
Spanish language: in Americas 69, 70, 71, 72; immigrants in Quebec 134
speech accommodation theory 113
sponsorship scandal 170–1
Standard Quebec French (*le français standard d'ici*) 107, 119–25; national dictionary project 123–7, 196
standardisation: of French language 107, 112–25; of Innu language 190
Statistics Canada 161–2, 207n.5
Stefanescu, A. 2, 91, 97

Stevenson, G.   154, 164, 167, 171
survivance ideology   27, 45–6, 54
Sweden   96, 101
Switzerland   33

Tajfel, H.   7–8
Tardivel, J.-P.   110, 111
Task Force on Aboriginal Languages and Cultures (Canada)   180
Taylor, C.   14, 53, 59–60, 61
Télé-Québec: *Pure laine* TV series   148–9
Termote, M.   157
Tocqueville's paradox   17
Travis, D.   151
Tremblay, M.   111
Trent, J. E.   164
Trent, P.   208–9*n*.4
trilingualism   145, 147, 148, 191
Trudeau, P. E.   36–7, 54, 97–8, 112, 204*n*.2; repatriation of the Constitution   37
Trudel, F.   178
Tully, J.   43, 161, 184
Turi, G.   112
Turner, J. C.   7–8
Tyler, B.   151, 163

UNESCO: Convention on the Protection and Promotion of the Diversity of Cultural Expressions   66, 77–9, 80, 172, 195, 203*n*.8, 203–4*n*.9, 204*n*.10
Union nationale   85

United States: *américanisation*   73, 74; Anglo-American hegemony   62–3; Anglophone community as link with   151; citizenship and nationality   33; economic and cultural integration   74–5; English as official language   101; instrumentalism and immigration   92; integration policy   28–9, 38; international relations with   63; language and new nativism   101; and linguistic diversity   78; *see also* Americas
Université de Sherbrooke   107, 123–4, 196
urban planning and French language   95–6

van Schendel, N.   140–2, 143, 144, 149
variation: linguistic variation   2, 114–17
Vassberg, L. M.   100
Vaugelas, C. F. de   114
Venne, M.   14, 33
Verreault, C.   113–14, 115–16
Villers, M.-É.   120
visage linguistique   102

Waddell, E.   152
Walker, B.   102
Weinstock, D.   18–20
White, D.   28–9
Wright, S.   96